H...., 

**ישראל**
Israel,

**יהוה**
YHVH

**יהוה את ואהבת אחד: יהוה אלהינו**
YHVH    And you    is One:   YHVH   our God
shall  love

**אלהיך**
your God

**בכל-**
with all

**לבבך**
your heart,

**ובכל-**
and with all

**נפשך**
your soul,

**ובכל-**
and with all

**מאדך**
your strength.

*God made the sunshine for us all*
*It falls on things both small and tall*
*The flowers bloom and smell so sweet*
*God gave them to us for a treat.*
*The beams reflect upon each stream*
*And "heavenly light" is not a dream.*
*It gives us warmth for work and play*
*This gift divine comes every day.*

*Naomi's Grandmother*
*Margaret Whittlesey*

Open Soul Surgery, English language edition
The Visions of Mrs. Naomi Levell
Autobiography
© Mrs. Naomi Levell 2014 anno domini

Dedicated to the cherished memory of our beloved young

# *Bonito*
# *Binkybunny*

(of whom, owing to the discovery of a significant error,
we rather belatedly changed her name to *Bonita*).

November 6, 2010-January 19, 2013

Many thanks to my aunts Rachel and Judith, and my mother Shoshanna Miriam, and to Susana Erickson, my dear sisters and true friends in Christ; and to Rodrigo Rivera, Pastor Pedro Bernabe, and Joey Bernabe, my dear brothers and true friends in Christ; and, above all, to my Lord and Best Friend Messiah Yeshua and to my other lord and best friend Benaiah Zechariah Levell, for believing in me and in this work when it was as yet only a hope and a dream.

Many thanks also to my beloved husband Benaiah Zechariah Levell for his great love and patience, and for waiting so patiently for my hands, and my eyes, and his supper. Without his patience and love, I know that I would not have had the time, or the strength, or the courage.

23    Examine me, *O* God, and know my heart:
        test me, and know my thoughts;
24    And see if *there is any* saddening way in me;
        and guide me in *the* way everlasting.

————Psalm 139:23-139:24

# CONTENTS:

### Section One:
## The Seer

## Section Two:
## Seven Flames: Letters to Manasseh

## Section Three:
## Alive and Kickin'

Section Four:
# The Storm

Section Five:
# The Daughter

16    Because God so loved the world, that He gave His
      only-born Son, so that whoever trusts[1] in Him
      does not perish,[2] but has everlasting life.
17    Because God did not send His Son into the world to
      condemn the world; but that the world through Him
      might be saved.

—John 3:16-3:17

INTRODUCTION:

# Times of Transformation
# by Pastor Pedro Bernabe

On July seventh, two thousand one, the Lord Himself took
me out of the business world; took me out of all control; took me out
of my (what I called) "good life," and put me into a place where I
had no control at all. And it's called Federal Jail. By this time (April
seventh, two thousand fourteen), I was supposed to be getting close
to ending my sentence—thirteen years.

But when I was in jail I prayed to God and I asked Him for
forgiveness; I gave my life to Him; and I told Him that I was a
broken cup, and if He wanted to use my life for any of His purposes
then He had to restore my life, put me back together for His
purposes. And God did.

He got me out of jail without paying one penny, restored my
records like nothing ever happened in my life; and took me into a
Foursquare Church where I was restored spiritually for three years.

Then He made my calling clear to me and He called me to be
a pastor to shepherd His people.

Then He called me to worship Him where I've been serving
for the last twelve years of my life.

From the time that He called me until now I have had many
experiences with Him: I have seen God saving the lost, healing the
sick, restoring family relationships, lifting up the poor; blessing
many, many people.

I have seen God's glory falling on the people that have
believed on Him—not because I am special, but because He is good.
God is a good God.

In nineteen eighty seven, I graduated from a Bible school. But I didn't walk with God nor did I serve Him. Nearly twenty years went by and He called me again.

God has brought me from what I called "good life," but was really only crumbs from the enemy; crumbs from Satan compared to the promises of God. Now I know that there is a living God. And He loves me, and He wants to be with me: He wants a relationship with me. And now I live my life for Him.

Πετρος [Κηφας] Βαρναβας

Son of Consolation
Hijo de Profetizar

Hijo de Consolación

כֵּף בַּר-נָבָא

Piedra
Stone

Kefá Bar-Navá
Son of Prophesying

Pedro Bernabé

3      When I see Your heavens, *the* work *of* Your fingers,
        *the* moon and *the* stars, which You have prepared;
4      What *is a* mortal, that You remember him?
        And *a* son of man, that You visit him?

—Psalm 8:3-8:4

# God is Love

My friends have asked me now and then how old I was when I got saved, and I really don't know how to give a simple answer. First, Messiah Yeshua[3] of Nazareth gave His life to save mine, many hundreds of years before I was ever born. Then, I grew up under the loving guidance of a Christian mother, and from her I learned to believe in Him since before my earliest memories. He saved my life when I was three years old, He spoke to me in a vision when I was four, and I asked to be baptized when I was seven. When I was eleven years old, and still not baptized, I gave Him my heart and I promised Him I'd be baptized just as soon as I had the freedom to make that choice. I kept that promise on March 21, nineteen ninety-three, when I was eighteen years old.

He had shown me His love in many ways during these in-between years, and He continues to do so, patiently saving me step by faltering step, vision by vision, Bible verse by Bible verse, mercy by mercy, miracle by miracle.

When I was about fourteen years old, I lived in a foster home, and my scowling foster mother was not a Christian, and she did not approve at all of the time I "isolated" myself by reading the Bible each day instead of watching television or staring back at her pet cats. As if I was somehow missing some kind of social activity—with who? Her? She was usually too busy to talk.

When she wasn't too busy to talk, she never once missed a chance to belittle me.

Her sister was a friend of mine, but moved away into her own apartment just as soon as she could afford one, saying I could visit her any time I wanted. But my foster mother only let me visit this friendly, pudgy sister about twice, even though the new apartment was quite nearby.

Fortunately, I did have one other human friend outside of school—my next door neighbor. She was in her early twenties, I suppose, and she was slender, and very kind. Her words always encouraged my heart and never once belittled me, and the only time she was ever too busy to talk was when she wasn't home.

Our apartments were joined together in a duplex, and they shared a single porch, which was the undisputed territory of her little black kitten Buster. (My foster mother's cats were not allowed to go outdoors.)

When Buster was first found, being a newborn kitten in a good-sized litter, all the other baby kittens had their little umbilical cords neatly nipped off—except for Buster. He still had his umbilical cord; but his tail was gone, except for a bloody stump. Hmm...

As it turns out, tails are mighty important to cats who own them. They not only steer with them when gracefully leaping, but more importantly cats use their tails to talk. A straight-up tail can announce his immense sense of accomplishment for two or three days after the cat catches his first mouse, or elegantly swish from side to side, twitching at the tip, to gracefully display by degrees his growing anger. Buster, of course, had never actually experienced the many uses of a feline tail, but he still had the instinctive feline ways of talking, and he did the best he could with just a stump.

And so it was that, every time that poor little Buster got mad, his stump would twitch.

And it just wasn't elegant at all: As a matter of fact, it made him look rather like a rabbit with short, pointy ears, which would make us both laugh (my slender neighbor and I), which would make the fluffy black kitten madder, which made him look even more bunnyish, which made us laugh harder, which of course only made poor Buster all the more angry—Poor, poor Buster.

There was just nothing he could do about it but stalk away in righteous indignation and hide his twitching fluffy stump...

As I said, "his" human was a good friend of mine, and had told me before that I was welcome to come over to her apartment any time at all, even when she was at work—she knew full well just how unloved I was at my house, because she could hear my foster mother through the wall.

But it wasn't the likes of my foster mother we would talk about together. We would talk about God, about cats, about strange science and history trivia, about food, or whatever. I felt comfortable and safe on her side of the wall, because this friend of mine shared my joy and wonder of life, and she didn't think any less of me because I struggled to learn names, or because my mind worked differently from the minds of everyone around me. I didn't know the phrases "Autism Spectrum Disorder" and "High functioning Autism" and "Asperger's Disorder." But I sure did know I was different, and I sure did know that it sometimes took me five whole hours to do a "fifteen minute" homework assignment, and—above all—I knew that none of the adults ruling over my life could understand, figure out, or even put a name to whatever it was that made me different. But here, on this side of the wall, that was okay—my neighbor wasn't "normal" either; she hadn't even ever met anybody who was: As far as she could tell, "normal" was merely a myth, and a cruel myth at that. So we would talk and laugh together.

On this day, however, I was alone. My friend was at work, and my foster mother was in a good enough mood to ignore me. On this side of the wall, my only companion was my tom kitten Theo. I don't rightly recall what I was doing in the basement, but it wasn't my tom kitten Theo whose pitiable mews I heard.

These meows seemed to be coming from my neighbor's basement, so I went into her apartment and ran downstairs. The meows were desperate and urgent, and I knew I had to find Buster fast; but where *was* he? Now that I was on this side of the duplex, Buster was nowhere to be found, and his frantic meowing now sounded like it was coming from my foster mother's basement instead. Upstairs I ran, and out, and in, and downstairs again into my foster mother's basement where I had begun. But still no Buster to be found anywhere: Only his distant meowing for help.

I searched in vain, then ran again to my neighbor's basement, but now the mewing was already weak and faint, while I tore through everything my friend had, searching vainly for her trapped and frightened tom kitten.

Finally, the faint meows stopped. I held my breath, straining to hear Buster's voice just once more.

Silence.

I froze. I had failed, but this failure was unbearable. I could do no more, but inaction was not an option my heart would accept. I didn't really know how to pray, but pray I did, and then listened again to the silence.

And in a heartbeat my prayer was both heard and answered: I saw a vision of a plastic ice chest, lying on its side, buried under the big pile of empty cardboard boxes. I didn't have time to doubt or to ask any questions—I ran, I flung boxes madly away to all sides until I saw it: The plastic ice chest, just like in my vision, lying silently on its side.

I grabbed that thing, and ran to the center of the room, and opened the lid.

A blast of hot moist air rushed out. I didn't want to see what I saw—Lifeless, silent, a mere limp pile of soft, thick, black fur.

Gently, I lifted out the tiny body, but Buster was breathing no more. His heart didn't seem to be beating either. Shame and Inadequacy were my two cruel companions, mocking me with the memory of how all my classmates had quickly mastered CPR, leaving the instructors free to patiently work with me for another hour or two before they were willing to accept the fact that I just couldn't do it—I couldn't keep a steady rhythm, couldn't track time, couldn't master a simple, necessary action they had *never in their lives* failed to teach to *anyone* before.

Confused, I stared heavenward—why would God show me how to find an already dead kitten? Buster just *had* to be alive—he just *had* to! I didn't pray a word; I just silently waited and dared to trust. Suddenly, with a deep shuddering breath, Buster's tiny furry chest began to heave again, and as if in a daze he staggered to his feet and onto my lap, and began to purr.

My mother had taught me long ago that "God is love,[4]" but I had known it only intellectually, as one of many facts and myths passed down to me in the traditions of my elders. Now, I didn't just know; I *knew*; I *knew*; with every fiber of my being; that God *is* love.

I don't know how long I sat there with that kitten in my lap, replaying in my mind the vision God had given me, drinking in deeply of the now-certain knowledge that God cared that much about the fleeting breath of a little black kitten who had trapped himself inside a hidden plastic ice chest.

I was drinking in deeply of the knowledge that the Author of all creation had taken the time to answer *me*; and I was rejoicing in the life that He had chosen to spare.

And as I look back on that simple prayer of faith and its awe-inspiring simple answer, I remember another miracle cat: This one I had only heard of and read about: Like Buster, it seemed that help had come too late.

But it happened that it was picked up off the ground by a woman of enormous faith, and she refused to listen when everyone told her that this life just couldn't be saved, and that it would be kindest to just let the dying creature die. Her name, I've been told, was Terri Schaivo. Like me, she prayed, and waited, and cared for a dying creature almost no one else believed could possibly survive. She knew of the power of her God, and she knew the mercy of her God, and He saved that cat just as surely as He would also save Buster. And for the rest of her life, Terri Schaivo never stopped telling people about God's mercy and compassion, and that none of us should ever give up on life, because even the smallest, least significant life truly is cherished by the Author of Life.

Terri Schaivo was a devout Catholic, and a woman of courage and faith, but her husband did not believe as she believed. There came a time when she, like the cat she and her God had saved together, would also be found on the ground.

There came a time when others would speak of giving up on Terri's life, even as others had once told Terri to give up on the life of that creature in her arms. Her husband was one of these, and an American judge gave this husband the authority to end the life of Terri Schaivo by starvation and thirst. Her voice on behalf of life is silenced forever from this world, but while I yet live her teaching will still be heard: Life is precious beyond all measure, and we have no right at all to give up on anyone's life while the all-powerful Author of Life even hears the cry of a tiny black kitten with no tail and no hope.

Who am I, that God would speak to me in a vision? Was I holy? Certainly not: I cussed; I lost my temper; I hurt God's heart by doubting in Him again and again and again.

Did I somehow deserve this amazing gift of love? No. But there it stands. And here I stand to speak of His deep and total healing love.

# Section One:

# *The Seer*

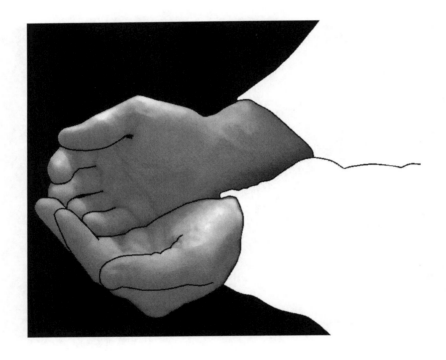

And I, I will remember my covenant with you
*which I made* in *the* days of your youth,
and I will raise up unto you *an* everlasting covenant.

——Ezekiel 16:60

...Of *a* truth *it is*, that your God *is a* God of gods,
and *a* teacher *of* kings, and *a* revealer *of* secrets...

—Daniel 2:47

# CHAPTER ONE

# Yeshua's Voice

Where does my story begin? Does it begin with my birth?
Does it begin with my conception? Does it begin with my
genealogy, carefully traced back in time all the way back to Princess
Pocahontas? Granted, my ancestress Pocahontas does have a good
story, well worth reading—and I'm not talking about the clever and
popular fiction tale by that rogue Captain John Smith: Princess
Rebecca Rolfe's true story is far better than any cheap ten-penny
romance yarn—but it is, after all, her story and not mine, and I'm
fairly certain that those of us who are so easily entertained can all
find royal ancestry in our lineage, provided that we'd actually bother
to go searching for it. I didn't. But I do admire the woman, and I am
honored to be called her descendant, but it certainly wasn't me who
searched out my genealogy; nor does it tell my story.

As for the details of my conception and birth, and the first
couple of years afterward, these are a part of my mother's story: I
certainly don't remember being born.

Where then, does my story begin? I choose to begin where
my walk with God began, in the small kitchen of a low-income
apartment on the poor side of town, in which dwelt me, my mother,
my four-year-old identical twin sister Drea (four minutes younger
than me), and our older brother Reuben David, about six years old.
There should have also been a father with us, and there had been,
but now he was gone: Our mother had fled with us from him.

The year was nineteen-eighty, and I believe that President
Jimmy Carter was just ending his term in the White House.
Communism, according to my brother's schoolteachers, was the
enemy; the Soviet Union seemed powerful, strong, and dangerous;
Africa was a place mostly ignored by the American and European
historians and the media; for many Americans taking care of the
earth or the ocean still seemed an idea as rare and absurd as taking

care of the universe itself, or of God; cell phones were a mythical device on Star Trek; America's wealth seemed infinite, secure, and undoubtedly a reward from God because this was God's Country; and millions of people thought that the U.S.A. was really, really progressive because the idea of someday having a African-American president had actually become possible—maybe, one of my more forward-thinking teachers later dared to imagine, I could even live long enough to see my grandchildren vote for him—(or maybe her).

One day in this time of my peace and security, I happened to be in the kitchen keeping watch while my sister played with the dishes. And then it happened: My first encounter with the Creator.

I saw a vision of another land in another time; and an appalling and terrible war, like none before: and I saw orbs like cannonballs, but burning with fire while in the air.

| 13:9 | Behold, *the* day *of* Adonai[5] comes: cruel, and *with* rage and burning anger, to put the land to destruction; and He will destroy her sinners out of her. |
| 10 | Because *the* stars of the heavens and their constellations will not shine their light; the sun will be dark in his going forth; and *the* moon shall not shine his light. |
| 11 | And I will punish the inhabited *world for its* wickedness; and *the* wicked *ones for* their iniquity; and I will cause *the* pride *of the* arrogant *ones* to cease; and I will humiliate *the* pride *of* tyrants. |

—Isaiah 13:1-14:28

And a voice (Which I knew not yet that it was the voice of Messiah Yeshua) said to me: "This war shall begin in Nasiriya, but it shall end in Nazareth: It shall begin in Nasiriya, but it shall spread to include Nazareth." And the Holy Spirit also spoke to me quietly, to warn me that my brother Reuben[6] would be tempted to worship his own people, to serve for the glory of his nation and for the glory of his own family, instead of the glory of God.

And thus I knew that the war would be in my brother's lifetime, while he was young enough to fight as a soldier. Now, I knew that to ask my sister anything about this would be a waste of time. And I asked my brother Reuben about the fiery cannonballs, because (for a six year old boy) he knew a lot about weapons and warfare: but Reuben said that there's no such thing as cannonballs that burn with fire in the air: but all cannonballs explode, rather, on contact: so he laughed. And I asked my mother where Nasiriya and Nazareth are, because (I said to myself) she knew a lot about the Holy Bible and about maps and cities; but my mother had never heard of Nasiriya.

And I forgot this vision, until I was more than thirty years old, when I saw Nasiriya burning and the flaming cannonballs in the air; because after all these things—after the manner of autistic children—I had lost the ability to speak until after I was ten years old: and not until after I had attained sixteen years could I speak fluently in my own mother tongue; and only because I first learned to read and write.

But when I saw these things come to pass in Nasiriya, Iraq (because the war began in this city in Iraq); and my brother Reuben a soldier in the Navy; then I spoke to warn my brother against idolatry. But he laughed anew, saying that he truly did worship his family before his God. And I know not whether this was only a joke to annoy me. And this was the last time that I saw Reuben until our tribulation.

Isaiah

14:4    …you will lift up this proverb against the king of Babylon, and say, How has the oppressor ceased!
*The* golden[7] *city* has ceased!

14:12    How are you fallen from *the* heavens, *O* shining son *of the* daybreak! You are hewn down to *the* ground, *which* did weaken nations!

14:16    *They that* see you will look upon you,
*and they will* consider you, *saying, Is* this the man
*who* made the earth to tremble, shaking kingdoms;

17    setting *the* world as a desert, and *who* destroyed its cities;

*who* never opened a home *of* his prisoners?

18    All *the* kings of *the* nations (*even* all of them) lie down in honor, every man in his *own* house;

19    but you *are* cast out from your grave like an abominable branch, *and as* the garment *of* those *that are* slain, pierced through *with a* sword, that go down to *the* stones of *the* pit; as a trampled corpse.

20    You shall not be joined with them in burial, because you corrupted your land: you have slain your people…

14:4    … How has the oppressor ceased! Madhebah[7] has ceased!

5    Adonai has broken *the* rod *of the* wicked, *the* scepter *of the* rulers;

6    *he who* wounded peoples in wrath *with* a wound without turning away, *he that* subjugated the nations in anger, from persecution without restraint.

14:12    How are you fallen from *the* heavens, O shining son *of the* daybreak! You are hewn down to *the* ground, *which* did weaken nations!

14:7    The whole land *is* at rest, and tranquil; they sing, shouting songs of joy.

—Isaiah 13:1-14:28

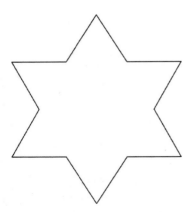

...Blessed *are* those who weep now: because you will laugh.

——Luke 6:21

CHAPTER TWO:
# Weeping (part one)

On the first morning of March, two thousand thirteen, I awoke to find myself doing something I had not done in perhaps thirty-three years: I woke up weeping for the man who should have been a father to me. His name was Dale Stuart Veach. He died suddenly during the night on December 16, two thousand two.

> The tears I cried
> You didn't see
> Wanting your love
> So desperately
>
> Needing you
> To want the love you'd made
>
> Not one thing changed
> The day you died
> Just one more soul
> You pushed aside
>
> You just still weren't there
> Same as always
>
> Baptized five times
> So I've been told
> Just five more lies
> A conman sold
>
> I wish the last one
> Had been true

It wasn't you
It was the wine
What can I answer
This painful line

When I never saw
Just who you were before the wine

I was not planned
You made that plain
One boy, one girl
But still I came

Wanting you
To want the love you'd made

Learned how to love
How to forgive
Learned how to trust
How to open up and give

But I did not learn these things from you
God is my Father

For the first time
In all my life
I want you here
I don't want to say goodbye

No second chances
In the grave




Goodbye forever

Beloved children in my true family—listen; please listen closely: It is good to weep, even for God's enemies; perhaps even especially for such as these; because these shall have no heaven, no joyous resurrection from their death. It is necessary to mourn them.

If we choose not to weep, a part of our own soul slowly dies. My sons and my daughters, fear those, more than all sinners; fear those who have refused to weep for so long a time that they cannot weep. And now, healed by my heavenly Father, ten years late I weep.

Beloved fathers and mothers, sons and daughters, brothers and sisters, fear those who are no longer able to weep. And, if you cannot weep, pray for our loving Father to heal your wounded soul—the answer is already "yes," before you even ask Him: This is one of His favorite prayers to answer. Beloved fathers, sons, and brothers, it is not manly or macho or in any way mature to hold back from weeping: It is a form of spiritual death: To weep is to be truly human and truly alive. Weep for the dead who shall not live again, weep for the harm they have caused and are still causing, and weep for those who cannot weep.

Because I love the One who truly loves them, I pray for the wounded souls of my enemies to be healed, and I weep for them. This was not always true: There was a time when I struggled continually to banish the Hatred and Rage and Fear which welled up from somewhere deep within my soul; and over and over again I would imagine that they were gone at last from my wounded heart, but in truth these three dark, wolf-like predators were always there; always waiting for every moment of spiritual weakness. I could not escape them: I could never escape them: None of us can—but Yeshua has now banished them for me. And so, because I could not escape these three dark, hidden predators dwelling always in the shadows of my heart, God had held me back from writing of three very important miracles of mercy.

But even while my Father held me back, in His eternal mercy He was casting them out: Slowly, slowly, line upon line, precept upon precept, with stammering lips and in a foreign language He has taught me the narrow path of true liberty: He has set me free from the three dark wolves named Hatred, Rage, and Fear. I am free: My Redeemer has set me free: I am free from the jaws of Hatred, I am free from the jaws of Rage, and I am free from the jaws of Fear. I am free to mourn for the dead who shall not live again. And so, after more than ten years, I am ready to write this chapter.

> …Blessed *are* those who weep now: because you will laugh.
>
> —Luke 6:21

Beloved brothers and sisters—because my brothers and sisters you truly are, being children of One Father: This is not just rhetoric or traditional Christian jargon: this is *real*: This brotherhood is *more* real than our temporary flesh connections of this passing world of dust and shadows—I write to you as your real and true sister, because we are born of the same Breath, and re-born of the same Blood.

We are the same, you and I; we are family, you and I, even if we have never yet met face to face, we are already brothers, walking the same path under the same sunshine, following the same Eternal Father. We struggle like brothers and sisters also—and sometimes with a little too much brotherly contempt, which we should daily strive not to do, not even with our temporary siblings—and we must also both weep together and rejoice together, as all siblings must share their sorrows and joy. And so, as both your sister and your daughter, here is my sorrow: that the man who should have been a father to me has both died, and is also dead forever.

In the days between Thanksgiving and Christmas of nineteen seventy-nine, when I was not quite four years old, I had just learned the word "adultery" in a sermon at my mother's church; so I started to tell my mother that Daddy was committing adultery.[8] But she thought I was talking about his regular habit of flirting with other women—right in front of her—so she told me that she also had long suspected him of committing adultery, but it was a sin to make such an accusation without proof—after all, it *was possible* that he never went beyond words with *any* of them. And, she added, to accuse my own father of a mortal sin without being sure would be a violation of the commandment, "Honor your father and your mother.[9]"

Although I believed he *was* sinning against my mother, and although I strongly suspected he was somehow sinning against me as well— although the preacher had never named any such sin—Even so, at three years old, I wasn't quite *sure* of *anything*. And I had no proof.[10]

A humble little child is easily silenced.

And so, I said nothing more to her about it, but I thought and thought almost all that night, wondering just what I ought to do about Daddy's nighttime adulteries with me. I had never heard of the word 'incest,' or of how adultery and incest could be interconnected. And before I fell asleep I prayed, asking God to keep me from the sin of dishonoring my father, and to keep my father from the sin of adultery.

In the morning, I woke up with a plan. *Grandpa Ding-Ding would know what to do.* I was sure of it. And so I asked my mother to take us to Grandpa's house. But she said that we'd just been there for Thanksgiving, and we didn't have the money to go visit Grandpa and Grandma all the time.

But I kept insisting that I needed to talk to Grandpa, so finally she said I could call him on the phone. So I agreed.

But then, Mommy waited until Daddy was home before making the phone call, and the whole family sat there together and listened attentively to every word while we took turns talking to Grandpa.

How could I possibly ask Grandpa what to do while Daddy was right there listening?

I wanted to run into my mommy's bedroom closet and cry, but I tried to be brave and keep trying. So I asked my mother what holiday was next. And when my turn on the telephone finally came, I told Grandpa Ding-ding that I missed him and Grandma, and I wanted to visit them again for Christmas. But this plan didn't work either—It seemed like half a dozen or more other relatives had made the same Christmas plans, and I couldn't get more than a minute alone with Grandpa the whole holiday.

Less than one month later, ten days after my fourth birthday, the man who should have been a father to me was seated at the dining room table, trying to calculate his taxes—while he had a hangover. Not a good idea; especially in a small apartment with small children. His breath and his shirt still smelled of his liquor indulgence of the night before. We were poor because he spent his money on wine. My twin sister Drea, eternally trusting and happy, was being her usual oblivious self, running at his feet in circles around the table, making what I think was supposed to be airplane noises while pretending a toy was flying. (I don't think it was even a toy airplane, but she had plenty of imagination; and whatever it was, it was flying in very noisy circles around Daddy and his tax papers.[11])

My brother and I both saw his anger starting to rise. We knew his temper all too well, and I knew to be afraid whenever he smelled like that.

I don't think we had ever yet thought there was anything different about our sister, but still we both felt particularly protective of her: Somehow, Drea seemed more vulnerable. Maybe this was because of her total and unfailing trust of everyone she met. And now, she was very trustingly annoying a violent Daddy while he was busy trying to do his taxes—with a hangover. To this day, I cannot tolerate the smell of wine, because it was the smell which permeated the air during all of his crimes.

I had already learned that my twin sister and I had one advantage over him—he couldn't tell us apart. So I began to run circles around the table with her; three times I ran all the way around, then I shoved her away and ran right at him, making an even louder airplane noise.

It worked.

She was safe.

But he was still so wiped out from the night before that he completely forgot to hide his violence from our mother. She was standing right there—he, like an enraged animal, picked me up by both shoulders and *shook* me forward and back, *hard*. My mother was a trained nurses' assistant. She knew full well that at my age, this was a *killing* move. Then she understood—she was not his only hidden victim.

She found an excuse to leave the house, and she went to the nearest pay-phone and called our Aunt Rachel. Rachel had never made any secret of totally distrusting him: She had been watching his alcohol abuse—and the violence with it—get progressively worse since the day I was born.

I later heard that Rachel had been clocked by a cop *entering* the freeway at a hundred miles per hour. He got one look at her face and followed quietly: He didn't need hear one word—he saw her face, and he knew better than to pull her over before she got where she needed to go. Now, Rachel is not a small woman, and she wasn't small back then either; and as a former bureaucrat in the Department of Environmental Quality she knew how to get angry; and she knew how to throw her weight around. They pulled up to our apartment door together.[12]

For me, that car ride signified the end of Daddy's adultery. We three children felt safe (most of the time, anyway) during this brand new part of our life. For us, these days were mostly days of peace and safety, and for our brother Reuben, they were days of high adventure:  For the first time, we were free to just be kids.

I praise my God that He answered my ignorant but passionately heartfelt prayer. And I weep that it was needed, and that it continues to be needed on behalf of so many other faithful daughters of our Father Adonai.

I have a tender Father
I call Him Adonai
He lifts me up when I fall down
He answers when I cry

On the day that I was born
He heard my feeble cry
He held me softly in His hands
He did not let me die

I had a human father
It hurts to say his name
He fled away into the dark
I cried out in my pain

On the day that I was born
He sold his soul to wine
He didn't want another child
To use up so much time

I have a tender Father
I call Him Adonai
He lifts me up when I fall down
He answers when I cry

2   I will say to Adonai, My refuge and my fortress:
    my God; I will trust in Him.
3   Because He will deliver you from *the* snare *of the* trapper…

          —Psalm 91:2-91:3

CHAPTER THREE:
# The Traffic Jam

In the days and months after our mother took us and fled to safety, she had to leave us behind nearly every day to go to work. She had to depend on daycares and babysitters to protect us, because the man who should have been a father to us continued to stalk both us and our mother. He tried to kidnap us from our babysitters, and harassed our mother at every job, in order to get her fired. And so she took care to show our daycare workers and babysitters the restraint order forbidding him from entering any building we were in, or from coming within so many feet of us. In addition, our mother strictly charged our caretakers not to release us to anyone but her: Because there was no telling what the man might do to us to punish our mother for divorcing him.

Then early one evening, while she was held up in a traffic jam on her way to pick us up from a Christian daycare facility, he found us. But our Christian caretakers didn't call the police: No! Rather, they were completely taken in by his charm: And without a second thought our caretakers called him our Daddy, and tried to send us with him. But I hid underneath a table, held tightly onto one of the table legs, and screamed; while Reuben[6] David bit him on the leg.

Our sister Drea Michelle, however, ever trusting no matter what, played happily at his feet. But of course he didn't dare grab just one child and run with her, because then the caretakers would have known he was a kidnapper and called the police.

As it was, they merely assumed that Reuben and I were being unreasonable brats, and they were still trying to calm us down and reason with us when our mother showed up. And this was the first time that I had ever seen human pride lead our society to betray us. Now, maybe you'd call it a miracle and maybe you wouldn't, but if the traffic jam hadn't suddenly cleared up just when it did, I don't think we would have been safe at home in our beds that night: A young blond man was already trying to forcibly separate my hands from the table leg.

2      I will say to Adonai, My refuge and my fortress:
my God; I will trust in Him.

3      Because He will deliver you from *the* snare *of the* trapper…

—Psalm 91:2-91:3

Psalm
22:9
Because You *are He* who birthed me out from *the* belly,
causing me to trust *when I was* upon my mother's breasts.

10  I was cast upon You from *the* womb: from my mother's
belly, You *are* my God.

Jeremiah
1:4  And it was, *that a* word of Adonai *came* to me, saying,

5  Before I formed you[14] in *the* belly I knew you; and before
you came out of *the* womb I consecrated you,
*and* I gave you *as a* prophet to *the* nations.

6  And I said, Oh, my Lord[15] Adonai! Behold, I do not know
*how to* speak: because I *am a* child.

——Psalm 22:9-22:10[16]; Jeremiah 1:4-1:6

CHAPTER FOUR:
# Babies in Paradise

Sadly, seven days after our seventh birthday, my twin sister and I were carried away captive from our home and mother. The kidnapper spoke to my mother with a smile and a soft voice. But with her words she half-revealed, half-concealed power, and potential for cruelty and violence. My mother returned smile for smile: Hers was the smile of the immigrant laborer to the landowner with unjust balances; and of the worker to the factory boss with a mattress hidden under his desk; the smile of the lesser gorilla toward the conquering gorilla. It was not out of courtesy that the smiling gentile opened the car door for me, which had no handles on the inside. As soon as the doors closed, the fake smile vanished, together with all her friendly words.

At our destination, the smile returned. She very kindly gave me to understand that the separation was only a temporary arrangement, and in six weeks we would return home, because our mother needed help to get back on her feet.

Our brother was separated from us in another house, and nobody ever gave us his address that we might write to him, nor his telephone number, nor any way to speak with any member of the family.

Our preschool teacher tried hard to replace our mother. Afterward I learned that she had called the kidnappers against my mother, and accused my mother because of my disability; but she thought that the matter would be searched out with great care to discover the truth; and that, if any cause should be found, that the truth would be established before a judge according to Constitutional law.

But all the investigations are corrupted[17] with bribery: Because every state in the union receives a bribe of twenty-thousand dollars for every child taken captive, and another five thousand dollars for every child adopted.

All this bribery is from the same taxpayers who are their victims (courtesy of William Clinton)—and we twins seemed very, very desirable for adoption, because we were very cute, and had very white skin.

Our teacher and her husband were Catholics, and although I had seen many churches, theirs was different—sad, ceremonious, distant: Not a bride so much as a faithful handmaiden: An impression which I recognized later worldwide among Catholics, and also among Muslims and Jews; and also in a few sleeping Christian churches.

And much later, when I was reading these words, I looked with a sad heart upon the Catholic Church, remembering the sorrow of this faithful handmaiden:

> And it shall be in that day, says Adonai,
> *that* you will call me My Husband;
> and you will no more call me My Master.
>
> —Hosea 2:16[18]

But in my childhood I thought that this little congregation was a sleeping Christian church: I saw no difference, but rather sought to revive and awaken the congregation. And the priest said that no one enters heaven without baptism, and no babies go to heaven without being baptized. And I was troubled because of these words; because how could the loving Lord that I know reject a baby? And with the humility of any little girl I heard the priest's words, and sincerely prayed to God for the babies that died unbaptized, to know whether they are alive in paradise, or dead.

And I saw a vision: I was in paradise, next to the shore of a pink, warm lake. And I saw children, from five to nine years of age, all waiting by the lake with soft blankets, each cloth of a different color: because each child waited for a particular baby, and each child knew when and where the baby for her blanket would appear from the lake. And babies, one too small to be born, each arose upward with a great splash; and without any visible wings each waiting child, with her colorful blanket, flew straight forward with arms outstretched for a baby.

And I saw no pattern to where or when the babes arose: but sometimes one baby here, and other times two, or four, or five, there, or there, or there, like fireworks.

And with great joy each child received her babe, and flew to the shore, and ran joyfully away.

And in the next time that we saw our mother, I asked her why the Catholics demand baptism for babies, but the Quakers prohibit infant baptism. And my mother said that a baptism is meaningless without consent: because baptism is a voluntary contract with God, and nobody can give another person's soul to Adonai. Therefore, she said, infant baptism is no different than circumcision for Jewish babies—A religious ritual only between the parents and God, and not the baby.

And my mother said, concerning the Catholics, that perhaps they think that baptism is a magical ritual. But, for the Quakers, it is a wedding with Yeshua, to give the soul to the Messiah forever.

And, from this day onward, I greatly desired baptism; but when the Catholic priest understood that my mother was a Jewish Quaker and no Catholic, he refused at first, because he required my mother's consent: Because the priest understood very well that it is a serious decision to baptize a child of non-Catholic parents (especially a Jewish child) without permission.

And when my mother heard, she wrote to the bishop (having no way to speak to the priest), asking the bishop to persuade the priest: And the bishop searched out the matter with great care, and granted authority. But in the course of the investigation the kidnappers heard of the matter, and hurriedly removed us to a new home, where both parents were a little crazy, but not Catholic.

And my mother wrote to the judge. And the judge, who had promised to protect us children until we returned home, withdrew himself from our case and from his own promise: Because the judge was also Catholic.

And we never again had any God-fearing judge to protect us from the pagans, and we never again lived with God-fearing parents of any faith.

> Therefore do not judge anyone before *the* time;
> until the Lord comes; who also will bring to light
> the secrets[19] *of* the darkness, and will make manifest
> the intentions *of* the hearts…

——First Corinthians 4:5

8    I have *seemed* weird to my brothers,
     and strange to my mother's children.

12   …They who sat *in the* gate talked about me;
     and I *am in the* drunkards' songs.
13   And I—my prayer *is* to You, *O* Adonai,
     *in* a time *of* God's desire: In Your great mercy answer me,
     in *the* truth *of* Your salvation.

                              ——Psalm 69:7-69:13[20]

CHAPTER FIVE:
# Speaking to Souls

According to our mother Shoshanna Miriam, my sister and I hated the sound of one another's crying so much that whenever either of us got started, we would cry about the other twin's crying for hours, until we both cried ourselves to sleep. Consequently, my mother—of necessity—was so attentive that by our first birthday we never cried about anything anymore, being confident that the slightest expression of discomfort would be answered right away. Our mother also said that our folks used to put a mirror in our one crib with us, and (seeing our reflection) we would both try persistently to play with "the other twins"…

I don't suppose we ever actually thought our reflections were exactly what we were, since we never sensed that they had their own separate souls, but we both certainly seemed to think they were some sort of somebody sharing our little bed.

Our mother finds twin stories fascinating, as do many people; but to us, twins were of course as ordinary as our own reflections in the mirror: And as a small child I never even thought about what it must be like to have my own unique DNA, or birthday, or my own clothes in my own closet, or even my own face: To have come in a matched pair seemed as natural to both of us as having two ears, two feet, two mirror-image thumbs on two hands, and two deep brown and slightly slanted eyes with two bushy eyebrows. For the first few years of my life, it never even occurred to me to think of the idea of "myself."

Then, when our mother brought us to church, we noticed that the other children almost never came in pairs. I recall wondering what could have happened to the other children's twins. But it didn't take those grownups long to teach me that twins are quite rare and special; and identical twins even more so.

Almost as soon as we'd mastered the art of running, my sister and I invented a game we came to call "church tag"—The ground floor of the whole chapel was joined room to room in a big loop, so that we could scamper from the chapel sanctuary to the entrance hall, from the entrance hall to the nursery, and from the nursery to the chapel sanctuary: And it was a delightful diversion to both run this loop at full speed, taking care to run the same direction at the same speed, exactly opposite from one another so that no one

in the building could see both of us at the same time; and our mother says that invariably there was among the ladies another newcomer to the church who hadn't heard about the twins: And with a worried look on her face she'd invariably say something to the effect that *Somebody ought to slow that speedy child down!*

Our mother was in on our little prank, of course, and without batting an eyelash or missing a beat in the conversation she just scooped up the next twin to run past her, and then the second child when she came near, and you should have seen the look our mother got to see on those ladies' faces! It was worth a good, long laugh every single Sunday morning.

Like a great many other identical twins, my sister and I could read each other's minds, share the same dream at night, speak our own mysterious language no one else understood, and my sister could always finish my sentences almost as soon as I opened my mouth to speak. Even as grown women, we never needed one another's phone number because, if it was anything important, the other twin always already knew.

But we were most certainly not the same person in two bodies: From the beginning I was the brave and rambunctious tomboy adventurer, while Drea knew full well, whenever I tried something new, to wait a few minutes to see what would become of me. I liked dogs, dirt, trees, and all of the games those unfair boys always played without us girls; while my sister Drea liked our frilly cute matching dresses, sugar cookies, baby dolls, and fat puffy pink curlers in her hair to cover her head with adorable auburn Shirley Temple curls. Now, time would eventually reveal my sister Drea Michelle to be the more reckless of the two; but when we were small she seemed more cautious than I, for no other reason than that she had the good sense to wait and see what sort of trouble my latest new adventure would lead to: And when we were still quite small girls, I learned exactly how to climb up to the top of our wooden crib: And climb up to the top is just what I did. Then I just perched there, puzzled, as the realization slowly overcame us both that I hadn't the slightest idea how to climb down.

I haven't any idea how long I perched there before I grew tired of being stuck, and with all my strength I leaped from the crib railing, with every hope and intention that I would somehow learn mid-air how to fly.

I remember perching on top of my crib that day, bewildered by the realization that I did not know how to climb down yet, and I remember the moment when I decided to jump out into the air with all my might.

I have no memory of hitting my little noggin on our big wooden dresser, nor of hitting the floor afterward, nor of the blood-curdling scream with which my mother says I announced my utter disappointment at the top of my tiny little lungs, nor of the quickly spreading puddle of blood in which my mother says she found me when she came running into our bedroom.

But to this day I have a bald scar on my left eyebrow to remind me that I can't fly, and by which I was evermore easily told apart from the other twin as Angel Naomi, the one who tried to fly while her sister Drea Michelle quite sensibly stayed behind in our crib, watching to see whether her sister could fly.

Unreasonable courage was neither the only nor the biggest difference between us two: And when we were seven years old, we met a chained-up dog who had been so thoroughly abused that she hated humans: By a vicious sinful man, an innocent sinless friend was made vicious. My sister and I were told to stay away; but I (the unseen soul) slipped away unnoticed and unmissed. I knelt at the paws of my fellow creature, apologizing to her for the sin and cruelty of man. And once she understood that I had come in peace, I gently stroked the soft fur on her shoulder.

The creature was so lonely that she was hungry for my touch: Fear of humanity had left her wounded unseen soul perpetually desperately lonely: I was one of only two people in her life whose hands she dared to trust, because God had given me the gift of talking to animals' souls.

When I turned to leave, my sister Drea was staying in the shadows watching; and so I reminded her that the dog was vicious, and could in no wise be petted because human cruelty had left the dog terrified of nearly everyone: Only her owner, over many patient months, had won this wounded soul's trust and could pet her fur without getting bitten. But although Drea seemed as if she understood, in truth she did not understand: Almost immediately my sister returned to the dog, thinking to herself that if I could pet the animal safely, so could she: We looked the same, we must have also smelled the same—but in truth God had not given my twin sister the same gift of talking to animal spirits.

And I was greatly ashamed because I knew that by my example I had caused my sister to get bitten by a big vicious dog. Our spirits were not the same:

I was a different creature than Drea Michelle, indeed, I was a different creature than all the children around me: There was no doubt in either of our minds that I was The Other One, the one the doctor didn't see on the ultrasound photo, the extra, uninvited, unexpected third child in our planned family of two parents, one strong, intelligent son, and one cute, dainty daughter whose greatest sorrow in life seemed to be that she had not inherited our mother's mane of incurably untamable curly golden hair.

I was The Other One, the one who was afterward called by my pagan caretakers an Ancient Soul; I was the child who, when my feminist schoolteachers asked me what I wanted to be when I grew up, chose mother, or prophetess, or superhero, or even light bulb; the one who was laughed at by other children because I would read dictionaries for fun; the one who saw and dreamed things before they came to pass; the one who would kneel at my grandfather's feet and hear his old stories rather than wiggle and giggle and play like a child; the one whose name was Messenger.

I was the Other One.

…thus says Adonai your Creator, *O* Jacob, and your Potter, *O* Israel: Do not be afraid: because I have redeemed you, I called you by your name: you *are* mine.

—Isaiah 43:1

Jeremiah
11:19
...and I did not know that they had schemed thoughts against me, *saying*, We will ruin *a* tree with its food, and we will cut him off from *the* land *of the* living, and his name will be remembered no more.

Psalm
52:8
Yet I *am* like *a* green olive tree in *the* house *of* God: I trust in *the* mercy *of* God for ever and ever.

—Jeremiah 11:19; Psalm 52:8[21]

CHAPTER SIX:

# The Everyday Miracle of a Tree

My sister loved to be a pretty little twin girl, and so for her sake I reluctantly tolerated the adorable little identical dresses which she was so fond of wearing. But in truth I couldn't possibly care less what I looked like; and so I was inclined to forget altogether about the frilly skirts which almost invariably adorned my scarred and calloused awkward knees. Up the nearest tree I would scamper and climb, neither noticing nor minding when a ruffle or a bit of lace remained behind where a rough twig had snagged it somewhere; and sheepishly I would apologize to my mother and to my poor sister, who through no fault of her own had lost yet another pair of cute matching frilly dresses to wear with her identical twin.

I was truly sorry for her loss every single time, but unfortunately I just loved trees the way she loved our frilly little twin skirts.

And because I didn't care one whit what I looked like, I also just didn't understand why it seemed so important to my family to dress us alike in the first place.

And so it happened, when we were about five or six years old, that I got some bubble gum stuck in my hair; and so after expending a great deal of wasted effort on removing the bubble gum, I cut it out with scissors. Now, neither of us minded at all when my mother gave me a very short and rather tomboyish haircut afterward to minimize the damage; but then, to our mutual disgust, she gave my poor sister the same tomboyish haircut so we would still look alike, which we both regarded as dreadfully unfair.

Although I remained totally indifferent to everyone else's efforts to make a young lady of me, there came a summer (when we were about seven years old) when I did start to care what I looked like. Two dresses which stuck in my memory from that summer were a matching pair of identical striped sundresses, brand new, which were handmade just for us twins; and we wore them for the very first time on a visit to a petting zoo. But while we were feeding the adorable little white baby goats, two mischievous twin goats snuck up behind us and nibbled two twin holes in our new twin sundresses! My sister and I were almost in tears, but everyone else couldn't stop laughing.

One day that same bright summer, as we were shopping for dresses in a second-hand store, I saw a fancy, colorful Spanish dancing dress just my size with a multicolored skirt which would spread out like a gorgeous bright flower when I twirled.

Seeing that there was only one, Drea frowned at it: My sister was still rather fond of dressing alike. But this only made me want the Spanish twirly-skirt more, and I was overjoyed when our foster mother bought it for me—I had never had a pretty little dress that was just my style, without any bows, frills, sashes or laces to catch on trees, a pretty little dress which swirled prettily out of the way so that I could run, leap, climb, tumble and twirl as much as I pleased, as freely as if I were wearing trousers instead. And, to my delight and my sister's annoyance, my Spanish twirly-skirt was unique and just mine, only mine! I had never actually had my very own clothes before, and I wore it nearly all that summer until it could no longer be mended, because even in my very favorite dress I kept on climbing trees.

I don't know if it's a sign, or just a coincidence that I was born on *Tu b'Shevat*, the Hebrew "New Year's Day for Trees", but from the very beginning I've had a love for and connection to trees of every kind, and also for objects made of natural wood. My sister's connection is different: She can hear how trees are feeling.

And when we were still quite young, we often visited the house of our mother's parents, Grandpa Ding-Ding and Grandmother Margaret. And we all called Grandfather Nathan "Grandpa Ding-Ding" because he sang "ding-ding" when we tugged his thick, bushy beard. And one day when we visited our grandparents' house, there were so many visitors that Grandpa Ding-Ding didn't have enough chairs to sit everybody down to dinner: So he cut some short logs and brought them inside to use for extra chairs. But I kept playing with them. And when Grandfather Nathan saw me drinking out of a tin cup while balancing on one of these logs, rolling it about on his kitchen floor, he sternly told me to get down and not to play that way anymore.

I obediently got down, but then I forgot right away what he had said, and I did the same thing all over again. And this time, the log rolled right out backwards from underneath my feet, so that I fell face-down on the hard kitchen floor, with the tin cup still at my lips, which cut my smile nearly an inch wider on both sides, as well as cutting a deep gash through the cartilage on my nose. And the two mouth cuts healed up pretty quick, but to this day I have a wide scar across the bridge of my nose, to remind me of when I learned to obey my grandfather, because his loving commands were meant to guide me on the path of righteousness and protect me from harm.

A few years later, when I was about nine years old, I was sent to a secular, government-run orphanage called Parry Center for Children, which had about ninety children living there at a time in three large houses.

One of the well-documented attributes of Autism Spectrum Disorder is that autistic children cannot handle large groups of people, especially crowds of playing children: It was irresponsible, damaging, and potentially deadly to put autistic children there, and if a private citizen had done any such thing to his own daughter, he would have lost custody for child abuse. And I was not the only autistic child they did this to.

But, unlike some less fortunate others, my autism was mild enough that I was able to devise coping strategies to stay sane in this abusive environment: And one such strategy was that at my very first outdoor playtime I decided to climb up into a gigantic oak tree in the large, grassy courtyard between the three houses.

What did those adults expect me to do—stay on the lawn with that disorganized mob of children and suffer a potentially fatal nervous breakdown from sensory overload? Apparently so: Because several of those so-called adults became very agitated as soon as they realized I was up there, and told me to come down and not climb that tree ever again.

But I had already noticed that their commands were unlike the commands of my mother and my grandfather: They were not necessarily for my well-being so much as for their own. And because careful, respectful spankings which cause no injuries are considered by the State of Oregon as child abuse, the accustomed method of disciplining us at this orphanage was instead to forcibly lay us down on our faces on the cold, dirty hallway floor and to sit upon our backs, pulling our little arms backward in order to hold both wrists in an unnatural and painful position behind our shoulder blades, so that we feared our arm-bones would be pulled loose[22] from their shoulder sockets; and if we dared to cry out from the pain, to stay there even longer until we fell silent from terror.

And so I, noticing that all of the angry adults were too awkward and fat to climb the tree to come after me, refused to come down.

I didn't want to return to those angry women, some of whom weighed two to three hundred pounds.

Nor did I want to return to the dangerously over-stimulating chaotic mob of children below.

So I stayed in the tree.

And the women called the head administrator of the orphanage out from the administration building, and he came out and asked me why I was in the tree (as if none of them had noticed that I could scarcely speak better than a weaned infant). And I told him it was a very nice tree to climb, and I invited him to climb up and see for himself.

And he laughed, and told me that the staff member standing next to him had told me to come down. And I asked the administrator whether there was a rule in the rule book against tree climbing, and he said he hadn't heard of one, but that I should obey anyway.

And I just shrugged my shoulders, and I laughed, saying that if any one of those city slickers was small enough to do it, then she should climb the tree and carry me down. Then I invited the head administrator again to join me up in the tree, and he commented that he wasn't sure just who was up a tree around there, and he walked away laughing.

And while this entire amusing ruckus was playing out, another little girl was up the tree with me, on a higher branch; a chubby little blonde child with a bright pink shirt; who also scolded me for being there; because she had already claimed the big oak tree as her own: And she imperiously commanded me to get out of her tree.

Indignant, I just scolded her right back, declaring that the giant oak tree was far too big for just one little girl to claim the whole thing for herself.

So she answered back, "Well, *this* is *my branch*, then. You can't sit on *this* branch." So I looked around, chose my own favorite branch—I didn't even like the one she was sitting on anyway, because it didn't even have much of a view—and I plunked myself down in my favorite spot, folded my arms across my chest in a mocking imitation of her posture, and said, "Then *this* is *my* branch, and you can only sit on it if I invite you." And we sat and stared at each other for quite some time without another word.

And the women below us called the police—they never seemed to even notice that the other girl was up there with me, and I wasn't about to bother tattling on my new tree-neighbor, whose perch did have the singular advantage of being much better hidden from the adults than my own. And a police officer came outdoors, and he looked up at me sitting there. And the police officer then told me that the adults who had been given charge over my well-being were concerned for my safety, and had therefore commanded me to come down, and that I should probably obey them. And I asked him if I was breaking any city or state law, and he said no. And I asked him if he was going to climb the tree and remove me if I should refuse to come down, and the officer said "no." And so I said, "Then I'm staying right here: None of these women are my mother, and I don't feel like coming down right now." Then, laughing, he commented that I had found a fine, strong climbing tree, and he told the pagan women that I would eventually come down on my own when I got cold or hungry enough; and then the police officer walked away, chuckling to himself as he went.

Seeing that she wasn't rid of me so easily, the girl began to talk. Her name was Dawn[23] Larsen, and (although we were about the same height) she was almost two years older than me, and we were to share a bedroom. From that day on, Dawn and I were best friends.

But, to continue the narrative of what happened when this nine-year-old ever so *scandalously* dared to *act like a child* by *climbing a tree*, the comically obese adults below us still were not satisfied, so they told me I had to come down because their insurance plan did not cover children climbing up into trees, and that I was, therefore, financially endangering all the children because Parry Center for Children could lose its insurance coverage for this *"outrageous and reckless behavior."*

As alarmingly irrational as these city slickers were, they were also rather entertaining.

Grinning, I double-dog dared the loudest one to send the insurance agent to order me out of the tree, and promised that I would immediately come down if their insurance agent came to me in person and said to my face that Parry Center for Children could lose their insurance because I was in the tree. I began to wonder just how many sane people these strange women would send at me before it dawned on them which of us was behaving strangely.

I was really starting to enjoy this game.

Less than an hour later, an insurance agent came and stood under the giant oak tree, staring up at me (utterly amused) for a short while as she listened to the fat caretakers explaining their predicament.

Then she asked me how I had gotten up there so high, and I answered that I had climbed up the trunk, and then from branch to branch. Then she asked me if anyone had helped me get up the tree, and I said no. Then she asked me if I had much experience with climbing trees before, and I answered that I'd been doing it ever since I could remember. Then she asked if I had ever gotten hurt falling out of a tree, and I said no.

Finally, she asked me if I understood why the adults wanted me to stay on the ground, and I said, "I don't know. Am I breaking any insurance laws? The police officer said I wasn't breaking any city or state laws. Can Parry Center really lose its safety insurance because I like to climb trees?" The woman laughed, and forbade me from climbing any higher up any of the trees than I could without help, and she walked away shaking her head, her shoulders heaving in silent laughter.

As I said before, from that day on Dawn and I were best friends; but when my best friend Dawn Larsen was removed to a different place we lost contact permanently, because Child Protective Services cares more about its "confidentiality" policies than it does about our need for continued friendship and love, and so telling either of us how to contact the other was strictly forbidden.

Now, my lifelong fondness for trees was not at all limited to climbing them. I also naturally excelled at woodcrafts, and I also built various tree-houses over the years, including one in the shape of a gigantic robin's nest about three feet across, in the lower branches of a little old pear tree, when I was about fifteen years old.

Each climbing tree I found became a comfortable quiet place for me; a refuge from the bustle and noise below, in which I could shut out the chaos and lean back against the smoothly swaying branches, listening to the wind as I read a book; and—as often as I could escape the planned chaos of the mad world below—I was almost always reading one book or another, because my mother had quite fortunately taught both of us twins how to read the Bible when we were quite young.

Whenever I got hold of a new book, I would bury my nose in the middle pages and breathe deep, filling my lungs with the scent of fresh new paper, and I would close my eyes and imagine the whole journey the wood pulp must have taken, from the moment the tree was cut down until the brand-new book was removed from the gluing press, and wrapped in its shiny new jacket, and boxed up to be sent to a bookstore.

I would spend nearly every free moment reading fiction novels, 'how-to' books, histories, joke books, social commentaries, comic books, textbooks from college and kindergarten and from every grade in between, and poetry. I would even spend hours reading Webster's unabridged dictionary. I especially adored reading poetry when I was a child.

My favorite book was usually the Holy Bible, but I was rarely allowed to have one, and when I did I was almost never allowed to read it: Reading the Bible invariably went onto my record as "self-isolation" and "withdrawing from social situations," even though the same was never said about the countless hours I spent reading poetry, or even the time when I spent the whole day from breakfast until suppertime reading the dictionary, stopping only reluctantly for lunchtime.

Years later when I had children of my own, I spent far less time climbing up into trees, and far more time with baby trees in my hands: I take great delight in saving every seed from every good fruit we eat, and planting them in every available pot, and then giving away the young fruit trees to anyone willing to accept one.

As soon as I find it has newly emerged from the earth, I joyfully welcome each new tree sprout into the world with a prayer: I ask Adonai to protect this new living thing from harm, and nourish it with His rain and sunlight, and use it to bless His faithful creatures with good nourishing food.

And I taught my children Manasseh, Elishevah, and Mattithias to pray likewise for their own baby trees.

Jeremiah

17:5     Thus says Adonai: Cursed *is* the strong *man* who trusts in man, and makes flesh his arm,[24]
and his heart turns away from Adonai.

6     And he will be like *a* juniper in *the* desert, and he will not see when good comes; but he will inhabit parched places in *the* wilderness,[25] *in a* salty and uninhabited land.

7     Blessed *is* the strong *man* who trusts in Adonai, and whose confidence is Adonai.

8     And he will be like *a* tree planted by *the* waters, sending out his roots to *the* stream, and he will not be afraid because *the* heat *is* coming: and his leaf will be green, and he will not worry in *the* year of drought; neither will he cease from yielding fruit.

——Jeremiah 17:5-17:8

42 …And in His departing, the multitude thronged Him.

43 And *a* woman being in *a* flow *of* blood since twelve years *of age*, who had spent all her living upon physicians, neither could be healed by any,

44 came behind; *and* she touched the fringe[26] *of* His garment: and immediately her flow of blood stopped…

—Luke 8:42-8:48

CHAPTER SEVEN:

# Double Pneumonia

When my parents were newlyweds, my mother wanted to have several children, according to the ways and beliefs of our people, that our God who loves creating children has commanded us to be fruitful and multiply, and fill the earth. But her husband *wasn't* interested in having children. And so it was, after much discussion, he agreed reluctantly to have exactly two children, preferably a smart, strong boy and a dainty little girl. And so it was that about one year after the wedding, just as they had planned, our mother bore to her husband a strong, smart, healthy, rambunctious son, who is our brother Reuben David Goldenstein, the father of Noah Ezra and the husband of Noah's mother Cindra. (But our mother had not named him Reuben, but rather she gave him the gentile name of Rick, which means "Wealthy"; but our brother had rejected this name as soon as he could talk, and he had it legally changed to Reuben soon after his eighteenth birthday.)

Then, about a year and a half later, our mother's doctor decided that it was time for our pregnant mother to give birth to her second child, having calculated its age by our mother's weight gain and belly circumference.

And he induced labor and went home, telling our mother that she would probably give birth on the afternoon of the next day. (And these are common practices among allopathic doctors; first, for men to specialize in childbirth; and second, to induce labor for the sake of convenient scheduling when it is not medically indicated.)

But the doctor had mistaken both our due date and our speed of delivery, because he thought there was only one baby in the womb; and our mother went into hard labor almost immediately; and so the man's vacation was ended quite abruptly.

Just as the doctor hurried back into the hospital building my head appeared, and at the moment he rushed back into the room, one of the nurses holding me announced, "It's a girl." Because they still did not know there were two of us, but until my sister's head appeared they kept telling our mother not to push for birthing the placenta, and they wondered why she wasn't obeying. And the doctor found himself presented not with one healthy full-term little girl, but with slightly premature twins; and we were both blue. And throughout our infancy we struggled to keep breathing, and remained at high risk for Sudden Infant Death Syndrome, which used to be called Crib Death. And every sickness of the lungs or throat was for us a brush with death, so that our mother became accustomed to listening constantly for our loud, raspy breath; and whenever she couldn't hear it she would rush into the room, for fear that we had stopped breathing yet again.

Nor did my health troubles end there, because the doctor had also failed to diagnose our mother's pregnancy-induced diabetes: And we had both adapted by helping to supply enough insulin for the three of us.

And I, being the larger of the twins, had the more productive pancreas; which even after I was born continued to make extra insulin for my mother: So I stopped breathing nine hours after the birth.

I continued struggling for breath until my seventeenth summer, when it pleased God to miraculously restore my badly scarred lungs and bronchia.

Earlier, when we were three years old, my sister and I both got pneumonia, which quickly became double pneumonia. But the doctors and nurses at the hospital kept reassuring our mother that we would be alright. But we kept getting sicker. Finally, the day came when one of the nurses couldn't look my mother in the eye and say we were going to live. So the next Sunday morning, my mother checked us both out of the hospital, carried us into her church, set us down before the altar, and prayed. And we were completely healed of our double pneumonia that same day,

whereas the doctors' Western Medicine had not been able to cure our lungs at all. And I grew up hearing this story of our miraculous faith healing, and so from my earliest memories I was aware of our own mortality, and of God.

11  Because I know the thoughts that I think toward you,
    says Adonai, thoughts of peace, and not of evil,
    to give to you *a* future and *a* hope.
12  And you will call upon me, and you will walk
    and you will pray to me, and I will hear you deeply;[27]
13  and you will seek me, and you will find *me*,
    because you will search for me with all your heart.
14  And I will be found by you, says Adonai...

—Jeremiah 29:11-29:14

CHAPTER EIGHT:
# Visions of a Joy yet to Come

When my sister and I were about nine years old, and living with crazy people—because our government had for religious reasons taken us away from our loving Catholic foster parents and placed us with a pair of slightly crazy people—I became afraid for our safety and begged our latest caseworker to move us to a home with sane parents in it.

But she decided to remove me only, despite the judge's promise that we would be kept together, because the judge had recently broken his promise to protect us until we were returned home, and had instead withdrawn himself from our case.

And I was separated from my sister Drea and placed in a government-run orphanage, because our caseworker had decided that my sister was slowing me down in learning to talk. (Drea always knew what I wanted to say and kindly spoke my thoughts for me.)

But without my twin I didn't learn to speak any faster: Instead I was the more deeply alone, having nobody to talk for me and therefore nobody I could talk to, except of the simplest things. (I often felt that I spoke like a toddler.)

Nor could I relate well to the other ninety or so children at the orphanage—the multitude, the throng, the anxious, squabbling crowded mass from which there was no escape day after day—because the ones I met all shared a child's innocent assumption of immortality, while I was very much aware of death. At times I felt that it was like a school in which the bell never rang to go home, but only the worst aspects of a school. Nor could I join in many of their games, because of my bronchial asthma, and my scarred lungs, and my occasional unexplained seizures.

Still, I didn't consider myself a weakling: I had stronger muscles and greater discipline and physical endurance than any of the other girls, and would probably have been an athlete if we hadn't been premature: But I couldn't run or jump with the other girls because of my scarred lungs.

I also had to avoid dust, and smog, and cigarette smoke, and many perfumes, and guinea pigs, and cold air, all of which could cause me to stop breathing; and I had to stay away from any child with a cold. And so, even in a home with about ninety other children, for four years I was almost completely alone.

When I was seven years old, and again when I was eleven, I asked to be baptized; but I had no such liberty: Because, seven days before our seventh birthday, my twin sister and I were carried away captive from our mother's loving arms by the Beast[28] with great iron teeth; and this Beast opposed my baptism, saying that Christianity is child abuse, and that the Beast is our benefactor, to save the soul from the gospel of Messiah Jesus.

And with great cruelty my request was crushed for the second time, when I was eleven years old; for the Beast with great iron teeth (not willingly, but after several redundant court orders) permitted me to attend church once a week, but only until I asked to be baptized. Then, claiming (from a fictitious law) that "Separation of church and state" is a constitutional law, the Beast commanded that I, a "ward of the state" had therefore to remain separated from the Christian Church. (But the Beast never says this of the Buddhist church, nor any other congregation in which the Living God is not worshipped.)

Neither was the Beast contented only to separate my body from the church, to prevent my baptism, but also the state cut off all visitations with both girls and our young brother, although my mother had with constant humility never rebelled against any of the dark, wicked regulations. Neither was the Beast contented with all this oppression, but also demanded of the court without cause to terminate all of her parental rights; although, even four years after our fly-by-night kidnapping, they had found no testimony against my mother, although many false witnesses were presented.

But in the end came false witnesses, who said that my autism is a symptom of child abuse. —And the psychologists at one time believed this lie in their pride: But this lie has already been tested and found false in nineteen sixty; nevertheless the witnesses spoke thus thirty years later: However, those psychologists have known

since nineteen sixty that autism is congenital: That is, that autistic children are in reality autistic from birth. And they also know that autism is physical and neurological.

But the religion psychology does not forbid lies, if the cause is advantageous to them—and to them there is no cause more advantageous than to fight against every religion that worships the Living God; and especially against those who trust in His Son Yeshua.

Of a certainty I say that I walked with God in my childhood; and that I heard the voice of Messiah Yeshua, and the quiet whisper of the Holy Spirit, when I was but a four-year-old girl, and that the Living Lord had given me a vision then, and that He also gave me three more visions in nineteen eighty-seven, when I was an eleven year old girl:

In my first vision in nineteen eighty-seven, I saw my husband Benaiah in rags, when he was already mine husband; and his appearance was the same as when Benaiah, seeing my afflicted childhood, prayed that God would comfort me: And in truth the vision of my future husband had comforted me.

The second vision which I saw in nineteen eighty-seven I saw twice again (although that third time it was a dream): It is written later in the book.

And the third vision which I saw in nineteen eighty-seven is this: Six youths were together, and four of them were as Choctaw Indians in form and clothing; but one of these four (the only girl) was dressed like the daughters of the tribe of Manasseh; and their captain was dressed like an American.

And the sixth youth was so short that I saw his face between the legs of the eldest, but I knew not whether he was a dwarf or without feet; and this short youth was Germanic.

All of the six had pale skin, and both the captain and the short youth had clear blue eyes and blond hair: but the other four had brown eyes and brown hair. And the eldest youth had my same likeness: so that I knew immediately that he was my own future son: And a silent voice said to me that the four like Choctaw Indians were all mine, and also a fifth; a little baby girl whom I saw not in the vision (although I did sense her presence with me); and that the short youth was my brother Reuben's son, and yet also not his son.

And the captain was not my son, the same is a wise man of God, and a perfect shot, but also crippled, unable to run: And my son of his same age, this son was his right hand man, very zealous for our Lord, and a faithful servant, and a fast, strong runner.

These six warriors were in a wood, in a forested valley, during wartime; and the father of my four I saw not, but he was hidden nearby at home, in a cave, and I knew the land by the plants and trees, in what part of the world was this wood. And I know that this war is the same war which I saw in Nasiriya, Iraq; which begins in Nasiriya, but ends in Nazareth, Israel: Because the war shall cover all the earth before the end.

3   Behold, children *are an* inheritance of Adonai:
    *The* fruit *of the* belly *is a* reward.
4   Like arrows in *the* hand *of a* strong *man*,
    so *are* the children of the youths:
5   Happy *is* the strong *man*
    who has filled his quiver with them…

———Psalm 127:3-127:5

...this *is* my name for ever, and this *is* my remembrance *from* generation to generation.

———Exodus 3:15

# CHAPTER NINE:

# God's Healing Presence

Although in truth I walked with God in my childhood; nevertheless, of a truth I say that almost, almost I lost my soul forever because of the soft deception called psychology, which is sorcerology carefully concealed: For of a truth I say that, although I walked closely to the living Lord until my eleventh year, when I was a child of twelve, very subtly and gently, so softly that I never felt the hook of the Enemy in my nose, and so that I knew not that I no longer walked with the true Lord of my soul, but walked with the wisdom of the world. In this way, many psychologists slowly drowned my soul in the waters of darkness, until the hands of Adonai my Father touched me.

In nineteen ninety two, when I was a young woman of sixteen, and almost drowned in my despair, the Holy Presence enveloped me in a thick invisible cloud.

But I knew not that this cloud was the God of my fathers, but only that it was a very big spirit, not human, and very loving and beautiful beyond all human words. So I asked, and said: "Who are you? *What* are you?" And the big Spirit said, "I AM."

And at His voice I trembled, and I bowed myself and worshipped the great I AM, but I knew not that I AM is the name of the living God, the God of my fathers.

And all the youths in this place had authority to paint this wall where I AM spoke to me, with only these rules: First, No obscenity, no disrespect, and nothing sexual or offensive: And second; that everyone also had authority to remove any painting which offends, with or without cause, and that in the end all the paintings are removed.

Then, to commemorate this amazing experience—because I was as a mute, but only beginning to open my mouth—therefore I created for a monument a painting with words, which said, "I AM was here, " so that my friends might ask what this was.

Then, for three days a controversy arose among the other young women, but no one spoke of this in my presence. And in the third day a friend disclosed to me the whole controversy: Because the majority of my friends said of the painting, that I had a civil right, in the United States Constitution, freely to write and to speak: Because in truth this is a sacred right to many of us Americans; and all of my friends also knew that this right was sacred to me.

But others, including my greatly beloved friend, were not able to bear this work of my hands: Because they considered my words blasphemy, as if I had called myself the Holy Name, I AM. (And this is the first time—that I remember—that anyone had ever said to me that the God of my fathers is called "I AM.")

And neither did this friend want to disclose to me this controversy: But she saw that only I was able to put an end to the incessant quarreling.

I was amazed, and shook my head, and finally I said that both sides were in the right: —because all of us had authority to paint these words, and all of us had authority to remove any offensive painting, with or without cause: Therefore I said, Remove: Because certainly my companions were offended, and certainly if all paintings are removed in the end, then no painter has any authority to preserve any painting.

And the house was at peace once again, but now all the girls were either my friend or my enemy; none remained neutral; no, none in all the house. Neither did my friends look upon my face the same, but as if they beheld some insect from outer space.

And the adults were also divided likewise into two groups: but the part in power was against all who believe in the living God; therefore the psychologists were against my soul, to break my will and my faith: And with wise deception they robbed me of every thought of this miracle: A youth is very easily distracted.

Senselessness; how foolish I was, even enough to exchange the sure guidance of the All-knowing Adonai—in whom is no deception—for the unsteady guidance of man! Thus I sunk in the mire falsely called science, and like a donkey in a pit I knew not to fight for my life until escape was already almost impossible.

Pride, hatred, bitterness, prejudice, despair, wrath, apathy— the dark waters of the pride of man almost devoured all memory of the Messiah in my heart, and with overwhelming pain I struggled to escape from the darkness. But I still believed in the human wisdom called psychology.

I believed when one psychologist after another said that the darkness and the pain must get worse first, and then heal. I believed when one after another taught me to think on much human wisdom which is false, deceptive, unjust, polluted, and cruel.[29] I believed when one psychologist after another taught me to think on slanders and on worthless and scorn-worthy thoughts.[29] In this way, many psychologists robbed my mind, to slowly drown my soul in the waters of darkness, without delay; even immediately after Adonai had touched me.

Eleven years of my life, from my seventh birthday, I saw that apart from God, man is evil, perverse, and depraved. I saw, and heard, and I bear testimony of more evil than my heart could speak and yet live; of such sins as which the apostle Paul wrote:

12     …Because *it* is shameful even *to* speak of the hidden *deeds* being done among them.

15     Watch, then, how diligently you walk;
       not as fools, but as wise,
16     redeeming the time, because the days are hurtful.

—Ephesians 5:12, 5:15-5:16

My faith was completely broken. My soul was submerged in the waters of darkness, and I saw no ray of light, neither knew I where to swim to find the air: I raised my voice and cried in the darkness, asking how a good God could possibly create such evil.

Then God answered me sadly, saying that He had not created evil: The world He created was good, and there had been no evil in it.[30] And He spoke to me of my Hebrew heritage, and of His Law, and of His holy son Yeshua; and again His presence enveloped me in a thick invisible cloud, and I bowed myself prostrate upon the floor.

Soon afterward, in the twenty-eighth day of the Hebrew month *Adar*, and in the twenty-first of March, I was baptized in my mother's church: And immediately, when I arose from the baptismal waters, my heart was bound with a severe longing for the land of the tribe of Manasseh: And before I ever saw the face of my husband Benaiah, I also saw that I would give birth to a son in the land of Israel, and that his name would be called Manasseh,[31] and that I would return to the United States with my son. (But I forgot his name right away, as soon as I had told my cousin; because I did not have a good memory for names.)

31     Behold, *the* days come, says Adonai, and I will cut with *the* house *of* Israel and with *the* house *of* Judah *a* New Covenant:

32     Not like *the* covenant[32] that I cut with their fathers in the day *that* I took them by the hand to bring them out of *the* land *of* Egypt—my covenant which they annulled,[33]
    —and I, I was *a* husband; *I was* with them; says Adonai:

33     Because[34] this *is* the covenant that I will cut with *the* house *of* Israel: After those days, says Adonai, I will give my law in their nearest *being*, and upon their heart I will write it; and will be to them for God, and they will be to me for *a* people.

34     And they will not teach any more *any* man with his neighbor, nor *any* man with his brother, saying, Know[35] Adonai: because all of them will know me...

—Jeremiah 31:31-31:34[36]

Manasseh

27 And you will know that I *am* in *the* midst of Israel,
and *that* I *am* Adonai your God, and there is no other:
And forever my people shall never be put to shame.

28 And afterward it will be *that* I will pour out my Spirit upon
all flesh; and your sons and daughters will prophesy:
Your old *ones* shall dream dreams,
*and* your young *ones* shall see visions;

29 And also upon the servants and upon the handmaids
in those days I will pour out my Spirit.

30 And I will give wonders in *the* heavens and in *the* earth…

—Joel 2:27-2:30[37]

CHAPTER TEN.

# An Undesired Prophecy

When I was four, a prophetic vision was given to me; and a prophetic premonition when I was six or seven.[38] And when I was seven years old, another vision was given to me; but I kept them in my heart, being only a small child. When I was eleven years old, three more prophetic visions were given to me. I kept these also quietly in my heart, being only a little girl, easily kept in silence. Soon afterward, I fell aimlessly into sin, and was no longer a pure hearted child. When I was sixteen years old, badly broken by the dark forces of the world, the living God caused me to feel His presence.

I began to show others what God had caused me to see. But, as before, my teenage friends mocked me into silence.

When I was seventeen, my soul was completely broken. I was at the edge of death, suicidal, because of the deep suffering within my soul.

I had stood by helplessly while my best friend was placed in the hands of someone who had publicly sworn to kill him. This was done for no other reason than the color of his skin. He was only a twelve year old boy, with a pure heart so full of life; rejoicing every day with me in the music of his beautiful people; rejoicing every day in our friendship; loving everyone he met with a beautifully open heart. And I never saw him again.

I also saw many other cruel sins done in the dark, many of which it is written that we should not even speak of them: This was only one of the cold daggers penetrating through my soul. I fell upon my knees in the darkness, broken, ready to die, alone in the darkness.

But God did not leave me alone; my Savior came to me; He spoke gently to me; He healed my dying soul; He promised me a joy equal to the pain.

He brought me into His church, where I rejoiced in my Healer, my Savior, my Redeemer—*quietly* I rejoiced. But my God wanted more.

From the moment of my baptism, God raised up within me a deep love for the Torah, and a painfully deep desire for my ancestral homeland: I was in love, painfully in love, with my heart as if it were in a vise every time that I tried to pull away. From the moment that I arose from the waters of my baptism, I was hungry and thirsty for the Law that God had given to Moses.

But the Gentile Believers within my mother's church understood not these things: Patiently they exhorted me against "judaizing", teaching me that we are all saved by grace, both Jews and gentiles—which is a beautiful truth—and, therefore, that my Jesus came to abolish the Law; and that, therefore, I need to eat pork with my gentile brothers: Because the Torah cannot save me.

I did not eat the pork, and without tears I hid my anguish.

In truth my soul knows clearly that my only Savior is Messiah Yeshua, who is called Christ Jesus. (But, it is not for hope of saving the soul that a woman enters all the dreams of her lover!) And I read:

17       Do not think that I have come to destroy the Law, or the Prophets: I have not come to destroy, but to make complete.

19       Therefore, whoever will destroy one *of* the smallest *of* these commandments, and will teach the men so, he will be called the smallest in the kingdom *of* the heavens: but whosoever does and teaches *them*, the same will be called great in the kingdom *of* the heavens.

—Matthew 5:17, 5:19

Then, the new pastor (son of our senior pastor) grieved my brother Reuben away from the church with anti-Semitic doctrines. And Reuben never again listened to another word of the gospel, but hardened his face against both of us, his mother and his sister. With great difficulty I have forgiven this pastor completely: Because I know that the pastor only spoke in ignorance, from an incomplete understanding of the Holy Bible, and saw not his own anti-Semitism.

But this was not easy for me to forgive; because my brother had searched diligently for the truth, whether Christ Jesus is the true Messiah or not, until that Sunday: And now I am a fool and an enemy in his blind eyes.

And I, for love of the Torah, and being called a Jew and a Judaizer, I sought fellowship and brotherhood among Jews, in an Orthodox synagogue.

And when I worshipped the Father there (in the second time that we worshipped our God together), I saw a vision about that synagogue and that congregation, that an elderly man would suffer a heart attack while the sacred Torah scroll was in his arms; and that the scroll would break. I sought to warn the congregation, and to point out the elderly gentleman in order to prevent this double accident: But the women severely reprimanded me: Because their doctrine said that God no longer speaks to men in visions: Therefore they believed not my words.

Neither would they suffer me to go to the men to warn them, because this is a thing unspeakable to us Jews, that the Torah scroll should break; and I was a false prophetess in their eyes, a very wicked liar.

And I was amazed and perplexed to hear that God no longer speaks to men in visions: Because this was already my seventh or eighth vision from the Lord. Then they said that this is a Christian doctrine and not Jewish, that God speaks to men today, and then they asked whether I believe that Jesus of Nazareth is the Messiah; and when I answered that I not only believe, but I know that He is certainly alive—because Jesus of Nazareth spoke to me—and also that He is the only Messiah and King of the Jews—because the living God told me so.

Then they said that I am only a Christian and not a Jew.

Religion without Yeshua is sweet starvation: In Matthew 15:21 through 15:28, and in Mark 7:24 through 7:30, a Greek woman from Lebanon cried out, "Lord, help me!" Behold, listen well: Because the Lebanese woman, she is the Catholic Church, and the tribes of Israel, and also the Muslims:

Mark

7:24     And arising from there, *He* went into the border *of* Tyre and Sidon; and entering into the house,
*He* desired no one *to* know *it*; and *He* could not be hidden:

25     Because *a certain* woman, whose daughter had *an* unclean spirit, *upon* hearing about Him, *she* came *and* fell at His feet.

26     And the woman was Greek, *of* the Syrian-Lebanese lineage; and *she* begged Him that *He* would cast the demon out of her daughter.

Matthew

15:22     ...Have mercy on me, *O* Lord, Son *of* David; my daughter *is* grievously tormented *by a* demon!

23     And He did not answer her *with a* word.
And coming near, His disciples begged Him, saying, Send her away, because she cries out after us.

24     And answering, He said: I am not sent but unto the perishing sheep *of the* house *of* Israel.

25     And coming near she bowed before Him, saying, Lord, help me!

Mark

7:27     And Yeshua said *to* her, Let the children first be filled: because *it* is not good *to* take the children's bread, and *to* cast *it to* the little dogs.

Matthew

15:27     And she said, Yes *it is*, Lord; because even the little dogs eat of the tiny crumbs which fall from the table *of* their lords.

28     Then Yeshua answering said *unto* her: O woman, great *is* your trust; be it unto you *even* as you desire.

Mark

7:29     ...By this word, go: the demon has gone out from your daughter.

Matthew

15:28     And her daughter was healed from that very hour.[39]

Mark

7:30     And coming to her house, she found *that* the demon
had gone out, and *that* the daughter was laid upon the bed.

—Mark 7:24-7:30; Matthew 15:22-15:28

In those days, Israel ate from the table, and the Lebanese
woman cried for their crumbs; but she returned to her house with
joy: Because the crumbs from Adonai's table are so very nourishing
that all who eat thereof are also satisfied, more than any soul with
one speck of humility could possibly ask for.

And now, the house of Israel is blinded and hardened for the
sake of the other nations:

25     Because I am not willing, brothers, that you should be
ignorant of this mystery... that, in part,
a blindness of the eyes and a hardening of the heart has
happened to Israel, until the fullness
of the nations comes in.
26     And so all Israel shall be saved: as it is written,

Out of Zion the Liberator will come,
and shall turn away ungodliness from Jacob:[40]
27     And this *is* the covenant from me to them,
when I will take away their sins.[41]

—Romans 11:25-11:27

And blind Israel sees not the table, but is quite content with
the crumbs: And every Hebrew brother who is so brave as to bring
to his people the gospel of Messiah Jesus, the same is a thief in their
eyes, trying to steal the holy crumbs from God: Without Yeshua, the
sweetness of the Torah is deadly.

But we are already in those days in which the fullness of the
nations is coming in, and already many Jews with great joy have
already come; we see and believe; but not all of us just yet: Because
this is only the beginning.

And other sheep I have, which are not of this fold: them also
I must bring, and they shall hear my voice; and there shall be
one flock, one shepherd.

—John 10:16

CHAPTER ELEVEN:
# Two Flocks

In those days I saw a vision of a narrow canyon, perhaps
thirty feet across, but too deep to gauge the depth. Two flocks, with
sheep like the stars of heaven for multitude, were going to the right:
One flock with me, all of one breed, was at my feet; and all the other
breeds of sheep were in the other flock, on the other side of the
canyon, and goats also were in both flocks.

I looked to the left, and saw that the canyon opened up wider
to the left, from whence went the sheep; and I looked to the right,
and saw that the canyon was slowly narrowing, until it closed
altogether in the distance, so that the two flocks were one flock far
in the distance.

14     I am the good shepherd, and I know my *sheep*,
and am known by mine.

15     As the Father knows me, I also know the Father;
and I lay down my life[42] for the sheep.

16     And I have other sheep, which are not of this fold:
I must also bring them, and they will hear my voice,
and *we* will become one flock, one shepherd.

17     Therefore my Father loves me,
because I lay down my life,[42] that I might receive it again.

18     No one takes it from me, but I lay it down from myself. I
have authority to lay it *down*, and I have authority to receive
it again. I have received this commandment from my Father.

—John 10:14-10:18

27   And he said: Blessed *be* Adonai, God of my lord[43] Abraham,
who has not abandoned from my lord His mercy
and His truth …

—Genesis 24:2-24:67

CHAPTER TWELVE:

# The Matchmaker

Then, after the vision of two flocks, in my search for another
synagogue, I saw two Messianic synagogues in the telephone book.
And then (half afraid that those Messianic Jews would announce
Rabbi Tom Green of Wisconsin or somebody to be the Messiah, and
half hopeful for true fellowship) I traveled to a synagogue by bus
from dawn until the evening.

On the way there, a disheveled and unkempt black
gentleman enthusiastically announced himself to be Jesus Christ,
returned to the earth. My disbelief [Luke 17:22-17:24] irritated
him…

From my seventh birthday (that is, when I was kidnapped), I
had been an unwanted foreigner. Then, from my baptism, I had been
a Jewess to the Christians, and a Christian to the Jews.

And from my earliest childhood, I never saw any other child
like me—even to my twin my soul was partly a stranger: Therefore I
knew not that anyone anywhere like my own soul existed upon the
earth, much less dozens of souls, only one bus ride away: After
nineteen years as a homeless foreigner, I was home. The weekly
Torah reading, the Davidic dance, the Hebrew language, the
freedom of worship; here I could freely worship my Jewish Savior
in the Jewish way, and not feel strange or awkward or alone.

In those days I also sought an earthly husband, for there is
nothing in all this world that I loved the way I love children and
babies.

I chose a man for a husband, desirable according to the
wisdom of the world: Handsome, intelligent, charming, and
civilized. And like many other young people in love, I did not ask
first about the will of God. Neither did I ask my mother: Because
she had chosen a violent drunkard, and a liar, and a terrible father;
no more a father to me than a breeder stallion is a father to his foal.

She chose him following only her own passions, and the wedding was primarily an act of rebellion, because—after she had already turned his marriage proposal down flat—my grandfather had forbidden the wedding. And my poor grandfather (a devoted and humble Quaker pastor, and a faithful father), blamed himself.

The man whom I chose was desirable according to the wisdom of the world, but not in the eyes of my Lord Messiah Yeshua; because my mother revealed to me this scripture passage,

14     Do not be unequally yoked together *with* unbelievers: Because what partnership do righteousness and anarchy have? And what communion *does* light *have* with darkness?

15     And what concord *does* the Messiah have with *a* wicked *one*? Or what part *does a* believer *have* with *an* unbeliever?

16     And what agreement *does a* temple *of* God *have* with idols? Because you are *a* living temple *of* God; as God *has* said:
        I will dwell in them, and walk among *them*,
        and I will be their God, and they will be my people.[44]

17     Wherefore,
        Come out from among them, and be separated,
        says Adonai, and touch not *anything* unclean.
        I also will receive you,[45]

18         and will be for *a* Father *unto* you, and you will be *to* me for sons and daughters, says Almighty[46] Adonai.

—Second Corinthians 6:14-6:18

And for three days I fasted and prayed, "Please, please, choose a husband whom You want for me: I am not able to understand Your will, and I only want Your will for my life." And the fourth day after these three days was the Sabbath; and so I returned to the Messianic synagogue.

After we worshipped, I was in the entrance hall of the synagogue, ready to leave, when I heard the silent voice of the Holy Spirit saying to me, "I choose him." And nobody was there in the foyer with me, except for Benaiah Zechariah Levell.[47]

I obeyed.

And, as with every word of my beloved Lord, I never, ever have regretted my obedience.

Your God has commanded your strength:
Strengthen, *O* God, that which You have done for us.

—Psalm 68:28[48]

CHAPTER THIRTEEN:
# A Heartbeat on Christmas Day

When in August of nineteen ninety-five I met my husband in the synagogue, I already knew by Yeshua's words that I would give birth to a son in the land of Israel, and that I would afterward return to the United States with my son.

And when I met my husband in the synagogue, I also knew that the Holy Spirit had betrothed me to Benaiah Levell; but Benaiah knew it not, neither sought he a wife.

And I would have required a lengthy courtship; but the day we met was the last possible day: His backpack was already filled with his provisions, and he had no intention of attending another service with us, but rather to go to the wilderness, in preparation for his emigration to Israel: Very probably, if I did not go with Benaiah right away, I would never see his face again.

Benaiah was not seeking a wife, neither sought he any female; but solitude is not easy for a father in mourning: Because he grieved his first wife, and his children—not dead, but prisoners of a pseudo-Christian anti-Semitic cult called "Blood Covenant."

(And his first wife's elopement and wedding was in July 29, nineteen eighty-two, on the fast of the fifth month; and the time from their wedding until we met in August 19, *Av* 23, nineteen ninety-five, is thirteen years and thirteen days by the Hebrew calendar: And in the fast of the fifth month, the children of Israel mourn, because in this day the army of the Chaldeans burned down the House of the Lord.)

Then, from the first of September, seven weeks we dwelt in the wilderness of Bend, Oregon: From the evening of September 1, *Ellul* 7, nineteen ninety-five, until the evening of October 13, *Tishri* 20, we lived in the wilderness; and Benaiah looked upon me with all the purity as his sister in the Messiah. And in the evening of October 13, to provoke his desires (full of doubt and exasperation because he looked upon me only as a sister) I said, "Do you want to adopt one another as brother and sister?"

After a short time he said, "No: Because if you're my sister, we can't get married." And before the end of the day, Benaiah asked for my hand in marriage. And so, on October 20, nineteen ninety-five, seven weeks to the hour of the day we departed, we were married on the evening, in the beginning of the Sabbath, *Tishri* 27, nineteen ninety-five.

We dwelt there in the desert until November, and then we lived in his little sister's house; where I conceived a son, according to the word of the Lord.

And from Christmas Eve of nineteen ninety-five, the seventh day of the Feast of Dedication, until the summer of nineteen ninety-six, we lived in Northern California.

Manasseh's heart began to beat on Christmas Day, in the last day of the Feast of Dedication, which in the Hebrew tongue is called *Hanukkah*.[49] And in the springtime; in the first morning that I knew I was expecting; the word of the Lord came to me, saying a second time: "You shall go to the Land of Israel, and you shall return with a son."

But the word came not to my husband; neither did he want to endanger his wife and baby in a military zone: But the God of my fathers drove us from the United States with His own hand.

Then, one Hebrew year from the day we departed together, in August 22, the seventh of *Ellul*, nineteen ninety-six, in Tiberias, Israel, I gave birth to Manasseh Raphael Levell ben-Benaiah.[31]

20 Children of your bereavement will say again in your ears,
The place *is too* narrow for me:
Come near to me, and I will dwell.

21 And you will say in your heart, Who gave birth to these
for me? And I *had been* bereaved of children, and desolate,
*an exile* stripped naked and removed; and these,
Who raised up *these*? Behold, I *was* left *alone*:
I *was* alone: these, where *were* they?

—Isaiah 49:18-49:21

34  Do not think that I have come to cast peace upon the earth:
    I came not to cast peace, but a sword.
35  Because I have come to set *a* man at variance
    against his father, and *a* daughter against her mother,
    and *a* bride against her mother in law;
36  and the man's haters[50] *will be* his *own* relatives.
37  Whoever loves father or mother more than me
    is not worthy of me: and whoever loves son or daughter
    more than me is not worthy of me…

—Matthew 10:34-10:39

# CHAPTER FOURTEEN:

# The Javelin

In the days in which we lived in the wilderness, I dreamed another prophetic dream, in which I saw my future son Manasseh Raphael as a pleasant, strong, slender youth, with long hair; and a javelin was in his hand. And I rejoiced in my handsome firstborn son, because his heart was faithful before our Lord. And with a loving smile, my faithful son speared me through my belly: And he saw no harm in this, neither had he any ill will toward his beloved mother. And he looked upon my dying face with innocent joy and love. And I awoke under the shade of a lovely tree: And the dream seemed so real that I still felt the spearhead in my belly for two hours.

From the moment of my baptism, God had stirred up within me a deep desire for my ancestral homeland: I was in love, painfully in love. The Holy Land and the motherland of my tribe filled my dreams, and I turned my face to the east or west in every idle moment; and likewise so for Benaiah: Therefore, when we were in Israel, a desire to immigrate and to remain took hold of our hearts as in a vise.

And men say, "Love is blind;" but I think that love is also *deaf*: Because my heart refused to hear the word "return" in the command, "You shall go to the land of Israel, and you shall return with a son," but rather I reasoned within my heart that our return may yet be many years into the future.

But the Lord of my soul did not call us there to immigrate, but rather to return and to bear witness against our peoples, that His bride Israel is unholy, neither is she faithful to her husband, and that bloodstains defile her wedding gown.

9 ...and you will be brought before rulers and kings because of me, for *a* testimony to them.
10 And the good message must first be proclaimed among all the nations.

—Mark 13:9–13:13

We wanted to stay and immigrate, but the God who commanded me "return," the same drove us from His promised land with His strong hand.

The birth of my Manasseh was after this manner: On the beach of the Sea of Galilee, my husband and I were camping, and the next day was my due date. Benaiah had been an assistant to the naturopathic midwives for his first wife, and also was a shepherd of many lambs in the time of lambing in Utah; and he had delivered them there. And my pregnancy was uncomplicated until that day, neither had I had any epileptic seizures since my childhood, but rather everyone thought[51] that I was healthy: (Neither had any physician ever found a cause for my seizures which I had suffered as a foster child).

Our determination, until then, was to give birth with the help of a naturopathic midwife; for which cause Benaiah sought a midwife; and that if we found no worthy midwife before the due date, to give birth in Jerusalem, in the renowned Hadassah Hospital. And we waited for the first symptoms of labor. But Manasseh came not with labor pains, plural, but rather with one big pain: Because he was born in precipitous labor, a frequently fatal complication.

In a panic, the ambulance driver was unwilling to drive to Jerusalem, but decided rather to drive to Tiberias, to the segregated hospital for Israeli Arabs. And Israeli driving is *really* bad; but his driving, on account of fear for my life, was *worse*. With both hands I clung to the stretcher like a lobster; and the stretcher was not fastened to the ambulance, but was rolling half the time, and flying the other half. And I yelled "Slow down, before you kill us!" But he just yelled back at me, "No! Cross your legs—I don't want to deliver your baby!"

And my husband Benaiah was not in the ambulance, but still at our camp on the beach.

And in the hospital for Arabs, when the midwives saw the final symptom before death, their faces were white, because (after they made the nearly fatal mistake of giving me oxytocin, assuming I had been in labor many hours) my womb had almost burst: But at the very last moment, with a double episiotomy, my baby shot out from the womb, and the head midwife literally caught Manasseh in the air: Because two midwives had held him back until both cuts were finished.

Even so, my womb was already wounded by the pressure, and had almost burst, in the exact place in my belly where I had felt the head of the javelin in my dream.

Consecrate[52] *a* child at *the* beginning[53] *of* his way,
and even when *he is* old he will not depart from it.

——Proverbs 22:6

INTRODUCTION:
# Silent No More

When Manasseh Raphael was one or two months old, soon after we returned with him to our home in California, I began to write a letter to our baby boy, intending it to be about seven pages long, teaching him what we have learned about God's love, so that if Manasseh should become an orphan he would still be able to learn the most important things we wanted to teach him about.

And I asked Benaiah to write a paragraph or two, and he refused, saying that his dyslexia made it too hard for him to communicate. So I showed him how, with patient editing, he could take his time and say exactly what he intended to say to our child, without his severe dyslexia scrambling up the meaning of his words. Seven pages? Benaiah had been waiting forty-three years to communicate, and now suddenly he could talk! Ben dictated his words to me, and I wrote them down and read them back to him hour after hour, day after day, making corrections according to his commands, until Benaiah was finally satisfied that he'd meant what he said and said what he meant. And when we had finally finished two years later, my little seven page letter had become a whole book, which Ben had named *Letters to Manasseh*. In this book, we criticized some mistranslations in the King James Version of the Bible, which I fear may mislead some people to believe that we considered it one of the least trustworthy translations, which is not the case at all—Please understand, beloved reader: Of all the English Bible translations I've studied, not one is more accurate than the Authorized King James Version.

Meticulously accurate translations of the Bible, of which the King James Version is the best I've seen, are a priceless treasure, and the many men and women who have dedicated so much of their earthly lives to give this gift to the rest of us, these surely deserve our deepest gratitude.

The King James Version of the Bible is—for the most part—a very accurate and reasonably literal translation of the original Hebrew Masoretic Text and the original Greek *Textus Receptus*, and has therefore come to be widely relied upon throughout the world:

Indeed, there are many educated and intelligent English-speaking Christians who sincerely believe that the King James Version is the absolutely infallible Word of God—(which is precisely why this translation has been singled out for our criticism).

However, in the days of the tower of Babel, God did more than to merely confound the words of human language: He actually transformed the way each different language-group *thought* in their new language. One way that He did this was by connecting words together differently in each language, which caused the different groups to see different connections between the same ideas. For example, in Hebrew, *kélev*—the word for "dog"—comes from the words "all heart", so that the words themselves teach us that dogs excel at loving their friends, and indeed at doing all things, wholeheartedly.

And so, because in truth it is not possible to perfectly translate the Bible into another language, it would be better if we all had the time, talent, skills and resources needed to read the original Holy Bible texts. But because this isn't possible for most of us, at least not here in this world, we continue to need these translations of the Bible.

Here, following, is Benaiah's and my first book, written to our son in nineteen ninety-six and in nineteen ninety-seven; I have taken the liberty of omitting the introduction which was added to its final form in *Seven Flames*:

# Section Two:

# *Seven Flames:*
## Letters to Manasseh

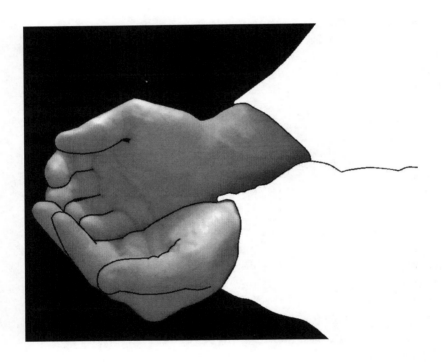

And *if* my people, which have called my name
upon themselves, shall humble themselves, and pray,
and seek my face, and turn from their wicked ways;
then I will hear deeply[1] from the heavens, and will forgive
their sin, and will heal their land.

—Second Chronicles 7:14

# *Letter to Manasseh*

# Preface
## *by Benaiah Z Levell*
## *[Abba]*

In my hour of darkness, as I was about to take my life, I called out to God. He, who is called Adonai, directed my soul to His Jewish son, Yeshua. I read Yeshua's words that said not to think that He, the Messiah, had come to abolish[2] the law; but Christian men and women told me that Yeshua had freed us from the Law. I read Yeshua's words that said to obey[3] the Law and the Prophets; but Christian men and women told me not to obey the Old Law. I read Yeshua's words that said for a cleansed leper to go show himself— as commanded[4] by Torah—to the priest. I read Yeshua's words that said whoever obeys[5] the Law and teaches others to obey it will be called great in the kingdom of heaven. I read the Law, obeyed the Law, and taught the Law. I discovered that the Law is good and that "eye for *an* eye[6]" is just and equitable. Yeshua did not corrupt the Law: He removed the corruption that tradition had encrusted upon the Law, and brought back the Law's clarity as in the days of Moses. Yeshua said, "And if you desire to enter into the life, keep the commandments.[7]"

There is a viewpoint that is faulty, yet it is common: Many of us seem to have the notion that mankind is primarily responsible for the creation of law and order on the earth; that we have brought order from chaos; that we have brought light from darkness; that we "the great human race" have mostly made things right. We have not.

Furthermore, we are deceived when we think that we are the source of what is good in the world. Here are some of the good things man did not originate and is not the source of: Man did not invent law and order; God did. Man did not invent math; God did. Man did not invent music, wisdom, loving, or any other good pleasure; God did. Everything of any lasting value, God invented. He is the one [who gave us] our life, liberty, and happiness—not man. Man, apart from God, is responsible for such things as disorder, noise, confusion, foolishness, hatred, perversion and war.

Each day we need to look out over creation, stop perceiving the world as if it belongs to man, and start seeing it for what it is: It is God's. Adonai is God's name.[8] And Adonai owns the world. Without exception, everything good comes from Him.

Each new generation is eternally responsible for the decisions it makes and the directions it chooses. It is our hope and desire that this letter to Manasseh will, in some way, help guide the eyes of this present generation toward a better viewpoint—one that comes not from the faulty eyes of man, but from the perfect heart of God.

—*Benaiah Z Levell (Abba)*

CHAPTER ONE:
# The Father

Beloved Manasseh, believe us in what we are about to say because it is trustworthy and—as best as can be—true, from true hearts. Liars also claim to be true, but they imitate integrity. We are not like them; they are children of their father Satan. We are children of beautiful Adonai and of truth.

Abba[9] did not know the truth until he was about twenty years old. He was a good-natured person: caring, polite, creative, strong, and sincere. However, he did not know the truth. By the time Abba was twenty, he was going to commit suicide because he did not want to be a part of this dark world any longer. To him, the world and society in general seemed a filthy, selfish, hateful, proud, violent, dishonest, disrespectful, and perverse place. He was ashamed to be a human being because he could also see signs of these horrible things within himself. He had never met a person that he could see truly loved anyone besides themselves. So Abba didn't trust people.

Just before he could kill himself, he called out into the universe and said, "If there's a God, stop me—because I'm going to end it!" Adonai stopped Abba by really hugging him. His spirit hugged Abba's spirit.

He then began showing Abba many things: Abba was shown that Adonai is the God of the Jews, the God of the Bible, and the father of Yeshua. Adonai revealed clearly to Abba that Yeshua was sent to be the Messiah of the Jews and the Savior of all who believe. Abba loved and believed Adonai because Adonai loved and embraced Abba.

Imma,[9] like a little angel thrown into a big dark jungle, was born into a world of trouble. She was scared: her abba was not an abba at all—he was [like] a devil. He (like a vicious, selfish monster) treated his little girl like a snot rag only to blow his sickness on. She ran and hid from him, but like some giant poisonous insect he continued to find and sting Imma with painful stings.

One day, her mother took her and ran to safety. Her mother also asked the government to help. Instead, the government—acting like some blundering, incompetent colossus—came and took Imma away. They took care of Imma by feeding her and clothing her;

however, they forgot to love her. When she became a lady her body was sound,[10] but her soul was dying and very hungry. She began to seek Adonai. He then fed and strengthened her spirit.

Some time later, while worshipping Adonai, she met Abba who was just waking up from a real-life nightmare. He had dreamed of being a good father to four beautiful little children. One morning he was suddenly shocked and bewildered—terrified to find that a hideous kidnapper had snatched all of his little children. He tried with all his might to rescue them but could not because the children were hidden in a deep hole filled with piles and piles of lies. Because he was powerless, all Abba could do was weep and pray, again and again, day after day, until he met Imma. She, with her kind words, comforted him and became his wife. He loved her and took care of her.

Manasseh, our little son, we're writing down what we know and what we have witnessed so that you can start out equipped with our few little bits of wisdom gleaned from our experiences in this tempestuous and sometimes nightmarish world.

Here is some wisdom for you: Beloved Manasseh, always put Adonai first—before all things. All things truly are His and for Him. He loves you. Love Him....

Adonai is bigger and more beautiful than what is taught by ignorant men. He is so big that He is bigger than size. He cannot be accurately described as "big" because "big" is too small to describe Him. There is nothing bigger than Him, nor more far-reaching. He is in[11] us, and we are in[12] Him. There is nothing outside of Him because there is not an outside of Him. He did not have a beginning;[14] neither is He young nor is He old—and the depths of His beauty are incomprehensible.

---

*11    Note added by Naomi: "He is in us, and we are in Him."—These two "in" statements are not equal: Every human being is in Him, but in His mercy God chooses *not* to be in every human being. Those of us who are called and saved and healed according to His mercy through the blood of Yeshua, God is in us, as it is written in the following verses: John 17:20 through 17:23, 1ˢᵗ Corinthians 15:28, Ephesians 1:23 & 4:6, and Colossians 3:11. However, in His mercy, God allows sinners to spiritually distance themselves from Him (John 15:4 & 16:7, & Romans 8:9). He does not force Himself on us—With pain in His heart

He allowed them in their confusion and shame to distance themselves, and said to Adam "Where *are* you?", allowing Adam and Eve to be the ones to draw near again to Him, and to make this choice of their own free will (although they did not—at least not back to the same deep emotional and spiritual closeness that He wanted and they needed, the closeness they had only been able to share with God before they had sinned).

We humans were designed to have God's Holy Spirit always within us, and to be always united with God—this is what all the empty souls long for and they are hungry and thirsty for (which is how He guided me to Himself)—but God also gave us the freedom to choose to go His Way or not, because He doesn't want merely to be united with His human creatures, but rather he wants even more—God wants us to *choose* to dwell in unity with Him, and to *freely give* our bodies to be the temple of His Holy Spirit through the blood of the Lamb Messiah Yeshua.

This is going to feel harsh to the New Age Christians, but the truth is necessary to say: These following words are born of my love for my sisters and brothers: There is a popular New Age teaching that because God is light, and all created things in this universe are made of photons, and therefore of light, that the concept that God is in everyone naturally follows. The problem with this reasoning is that it depends on what students of logic call "confusion of terms"—If God is made out of the same kind of light that is photons, then obviously He did not exist until He created photons by saying "*Let there* be light." How can He be Creator and creation at the same time of the same thing? God is indeed light, but in a different sense: He has a personality: He is not just energy: Photons are a creation of His which He made on the first day of our universe's history, saying, "*Let there* be light." (Genesis 1:3)

While there are many genuine Christians who sincerely believe this doctrine, these "politically correct" New Age "Christians" are in fact theologically identical to Hindus, and they are also in disagreement with the Gospel message, as follows:

1. ***If*** God is in everyone, and if God will be in heaven, then it naturally follows that everyone will go to heaven, including Lucifer himself—or perhaps *especially* Lucifer, since "Lucifer" means "Shining", and our nature as photon-creatures is why God is in all of us.

2. ***If*** everybody gets to go to heaven, then it is *not the truth* that no-one can come to the Father except through Messiah Jesus (John 14:6), therefore Jesus is *not* "*the* Way", but rather He is (at best) only one of many Ways, all of which are equally correct.

3. ***If*** everybody gets to go to heaven, then we are eternal creatures, for whom eternal death is impossible, and for whom eternal life is inevitable (which would be terrific if it were only true), and

therefore it is *not the truth* that Messiah Jesus is "*the* Life"—I'm OK; you're OK; everybody's point of view is just fine, so let's just all go to heaven our own individual ways...

4.    And *if* there are many Ways, many Truths, and many Lives, then Jesus didn't die to accomplish *anything*: His death of the cross did not save anybody from sin and eternal death, because neither sin nor eternal death actually ever existed: The question then becomes, simply, *if* God is in everyone,

### Who needs Jesus Christ?

As it is written in John 14:6,

Yeshua said *to* him, **I am the way, the truth, and the life: no one comes to the Father, but by me.**

Ignorant people sometimes say that Adonai is small, that His words are trivial, that His ways are inferior, or that He does not exist. They have said that His form is clearly definable; it is not. They have said that His magnitude is humanly perceivable; it is not. They have thought to measure Him in their minds; they cannot. They have said that His substance has limits; it does not. In truth, Manasseh, the scope of His beauty and substance is without limits. And the expanse of His form is without end.

We, however, are like a miniscule pinpoint; the nations are like a tiny drop;

◆

and the earth is like a small pebble compared to the extent of Adonai. Yet, as small as we are, Adonai cares so much for us that if we love Him with all of our heart, He will give us good things just as a wise and loving father gives good things to his children—He loves us very much.

Though we do not have the exact date, we are fairly certain that Adonai made everything that humans know about more than five thousand years ago. He, in His infinite wisdom, took six days to make all things[15]...—such as the universe, the galaxies, the stars, the earth, and all things on the earth. Read about this in His Holy Scriptures.

Truly, in unquestionable and definite reality, we know that God exists; that He is perfectly beautiful; that He is the God of the Jews[16] the father of Yeshua, whom He sent to be the Messiah of the Jews and the Savior of all who long for life everlasting.

CHAPTER TWO

# His Words

Adonai's words are very important: they teach us, they strengthen us, they heal us, they comfort us. His words are perfect and holy because He is holy. And though Adonai is the most beautiful of all, His words are next to Him in loveliness. They are sharper than the sharpest sword, brighter than the brightest light, more fragrant than the sweetest garden, and more satisfying than a cool rain on a famished desert. His words give life to the dead, sight to the blind, and strength to the weary soul. However, though they are of paramount importance and priceless in value, they are not easy to find—they (like a buried treasure) are hidden in a foreign language surrounded by bad translations, false teachers, and double-minded believers.

Most of Adonai's recorded words are written in ancient Hebrew and in Greek. But because the people of this world speak in many different languages, various translations from the Hebrew and Greek have gone forth into the world. By and large these translations are useful but not to be entirely trusted. If they are used, however, they must be considered only "tools" for the Holy Spirit to control. He is our guide, sent to us by the great Yeshua. Translations in the Holy Spirit's hands are not dangerous; He faithfully leads us into all truth. But in human hands, translations confuse and mislead. Remember: There are no infallible translations, only imperfect paraphrases.

In addition to the pitfalls of unreliable translations, we who love God's written word are plagued by false teachers who try to deceive us. For example, the apostle Paul knew clearly (as did the other apostles) not to obey ungodly commands; for when the rulers commanded them not to obey Adonai, the apostles proclaimed plainly: "*It is* necessary *that* we obey God more than men.[17]" Yet, many of today's false teachers distort a portion of Paul's letter to the Romans to mean obey the ungodly commands of ungodly rulers.[18] These teachers ignore the recorded fact that when Elijah, the holy prophet, was commanded by the king of Israel[19] to come down from a certain mountain, Elijah rightly did not obey. They ignore the fact that when righteous Shadrach, Meshach, and Abednego were commanded by the king of Babylon to disobey Adonai, they rightly did not submit to the king. And they ignore the fact that when Daniel was commanded by king Darius not to pray, Daniel rightly did not conform. In like manner, Manasseh, do not conform to commands that are contrary to the will of Adonai—and beware of false teachers.

In addition to bad translations and false teachers, there are many double-minded believers who desire to worship two masters. To worship means to give great love, devotion, and allegiance to something or someone. But only Adonai is to be worshipped.[20] On June 14, seventeen seventy-seven, the people of the United States of America proclaimed the stars and stripes to be their banner. Many of them now worship this banner and what it stands for. They give great allegiance to their flag and great love and devotion to this republic.[21] But Adonai is *our* banner. Worship Him and what He stands for; give great allegiance only to Him; and give great love and devotion only to His kingdom.

Manasseh, trust Adonai—*talk to Him*—praise Him! Listen very carefully for His beautiful, holy voice each and every day.

Then, read His holy words in their original form; seek for the treasure of His word; fight for the light of truth; and overcome the false teachers with fact.

Manasseh, do not be afraid of those who kill the body. Being killed will simply send you to heaven sooner and make their punishment greater.

When Abba was a little boy, he had the same scary dream again and again. In this dream, Abba was climbing on a giant web hanging high in a vast, dark space. A dark manlike creature—much bigger and stronger than Abba—was a short distance below, on the same giant web. This insubstantial, shadowy creature was scrambling higher and higher to catch Abba. Just before it could grasp Abba's legs, Abba would wake up and cry. One night, Abba was told to turn and fight this dark enemy. So in his dream, Abba stopped climbing, turned around and bravely killed it with the power of Yeshua.[22] That dark, violent creature was the fear of death..

Do not be afraid of death, Manasseh. Instead, join with Moses, Elijah, the apostles of King Yeshua, and all the other living multitude of heaven; and proclaim that you ought to obey God rather than men. And remember—the Holy Spirit is promised to all God's children to guide us into all truth. Ask for Him in prayer. He is a free gift.

CHAPTER THREE:
# Prayer

Manasseh, prayer is talking with Adonai. How do we, such insignificant creatures, talk to someone so infinitely big? Fortunately, our big God also has big love. He is all-powerful and all-mighty, but He is tender and gentle too. We must remember, though, that He is neither a man nor to be approached as a man. He is merciful and His compassion is great, but He is holy. We are not holy. We must, therefore, come before Adonai with humility, reverence, and patience.

We must be humble to approach Adonai. Humility is magnificent and powerful. It is the source of eternal strength that everyone must acquire and maintain to approach Adonai. But Adonai hates a proud look—it is an abomination to Him. Neither will He hear the prayer of anyone who has a proud heart. Humility begins our walk on the path to paradise, clearing the passage to the delights of holiness. But pride is the reason for man's fall and the root problem of his separation from Adonai. Get rid of all pride when you pray; it is the core of man's difficulty. Adonai said that whoever humbles[23] himself and calls upon the name of the Lord shall be saved.

Besides being humble, we must be respectful when we approach Adonai. Listen, Manasseh—because God is holy, He is very strict. Approach Adonai reverently and in all seriousness, and all your requests will in faithful certainty be heard. Adonai is indeed strict, but He is also faithful, merciful, and just.

Also, to approach Adonai perfectly, we must have patience. Patience is a hard thing to have, Manasseh; but we must learn to wait patiently. Sometimes, when we pray, Adonai doesn't answer. When this happens, the foolish will walk away, for there is much to do and life is short. Adonai knows this very well. He said all flesh is like grass and all the beauty of our earthly lives is like the beauty of lovely meadows. As the grass withers and dies and the lovely meadows fade, so does our beauty fade and we die. He knows that our time is short. When we give Him some of our precious fleeting moments by waiting patiently for Him to answer, He sees that we love Him more than our very lives. Remember, whoever loves his life in this world will lose it, but the one who loves Adonai more than all things will gain life eternal. Do not walk away like the impatient ones; wait upon the Lord—the reward is great indeed. All things belong to Adonai. He wins all battles. His words never see defeat. And our prayers never go unanswered when we humble ourselves, reverently seek His will, and wait patiently.

Yeshua said to pray like this[24]: "Our Father who *is* in the heavens, sanctified be Your name; Your kingdom come; Your will be done, as *it is* in heaven, also on earth; give us today our bread for tomorrow; and forgive us our sins because we also forgive *all of* our debtors; and do not lead us into temptation, but deliver us from the evil *one*." Yeshua is the great high priest. He must go before us into the holy courts of His Father and open the gates for us. Once the way is open, we can then, with full confidence, enter the holy place with our praise and requests.

When Abba prays, he humbles himself before Adonai. He kneels before Adonai. He raises his hands high to Adonai. He gives his utmost attention to Adonai. His eyes fervently seek Adonai's face. With all his might, Abba tries to love Adonai with all his heart and with all his soul.

As Abba kneels and struggles to mightily love Adonai, the enemy tries to distract him. Thoughts of everyday concerns begin to vie for Abba's attention. When Abba recognizes this, he turns his thoughts back to Adonai. In a sometimes painful twist of the brain, Abba wrestles his thinking back to the one who loves him more than anyone loves him:

Adonai, his beloved God, his beautifully beautiful Father and glorious Creator. Adonai is tender. He snuggles Abba in spirit. Abba responds: He sings to Adonai.

The world cannot understand. It is a private time between a loving father and His adoring child. Love Adonai, Manasseh.

Manasseh, think of Adonai every day throughout all your days, walking and talking with Him at every good opportunity. Have harmony with Adonai when you pray. Want only what He wants. Be of one mind and of one will with Him. Delight in Him.

Walk with Him. And let your actions reflect the will of Adonai like a clear, blue lake on a bright day reflects the brilliant colors of the surrounding forest.

Prayer is a great and powerful weapon, Manasseh. (The fervent prayer of a righteous soul avails much.[25]) Prayer is not a monotonous religious ritual; rather, it's an exciting and real-life relationship with your incredible Creator, who is your best of all friends.

*"Lake" by Momo Tia*

CHAPTER FOUR:

# The World

Manasseh, there are two kinds of people and two kingdoms on the earth today: the children of Adonai and the children of the devil. When people first walked this earth they did not know as much as we know today, but the earth was perfectly clean. The waterfalls, streams, rivers and lakes were deliciously pure. The first people could drink at almost any water source, and it would be safe. (Mankind's own evil created the modern-day pestilence and widespread pollution that now exist.[26])

Back then, any of the healthful fruits and vegetables of the earth could be safely eaten, for there were no poisons on them. The grass of the field did not cause the grievous allergies of today and was as safe and pleasing to roll in as it still sometimes appears. The air was magnificently overflowing with bird song and animal sounds. The fish of the streams, lakes, and oceans were healthy and beautiful; and the feathers of the birds were shiny and bright.

The children of Adonai, who lived in this real-life wonderland, were humble and called upon Adonai for help; but the children of the devil were proud and did whatever they pleased. The children of Adonai were kind and considerate, and kept the earth clean; but the children of the devil were violent and selfish, and made the earth dirty.

Today, more than five thousand years later, there are still just two kinds of people on the earth, but the knowledge of how to use deception has been greatly increased. In addition, mankind has learned how to make all kinds of poisons, and much of the earth is contaminated. The children of Adonai are still humble and call to Adonai for help; but the children of the devil are proud and do whatever they please. The children of Adonai are kind, considerate and compassionate; but the children of the devil are violent and selfish.

The world is also like a painting of two pictures, a land of two creatures, and a garden of good and evil: Adonai's people are like a poetic picture of Him. Their eyes of joy sparkle like a billion radiant stars in the night. Their sweet singing voices are like happy little birds of every sort. Their hands—performing holy duties with diligence—are noble servants reaching high to heaven. Their feet are lovely like brave and gallant soldiers. Their thoughts are high and majestic like tall mountain peaks against a brilliant blue, and their words are true and finely sharpened like the dazzling steel of Adonai's swift sword.

The other painted picture is not so grand, for the devil's people are full of pride and deceit. Their eyes are like their father's eyes. They are eyes of lifelessness, dull colors, and dreary tones. Their gloomy voices wail of despair, sounding like a moaning beast ready for slaughter. Their hands are horrible to look upon—hands covered with the blood of abortions, the diseased slime of perversions, and the shameful bruises of violence. Their feet are weak, disfigured and grotesque, painfully packed into pretty shoes (a symbol of their oppressive rule upon the earth). Their thoughts are of ungodly gain, evil ambition, and wicked desire—thoughts so grossly immoral that their imaginations are like frenzied scavenger fish, deep in the putrid sewers of hell itself. Their tongues are clever, crafty, and quick to deceive. Like maggots feeding on a carcass, they gather and squirm to delight in their delicious lies; and with their lies they cover every appearance of their shameful deeds so as not to be detected by Adonai's people.

The world is also like a land of two creatures: Adonai's Law is perfectly beautiful. Like a noble lion, it bravely attacks and battles against the enemies of Adonai. Like a strong ox, it carries the people of Adonai over the rough and rocky ground. Like a wise priest, it instructs Adonai's people in the way of holiness. And like a majestic heavenly bird with eyes seeing great distances, it flies Adonai's people high above the foolish and undiscerning world.

The other creature that shares this land is man's law. It has a proud man's head speaking great lies. It is not brave or noble, but oppressive and cruel. It does not carry people to safety, but hammers them into submission. It does not instruct them in wisdom, but teaches them the folly of deception. And, it does not have far-seeing eyes, but eyes that see only itself. It appears like a creature of light, but speaks like a beast in the dark. It is clothed in royal robes, but stinks like death. It has great authority and is respected by the world; but at its core, it is a rebel to Adonai, an opponent to holiness, and a hellish, barbaric brute.

The world is also like a flower garden of good and evil. It appears mostly good, but it is mostly evil. The many evil forces disguise themselves so as not to be discovered. Like pernicious insects, they hide under the rocks, under the leaves, and under the dirt.

The great flower of pure love blooms bright in this garden, but the ungodly of this world do not give glory to Adonai. Instead, they suck love's sweetness and then hide under the rock of perversion. "Love is what makes life worth living," they say, as they abuse their spouses, fornicate with their neighbors, and molest their children. The glorious flowers of holiness are fragrant in this garden, but the ungodly of this world do not give glory to Adonai. Instead, they enjoy His mercy, kindness, compassion and care. Then they bury these things and oppress the poor under the dirt of deceit. The perfect flower of peace is a precious gift in this garden, but the ungodly of this world do not give glory to Adonai. Instead, they enjoy the shade and security of peace while they devise strategies to war against Adonai's people.

Manasseh, in the later part of winter, on a high mountain, at the beginning of sunset, Abba saw a vision: He looked to the left and saw the beginning of time, the creation of the world, the violence of mankind, and the faith of Noah. Next to that, in the middle and straight ahead, Abba saw a rainbow of Adonai's love covering the earth. He saw millions of people and animals scatter in all directions over the whole earth. A law was set in place; it was protected by the Jews. (This holy writ thundered and echoed in the midst of the earth.) Rays of sunlight and lightning flashes came from it, surrounding the earth with light.

Then darkness came up from the earth; and like billions of fingers, this darkness covered the faces of men, women, and children from the light of Adonai's Law. These dark fingers became a giant iron cage that imprisoned the whole earth. The light shone through the iron lattice of the cage, but this latticework became thicker and thicker. Abba called out to Adonai to deliver the people of the earth from this iron cage, but Adonai said it must remain. Abba looked to the right and saw a beautiful clean meadow. Then a road was made through the midst of the meadow. The road became black with greed, and was first covered with innocent blood; then it was covered with hordes of devouring insects and their pollutions until the road became thick with death and disease. Toxic chemicals were sprayed over much of the earth to clean the road. All nations became sick, but the insects became strong and covered the whole earth. These insects are wickedness, the chemicals are the elaborate mixture of the lies of the nations, and the iron cage is the governments of men.

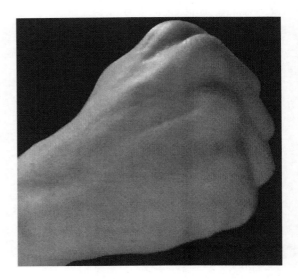

CHAPTER FIVE:
# Yeshua

Dearest Manasseh, our precious child, believe in our love for you. From the moment we first perceived the wonder of your tiny presence in Imma's womb, we loved you—you were our special delight.

Adonai's love is like this. He has taken delight in mankind from our very beginning. Since the days of the first man and woman until now, Adonai has faithfully and tenderly loved us; yet we have only sometimes loved Him. From the beginning of human history, we have acted proud and have many times ignored Him, yet He still loved us. We have acted rude and disrespectful to Him, yet He still loved us. We have rebelled against Him and rejected Him, yet He still loved us. We have hurt one another and were not sorry, yet He still loved us. We have created our own evil kingdoms and tried to destroy His good kingdom, yet He still loved us. We have even claimed that He did not exist, and He still loved us.

After thousands of years of suffering such cruel abuse from us, Adonai's great and gentle heart was broken. Yet because He still loved us, He sent His precious Son into the world. He had already sent many other messengers, but the evil people of this world hated them and mistreated them. Then about two thousand years ago, Adonai sent Yeshua. He was born of the virgin Miriam by the Holy Spirit (*Rúakh HaKódesh*[27]). When Yeshua was born, the godly people and all of heaven rejoiced, but the world did not rejoice. The forces of evil rallied together and tried to destroy baby Yeshua, but Adonai rescued Him.

Listen, Manasseh. Yeshua is distinctively unique: He is unequaled among humanity: He is a beauteous and wondrous miracle. And He is not just a man—He is both God and man.

Adonai does many miracles for us, but Yeshua is His most awe-inspiring one. The people who saw Yeshua actually saw Adonai in the form of a man; they saw a man with no human flaw, and they saw perfection in motion. The people who heard Yeshua actually heard the voice of Adonai. Yeshua's face was Adonai's face. Yeshua's eyes were Adonai's eyes. Every step of Yeshua on earth was the step of Adonai. Every movement of every cell of Yeshua's body was Adonai's movement. Every heartbeat was

Adonai's, and every drop of Yeshua's blood was Adonai's blood. The world murdered Yeshua, but Adonai raised Him from the dead and made Him King of kings over every authority, everywhere.

When Yeshua returns, all man-made governments will be uprooted and destroyed because they are all built on faithlessness. The beginning of man's trouble was because the first man and woman did not believe Adonai. Ever since their disbelief, Adonai has been purifying the human race from this ugly sin of doubt. Adonai is true, and He hates not being believed in—it is an abomination to Him. Whoever does not believe in Him shall not live.

We create unrighteous governments because we doubt Adonai and believe in ourselves. Adonai said to have no other gods; we worship ourselves. Adonai said to love Him more than anything; we love ourselves more than anything. Adonai said to love and obey His Laws; we prefer to love and obey our laws. Adonai said to do what is right in His eyes; we do what is right in our eyes. We are indeed faithless and disobedient, and our governments reflect our faithlessness.

On the other hand, people who love and obey Adonai and His Son are like wise children in a secure castle protected by a strong army. Yeshua said that whoever hears His words and obeys is like a wise man who builds his house on a rock.[28] The storms beat upon that house, but it will stand firm.

Manasseh, there was once a family of settlers that lived on a prairie; they were a good family, and their hearts were true and kind. One day, the father was out in the field with his children, and suddenly he told them to drop to the ground and lay still. This did not make any sense, but the children were good and wise, so they obeyed. No sooner had they obeyed, than a great fire swept over them quick as a flash, leaving the once tall prairie grass short and burnt. Because they were wise and good children, heeding their father's command, they were saved.

Yeshua is the miraculous child of Adonai, perfect in His obedience. Whoever trusts in Yeshua will be saved from the great sweeping flames of eternal death.

# CHAPTER SIX:

# Christians

Manasseh, Yeshua said, "Do not think that I have come to cast peace upon the earth: I came not to cast peace, but a sword.[29]"

The devil is a liar of unsurpassed skill; we honest folk cannot easily cut through his tangled, sticky webs. He is like a great ancient spider in a deep cave, and his webs have many layers and connections. He has a vast array of helpers, and his children have been strategically placed over the whole earth. It is not a simple battle, Manasseh; but take heart, for your commander Yeshua is not simple minded. His intellect is more than sufficient to outwit every tangled idea and every twisted thought of the enemy. Even today, though the battle rages and true believers are feeling crushed, Yeshua helps His few faithful ones endure; and by undeserved suffering, their righteous souls are strengthened.

When Abba was a boy, he discovered, near the edge of a vacant field, a most remarkable little creature. As Abba kneeled close to observe its beauty in more detail, he noticed that it was as small as his finger, yet as colorful as a rainbow. It was a simple grasshopper, but its beauty was like that of a treasure of dazzling emeralds and shiny ornaments of gold. Its metallic-like armor was like shimmering silver elaborately overlaid with sparkles of light, and its eyes were lovely examples of glimmering innocence. As Abba beheld this wondrous little creature, a thoughtless boy came along and disdainfully brought his heavy boot swiftly down upon its fragile little body—crushing its tiny organs into a smear of ruptured flesh and splintered armor.

Its life was instantly gone, and Abba's delight instantly turned into rage at that thoughtless boy. Bullies like him rule the world today, Manasseh: stomping their violent boot with flagrant pride, they try to destroy Yeshua, His people, and anything else divine that crosses their path.

In addition to this visible foe, there is another particularly dangerous enemy. This enemy is the false church: The multitudes of people that live a double life of sinner and of make-believe saint. They act as distressed as we do to hear of the existence of the apostate church, yet they themselves are the apostate church. When not in the direct observation of true believers, they practice wickedness and delight in sin; but when they are with Adonai's people, they act like perfect replicas of saints. This is confusing but true. Beware of them, Manasseh; they are like Judas Iscariot who, appearing like a friend, held close to Yeshua for a season but later betrayed Yeshua.

Excellent actors, these backstabbing betrayers are hypocrites, fakes, and frauds performing beautiful counterfeit prayers. Often, they mimic sermons that were created by genuine believers and offer these sermons as their own. While pretending to love God and His people, these smiling impostors are really snakes in disguise, clever spiritual magicians that we rarely detect. To be rich and powerful is their goal; to steal and destroy is their scheme; and, like their father the devil, they are treacherous. This apostate church is a very real threat to Adonai's people. Likely to be in every sect, denomination and group, they are not detected easily because they take great pains to keep their outer appearance adjusted perfectly. This is their mask; beware of them, Manasseh.

Abba had four beautiful little children that he loved deeply— they were his delight. He loved them and cared for them with all his might. He thanked Adonai for them. Each day, Abba would teach them Adonai's words, pray with them and try to be an especially good parent to them. As a matter of fact, it was one of Abba's utmost goals in life to be an exceptional parent, like Adonai Himself.[30]

One night, Abba dreamed that he was standing before a steep, grassy mountainside with a cute collection of little creatures happily living in it. Suddenly, an explosion of great force ripped the mountainside apart, leaving only bare bedrock. Abba was greatly distressed to see all these little creatures torn violently from their grassy home, thrown into the air, and scattered. Immediately, a strong hand reached into the bedrock, brought forth an ingot of polished gold the size of a man's hand, and held it before Abba's face. Inscribed on it, Abba saw what looked like a profile of an Egyptian pharaoh. It was an image of Joseph, the Hebrew who became the great governor of Egypt. This dream meant that Abba's family would be painfully destroyed; that Abba would be tested like gold; and that his heart would become like Joseph's heart.

Abba had a precious family that flourished (by the grace of God) for ten years. But there was an enemy lurking about that Abba did not recognize. This enemy wanted to destroy this beautiful family; and it *did*. It stomped it—like that grasshopper had been stomped—into a bloody smear. Abba's innocent little children had their tender hearts and their lives ripped in half by the lies, riches, and great acting ability of enemies in Christian disguise. These enemies appeared to Abba to be friends, but they were not. They smiled brightly as they told Abba that they loved him; then, while Abba was sleeping, they kidnapped his little children. When Abba awoke to pray with his children, the house was empty....

Abba searched for two weeks without sleep. He became emotionally shredded trying to save his little children. He went blind in one eye because of this trauma; and when Abba finally found where the children were kept, it was too late to help them.

Abba sought out help wherever he could, but was commanded by the government to be silent. His pain was unbearable: His little children were in danger and needed his help, but he was prevented! Abba had not wept much his whole life; but after this tragedy, his eyes became like pools of a trillion tears, and his chest was burst open with the great pain that only a loving Abba or Imma can experience by losing their children.

Abba now understood some of the pain of the Holocaust; he hurt so bad that he felt like he had been killed. His heart had been broken so severely that he began to understand Adonai's broken heart for Israel. Israel—Adonai's special family—has also been kidnapped: they are being separated from their Father by false ideas, and they are being kept from their Messiah by false beliefs.

Beloved Manasseh, you are named Manasseh[31] for the same reason that Joseph's son was named this—you make your Abba to forget his pain; therefore, you are called "making to forget." But just as Joseph's son could not make Joseph to forget his lost family, likewise you cannot make your Abba to forget his other precious children. Abba must endure the pain of never knowing whether these children he loves are being hurt, or even whether they are alive. They had been with Abba every day of their lives; then, suddenly, they were gone.

Two weeks does not sound like a long time, but those first two weeks were like a cruel eternity inside an agonizing torment with no end in sight. Then, at the worst part of Abba's anguish, as he lay on a mattress soaked with his own tears and sweat, feeling like he was literally dying, Abba saw a vision of Yeshua's face, hidden behind a misty cloud. Only Yeshua's eyes were clearly visible. They were not like the eyes of any human that Abba had ever seen—they were more powerful. Moreover, they were eyes burning with great seriousness and deep concern: Yeshua saw the great depth of Abba's agony.

To see Yeshua's eyes of fire brought Abba's soul out of complete despondency and healed a very deep wound. Abba then understood that Yeshua had been watching, with a sad heart, the whole painful tragedy. Abba now knew that his little family was in Yeshua's thoughts, and that they were a special part of Yeshua's heart.

In the image:

And Adonai spoke unto Moses, saying

Speak unto *the* children of Israel, saying, In *the* fifteenth day of this seventh month *shall be* a celebration *of the* booths *for* seven days unto Adonai.

In the first day *shall be* a holy gathering: you shall not do any work of service.

...in the first day *shall be* a little sabbath, and in the eighth day *shall be* a little sabbath.

And you shall take to yourselves in the first day the fruit *of the* citron tree, leaves *of* date palm trees, and branches *of* interlaced trees, and willows *of the* brook; and you shall rejoice before the face of Adonai your God seven days.

And you shall celebrate it with dancing as a celebration unto Adonai seven days in *the* year, an eternal statute unto your generations; in the seventh month you shall celebrate it with dancing.

In booths you shall dwell seven days; every native in Israel shall dwell in booths:

that your generations will know that I caused *the* children of Israel to dwell in booths when I brought them out from *the* land of Egypt. I *am* Adonai your God.

*Sukkot b'Yerushalayim*

**1994**

Leviticus 23:33-23:44

CHAPTER SEVEN:

# Israel

After these things, Abba was taken to the land of Israel and into the Judean wilderness. There, while he walked with Adonai in spirit, he experienced the most beautiful day of his life—Adonai spent the whole day with him. Adonai healed him, strengthened him, guided him, encouraged him, and gave him rest, and peace, and tears of joy.

As Abba entered the wilderness, ravens followed him overhead while sweat poured down from his face and brow. The land had only barren rock in every direction; and the ravens were quietly gliding upward and downward overhead as he hiked over this scorched territory. He considered climbing upward into the mouth of the ravens' mountain, but he took the path instead. At every opportunity, he would kneel in the narrow slivers of shade cast by the massive rocks along the steep path. The rough, hot ground hurt Abba's knees to kneel on; but he especially humbled himself before Adonai because he was on Adonai's special land. Abba would kneel and pray, again and again, every few steps, until he became parched and weary.

As he climbed higher and higher into this burning, stone-laden land, he asked Adonai for somewhere to rest. Adonai led him off the path to a small pool of water. It looked inviting and good from a distance, but Abba was disappointed to find it badly polluted. He was also disappointed in himself to think that he might somehow have been badly polluted by giving way to the wicked. When he asked Adonai about this, Adonai spoke to Abba's heart and told him to avoid the wicked and seek higher ground (both in spirit and literally).

Abba obeyed and climbed up over the nearest rise. There, before his tired eyes, was a most beautiful little oasis just the right size for Abba—tiny exotic creatures, gorgeous flittering insects, and busy colorful bees dashed about in a lively dance of exuberant activity. At the very center of all this colorful activity was a clean jet of water, shooting forth from a small round hole in the rock. Abba washed, refreshed himself, and lay down to rest in the coolness of this small oasis.

He awoke later, startled to see a pretty olive tree a short distance in front of him with seven beautiful doves in its branches. Tears of joy filled his eyes as his soul revived and he thanked Adonai. Then he hiked a little farther into a box canyon with high jagged walls on three sides where he saw, in the clear blue sky, a rolling, swirling, pink and purple cloud majestically moving over the canyon. This wondrous, swelling cloud with an ever-changing shape seemed to appear from nowhere as it billowed around the top of the canyon walls; and a soft, muffled thunder came from the cloud— like a great hidden heartbeat.

It was now evening, and Abba continued hiking until he saw an inviting cave at the top of a peak. "There would be enough time to get there," he thought, "but no time to seek another place afterward." Abba prayed, then took the chance, making the climb upward as the evening darkened. When he arrived with only a hint of light left, he saw that there were no flat places in the cave—only sharp, jagged, knifelike protrusions. It was getting pitch black, and he could not hike anymore. He was dismayed (having trusted that Adonai would tell him not to come to this cave if it were not good). Then Adonai showed him a big, flat rock nearby; and under this rock, there was soft flat earth in a space the size of a large bed. Surrounded only by the warmth of the night and his tender thoughts toward Adonai, Abba slept soundly under the giant tilted stone.

In the morning, Abba hiked down a tortuous trail on another side of the mountain; and all the way down, he quietly praised Adonai in joyful exultation. The landscape was a jumble of tumbled stones as far as the eye could see, and the day was hot. Down below, in the distance, Abba could see a refreshing, manmade spring. He hiked swiftly downward. However, just before he could arrive at the spring, he was reminded that he had left his Bible far back up the trail behind him—it was high up into the hot stones where he had stopped earlier to worship Adonai. The day was getting hotter, Abba was very thirsty, and the trail leading back up to his Bible was steep, rugged, and exhausting to climb. He longed to refresh himself at the spring; but because Abba cared for Adonai's written word more than himself, he hiked all the way back up the hot, twisted trail, struggling and climbing over its steep, rocky places until he finally reached his Bible.

A voice then spoke to Abba's heart and said, "See all these stones, as far as your eyes can see? They are dry and thirsty like you. To you, my words are more important than your thirst. These dry, thirsty stones are like my people Israel: Their souls are dying of thirst, but they choose the man-made springs of this world rather than the living waters of my Son, Yeshua."

With Bible in hand, Abba hiked back down to the beautiful spring and quenched his thirst. He then hiked around the brushy base of the mountain. Suddenly there was a wall of rock on his left, overlooking the trail; it looked to Abba like a broken stone wall of an ancient shrine. A shiny snake was somehow crawling up the wall's flat, vertical surface. Abba stopped and stared in amazement—he had never seen such a feat. This exotic-looking serpent was two to three feet long with golden bands encircling its slithering body. He watched this acrobatic serpent until it reached the top of the stone wall. When it reached the top, it turned around, securely situated itself, exalted its golden head, and looked down upon Abba's head with fearless disdain. The creature stuck out its black flickering tongue. Again, Abba was amazed at the spectacle; he had seen many snakes, but this one behaved strangely. A silent voice seemed to come from the serpent's eyes, exclaiming that it was exalted over the things of God; and it caused Abba to envision the mosque[32] exalting itself over the broken wall of Adonai's Temple.

Abba quickly retrieved a nearby stick from the bushes to confront this proud reptile, but when Abba looked again the snake had vanished.

Immediately, there was a short tunnel before Abba, carved out of the bushes. This shadowy corridor of crooked bushes was a hedge of high, twisted shrubs and intertwined thicket, whose center was roughly carved out into the shape of a gigantic snake hole of some length.

A glimpse of light could be faintly seen coming from the other end of this dark and prickly passage of tightly trimmed brambles. Until this time, Abba's walk with Adonai had been out in the open, under the bright blue sky; this prickly thicket reminded him of the twisted darkness of man's ways. The trail went through this tunnel, so Abba went through and out the other side.

There, he found a man-made water trough which created a small waterfall, and dipped his head into the rushing water to cool off. When Abba opened his eyes, a young man exalted himself in Abba's face. He was standing above, on the rocky ground. Speaking in broken English, this young man (named Gaal) commanded him to pay a fine and said that he would be imprisoned if he was caught spending another night on that mountain. Abba felt like he had just walked out of a glorious cathedral and into a misbehaved kindergarten class....

Abba's prayer, after being cast out[33] by Gaal from Adonai's mountain:

Heavenly Father, majestic and true, I thank you because you have regarded my pain and suffering and have lifted me up with your strong hand. I will dance to you like the satisfied bees. I will follow you like the ravens and rest with you like the doves. I will stand firm like the olive tree. And, like the little hole in the rock, I will let good waters gush forth from my fountain of your spirit. I will behold your glory and hear your heartbeat from the sky; and because you will cover me with your safety—like the great stone shelter—I will not be afraid of the evil deeds of proud men. Amen.

# Afterword

Manasseh, when Imma was a little girl, she was told that she was going to visit a beautiful cathedral, and Imma was very excited. She knew that a house made to worship God in must be truly grand and very beautiful. She had never seen a cathedral. When Imma got there, they got out of the car; walked past the soft, enjoyable grass; past the nice, fun trees; out of the bright, warm sunshine; and into a dark, empty building of bleak, somber tones.

Yet Adonai is not a gloomy, depressing, dismal God; nor is He a God of false smiles, foolishness or fakery. He is real and alive and surrounded by miracles.

Many people think that Adonai's only words are those written in Holy Scripture. These people are wrong. Adonai often hides His wisdom from the intelligent scholars and gives His wisdom to little children, whose hearts and minds are humble and open to Him—These little ones do not trust in their own minds but in Adonai's perfect thoughts.

We see an example of Adonai's perfect thoughts in His beautiful Law to the Jews. This Law (the Torah) comes from the heart of God and is full of love, justice, mercy, and truth. King David said, "Your mercy, *O* Adonai, fills the earth: Teach me Your statutes.[34]" He also said, "*The* law of Your mouth *is* better unto me than thousands of gold and silver.[35]" King David understood how to fully obey the Torah. He knew that its voice must come only from the mouth of God, that its eyes must see only with the light of truth, and that its hands must uphold justice only with love and mercy. It proceeds from the heart of God, and it is truly better than thousands of gold and silver.

Listen, Manasseh, there are some laws that are more important than others. We need to understand this. Yeshua said that the greater laws and lesser laws must work together in harmony; for example, do not neglect to tithe, but be merciful first. Certainly, we should obey every law of God, but always in good judgment—never at the cost of being unloving to Adonai or unmerciful to people. Ask for wisdom and Adonai will give it to you.

Remember, Manasseh, the Law is meant for every man, woman, and child (Jew and Gentile alike). Some commands are specifically for the Jews, some are for the Gentiles, and some are examples for all. If we obey the ones for us as best as we can, it is sufficient.[36] Adonai is merciful, and His Law is a merciful gift for us all, not just an eminent crown for the scholars.

Once there was a boy named Shlomo who was born blind. He was not less important because he was blind; Adonai loved him just as much as the other children who had the gift of sight. His good friends spoke kindly to him and described many sights; however, their wonderful descriptions still did not give him sight. Though he gave them his utmost attention, listened carefully to their vivid descriptions, and gave great thought to their words, he still could not see as they could see.

One day, a man came to blind Shlomo and began giving him descriptions that were different from all the descriptions Shlomo had heard; he told Shlomo things that sounded strange and false. Shlomo was angry with the man and didn't trust him. He asked his good friends about the strange man, and they also thought that the man's words sounded false. So Shlomo did not believe him. Shlomo's friends, being foolish and arrogant, began thinking that there was no truth in the stranger because there was no proof of the stranger's words. Shlomo, however, did not become arrogant; he believed that there were many unknown, unseen and unprovable things, even though his friends claimed otherwise.

One day the strange man returned. But this time, in humility, Shlomo called to Adonai for help to understand the man. Adonai opened Shlomo's eyes, and Shlomo saw the things that the man had said—The man's words were not false!

Manasseh, do not ever think that only what you see and understand is true: Truly, there is always more to be seen beyond our best efforts to see. Adonai hates a proud look, but the humble find favor in His eyes. Each time Abba prays, he must re-humble himself; he knows that he is blind until Adonai gives him sight. When Abba meekly prays he asks for sight, instruction, and the spirit of wisdom, then waits for them to be given him. He asks for humility, then waits for it to be given him. He asks for compassion, diligence, strength, courage and faith, then waits for them to be given him. Adonai gives these things to Abba because Abba humbles himself when he prays.

God hates the blindness of pride and is silent until Abba humbles himself. Humble yourself and re-humble yourself, Manasseh, and you will meet God again and again.

Love, *Abba & Imma*

P.S.    We send our love and blessing of peace upon all who, because they know Adonai, know that our words are true. May the compassion of Adonai and Yeshua protect you forever.... Come soon Lord Yeshua; this world is becoming very painful for all your little ones.

Amen.

# 2*nd* *Letter to Manasseh*

26 He said to him, In the law, what *is* written?
How do you read?
27 And he answering said, You shall love Adonai your God
from all your heart, and with all your soul,
and with all your strength, and with all your understanding;[37]
and your neighbor as yourself.
28 And He said to him, You have answered right:
do this, and live.

—Luke 10:26-10:28

# Preface
## *by Benaiah Z Levell*
## *[Abba]*

One night, when I was a twelve year old boy, my friend Scott and I were standing on a dirty sidewalk out in front of an old brick schoolhouse. It was an unfamiliar part of town—a musty place of faded, grey buildings, dingy sidewalks, and glaring streetlights.

Suddenly, in the middle of our conversation, Scott's face turned disturbingly pale, his eyes widened, his voice fell silent. In a panic, he bolted away from me and darted swiftly along the middle of the dark street. In the distance, I could see him flagging down a city bus. What's wrong? I thought, as I peered down the long sidewalk toward Scott's bus disappearing into the night. Scott did not want to come alone to this high school festival where his older brother was celebrating. Why then did he leave me alone? He was the one who knew this place and the way home, not me.

All at once, behind me, I heard something. I turned and saw why Scott ran. It was a street gang. And in my face the leader—a fierce black teenager with a nylon stocking stretched tightly over his greased hair—spoke loud and penetrating: "You got heart trouble?" I didn't know what to say. His ill-sorted group with violence in their eyes crept around me. He spoke louder: "You got stomach trouble?" I kept silent. Gang members now entirely surrounded me as the leader's savage fist slammed into my throat. I blacked out. My body seemed no longer mine....

I don't remember what happened next; but when I awoke, I was down on the sidewalk being viciously kicked in the ribs. Above me, in a blur, I could see a tall black man with a large, indistinct object fighting the gang off of me. He lifted me up and helped me walk to the door of a nearby building. Disoriented and confused, I knew I must flee this neighborhood and get home.

With bloodied, disheveled clothes and my mind in a fog, I stumbled down the dark, dizzy street to the first friendly spot I could perceive. It looked like an old-fashioned hamburger stand. I asked for directions, but when they saw my beat-up condition, they rudely slammed the window down in my face.

As I walked farther across town, I was astonished by the disregard. Everyone whom I expected would help me seemed to want to hide. I became disillusioned with the world. My trust in humanity melted as my once friendly world turned into an alien place of apathetic faces and frightening shadows. I couldn't walk normally or think straight. Yet somehow, after about ten anxious hours of staggering and stumbling lost over ten miles of dark city streets and strange neighborhoods, I found my way home. I slept for two days.

Scott was my friend; however, on that night, I learned that he did not love me as a true friend should.

That was my first experience with gangs. Since then, I've seen other gangs hurting people. Once, I even recklessly steered my speedy car off a mountain road and up into a frenzied gang on a steep mountainside to frighten them away from beating their hapless victim. Gangs are all over the world because there is not enough love in the world. But the violence of gangs is just one of the many shameful conditions resulting from too little love. Soon after Imma

and I were married, we were interested in purchasing a small trailer.
Seeing an empty one for sale, I called the owner on the phone. He
said to go out and look at it any time. He said it was open and to go
right in. That afternoon, I took a bus to the trailer's location.
Because it took longer than I expected, by the time I arrived, the sun
had set. Using a small flashlight that I sometimes carry with me, I
thoroughly inspected the trailer inside and out. The outside looked
fine, but the inside was not in good condition—definitely unsuitable
for our purposes. I then began to walk back to the bus stop holding
high, under the streetlights, Herman Wouk's book "This is my
God[38]" (a book about how the Jews go about trying to obey Adonai).

As I was reading, I noticed flashing colored lights dancing
around the edges of the page. They were coming from an
approaching group of police cars which swiftly surrounded me. At
once I lowered my book. Not realizing that I was the object of their
attention, I glanced around to see what the trouble was. I saw
nothing behind me but an empty field of grass and the dark sky.
Immediately their police guns and rifles were aimed at my chest.
"Get down!" they shouted, glaring at me as they cocked their
shotguns. I was puzzled. I thought to myself, "Could they be talking
to me?"

"Don't you hear!" They shouted, ready to pull their triggers.

I looked at the gun barrels pointing into my chest, then at the
grimy asphalt beneath my feet. I was wearing clean clothes and did
not want to get soiled. Nevertheless, explaining that I had a ruptured
spinal disk, I lowered myself down to the dirty road, hoping they
wouldn't shoot me for not flying to the ground. Quickly, they
shackled my wrists. My face and beard became encrusted with the
grime of the street as the female officer at my back frisked me
saying, "Do you have any needles in here? I don't like needles. You
better not have any needles in here."

My eyes could see only the darkness of the cold, dirty road
as I heard them say that they had found only Bibles in my
possession....

After a long while, they unhandcuffed me and sent me away.
I felt violated and besmirched. They should not have treated an
innocent person this way. But because of lack of love, innocent

people are mistreated, misjudged and shamed every day in this world.

I once wrote a college paper on the need for more love in high places such as national governments. I was attending a certain university, studying political science in order to get a degree in liberal studies.

The professor was a man who cared deeply about the well-being of the world, and he searched for the solutions to the many political struggles between the nations, hoping to heal the world with the best political strategies. I also wanted to help heal the world, and I studied diligently all that this professor taught.

In time, the students were called upon to write papers showing what they had learned of this. I knew the answer because Adonai was also teaching me; and when I turned in my paper, it said that love is the answer. The professor was upset; he asked me to rewrite the paper, not believing that such an abstract idea could be a workable political solution. At that time I did not rewrite the paper, painfully accepting an incomplete grade instead.

Now, after twenty years, I find that love is still the answer: Where love is, families flourish; nations thrive; authorities of all sorts succeed. Without love, they fail. Gangs hunt the helpless, police harass the poor, governments punish the innocent—not so much for lack of learning but for lack of love.

This second letter to Manasseh is devoted to one of the most important things in life: love. This does not refer to the mixed-up ideas of a sodomizing society, nor to some popular psychological or scientific approach. This letter is about a higher, yet unfashionable love—one that is shining and brave.

Mahatma Gandhi[39] said, "A coward is incapable of exhibiting love; it is the prerogative of the brave." Is this why our governments find it so difficult to express undefiled love? Are they not brave enough to admit to the power of pure love? Our world is in a bad way because of this apparent cowardice. We who have the courage need to stand up for what is right: Love of God is right... Love of our fellow man is right...Love of animals is right...And any endeavor devoid of love is wrong.

*—Benaiah Z Levell*

# CHAPTER ONE

# Heart

The greatest thing we can do is to love God with all of our heart, soul, strength and mind. This chapter is about loving God with all of our heart.

Manasseh, in the nineteen-seventies—when Abba had just reached adulthood—there was a little creature who lived in a small box. One day, a man's hand reached in and picked up this fragile little creature. Abba watched carefully because this man was thought to be much wiser and more knowledgeable than Abba. The man, a scientist, took a sharp knife and without a hint of compassion coldly cut the little creature's chest open. The creature screamed and screamed. However, the man just cursed God while meticulously probing the creature's tiny beating heart. Abba was angry: this so-called great scientist was not great at all. In Abba's eyes, the man seemed a monster.

On another day, in the same medical facility, Abba was called upon to assist a professor of biology. In a back room, Abba watched in sadness as the professor intentionally injected cancer into a helpless animal. This professor was a researcher who studied how the heart worked by filling its blood vessels with plastic and dissolving its more tender parts. What was left was a semblance of the real thing. It was gained at the cost of an innocent creature's needless suffering and profound agony. This is an evil way to study,[40] yet this is what is done because we are lacking the love that comes from a good heart. God has a good heart, and He desires us to have a heart like His: a heart full of love and compassion, not one of disregard and apathy.

The love in His heart is shown by the marvelous and wonderful things He has given to all the world. Light is just one of the many things He gave to us. Look at its brilliance. Feel its warmth. Embrace its rainbow colors with all your soul. It is ours forever, given to us from a God of blue skies, vivid sunsets, and shooting stars. The list goes on: for example, He gave us fruit trees, bird song, and the aroma of the rose. He gave us friendship, laughter, and His only Son. Truly, His love is shown for all to see.

In addition to love, God's heart is also full of compassion. Adonai cares deeply about all His creatures. With love, He affectionately shaped them in each minute detail. He has every hair counted, every blood cell measured, and every feather weighed. This is true; and every human soul which has not embraced this divine compassion is without a good heart.

Manasseh, in nineteen-ninety-six, just a few days after you were born in Israel, you and your Abba and Imma had a bad experience. It was in the hot summer when an apparent computer error left us stranded in Israel with no money. At first we were not afraid, trusting that the error would soon be fixed; but no matter what we tried to do, our money stayed stuck and we stayed stranded.

Because we had no food or shelter, we needed help as we waited for some relatives in America to wire money to us. A righteous friend told us of a Christian place called Baptist Village that he thought might help. It was about a day's journey outside of town. When we arrived at the village, we had sore feet, we were weary and hot, and you lay faint in Imma's arms. The delicate skin of your newborn face was red from the heat; yet we were hopeful, even though we were out of money, for we were now at the Christian refuge.

While offering to help them in any way we could, we asked to stay for the sake of your health in the shade of their village for a couple of days. (They had much property.) We did not ask for food or for money. We only asked not to be sent away, because you were overheated and faint.

The man in charge (supposedly a Christian) clearly understood our desperation, but to our surprise had no mercy whatsoever. This man smirked as he rebuked us and said he had no sympathy for us.[41] As Imma held your tiny, hot body close, tears began to stream down her dusty cheeks. The man then turned and sauntered back into his cool, shady village while we sadly headed back into the crushing heat.

As we hiked farther and farther up the hot highway, we looked for somewhere to rest. There was none. We now realized we were homeless on the streets of Israel. We wearily trudged along. Imma was weak and bleeding because of the birth, while you, Manasseh, were developing a burn from the long exposure to the heat. We finally found some shade behind a gas station and, to avoid the heat, stood there for what seemed like several hours until the sun began to set. Then we tiredly hiked off into the night to find a place to rest.

The only place we could find was an abandoned dump. It had piles of debris, thick weeds, tall scratchy grass and various bothersome rodents. Nevertheless, it was the only place available in the dark night; so we blindly climbed and stumbled over and around the various shin and ankle scraping obstacles until at last we found a small section of fairly decent ground. There, surrounded by tall tangled weeds and bits and pieces of garbage, we laid down on the lumpy dry grass. We looked up at the stars and took turns trying to rest, but the bugs, our hunger, and the noisy rodents kept us awake most of the night.

We didn't realize how really miserable we were, though, until the sun rose; we then felt stiff, sweaty, hot, and about as dirty as the dump itself. As Abba looked at Imma's misery and his baby's fragile condition, and thought about our having to sleep in the dump, he wondered if that Baptist man back in the comfort of his riches was really a Christian at all.[41] How could a believer saved by the compassion of God have so little compassion himself?

Because we were homeless now, the next few days and nights were dangerous for us. Imma, in her weakened condition, was sexually assaulted in the night by an evil man who tried to unclothe her as we lay exhausted and asleep on the beach of Tel Aviv. On another day while we tried to rest, sitting on a bench in the shade of a small deserted playground, an unkind man tried to chase us away with his trained attack dog. We could talk about how senselessly mean this man was, but it is not really the whole story if we don't talk about the dog. The dog refused to attack: he looked at us for who we were. He was not going to attack an innocent couple with an innocent baby.

Because this pit bull dog was not responding to his owner's commands, the man was bewildered. Apparently, the dog had more compassion than his owner.

After this, and on another day, Manasseh, your tender face could no longer endure the heat. Even though you got almost no direct sun, you developed such a severe burn that we ended up having to take you to a hospital. At last our money came in, Manasseh, but because of your severe sunburn you had to be kept out of the direct sun for nearly a year.

We learned from this perilous experience that apathy is commonplace on the streets of Tel Aviv. But Adonai commands us to love Him with all of our heart, and this means, among other things, to have compassion on His creatures.

Compassion is high and lifted up; it is a thing of kings and of greatness. More importantly, we honor God by being kind, and reveal our hearts to be like His.

Although most of the people we met made no attempt to help us protect you from your dangerous predicament, Manasseh, we also saw God's mercy in Israel. For instance, in the little patch of ground in the dump, it was like the land herself was reaching her arms around us and hugging us: Although the people had polluted her and covered her with refuse, she said, "I am kind of covered with garbage, but I'll give you all I have."

In addition, and in stark contrast to the man at Baptist Village—who had much to offer and gave nothing—there was another man we met, in the grayness of the dawn: a ragged beggar who also saw that we were homeless. Hearing you crying in the twilight, he came over and silently blessed you, Manasseh, with deep compassion in his eyes. He had no money or shelter to offer, but he gave us everything he had—he encouraged our hearts. And on another day, when we were put out from a small inn because we could not pay, one kind Australian lady completely emptied out her purse in our hands, saying it was all she had and that if she had more, she would give it.

This lady will be in our hearts forever because she had a heart like Adonai's: a heart full of love and compassion.

Besides having a heart full of love and compassion, Manasseh, Adonai also loves you with a generous heart. Love Him this way. Appreciate Him. Respond to His abundant generosity with abundant praise. Tenderly love the Lord with all the depth of heart you can muster. Take a long, hard, appreciative look at His handiwork. Then stand back and behold, as He causes an ever-mounting eruption of the heavenly pleasures that come from a thankful heart to burst forth in your soul. Truly, you will see the stones of the earth turn to jewels; and the dewdrops, to diamonds.

This chapter was about loving God with the heart. The next chapter explores how to love God with our soul.

CHAPTER TWO:
# Soul נֶפֶשׁ

Manasseh, with our outward eyes we see the natural things of the flesh; but with our inward eyes, we see the supernatural things of the spirit. With our outward self we sense the physical things of the world; but with our inward self we sense the spiritual things of eternity. This inward self is our soul.

In Leviticus 24:17-18, the Hebrew Bible tells us that both people and animals have souls (נְפָשׁוֹת).[42]

Woe to the ones who deny their soul and give themselves over to their dying body: Misery is theirs forever because they trade their eyes for mere orbs of flesh. Woe to the ones who deny their soul and give themselves over to their dying body: they plug their ears with the decaying fungus of their earthly shells.

Woe to the ones who deny their soul and give themselves over to their dying body: They suffocate themselves with the stench of their rotting carcasses. Eternal life could be theirs; instead, they spend their short lives blindly groping about in their unholy beds of ignorance and deceit.

Our soul is our eternal self; it resides within our body and is more important than our body. Adonai commands us to love Him with all of our soul.

Strange to say, many decent people in these last days do not believe in their soul. These imperceptive individuals are not unintelligent—just spiritually deficient when it comes to self-awareness. Apparently, they have been so engrossed in fleshly pursuits for so long a time that all sense of soul has disintegrated. Sometimes they act like mindless seascape artists who are so enraptured with their own brush strokes that they become wholly unaware of the teeming life beneath the ocean waves. For instance, it is recorded that the famous inventor Thomas Edison said, "My mind is incapable of conceiving such a thing as a soul. I may be in error, and man may have a soul; but I simply do not believe it." Beware of these people, Manasseh. They will deeply pierce an unsuspecting soul and mistakenly diagnose the wound they made as a minor scratch in need of only a Band-Aid.

Here is a true story about one little soul who was pierced:

When Abba was a baby and before he could walk, he would be in his playpen and his little friend would hold his hand. Soon Abba learned how to walk, and he and his friend would play together every week. They grew into boys and were very close— they loved one another as brothers.

When the two of them would meet other people, though, Abba was treated well because he was physically attractive; but his friend, who was not pleasing to the eye, was treated badly. Abba knew that he and his friend were both important, and it made Abba angry when the two of them were not treated the same.

Because he was repeatedly rejected, this young man felt the need to search for ways to cause people to like him. He tried to be funny, but that didn't work because he wasn't a talented enough comedian. He tried to change his appearance, but he wasn't artistic enough. He then began giving gifts to people to try to gain their respect. But not even this worked: people began speaking his name with contempt. He learned that going to the altar while in church caused people to give him some loving attention. But after repeating this method time and time again, it too began to fail.

When he grew into a man, he was bitter; for he had never gained the respect that he had searched so diligently for. He began seeking affection on the streets, and found some in the bars and from whores. But this didn't last, and it was not the real thing. Eventually, he learned that having lots of money attracted fair-weather friends. But, of course, they didn't last either.

He got married and raised a family. However, because he was bitter and confused, he committed sin against his own family— sin so bad that he ended up in jail. Now, because he had been treated as if his body was him, his soul matched the undesirable features of his outer shell. Like most human beings, Abba's friend loved himself more than he loved God. If this young man had recognized his own soul and had loved Adonai with it, he would have gained all that he was lacking.

The greatest commandment tells us to love Adonai with all of our soul. This means that the seed of our every desire is to begin its life only in the grand garden of Adonai's ideas, not in the dirt patch of ourselves.

Our desires must spring from Adonai's desires: If we are to be pleasing children to Him, we need to want what He wants. When Abba was a boy with long legs and short attention, his parents would often take him to the wilderness. His father loved to fish and to hunt, and his mother loved the beauty of the wild forest.[44] On one such camping trip, the three of them set out for a walk through the woods. His father strictly commanded him to stay right with them and not to leave the trail.

Abba obeyed for a little while, but then he thought of a fun trick to play on his parents. Because they were walking leisurely and Abba wanted to be faster than that, out into the forest he leaped, planning to jump out in front of his parents just a little up the trail. As he ran through the twisted twigs and the gnarly branches, he reasoned to himself that this tiny little disobedience didn't really count because he would only be off the trail for such a small while. The air was crisp and the run invigorating as Abba looked around for a clearing. The beauty of the forest was a mossy green with hints of a variety of browns.

Abba saw an opening leading back to the trail. He rushed through the opening, hoping to surprise his parents. After plunging through the crackling twigs, he landed on what he thought was the trail; but it was not the trail, just a soft flat spot. The sun shone through the tops of the towering pine trees and warmed the moist earth where Abba stood. Again, he rushed headlong through another clearing, knowing that the trail was just on the other side. But it wasn't there either, just more beautiful, fragrant forest.

The surprise was on Abba.

Abba began to feel a little worried. He couldn't believe the trail was not where he thought it to be. Just a few minutes before, he was with his father and mother. Now, he stopped and listened carefully, but he could not even hear their footsteps or their voices. Abba's heart began to throb faster. He felt somehow embarrassed. He *had* disobeyed.

Seeing sparkles of flowing water nearby, he remembered that his father had told him "If you ever get lost in the mountains, follow a creek downstream because it will eventually come out at civilization." Being very eager at this moment to prove to himself that he was not disobedient, Abba hurled himself toward the stream's mossy, wild edge and ran fast, with all his might, down the cold, glistening stream. To Abba, the stream was now his life—his savior. If this shimmering, hissing, bubbling path of water did not somehow bring him home, he might never see his father and mother again. He ran like a hunted animal—panicked and impervious to pain. He slipped on the slick rocks, twisting his ankles, but this didn't slow him. Time and time again he fell, scraping his hands and face on the wet sticks and stones alongside the water's edge. His heart was a pounding giant forcing him ever forward. His pant legs were wet with the cold icy water, but his face was hot with the sweat of determination and fear. All around him, the colors of the exciting forest were now just fleeting blurs of tall, grey trees and flashing streaks of sunlight.

After hours of running, the blue sky began to dim. The smell of the damp decaying earth and the coolness of the evening breeze reminded Abba of the approaching night, of coldness and possible death. He strained his eyes to see some sign of civilization down beyond the farthest glimpse of the serpentine stream. There was just more dark forest as far as the eye could see. Abba was getting weak. In his chest he had a sick empty feeling, and he missed his father and mother. He felt small and very alone.

To his knees he fell, then to his face. He began to cry, but only for a moment. He was too scared to cry. After washing his face with his marred and muddy hands, he took a quick drink of the crystal cascading water. It was sweet and cold and good, but Abba trembled, jumped up, and continued his hard running down the stream into the demon forest.

This once beautiful, seductive forest now seemed to Abba an unkind, dark magician casting its evil spell to keep Abba from his family. Abba felt like screaming, but he just continued to silently run. Only his loud breathing would be his call for help. Only his fast persistent running downstream would be his savior. His obedience to his father, he hoped, would clear the way to safety.

On and on and on—Abba ran for hours. The sun was setting, darkness was soon approaching, but Abba did not stop. He couldn't stop; what was there to stop for—a thick, uncaring, cold dark forest? Death?

All at once the stream started to cross a dirt road as an old jeep quickly passed before Abba's startled face. The Jeep stopped a few feet away. Abba stood still, glancing back and forth at the Jeep and at the stream. He wanted to continue running but somehow knew that his bond with the little wild stream was broken. The Jeep backed up, and the two smiling hunters inside stared at Abba.

"Are you okay?" the driver asked. After a short pause, Abba said, "I think I'm lost." "He *THINKS* he's lost!" one exclaimed, as the men laughed.

They drove Abba many miles back to his father and mother's campsite. The hunters commented that they couldn't believe a little boy could travel so far in just one day.

At the camp, Abba's parents were waiting in extreme anxiety. The hunters left quickly and Abba stood silently in front of his father. It was dark, but the flickering light of the nearby campfire revealed the strong emotions in his father's eyes. Abba saw love, anger, relief and compassion in those fiery portholes of his father's soul. He had not seen so deep into his father's eyes before.

Abba does not remember the actual hugs and kisses of that happy reunion with his father and mother, but he does remember his father sending him back into the nearby forest to choose a switch from a tree. He chose that switch carefully and also cautiously obeyed all the other instructions that proceeded from his father's mouth.

Abba was an obedient son that night, and that is when he began to love his father with a perfect love.

In the grey darkness of the twilight, his father's blazing eyes of love, anger, relief and compassion made the painful strokes of Abba's spanking a welcome, satisfying experience of love.

Abba had at first desired the beauty of the forest more than the wishes of his father. He should have desired the goodness of obedience—he should have desired what his father desired.

Manasseh, most people in this world have disobeyed Adonai, and they are lost in the darkening forest of their own ideas. They are doomed to die unless they follow, with all their soul, their little stream of humility back to their heavenly father. Then, they need to strictly obey Him: doing not what is right in their own eyes, but doing what is right in Adonai's eyes. We need to desire what He desires. He desires us to safely walk through the forest paths of life with Him—not to be lost with ourselves.

Loving God with all of our soul is important, but this must be combined with loving Him with all of our strength too.

CHAPTER THREE:

# Strength

Dearest Manasseh, our lifetime on earth may seem long, but we mustn't be fooled—it is short. While you have a voice, shout praise unto the Lord. While you have a song, sing to Him with all your might. While you have strong legs, march for Him. If you have any power at all, use it for Him while there is time. When Adonai alerts you, wake up, stretch your God-given muscles, set your course, and try to make each and every action please Him. This is the life we were made for, and it is full of pleasant surprises and delightful rewards.

Once there was a strong horse whose name was Joe. His big, powerful lean body was muscular and his scarred face, noble. He was mature and had much experience with rounding up cattle and with other rough work.

One day, a young, inexperienced sheepherder put a saddle on Joe and rode him out into the rugged Rocky Mountain wilderness to care for some sheep. For hours, they galloped over bumpy meadows, meandered through thickets, jumped over stout boulders, and tripped over twisted timbers until they came to a sandy riverbank. There, Joe stopped. He was hot, wet with frothy sweat, and his breathing was labored. He had obeyed every command of the sheepherder but now refused to budge.

This place in the river was shallow and wide. Underneath the clear, calm water, the riverbed was dark grey sand covered over with a thin layer of mud.

The sheepherder did not understand the meaning of Joe's hesitation, so he commanded Joe to cross the shallow river. Joe wanted to refuse; nevertheless, because he was an obedient horse, he tried with all his might to leap across the wide river. He only made it partway. His big body sank deep in the sucking sand, and in a panic the sheepherder jumped off Joe's back and swam to shore.

Joe, however, struggled to get free of the deep muck surrounding his legs and clinging to his big chest. For a fearfully long time, he fought for his life as the sheepherder watched helplessly.

Joe snorted and pushed and strained with such force that the soupy water and sand eventually gave way, and somehow he managed to get back to shore. The sheepherder was ashamed of himself. He apologized for being foolish, and let Joe take a long, well-deserved rest in the warm sun. He removed Joe's muddy saddle and wet blanket, and let him feed for a while on some tender green grass.

The sheepherder had never seen such dedication and effort in a creature before. He admired Joe, who not only obeyed when the going was tough but even fervently obeyed in a dangerous situation.

This is the kind of strength we should love Adonai with: self-denying effort demonstrated with full physical force. Do this, Manasseh. It will make you a champion for God. It will make you one of the best.

When Yeshua was on the earth, He taught us how to love and fight at the same time. He made a whip[46] and drove evil out of the holy place. He said that whoever does not have a sword should[47] obtain one; that if His kingdom were of this world,[48] he would fight; and that He came not to bring peace, but a sword.[49] King David—a man after God's own heart—says in Psalm 24:8, "Who *is* this king *of* glory? Adonai *the* powerful and strong, Adonai strong *in* battle." And in Psalm 144:1 David proclaims "Blessed *be* Adonai my rock, who teaches my hands for warfare, *and* my fingers for *the* battle."

David fought for his God, his loved ones, and his homeland; and he killed when necessary. We need to follow David's example, and when Adonai or Yeshua commands us not to have pity,[50] we must obey.

Manasseh, when you grow up and become righteous like your heroic fathers Abraham, Isaac and Jacob are, teach the children of God to be strong in loving Adonai. We must learn to love Him like He loves us. If we do not, we will become weak.

Many of the Jews in Israel have become weak. They behave as if the Bible is an unquestionable authority when it comes to who owns the land of Israel. Yet when it comes to how to behave on that land, suddenly the same Bible is not an authority; suddenly they do not want to obey the holy commandment: "Whoever sheds the human *being's* blood, by *a* human *being* his blood shall be shed.[51]" They have taken unto themselves democracy rather than godliness and have, among other sins, abolished capital punishment.[52] This has caused many of the good citizens of Israel to become afraid, for they do not live under the safety of the Torah. These citizens have resigned themselves to obeying democracy, to obeying the will of the wavering multitude.

However, the mind of the majority has never been the best mind: champions, heroes, and great leaders are always few in number and hardly ever in agreement with the crowd.

As long as the vote of the vulgar people controls, the people will remain vulgar, the exceptional ones will remain powerless, and mediocrity will continue to cause debilitating weakness. Like a thickheaded, lethargic leech, mediocrity will suck the life blood from the nation.

No more will such a people behold the glory of a king like David. No more will they hear the wisdom of a king like Solomon. No more will they experience the greatness of a king like Josiah. As long as God's holy nation is afraid of the golden wisdom of Torah, this nation will only be given the iron and clay of democracy. It will be ruled by the crowd, and it will go down in history merely as a corrupted evil creature without much sense.

History records that the common people have sometimes overthrown wicked kings because these kings have threatened the life of the common people. Yet today, Manasseh, the citizens of some democratic nations have become their own wicked king. They have become "King Majority," a high-handed, tyrannical king with destructive, absolute power. Yeshua warned us when He said, "Enter in through the narrow gate; because the gate *is* wide and the way *is* broad that leads away into the destruction, and many are those who enter through it.[53]" Also, the Law of God in Exodus 23:2 commands us: "Do not be *followers* after *a* multitude toward evil *deeds*."

Many nations solemnly declare democracy to be the best form of government. It is not. Love of God and love of His Torah is the best form of government—one to which democracy, as well as all other forms of government, should learn to bow. For truly the Torah is written with the finger of God.

Manasseh, Adonai commands us to love Him with all of our strength. This means that we must not only be faithful to obey His perfect Law, but we must strive to obey with every ounce of our ability.

In addition to loving God with all of our strength, we need to love Him with all of our mind. The next chapter discusses some important ways to love Adonai with our mind.

# CHAPTER FOUR

# Mind

A democratic nation having an ungodly majority is like a tyrannical king with a crazed mind. And, like a tyrant, this majority is also an oppressor. Over time, it distorts its constitution further and further until at last its crooked constitution becomes a twisted scourge to torment the minority and the good people of the land.

This is one of the many problems of an ungodly society whose people respect their own minds more than the mind of God. Adonai says, "For *as the* heavens *are* higher than *the* earth, so *are* my ways higher than your ways, and my thoughts than your thoughts.[54]" He gives us guidelines in His Law and shows us the correct way to rule ourselves. Here, following, are examples of some of God's guidelines for a good government.[55] They are not based on the pursuit of an ill-defined happiness that may hurt others, but they are based rather on the pursuit of a sure way of happiness—love.

You shall not murder.[56]

Whoever sheds the human *being's* blood,
by *a* human *being* his blood shall be shed:
because in *the* image *of* God made *He* the human *being*.

You shall not commit adultery.

And *a* man who commits adultery with *another* man's wife,
*even he* who commits adultery with his neighbor's wife,
the adulterer and the adulteress shall surely[57] die.

You shall not steal.

You shall not speak false witness against[58] your neighbor.

Judges and officers you shall give yourself in all your gates,
which Adonai your God will give you, to your tribe;
and *they* shall judge the people with just judgment.

These few laws from the Torah of God are examples of a Law that works. It is founded on love, and it is efficient and practical.

Until men and women of valor rediscover their God and begin to practice and enforce His Law, the earth we dwell upon will remain an ungodly house of ill repute, a prison for the powerless, and a swamp of despair for the poor.

Man-made governments all over the world give false promises of life and liberty. And they institute ungodly constitutions that appear wise to foolish eyes. These governments and their half-truths are doomed. But the Torah, like the strong voice of a good and brave king, is resounding from the high places to those of courage who will hear. It is the voice of God. And, unlike the other voices, because it comes from the mind of Adonai it is forever trustworthy.

Manasseh, loving God with all of our mind means earnestly and deeply desiring His wisdom. And part of what this means is that we would never make a false translation of His wisdom, nor would we choose to depend upon a false translation someone else made.

Below are some examples of Scriptures that Imma carefully translated for you from the original Hebrew language, followed by some questionable translations. Read these examples and compare them. Note their differences.

Example One:

**Exodus 20:13**

Imma's translation[56] from the actual Hebrew says:

You shall not murder.

In comparison, the less precise King James Version says:

Thou shalt not kill.

*Consider that many good people (being afraid to kill) have not executed brutal murderers, defended their households from violent enemies, or rescued their neighbors from vicious attackers. Consider that right and proper killing is never murder.*

Example Two:

### Isaiah 9:6

Imma's translation from the Hebrew says:

> Because a boy is born to us,
> a son is given to us,
> and the government is on His shoulder;
> and His name will be called
> Wonderful,[59]
> Counselor,
> Mighty God,
> my Everlasting Father,
> Prince of Peace.

In contrast, the Jewish Family Bible, Revised says:

> For unto us a child is born, unto us a son is given: and the government is upon his shoulder: and his name is called Pele-Joez-el-gibbor-abi-ad-sar-shalom (The mighty God, the everlasting father, the Prince of peace deviseth wonders[54]).

*Consider that the phrase "deviseth wonders" can cause the reader to misinterpret this scripture's true meaning by causing him to think that it refers to the Father, rather than to the Son.*

Example Three:

### Numbers 14:34

Imma's translation from the Hebrew says:

> By *the* number *of* the days which you spied out the land, forty days, *a* day to *a* year, *a* day to *a* year, you shall bear your sins, forty years; and you will know my alienation.[60]

Contrast this with the King James Version which says:

After the number of days in which ye searched the land, *even* forty days, each day for a year, shall ye bear your iniquities, *even* forty years, and ye shall know my breach of promise.[60]

*Consider that this last example from the King James translation seems to indicate the false notion that Adonai does not always keep His promises.*

Even though many Christians claim that their favorite translations are inspired by the Holy Spirit, we can see that these inaccurate translations are not inspired, because the Holy Spirit does not try to change or misrepresent Adonai's words. That is what men do.

In addition, ever since the days of the tower of Babel, the various peoples of the earth have had incompatible languages. And when God records His words in one of these languages, His words can never be perfectly translated into another. Therefore, Manasseh, do not entirely trust translations. Believing that all the words of popular translations are creations from God is like trusting that all the pretty flowers of the world are alive and real. Many are alive, but many are showy imitations.

Beloved Manasseh, trust only what is true. Sharpen your intellect. Cut away false ideas of the world from your thoughts. Purify your whole mind and give it—with all your heart, all your soul, and all your strength—to your beautiful heavenly Father, Adonai.

Following, (*read from right to left,*) are the original Holy Scriptures of the above translations. Below each sacred Hebrew word we have placed the English definition of that word:

# Exodus 20:13

לֹא תִּרְצָח

you     Not
shall
murder.[56]

# Isaiah 9:5[61]

נִתַּן-לָנוּ  בֵּן  יֻלַּד-לָנוּ  כִּי-יֶלֶד
given      son    to    born   Because
to              us             a
us                             boy

עַל-שִׁכְמוֹ  הַמִּשְׂרָה  וַתְּהִי
his      upon      the        and
shoulder           government  is
                              [/shall be]

אֵל  יוֹעֵץ  פֶּלֶא  שְׁמוֹ  וַיִּקְרָא
God  counselor wonderful[59] his    and
                            name    will be
                                    called

שַׂר-שָׁלוֹם:  אֲבִי-עַד  גִּבּוֹר
peace.  prince  my        mighty
        of      everlasting
                father

131

# Numbers 14:34

בְּמִסְפַּר הַיָּמִים אֲשֶׁר-תַּרְתֶּם

you  which  the   by
spied      days  number
out

אֶת-הָאָרֶץ אַרְבָּעִים יוֹם יוֹם

day  day  forty  the
           land

לַשָּׁנָה יוֹם לַשָּׁנָה תִּשְׂאוּ

you  to  day  to
shall  a      a
bear  year    year

אֶת-עֲוֹנֹתֵיכֶם אַרְבָּעִים

forty    your
      sins

שָׁנָה וִידַעְתֶּם אֶת-תְּנוּאָתִי:

my    and  year
alienation.[60] you shall
      know

(In addition to Hebrew Scripture being read in the opposite direction of English, it was originally written without vowel points and without standard punctuation.)

This chapter has been primarily about loving God with our mind. The next chapter focuses on loving our neighbors as ourselves.

CHAPTER FIVE:
# Neighbor

Manasseh, sometimes the weak can overpower the strong. This seems confusing, but it is true. There once was a man swimming in the cool, green ocean near your home. A powerful sea creature with sharp teeth attacked him, biting deep holes in one of his legs. This vicious sea creature was the man's enemy.[63] It wanted to destroy him and eat his flesh.

As the man's life blood spilled into the ocean and severe pain surged through his leg and up his spine, he began to fight for his life. He did not consider for a moment letting the creature eat him, nor did he offer this violent creature his other leg for dessert. He would have been foolish to do that. This man pounded on that vicious beast with all his might, over and over again, until the beast let go and swam away. This man survived to tell his story because he defended himself. Yet many of God's people do not defend themselves against the dangerous bullies that attack them: Many of us have been deceived into feeding ourselves to our enemies.[63]

We have been victimized repeatedly because we have been taught that the doctrine of "turn the other cheek[62]" means give the shark the other leg. The people of God must stop giving pieces of themselves over to Lucifer for dessert. Instead, we need to pound at the devil and defend the righteous.

Yeshua said, love your enemies and do good to them.[63] But this does not mean that He came to destroy the Law of His Father. We are never to think that the royal prince of God would ever be against His Father's perfect Law.

One person with wrong thinking says: "Every minor insult, every opposing viewpoint, every slight injury needs to be paid back in full!" On the other extreme, another person says, "Every mortal wound, every tyrant, every murderer needs to be entirely forgiven!" Both of these people are unlike God, and they do not have the wisdom of God's Son, the Messiah.

The wisdom of God and the wisdom of His Son say: When slapped on the cheek, turn the other cheek. When slapped hard in the face, rebuke the offender as Yeshua and Paul did.[64] When slapped repeatedly, defend yourself; and, without malice or hate, report the offender to the judge. If any damage results from the slapping, the just wise judge is to require eye for eye and tooth for tooth.

This is the wisdom of God and His Son. By this, we do good to our enemies.[63] By this, we love our enemies[63] as Yeshua commanded.

Manasseh, when rightful authority is mildly over-strict with you, continue to love and obey. When the authority is unfair, tell him so. When the authority is evil and violently abusive, flee and defend your family. When the authority is a complete tyrant, pray that God's army will overthrow him.

Yeshua came the first time to be the Passover lamb for the slaughter, but He did not intend to turn His disciples into lamb burgers for the world to feed on. At the end of His earthly walk, Yeshua indeed became the sacrifice; but He did not have His bones broken or His spirit crushed. In like manner, we are not to invite the world to break our bones or allow tyrants to crush our spirit. We must be innocent but also wise.

In addition to preventing the devil from destroying us, we need to reach out and keep him from destroying our brothers and sisters around the world.

Manasseh, we have many God-fearing brothers and sisters on the earth that we do not know. They may seem complete strangers to us, but they are not strangers at all. They love Adonai just as we love Him. They obey Adonai just as we obey Him. And they strive to be one with Adonai just as we strive to be one with Him.

Loving our brother means to unite with him, to lift him up as high as we can, and to even die for him. This is true brotherhood, and this is a light for the world.

Put it on a hill and make it shine. Let all your brother's enemies become yours, and fight all his battles as if they are yours; for in truth, they are yours. Lift him up as if your own body had fallen to the ground, and fill his heart with the same joy that fills yours.

Have a brave love like Moses, who put his life on the line for his brother Israelites. And have a love like the Apostles, who sacrificed much for you. Yeshua said "Love one another as I have loved you.[65]" And He died for us to show us how. Be willing to put your life on the line, Manasseh, as Yeshua and His Apostles did for you.

This chapter was about how to love one another, but more importantly, we must first remember to love Adonai. We must continue to perpetually put Him first, above ourselves, above all things. Do this always, Manasseh. Take root in Him. Take deep root and forever grow.

# Afterword

Adonai said, "Vengeance *is* mine; I will repay.[66]" And He will. With every new moment, we are a moment closer to Judgment Day. It is real. It is good. And it will be a relief.

For all the little babies that have been aborted or abused, for all the animals that have needlessly suffered, for all the grandparents that have been coldly pushed aside, and for all the unwanted children and righteous souls that are crying out in their pain, the day of Judgment is beginning to dawn. It is both a day of gladness and a day of sorrow. It is a day of gladness for the people of God. But for those who are laughing at God, at His people, and at His Law of love, it is a day of sorrow and of doom. Truly the heavens and the earth will soon pass away, but the people of God will rise forever.

Manasseh, just like there are falling stars descending across the dark sky, and just like death is descending across the frail living bodies of all those walking the earth, so all earthly things come to an end. From dust we came forth, and to dust we shall return.

This short life that we now live, millions of others have also lived in like manner before us. There are tombstones, cemeteries, all manner of carcasses and scattered bones for all to see. It is evident that the end of each and every one of us is near. This body of flexing flesh, surging blood and crooked bone is merely a temporal earthen vessel intended for godly uses. It is our brief chance to demonstrate a light of love toward God and toward others.

Be brave. Let your light shine from the highest mountains to the lowest valleys. Lift up the fallen, and protect the helpless. Do not let the dead ideas of the world overcome the wondrous life that is in you. Your life is forever, and forever it is yours. Grasp it with all your strength. Give it to God, and fly higher than you can ever imagine.

To conclude, love is not weak. It is strong. But the pride of this world is weakness. It is a decaying, feeble thing on its way to the grave. Love, however, is growing stronger and stronger, and in a short while it will burst the seams of eternity.

Love, *Abba & Imma*

# Section Three:

# *Alive and Kickin'*

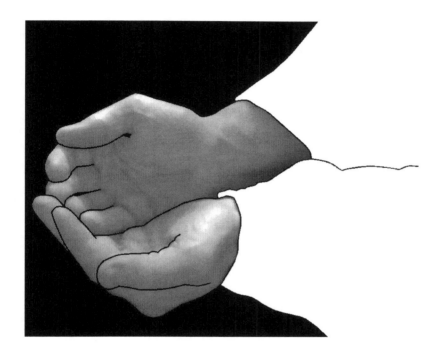

12 Therefore prophesy and say unto them,
Thus has said the Lord Adonai: Behold, I will open
your graves, and cause you to come up from your graves,
*O* my people, and I will bring you to the land of Israel.

13 And you will know that I *am* Adonai,
when I have opened your graves,
and lifted you up from your graves, *O* my people.

14 And I will give my Spirit in you, and you will live…

—Ezekiel 37:12-37:14

And God blessed the seventh day, and sanctified it:
because *that* in it He rested from all His work
which God *had* created to make.

—Genesis 2:3

# CHAPTER FIFTEEN:

# A Sabbath of Rest for His Children

In the day that we circumcised Manasseh Raphael, Benaiah
drank of the fruit of the vine for the last time: Because in that same
day Benaiah dedicated himself to the Lord as a Nazarite:

Numbers

6:2    Speak to *the* children of Israel, and say to them,
When *either* man or woman shall secretly vow *a* vow,
a vow *of a* Nazarite,[1] to separate *themselves* unto Adonai,

3    *He* shall separate *himself* from wine and intoxicating *drink*;
he shall drink no vinegar[2] *of* wine, or vinegar[2] *of* intoxicating
*drink*, neither shall he drink any juice of grapes,
nor eat moist grapes, or dried.

4    All *the* days of his separation, of all that *is* made of the
grapevine,[3] from the seeds even to *a* skin,
he shall not eat *them*.

5    All *the* days of *the* vow *of* his separation no razor
shall pass over his head: until the days are fulfilled
which he has separated unto Adonai, he shall be holy;
he shall grow *the* exposed hair *of* his head.

6    All the days of his separation to Adonai,
he shall come at no soul *of a recently* dead *person*.

7    To his father, or to his mother, to his brother, or to his sister,
he shall not pollute himself for them when they die:
because *the* separation *of* his God *is* upon his head.

8    All *the* days of his separation he *shall be* holy unto Adonai.

—Numbers 6:2-6:8

And after our son was circumcised, we remained encamped
in the same place, until he was healed, from Thursday until the

following Sunday: Because from the hospital we had returned to our camp on the beach, where we also sat at the table for the Sabbath feast with a young Israelite family; a father, and his pretty wife, and their little children.

The parents of this father and mother had faithfully kept the Sabbath every Saturday, very carefully and very thoroughly—but they understood not its meaning: They had worked very carefully to keep in every detail all of their convoluted doctrinal regulations, so that all the family was exhausted every Saturday night. Therefore, neither this man nor his wife obeyed their parents' overcomplicated traditions (whose rest was too much work).

The wife knelt gracefully in the sand. She lit a candle on a makeshift table, even though the moonlight was sufficient. As she carried the candle to the dinner table, I shook my head: Because it is written:

> You shall not kindle[4] fire in any *of* your dwellings
> in the Sabbath day.
>
> ——Exodus 35:3

A sudden whisper of wind extinguished the flame. She relit the candle. The wind again extinguished the flame. She relit the candle. The wind again extinguished the flame.

When the woman relit the candle again, and also melted a plastic bottle in her vain struggle to protect the flame, Ben quietly smiled. I laughed, still shaking my head: Because just as her parents had worked hard to avoid working on the Sabbath, likewise she worked hard to avoid their hard work—to avoid working on the Sabbath.

The confusion of her failure covered the Israelite woman's face. And I felt not one whisper of wind on the beach until the woman lit the candle, nor one whisper of wind afterward. (Was God laughing?)

As for my family, we never lit candles on the Sabbath after that Saturday. Yet, both my family and that family on the beach of the sea of Galilee are both Jewish; and the Law is not the same for all nations: God desires that we keep His day of rest in every tribe and nation, according to the different laws and different understanding which has been given for the peoples in His Kingdom.

Therefore, I know not whether God accepts it when Christians of other nations offer to Him, on the Sabbath day, beautiful candlelight with sincere love—but I believe that He does accept their offering, because it is written,

14      Because when nations,[5] having no law,
      do by nature that which is lawful,
      these, *although* having no law, are *a* law *unto* themselves,
15      who show the work *of* the law written in their hearts;
      their conscience bearing witness together with *them*,
      and *their* thoughts accusing and defending one another,
16      in *a* day when God judges the secrets *of* men
      in agreement with my good message by Messiah Yeshua.

—Romans 2:14-2:16

Therefore, I think that God accepts it when gentiles offer to Him their beautiful candlelight in any day with sincere love.

But this would be disobedience in *our* hands and hearts, to light even the smallest flame for a single candle, because to my people it is written, "You shall not kindle[4] fire in any *of* your dwellings in the Sabbath day."

And I bear witness not only that the Israelite woman worked to light her candle, but also that, when our daughter Elishevah Yael was eight or nine years old, our family no longer lit candles on Friday night (according to our former tradition). With Elishevah, even to protect the flames was work on the Sabbath: She would leap about like a field mouse, and could not understand fire, nor any other danger. Therefore I say that even if it is *not* work to light one single candle on the Sabbath, even so we shouldn't light it: Because it is easy for even a very small flame to *create* work. Nevertheless to the Jews I say, Judge not our non-Jewish brethren in this, because this law against fire is unto us. To the Christians of Colossus Paul wrote:

2:10    and *you* are completed in Him,
        who is the head *of* all rule and authority:

11      and in whom you were circumcised *with a* circumcision
        done without hands, in the putting off the body *of* the sins
        *of* the flesh, in the circumcision *of* the Messiah:

13      …And you, being dead in the fallings and *in* the foreskin
        *of* your flesh, He has made *you* alive together with Him,
        forgiving you all your fallings;

16      …Therefore *let* no one judge you…in participating *in*
        *any* holy day, or new moon, or Sabbaths:

17      *all of* which is *a* shadow *of* the *things* to come,
        and the body *is* the Messiah.

It is written by the prophet Isaiah,

56:2    Joyful *is a* mortal *man who* does this, and *a* son *of* man
        *who* strengthens himself in it; keeping *the* Sabbath
        *rather* than desecrating it, and keeping his hand
        from doing any evil.

56:6    And the sons of the foreigner, who join themselves to
        Adonai to serve Him, and to love *the* name *of* Adonai, to be
        to Him for servants: all *who* keep *the* Sabbath *rather* than
        desecrating it, and strengthen themselves in my covenant;

7       and I will bring them to my holy mountain,
        and make them joyful in *a* house *of* my prayer:
        their *offerings* sent up[6] and their sacrificed *animals*
        *will be* accepted upon my altar, because my house
        will be called *a* house *of* prayer for all the peoples.

8       My Lord Adonai *who* gathers *the* exiles of Israel says:
        I will even gather *others* to him,
        *and* to his gathered *congregations*.

66:18   …the hand[7] *of* Adonai is coming to gather all the nations and
        the tongues; and they will come, and they will see my glory.

And *there* will be *more* than enough[8] new moon
in *every* new moon, and *more* than enough Sabbath in *every*
Sabbath: All flesh will come to bow *down*
before my face, says Adonai.

—Isaiah 56:2; 56:6-56:8;
66:18-66:23; Colossians 2:10-2:17

Our living Lord has blessed His people with one Savior, for
everyone, but I have found seven different laws in the Torah: One
law for everyone who calls upon the name of Adonai; and another
for the strangers who live among the sons of Jacob; one for the
Israelites; one for the Levites; one for the Nazarites; one for the
kings and bishops; and another law for the priests.

Therefore, it is good for every child of God to rest in the
Sabbath day—the Israelites with wine, and the Nazarites without
wine; the kings with their peoples, and the mothers with their
families.

All faithful observances of the Sabbath are pleasing to God,
from the loving hearts of His children. God created the Sabbath for
mankind, because of His great love for us; as it is written in the book
of the words of the apostle Mark, which say:

27  And *He* said *to* them, The Sabbath was made for man,
*and* not man for the Sabbath:

28  Therefore the Son *of* Man is Lord also *of* the Sabbath.

—Mark 2:27-2:28

For the sake of His great love for us, our *Abba*—our
Daddy—gave us the Sabbath, a gift from our loving Daddy to his
little children. Therefore, if we never want to reject a birthday
present from any loved one (even if the gift is a very ugly sweater),
then it is not good to reject the perfect birthday present of the first
birthday, the Sabbath, from the only friend who loves us completely.
(And the Sabbath is indeed the first birthday present ever, even as
Messiah Yeshua is the first Christmas present ever.) And our

*Abba*—our Daddy—only asks of us an easy thing—to rest; that is, to dedicate to Him one day in seven (simply to be); simply to remember that man was not created for the purpose of working, but to sing praises to God our Daddy.

Therefore, to reject this gift breaks His big heart; because He only asks us to rest; as grateful little children, accepting with gratitude this perfect gift—which is certainly no ugly sweater!

Although to reject His gift breaks His great heart, He does not use His great strength to force His non-Jewish children to rest, even as we do not force our children to accept their cake and ice cream. But I know deeply, with all my heart, that my beloved Lord weeps over His rejected gift: Because from my eyes God has not hidden His tears.

And (in the case of our beloved Israelite friends on the beach) because their parents broke God's commandments for the sake of tradition, this adorable family broke the tradition of the elders—but, in their ill-advised rebellion, this family also broke the commandment of God. Thus do many err.

And in many other things also the Israelis have rebelled against the words of the Lord (in part because Israel cannot discern the holy Torah from the tradition of the elders), as it is written,

2    Hear deeply,[9] heavens, and give ear, *O* earth: because Adonai is speaking: I nourished[10] children, and I brought them up, and they rebelled against me.

3    *An* ox knows his owner, and *the* donkey his master's manger; *but* Israel does not know, my people does not understand *at all*.[11]

—Isaiah 1:2-1:3

And afterward we saw the rebellion of many Israelites and Palestinians, and we also saw the obedience and suffering of many Israelite Believers and Palestinian Believers (that indeed all of Israel's accusations against the Palestinians are true; and also all of Palestine's accusations against the Israelites); then, afterward, our Lord *Yahweh Yireh*—Adonai who sees—drove us out from the land that we might return to bear witness.

11  I was watching then because of *the* sound
    *of the* immense words which *the* horn spoke:
    I was watching until that beast was killed, and its body
    was destroyed and given to *the* burning of *the* fire.

12  And *as concerning* the rest of *the* beasts, their dominion
    was *also* taken away; and prolonging in life[12]
    was given to them until *a* set *time* and *a* set *time*.

13  I was watching in visions of *the* night; and behold,
    with *the* clouds of *the* heavens *one* like *a* son *of* mortal
    *man*—He was coming; *He* came to *the* Ancient *of* Days,
    and they brought Him near before Him.

14  And to Him was given dominion, and honor,
    and *a* kingdom; and all *the* peoples, *the* communities,
    and *the* languages will serve Him: His dominion
    *is an* everlasting dominion: it will never be taken away;
    and His kingdom *one* that will not be destroyed.

15  I, Daniel, my spirit was grieved in *the* midst of its outer
    shell; and *the* visions of my head troubled me.

——Daniel 7:11-7:15

CHAPTER SIXTEEN:

# Come Out of Her, My People

When we returned to the United States with my firstborn son Manasseh Raphael, in the airplane, I dreamed a dream: A beloved family member was with us in a great ship; and with a loving smile and innocent joy she snatched my baby Manasseh from my arms, and tossed the baby into the sea.

And in helpless horror I saw his little arms flail in desperate astonishment while he disappeared beneath the dark waves; and I could not move my feet to save my little son.

And I woke up shaking.

Three times I dreamed this dream; and each time I woke up trembling; but no one could interpret this dream.

And in the second month after Manasseh's birth, we returned to our home in California, and there we stayed. And in the first year after Manasseh's birth, I began to write a letter to our little child; in order that, if I were to die in his childhood, my son might hear my words, and know thereby my tiny bits of wisdom which his mother had from God.

And Benaiah was as a mute, because of his severe dyslexia: So that when I asked him to also write one part of my letter to our little son, he did not believe that he could possibly communicate to his son with words. But when Benaiah saw that he could, he began to write a long letter, which quickly became a small book: He dictated to me his words, and I wrote them, and then he changed the words until their meaning was correct: In this way I wrote both his words and my own, in our first book *Letter to Manasseh*: [which in time became the first section of *The Book of Seven Flames and Burning Coals*].

Then, with the writing of *Letter to Manasseh*, we also read the entire Holy Bible (—not for the first time, but for the first time together). And when we began to read the Revelation of Saint John together, but we understood not this book; then, we read many history books, and prayed, and we asked our God to open up our eyes to understand the Apocalypse.

And I heard in my heart (and Benaiah also in his heart separately) the voice of the Holy Spirit; which said that for our own good this book was dark and enigmatic: Because to understand these things is to know deep sorrow; and our loving *Abba* does not want to give His beloved little children any sorrow.

But in our great love for His words—for we were truly in love—we prayed all the more; and we fasted, and we begged, "Break our hearts, please, please, break our hearts with Your beautiful words."

For three days we prayed and fasted.

Then little by little, very gently, our loving *Abba* opened for us first Isaiah and Jeremiah, then Ezekiel and Daniel, and then the Revelation little by little, bit by bit: And I saw the tears of my *Abba*, the Lord of my soul; His unbearably deep sorrow, indescribably deep; and my heart was broken for His big, big heart so deeply broken. And my heart was filled with anguish and terror; because I saw the dragon, and the false prophet, and the Beast of the

Apocalypse, of which Daniel also spoke: And that the Beast is already in the world (but it is still only a naughty child).

And we wrote Seven Flames to give this painful wisdom to Manasseh and his brother and sister: But not all: For God did not permit us to write all these things: For Benaiah wrote in the Holy Spirit to our brothers in New York,[14] "Come out of her, my people, that ye be not partakers of her sins," but God commanded him to seal this prophecy until after the first punishment.

And also I dreamed another dream three times; in which a great silver missile, with Ishmaelite enemies inside the giant missile, pierced a silver skyscraper with an enormous explosion; and I recognized this building, that it was in New York. And again I saw what I thought was the same strike, and I also saw a captive slave with the enemies, also an Ishmaelite, and a brother of one of them.

And I saw another missile strike, in a field, so that I thought at first that perhaps the missile's future was still changeable and uncertain.

But when I dreamed the dream a second and a third time, I knew that both futures were certain: But I never saw the other which pierced the Pentagon, until the entire nation saw it with me on September 11, 2001.

And my broken heart cried out.

But after the third time that I saw the dream, I dreamed also another dream three times: And an angel[15] said to me, Seal this prophecy until after the crashes; and he said that if I seal them not, but reveal them, all that I saw was nonetheless certain, but I could change my own future: Because if I were to reveal the dream before the crashes, I would have become a scapegoat, an enemy of my own people, and with cruel, blind vengeance I would be tortured, and my family with me, to punish my soul with cruel revenge.

Then I dreamed yet another dream, also three times, that I stood in a big, beautiful synagogue: And the synagogue was burning. Painted wallpaper of Holy Scriptures in Hebrew letters was upon the walls, also burning. And then (in the second part of the same dream) I stood in the same synagogue before the fire: And I sought to warn the chief rabbi and another rabbi, but my words were

146

as foolishness to them: For there was no painted wallpaper upon the walls, but natural cedar.

And I dreamed still another dream, also three times, that the same angel[15] said that this prophecy is also certain; but this time he did not command me to seal these things and reveal them not, nor that any harm would come should I reveal; but the angel did say that this future is certain.

Moreover, I know not whom to warn: I know only that this is the second punishment.

And my broken heart cried out.

## Revelation Translated

17:1 And *there* came one of the seven angels[15]
who had the seven bowls, and talked with me,
saying to me, *Come* here: I will show you the verdict
*against* the big whore who sits upon the many waters,

2 with whom the kings *of* the earth have fornicated,
and the inhabitants *of* the earth have become intoxicated
from the wine *of* her fornication.

3 And *he* carried me away in *the* spirit into *a* desert;
and I perceived *a* woman sitting upon *a* scarlet beast
*which was* full of blasphemous names,
having seven heads and ten horns.[16]

4 And the woman was clothed *in* purple and scarlet,
and gilded, *adorned with* gold and precious stones
and pearls, having *a* golden cup *in* her hand full of
abominations and filthiness *of* her fornication;

5 And upon her forehead *was a* name written, *a* mystery:
Babylon the Great, the Mother *of* the Whores
and *of* the Abominations *of* the Earth.

6 And I perceived *that* the woman *was* intoxicated
from the blood *of* the holy *ones*, and from the blood
*of* the witnesses *of* Yeshua: and when I perceived her,
I was astonished *with* great astonishment.

17:7 And the angel[15] said *unto* me, Why are you astonished?
I will tell you the mystery *of* the woman...

15 ...The waters which you saw, where the whore sits,
are peoples, and multitudes, and nations, and languages.

18 And the woman who you saw is the great city
which reigns[17] over the kings *of* the earth.

18:1 And along with these *things* I perceived another angel[15]
descend from heaven, having great authority;
and the earth was lit up from his glory.

2 And he shouted in *a* very powerful voice, saying:
The great Babylon has fallen, has fallen; and has become
*a* dwelling place *of* demons, and *a* prison *of* every unclean
spirit, and *a* cage *of* every unclean and despised bird:

3 because all the nations have drunk of the wine *of* the raging
*of* her fornication, and the kings *of* the earth
have fornicated with her, and the merchants *of* the earth
have become rich from the power *of* her luxuries.

4 And I heard another voice from heaven, saying, Come out
of her, my people, so that you will not be partakers of her
sins, and so that you will not receive *any* of her calamities;

5 because her sins have followed as far as heaven,
and God has remembered her iniquities.

6 Reward her even as she rewarded you,
and double *to* her double according to her works:
in the cup *in* which she has poured, pour *to* her double.

7 As much as she has glorified herself, and lived luxuriously,
so much torment and mourning give her:
because she says in her heart, I sit *a* queen, and I am not
*a* widow, and I will not see *any* mourning at all:

8 Therefore her calamities will come in one day—death, and
mourning, and famine; and in fire she will be utterly burned
up: because powerful *is* Adonai, the God who judges her.

9 And the kings *of* the earth who have fornicated with her
and lived luxuriously will weep *for* her and lament over her
when they see the smoke *of* her burning,

18. 10   standing far away because of the fear *of* her torment,
saying, Alas, alas the great city Babylon, the mighty city;
because in one hour your condemnation came!

11   And the merchants *of* the earth weep and mourn over her,
because no one buys their cargos any more:

12   cargos *of* gold, and silver, and precious stones, and *of* pearls,
and fine linen, and purple, and silk, and scarlet, and all
fragrant wood, and every commodity *of* ivory, and every
commodity of precious wood,
and *of* bronze, and iron, and marble;

13   and cinnamon, and fragrances, and myrrh, and frankincense,
and wine, and olive oil, and fine flour, and grain,
and livestock, and sheep, and horses, and chariots,
and bodies and souls *of* men.

14   And the fruits *of* the lust *of* your soul are departed from you,
and all the *things which were* lusciously rich and glistening
are departed from you, and you will never find them again.

15   The merchants *of* these *things*, which were made rich
*because* of her, will stand far away
because *of* the fear *of* her torment, weeping and mourning,

16   and saying: Alas, alas the great city,
that was clothed in fine linen, and purple, and scarlet,
and was gilded in gold, and precious stones, and pearls!

17   Because *in* one hour so much wealth had been desolated.
And every pilot, and all the community on the ships,
and sailors, and as many as work *in* the sea, stood far away,

18   and they cried out *upon* seeing the smoke *of* her burning,
saying, What *city is* like the great city?

19   And they cast dust on their heads, and cried out,
weeping and mourning, saying, Alas, alas the great city,
wherein were made rich from her opulence all who had ships
in the sea; because *in* one hour she was made desolate!

20   Rejoice over her, heaven, and *you* the holy apostles
and the prophets; because God has decided the judgment
for you *who came* from *within* her.

18:21    And one powerful angel[15] lifted up *a* stone,
like *a* big millstone, and cast *it* into the sea, saying:
*With* such violence the big city Babylon will likewise
be thrown down, and will never be found any more.

22    And *the* sound *of* harpists, and musicians, and flute players,
and trumpeters will be heard no more at all in you; and no
craftsman *of* any craft will be found any more in you; and *the*
sound *of a* millstone will be heard no more at all in you;

23    and *the* light *of a* candle will shine no more at all in you;
and *the* voice *of a* bridegroom and *a* bride
will be heard no more at all in you: because your merchants
were the greatest *ones on* the earth because
in your shamanism[18] all the nations were led astray;

24    and *because* in her was found *the* blood *of* prophets, and
*of* holy *ones*, and *of* all the slaughtered *ones* upon the earth.

19:1    And after these *things* I heard *a* voice *of a* very big multitude
in the sky, saying, Praise Adonai! The salvation, and the
glory, and the honor, and the power, *is* Adonai our God:

19:2    because His judgments *are* true and equitable:
because He has judged the big whore who had corrupted
the earth in her fornication, and He has avenged
the blood *of* His servants[19] out from her hand.

3    And *a* second *time* they said, Praise Adonai!
And her smoke rises up to the ages *of* the ages.

4    And the twenty-four elders and the four living *creatures* fell
down and worshipped the God sitting on the throne, saying,
Truly: Praise Adonai!

20:11    And I saw *a* big white throne, and the *One* sitting on it,
from in front of whom the earth and the sky fled away;
and no place was found *for* them.

12    And I saw the dead, small and big, standing in God's sight;
and books were opened; and another book was opened,
which is the *book of* life: and the dead were judged
out of the *things which were* written in the books,
according to their actions.

20:13 And the sea gave up the dead *who were* in it;
and death and Hades gave up the dead *who were* in them;
and they were judged each *one* according to their actions.

14 And death and Hades were thrown into the lake *of* fire.
This is the second death.

15 And whoever was not found written in the book *of* life
was thrown into the lake *of* fire.

21:1 And I saw *a* new sky and *a* new earth:
because the first sky and the first earth were passed away;
and the sea no longer existed.

2 And I John[20] saw the holy city, *a* new Jerusalem,
coming down from God, out of the sky,
ready like *a* bride adorned *for* her husband.

3 And I heard *a* great voice out of the sky saying, Behold—the
tabernacle *of* God with men! And He will dwell with them,
and they will be His peoples,
and God Himself will be with them, *and be* their God.

4 And God will wipe away every tear from their eyes;
and death will no longer exist, neither sorrow,
nor outcry, neither will there be any more pain:
because the first *things are* passed away.

5 And the *One* sitting upon the throne said,
Behold: I make all *things* new. And He said *to* me, Write:
because these words are true and trustworthy.

6 And He said to me, *It* is done. I am the Alpha and the
Omega, the beginning and the end. To the *one who* thirsts I
will give freely of *the* fountain *of* the water *of* life.

7 The *One who* overcomes will inherit all *things*;
and I will be His God, and He will be my Son.

8 But fearful *ones*, and untrusting, and *the* abominable,
and murderers, and *the* fornicators, and shamans,[21] and
*the* idolaters, and all the liars, their part *will be* in the lake
burning *with* fire and sulfur, which is *the* second death.

22:20 The *One who* testifies these *things* says, Yes, I come quickly.
Truly; yes, come, Lord Yeshua.

—Revelation 17:1–22:20

151

The pure *in* heart *are* blessed:[22] because they will see God.

3 Who will go up into Adonai's mountain?
  And who will arise in His holy place?
4 *One who is* clean *of* hands, and pure *of* heart…

5 He will lift up *a* blessing from Adonai,
  And righteousness from *the* God of his salvation.

—Matthew 5:8; Psalm 24:3-24:5

CHAPTER SEVENTEEN:

# A Pure Soul

When my firstborn daughter Elishevah Yael[23] was in my womb, before I knew of it, I dreamed of a furry creature like a tailless monkey, and almost human, but more like a giant mouse: And its color was also brown like a field mouse, and it also leaped about like a field mouse. And its soul was almost like a human soul, but only almost: Because its soul was pure and caring like a critter. And I guarded her leash and her harness, so that the friendly critter should not escape to its own harm.

Then a friendly mouse was in my hands, and I knew that this creature and the first creature were the same one: They were a single creature. And my Lord put His hand upon my shoulder and said gently, "Do you want this living creature I have created?" and I said, "Yes."

And the next morning I learned that I was pregnant with a second babe: And when the baby was born, she was covered with mouse-brown fur like the critter in my dream.

And when the midwife saw my amazed face, she said that the hair was only temporary; and that every baby is covered with soft hair in the womb, and that her hair was still on her body because she was born just a tiny bit early; and the midwife showed me the baby's ears, that they were "early ears"—but in truth I was amazed because I knew that my Lord had given me the pure soul in my dream.

We lived in Smith River, California from Christmas Eve of nineteen ninety-five until the late summer of nineteen ninety-eight;

152

when we returned to Oregon to seek a midwife for Elishevah Yael's birth, and also to search for a job: Because in Smith River, the people had few job opportunities except for prison guards, and the laborers in the Easter lily fields.

And Elishevah's birthplace was her paternal Aunt Annette's ranch, in her barn; and the bed where I gave birth was under the place of the manger: Because although the room was a photographer's darkroom at that time, the marks of the manger were still on the wall. (And we had not chosen the place because the marks were there; rather the midwife—who knew not the meaning of the marks—chose this place for her own convenience, in case of emergency.)

And from the moment of her birth, my little daughter showed in her own face all the feelings of her father and mother: She felt all the feelings of anyone in the house with her, and showed our adult feelings on her new little face. Her daddy was so amazed by this, again and again.

When we had just moved into our small apartment in McMinnville, Oregon, I was sitting cross-legged on the well-worn carpet of a bedroom floor, reading silently to myself from a history book of famous cases of the United States Supreme Court. Benaiah was at work, at his night job caring for disabled men, and Manasseh and Matt were asleep; but Elishevah Yael was playing happily on the bedroom floor about ten feet away. At three years old, her favorite game was arranging and re-arranging her paper flowers all across the floor. Except for the cute, almost musical sounds of our daughter's baby chatter, the apartment was silent. Light had just begun to stream into the unadorned window.

From where I sat reading, the window showed only a beautiful view of a bright, clear sky, slowly changing from white to blue. My back was toward that window, and my gaze locked on the words on the large, yellowed pages which lay open before me. As I said before, this book was filled with true stories from the United States Supreme Court. I had considered reading the stories out loud for my three year old daughter, as I often did; but instead, this time, I had chosen to enjoy her baby sounds.

I had been silently reading every case in order, from the earliest toward the latest, but then when I came to the infamous

Dredd Scott[24] decision I turned the page, because I already knew that case by heart.

The happy chattering behind me stopped.

Two little feet stomped over to my side, two little arms folded sternly across Elishevah's tiny chest, and her lips pursed together, and her eyebrows went down. Elishevah Yael bent over,

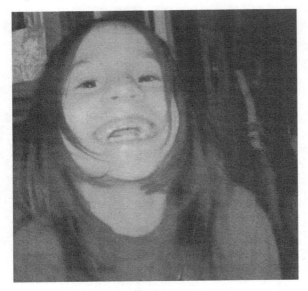

flipped the page back to the Dredd Scott decision, and folded her arms again across her little chest, and scolded, *"READ DREDD SCOTT!"*

And so I silently began to read the Dredd Scott decision, because she wanted to "listen to" the *whole* unspoken history of the Supreme Court, *without* skipping *any* stories. (And this was by no means the last time that Elishevah Yael got bossy about other people's unspoken thoughts.)

And after the beginning of our tribulation, her "psychologist" mocked to scorn the true belief of the pure creature, that she feels what human science does not say anyone can feel, the thoughts of others, and also where her parents are: Because our loving creature had told the worldly man that she knew in which direction we were, and pointed with her hand. And the psychologist mocked the child, because Elishevah Yael "thought" that she knew where her mother and father were.

Neither did he make any tests to discern whether she had such a rare ability as she had said.

Hosea

9:7 ...the prophet *is a* fool, *the* man *of* the Spirit *is* insane,
to your great iniquity and great hatred.

1 Co.

2:9 ...Eye did not see; and ear did not hear; neither have come up upon *a* man's heart, the *things which* God has prepared *for* those *who* love Him.[25]

10 But God revealed *them* to us through His Spirit: because the Spirit searches all *things*, and *even* the depths *of* God.

11 Because who *among* men understands the *things of* man, except the spirit of man *which is* in him?
And likewise no one has understood the *things of* God, except the Spirit *of* God *does*.

12 And we have not received the spirit *of* the world, but rather the Spirit which *is* from God, so that we might understand the *things that are* given to us from God,

13 which *things* we also speak, not in words *which* human wisdom teaches, but in *which the* Holy Spirit teaches, judging *the* spiritual by *the* spiritual.

14 But a natural man *does* not receive the *things of* the Spirit *of* God: because *they* are foolishness *to* him; and he cannot understand *them*, because *they are* spiritually discerned.

——Hosea 9:7; 1 Corinthians 2:9-2:14

Ezekiel

3:17 Son *of* Adam, I have given you *for a* watchman
to *the* house *of* Israel: and hear deeply,[9]
*therefore, the* word from my mouth,
and shine *to* them *a warning* from me.

18 When I say to *a* wicked *person,* Dying you will die;
and you do not shine *a warning to* him, nor speak
to enlighten *the* wicked from his wicked way,
to save his life; he, *the same* wicked *one,* will die
in his iniquity; but I will require his blood from your hand.

33:14 And when I say to *a* wicked *person,* Dying you will die;
and he turns from his sin, and does judgment and justice;[26]

15 *if the* wicked returns *the* surety, restores *what was* robbed,
*and* walks in *the* statutes *of* life, without committing iniquity,
living he shall live...

Isaiah

62:6 Upon your walls, Jerusalem, I have set guards:
they shall never be silent all the day and all the night:
those *of you who* remember Adonai, do not be silenced.

—Ezekiel 3:17-3:18; 33:14-33:15; Isaiah 62:6

CHAPTER EIGHTEEN:

# Revelation Revealed

After we had finished writing *Letters to Manasseh*, we also read through the whole Bible together. (We had each read all the way through the Bible before we married, but we wanted to do it together this time.) And because Ben had begun educating his firstborn son Elias Luke to be a preacher, Benaiah had several good Biblical reference books, the two most important of which proved to be Strong's Exhaustive Concordance of the Bible, and an interlinear Hebrew-English and Greek-English Bible with Strong's Concordance numbers. And we would stop at every Bible verse either of us didn't understand, and pray and study until we both understood.

After we had finished writing *Letters to Manasseh*, our plan had been to self-publish *Letters to Manasseh*, get a good job, save up enough money to move to Israel, and then raise our family in the land of my fathers. And so we also read every book we could find about the modern Judean nation called Israel, and studied the Hebrew language, as well as a little Arabic.

But when we reached the book of Revelation in our Bible study, we couldn't understand hardly any of it: The book of Revelation cannot be understood from a human point of view,

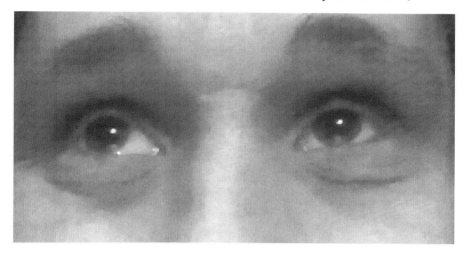

because it is written from Adonai's point of view.

And so I fasted and prayed for three days (and Benaiah prayed also, but he ate a little because his body was in no condition to endure so long a fast). And finally the Holy Spirit spoke to me, and warned me strictly that this book had been hidden in riddles as an act of mercy; and that if He opened my eyes to its secrets I would suffer great sorrow, such as I had never known. And He also answered Benaiah in like manner.

But, after I had rested and had meditated upon the Holy Spirit's warning for nearly a week, I fasted and we both prayed three more days; and then Adonai began to open up to us the Revelation of Messiah Yeshua, as well as the books of Daniel and Ezekiel (which we had understood well enough to keep reading, but not deeply enough to prepare us for the book of Revelation).

Here, below, is one chapter of what Adonai opened up to us, written in *Seven Flames: Letter to Elishevah* to our baby daughter Elishevah Yael:

# Authority (εξουσια)
### (An excerpt from *Seven Flames*)

There is a big difference between "power" and "authority". Remember this when you encounter someone who claims to have authority over you.

Elishevah, just because someone has power over you does not mean that they have authority over you. Δυναμιζ (DOO-nam-iz) is a Greek word meaning "power." Εξουσια (ex-oo-SEE-ah) is a Greek word meaning "authority." Εξουσια is also, quite possibly, the most misunderstood word in the New Testament, and thus a source of endless trouble, simply because it has been mistranslated as "power" (δυναμιζ). Although the King James Version of the Bible translates εξουσια as "power" no less than sixty-six times, this word always means "authority."

It appears that Satan enjoys these mistranslations, Elishevah, and that he will fight to defend them. Furthermore, Satan probably finds it flattering when we suggest that he is capable of fighting Adonai (Acts 26:18). And he surely thinks it is funny when we, by our mistranslation, speak of darkness as having power over light (Luke 22:53). But possibly his favorite mistranslation of all is the much quoted Romans 13:1.

Thousands, maybe millions, of God's people have been fooled by this mistranslation into obeying whoever happened to have power over them. Nowhere does Holy Scripture tell us to obey the powers (δυναμειζ) that be. Obey Queen Jezebel? Obey Hitler? Obey the Antichrist? How about the devil himself? God forbid!

To obey the higher authorities, however, the authorities that truly exist, this is godly. Rome did not do this when they met the Holy Messiah. The Roman guards thought that Yeshua (the physically powerless man before them) was not a king; yet they were very much mistaken.

Power and authority are not the same thing, Elishevah. The true authorities are not always those in power. The true ones are dressed in the royal robe of the Torah, and adorned with the mantle of godliness. These are the ones created in the likeness of God, and they continue to walk in His likeness. They are the real authorities, Elishevah. They love you deeply, and their love is genuine.

Numbers
23:19 God *is* not *a* man, that He should lie,
Neither *the* son *of a* man, that He should repent…

James
1:17 Every good giving and every complete gift is from above,
coming down from the Father *of* lights, in whom is no
variableness, neither shadow *of* turning.

———Numbers 23:19; James 1:17

# CHAPTER NINETEEN:

# The Everyday Miracle of Parenthood

Beloved fathers and mothers, sons and daughters, brother
Christians, I write to you as a mother, for your mother I am: And,
indeed, it is written not only of biological parents, but even more so
it is concerning you and your spiritual and theological fathers the
Jewish people, that it is written:

5    Behold, I am sending you the prophet Elijah,[28]
before the great and terrifying day *of* Adonai comes.
6    And he will turn *the* heart *of the* fathers to *the* children,
and *the* heart *of the* children to *the* fathers;
lest I come and strike the earth *with a* curse.[29]

———Malachi 4:5-4:6[30]

Our loving Daddy Adonai also said,

26    See, I set before your faces today *a* blessing and *a* curse:
27    the blessing, if you will hear[31] deeply *the* commandments
of Adonai your God, which I command you this day:
28    and the curse,[29] if you will not hear[31] deeply
the commandments *of* Adonai your God…

—Deuteronomy 11:26-11:28

But this does not match our idea of our loving Lord Jesus—
this is the Old Testament God; the God of Jacob; the God of
judgment—Why would our loving Daddy say such a thing? This

doesn't sound like our nice, friendly Savior Jesus healing our diseases, or making one young man's ordinary afternoon snack into a huge feast for five thousand people, or taking little children on his lap and blessing them.

But God has not changed.

God has not changed: He has *always* loved mercy; He has *always* been quick to forgive; He has *always* cared deeply about each and every one of us. God did *not* start loving us because His Son came—Rather, God loved us first: And, indeed, there is no better-known verse in all of the New Testament that John 3:16, which bears witness to this very thing: "because God so loved the world that He sent his only-begotten Son, that whosoever believes on Him shall not perish, but shall have everlasting life."—Jesus of Nazareth was our heavenly Father Adonai's idea.

God loved us first.

The indescribable and the amazing mercy of Yeshua freely choosing the Cross for our sakes, for my sake, was His Father Adonai's idea.

Yeshua did not change God: God *always* loved us so much that He gave us—How can I even *describe* what He gave?

How can I find the words to express the reason my heart is so full and almost trembling right now?

God was *never* the kind of deity who would go around like an angry warlock cursing people. The curses promised in the Torah are not motivated by some emotionally immature and unforgiving Zeus nursing a grudge with a thunderbolt in one hand: These curses of which Adonai speaks, He's speaking to all of us, today and for always, both before and after Calvary; because of His immeasurably vast love for us, our loving, tender Daddy Adonai is speaking to all of us, to warn us that if we disobey His loving Law, we curse ourselves.

In the Garden of Eden, God did not curse Adam and Eve with death to get back at them for disobeying. They cursed themselves with death. God did not curse Adam with hard work and adversity in nature; He did not curse Eve with difficulty in childbirth; He did not curse the serpent with crawling on its belly in the dust. Rather, He blessed them with the freedom to choose whether or not to obey His loving perfect Law, and they used this freedom—indeed, they abused this freedom—to curse themselves.

There once was a little boy named Manny who loved to explore, and who loved to discover all of the sparkly and colorful creations in Adonai's amazing creation. Little Manny was brand new to the world, and the world was brand new and very exciting to him. This curious little child also had a daddy who understood his son very well, because Daddy also loved to explore. But sometimes, for some reason, Daddy was bossy.

One bright and fragrant summer day, Manny's daddy told him to stay away from Auntie Annette's beautiful and brightly sparkling swimming pool. Daddy warned the little boy that if he did not stay away, he would fall right in and would not be able to breathe under the water.

The very next summer morning, the sun kept shining, and the water kept shimmering, and Daddy took Manny's hand inside his own big grownup hand and led him past the exciting sparkly water, and out onto the nice soft grass, saying again that if Manny did not stay away from Auntie Annette's swimming pool, he would fall right in and would not be able to breathe under the water.

Then, the very next summer morning, the sun was still shining, and the swimming pool still sparkled, and Daddy still had the same bossy unfair rule. But Daddy could see that little Manny wasn't interested in the miracle of breathing: Manny breathed all the time: Breathing was boring. The sunlight on the water was *not* boring—it beckoned to his little eyes, the tiny waves playing musically with the edges of the pool; cool fresh air wafted invitingly upward toward the child's outstretched hand.

One more time, just like before, Daddy said that if Manny did not stay away from Auntie Annette's swimming pool, he would fall right in and would not be able to breathe under the water.

Then, Daddy decided to stop being bossy and unfair. He let go, he lovingly gave his little son the freedom he wanted, and just stood there, quietly waiting for the inevitable *plunk*.

Then he fished his flailing boy out of the pool, patted Manny's back to help him cough the water out of his little lungs, and then just stood there and looked at his son. For a while, Daddy didn't say a word. Manny didn't speak either. He was too busy shivering and crying. Now, he knew very well just how important breathing really was. He *did* want to always breathe. And from that day onward, Manny was always very careful about sparkly, inviting swimming pools.

Years passed, and Manny was a big brother. He had a very curious little brother named Matt who loved to explore. One bright summer day, when they were visiting their fun-loving young Auntie

Annette, Manny told his little brother to stay away from the swimming pool…

I thank Adonai for His Torah, and for its promised blessings for His faithful nation. And I weep that we, in our stubborn pride, all too often choose the curse instead of the blessing; expecting His yoke to be too hard; expecting His burden to be too heavy; seeking liberty from His Law instead of the true and glorious freedom, which is liberty from lawlessness; we have confounded[32] Mount Ebal with Mount Gerizim: We have confounded the curse with the blessing. Let us now, therefore, return to the holy mountain of Adonai our God.

Before I formed you[33] in *the* belly I knew you;
and before you came out of *the* womb I consecrated you...

—Jeremiah 1:5

CHAPTER TWENTY:

# Twin Cousins

When I was pregnant with my third child, the Holy Spirit commanded me not to drink wine or strong drink, for the child would be a Nazarite to God from his birth. And this baby was my third child, but Benaiah's seventh. Then, throughout *Hanukkah*, the Feast of Dedication[34] (which is eight days for the eight days required to dedicate the altar in Jerusalem), from the first evening until the last evening, I could eat nothing, because of the morning sickness. And the labor for my Nazarite child was from seven o'clock until three: And I gave birth at exactly three o'clock.

In the same day, before the birth and again afterwards, the Holy Spirit commanded me to pray for my newborn cousin, the son of my maternal aunt, because his life was in mortal danger.

But I had not heard that any of my six aunts was pregnant; neither were any of them so young as to hope for another baby (except for Lydia, who no longer had a womb). Therefore I called my aunt Rachel, and asked her which of her sisters was expecting; but she said, "Nobody as far as I've heard: Neither are any of us all that young." But when I told my Aunt Rachel why I had asked, she asked with me in prayer for the safety of my new cousin, who shared a birthday with my own newborn son.

And we called our baby Mattithias,[35] after the famous hero of the Feast of Dedication, because I could eat nothing during the whole holiday because of him.

And after Mattithias was four years old (and we lived in Newberg, Oregon), my maternal aunt Judith and her husband brought their adopted children to visit the family in Oregon. And behold, the birthday and age of her third child Benjamin were the same as my third child Mattithias. Moreover, Benjamin was in mortal danger two or three times on the day he was born: Because of his *spina bifida*, and also because his birth mother would not suffer the nurses and doctors to save his life: Because she'd had no intention of giving birth to Benjamin: Her intention had been to abort her son. But God had other intentions—for his birth the very day before the scheduled abortion. And the mother was not willing to sign the papers authorizing the surgeries to close his spine, and to relieve the pressure on his brain. And only if her child already had adoptive parents, then the mother would agree to sign. And thus, with all possible haste, my Aunt Judith gained her third child Benjamin.

And when I saw his face, and knew also the day on which he was born, I knew that Mattithias' second cousin Benjamin is the captain of my teenage children in the war which I saw, when I was but eleven years old, of whom my Nazarite son Mattithias was his servant and faithful comrade.

And I told his mother Judith that her son Benjamin would be a holy man; and she said with a smile, "I know."

Many[36] *things* You have done, *O* Adonai my God;
Your amazing *works*, and Your thoughts
*which are* toward us: there is none *to* reckon *them* up
in order unto You: I will declare and I will speak:
*they are* more[37] than *can be* numbered.

————Psalm 40:5[38]

# CHAPTER TWENTY-ONE:

# A Traffic Light

In the early winter of nineteen ninety-eight, after the birth of Elishevah Yael, we returned to California, because Benaiah had found no work in Hillsboro, Oregon; and we were out of money: because my Social Security Income was two hundred dollars less in Oregon than in California. And we lived in Smith River, California, where our Nazarite child Mattithias Lazarus was born. And when Mattithias was born, his umbilical cord was uncommonly long: So long that the cord encircled his neck thrice; but no harm followed: Because Benaiah was a skilled midwife and he knew what to do.

Mattithias was a precocious and very strong child from the very start; and so it was that his father nicknamed him "Little Samson," because in the first hour following his birth he looked right into my eyes; and in his fourth day he raised up his head to see his parents; and also because he was so strong that I needed his father's help to change his diapers.

Then, in his eighth day, in accordance with the Law, we drove our car in order to bring our baby to the *mohel* to circumcise him: We left on Saturday night at the beginning of the first day of the week. And the car was a gorgeous antique, a gift to Benaiah from his dad. And our antique car was the only car on the twisting and turning unlit road, alone in the night.

When we had just passed the final crossroad and the last shoulder, all on its own the car began speeding up, and the brakes failed; and to our left was the foot of a steep, high cliff; and to our right the top of another cliff dropping down into the Pacific Ocean. This car was a very big automobile, with a racecar engine. Faster and faster it hurled around the corners in the dark, without any foot

on the gas pedal, past a couple of traffic signs which read
"*UNSTABLE ROADWAY*," and "*ROCKS AHEAD*."

Between the cliff and the cliff, without any other car on the
shoulderless road for miles behind us, I began to pray.

Then around the next curve, still without any crossroads,

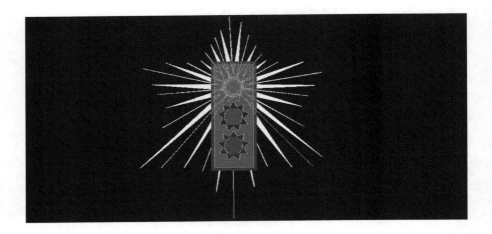

a lone traffic light shone red: and the only other vehicle for miles in
either direction came to a stop: And this vehicle was a huge,
powerful pickup truck.

When our automobile struck the huge truck, the pickup slid
more than six feet forward—which distance we were able to
measure by the truck's skid marks on the pavement. (Years later, we
saw this same car at an antique car show in Oregon; and we knew it
was the same one because of the enormous bowl-shaped dent in the
front bumper, where our car had plowed into the biggest tow-ball I
had ever seen in my life.)

And what if the traffic light had been broken, or had shone
green, or had not been there; and what if the truck had been a little
earlier, or later, or in the other lane headed north, or smaller, or not
there at all? God is great, God is good; God is very good. And
nearly eleven years later, I still have tears of gratitude when I
remember this big, beautiful miracle.

Zephaniah

3:17 Adonai your God *is* in the midst of you; *He is* strong;
He will save; He will rejoice over you with joy; He will
be quiet in His love; He will rejoice over you with singing.

Isaiah

31:4 Because Adonai said to me, in this manner,
*Just* like the lion and the lion cub roars over his prey,
…so Adonai *of* armies will come down to muster *His armies*
over mount Zion, and over its little hill.

5 As birds fly, so Adonai *of* armies will shield Jerusalem…

—Zephaniah 3:17, Isaiah 31:4-31:5

CHAPTER TWENTY-TWO:

# Guardian Angels

We returned to Oregon a second time, to seek work. And in
the night of May 13, Iyar 21, two thousand one; while we were
returning from a relative's home, on a dark, rainy, busy road; a new
minivan began to tailgate our car, and I sensed in the minivan five
almost catlike hunters, rejoicing in the chase, and that our car was
the prey; but I sensed in them no ill will nor any malevolence, but
only the excitement and joy of the chase. And the sixth person, the
only one with a human soul (I think that she must have been the
driver), I never saw nor sensed that she even saw our car. And this
minivan ran our car off the busy road into the shallow ditch: And in
the same moment that our car left the street, the gearshift handle
broke off in Benaiah's hand. Then, I knew that the five nonhuman
spirits must certainly have been our five guardian angels.

For almost an hour we bowed our heads and worshipped,
because, What if this minivan had been one moment later, or earlier,
or not there at all tailgating our car?

God is good.

7   If I walk in the midst of distress, You will revive me:
    against *the* wrath *of* my haters[39] You will stretch out
    Your hand, and Your right *hand* will save me.

8   Adonai, *You* will forever complete Your mercy through[40]
    me, *O* Adonai: do not abandon *the* works of Your *own* hands.

—Psalm 138:7-138:8

CHAPTER TWENTY-THREE:

# A Nation Changed by Fear

And Benaiah found work in McMinnville, Oregon, the city of my birth, as a caretaker for disabled men. My beloved cousin also lived with us in McMinnville, so that Benaiah could go to work without worrying about my safety: Because I had epilepsy. But I only had three or four *Grand Mal* seizures[41] in my lifetime until the year two thousand three.

In our new apartment I dreamed a dream, that Mattithias in his cradle and a beloved relative were on a high scaffolding; and my beloved kinswoman gently rocked Mattithias; and another woman I love was with her (whom I knew not, but still I knew that I loved her). And neither of the two women saw that the place was dangerous, and very high.

Three times I dreamed this dream; and my frightened heart cried out; therefore, God gave me the same dream a fourth time.

And our family still lived in this apartment on September 11, two thousand one: And on this morning my husband was at work—because he had graveyard shift—and I kept watch while the children slept. And we had a telephone only for emergencies, and he called me and said, "Turn on the television right now!" And when I asked "Which channel?" he said, "Any—**now!**"

And I saw the same image on every channel: The same tower which I saw in my dream[42] three years earlier: But instead of one silver missile, twice, I saw two passenger airliners; and two towers; and two crashes. Then I saw the other crash in the field: Because the hostages in one airplane had overcome their conquerors. And a fourth airplane pierced the Pentagon, so that fat politicians fled waddling away in terror. And thousands died, including many that came to the towers to save others. But the living God turned thousands of others aside from going to work in the two towers.

And the face of our nation changed, perhaps forever.

And I could not speak for three days because of the anguish and astonishment.

Soon afterward we moved near Benaiah's mother, so that Manasseh could help his grandmother and comfort her heart: But some of our neighbors thought that we were terrorists; because the fear of the Muslim terrorists had fallen upon the people: And these neighbors could not distinguish between Muslims and Jews, nor between Sunnis, and Shiites, and Islamists: But they thought that every foreign woman who covers her head is the same. And our fanatical neighbors drove out our family with cruel terror.

Therefore we returned to the apartment in the city of my birth, where we had lived on September 11, two thousand one, where we had lived while Benaiah worked as a caretaker for disabled gentlemen.

Proverbs
17:15
*Whoever* justifies *a* wicked *person,* and *whoever* condemns *a* righteous *person, are* abomination *to* Adonai, even *the* two *of* them.

21:15
*It is* joy to *a* righteous *person* to do justice; yet *it is* consternation to *the* doers of iniquity.

Psalm
116:15
Precious in *the* eyes of Adonai *is* the death of His merciful[43] *ones.*

——Proverbs 17:15; 21:15; Psalm 116:15

1    And now, Israel, hear[31] deeply[9] the statutes
and the judgments which I am teaching you to do,
so that you will live, and come in, and possess the land
which Adonai *the* God of your fathers *is* giving to you.
2    You shall not add to the word which I *am*
commanding you...

———Deuteronomy 4:1-4:2

CHAPTER TWENTY-FOUR:

# A Crack in the Door

Beloved Brothers and Sisters, when one of my sons was very small, about three years old, he got the foolish notion stuck in his little noggin one day that he needed permission each time to use the toilet; and then, for three or four weeks, it was a new tradition that he *insisted* things *had* to be so, and each and every time he asked and waited for permission, without which he would feel obligated to wet his little trousers.

This became just plain annoying after a while, because sometimes we were both asleep, or busy with another child's needs, so we did not always have enough time to say "yes" before this child peed his pants. I don't know where this silly notion of needing permission to pee came from, but nothing we said could persuade that boy otherwise: So finally, after he'd made a puddle on the carpet in the middle of the night because Ben was at work and I was asleep, I put my foot down and said *No. No more permission for toilet using*, and if he wet his pants because of it he'd be in *very big* trouble.

So now our poor little tot was in tears, begging and begging desperately until he couldn't hold it anymore. He had been perfectly potty trained until this new ordinance of his was decreed, even sleeping at night without a diaper and never once wetting the bed. This child had been potty trained younger than any of his brothers and sisters: We weren't stricter with him, of course, but he was certainly strict with himself:

This son was the sort of child who *always* obeyed, and *always* did his best. From the beginning, he wanted with all his heart

170

to be a perfect son. No matter what anyone said, the boy *demanded* perfection of himself.

So when he made that puddle, I didn't need to punish him. I didn't even need to say a word: My frown of disapproval was punishment enough already. Even when this son was only one year old, and had never broken a rule in all his life, every time we'd scold his perpetually mischievous brother Manasseh, this boy would burst into tears, assuming he *must* be the child in trouble *this* time. Twice more, he wet his pants for lack of permission; but when he finally saw that we would truly never again grant him any more permission to pee, he stopped asking and potty-trained himself again without another word.

But the root of the problem remained: This son always demanded perfection of himself; and he continued to set impossible rules for himself that we had never made. To this day, I have a cute collection of drawings that our children colored for us, but unfortunately almost none of them are from this little son: His drawings were of course always imperfect, so he would tear them up in angry frustration: He was determined to be another Leonardo DaVinci, or else not an artist at all.

Beloved Sisters and Brothers, among all the people of Israel, this child was like some Jews among the ultra-Orthodox in their long, black coats, complicating Adonai's beautiful Torah with tradition upon tradition until resting on Shabbat becomes an exhausting endeavor.

Also, many are they who laugh at the Orthodox Jews' refusal to eat a chicken and cheese sandwich because the Torah forbids simmering a young goat in its own mother's milk: But their intentions are honorable—even cute—because they come from a sincere desire to do even *more* to please Adonai than what He had told us to do. *But He didn't say not to eat chicken and cheese together.*

I have heard of and seen a traditional festive meal which our Bedouin cousins prepare, by gathering up all the milk from their herd of goats and making yogurt, and taking a tender suckling from the same herd, slaughtering it, and simmering it in this yogurt. I'm sure it must be a delicious and healthy meal for the tribe's honored guests, but for one poor mama goat in the herd the experience is very different: She knows very well the smell of her own baby, and this poor bereaved animal, already in mourning, must endure smelling behind the tent curtains her child's flesh being cooked in the very milk God had given her to feed to her baby.

God does not like this meal at all. In fact, God dislikes it so much that He forbade it three separate times in His holy Law.

Now, it's just fine with me when my Orthodox brothers choose to strictly separate meat meals from dairy, in order to honor the animal our food came from by refusing to mix the life-giving element of milk with the dead muscles. This is an honorable discipline. I think that God even finds it amusingly attractive. But as endearing as their desire is to do even *more* to please Adonai than what He told us to do, the consequent rules are just plain absurd: We human beings, compared to God, are only slightly smarter than rocks.

So when we go further and add our own manmade traditions to Adonai's perfect Torah, what do we get but sillier and sillier, like a toddler demanding permission to pee?

It isn't cute at all, though, when humans make this ridiculous human tradition equal to Adonai's holy Law, and start oppressing nice, friendly children of God who love them and who are counting on them to teach the true Torah. In my own life, I avoid eating milk and meat foods together, because I enjoy honoring the life of God's animals according to the way of our people, and I also enjoy honoring the teachings of the rabbis who invented this custom out of their sincere love for Adonai and His creatures: Because Yeshua said:

2      The writers[44] and the Separatists[45] sit upon Moses' seat:
3      All therefore whatsoever they tell you *to* keep,
         *that* keep and do…

But then to this he added,

3      …but don't do in accordance with their actions:
         because they say *things* and don't do *them*:
4      because they bind heavy and hard to carry burdens,
         and set *them* on the men's shoulders…

—Matthew 23:2-23:4

I do not force this nonsensical human tradition on anyone else. I don't even always demand it of myself, because I don't want my brothers and sisters to feel burdened or oppressed when they want to show their love by feeding us a home-cooked meal from their own culture's traditions.

We all have funny ideas, Beloved Sisters and Brothers, especially when we are just beginning to learn: And this is one of the biggest reasons why we all need to humbly obey Adonai's Torah, and not try to go beyond it: When we try to go further than where Adonai is leading, we always get lost, and we usually also end up acting, or looking, or feeling odd.

This son's mother can be just as weird too. My earliest clear memory is of a moment when I was a small child, newly aware that my twin sister and I were called girls, female like our mother; future mothers; but our brother was not so: He was called a boy, a future father. And as my twin sister Drea and I stared through the crack in the door, I wondered for a whole moment at this serious and unchangeable rule and its message. Our brother played alone outside in the back yard, happily digging roads in the barren soil for his toy cars: Our mother had ruled that he may go outside to play, but we girls must stay inside. Why, I wondered, must we girls stay inside on that bright sunny day? Why were we twins called girls, and what did it have to do with playing or not playing in the dirt? Who decided we were girls? Was it God? Did He send a prophet to tell our mother that we were female; that we were future mothers?

Side by side, we both gazed longingly at our older brother's fingers in the soil. Imagining that I could almost feel the soft dirt, I pressed close against the cool, smooth wood of the back door, smelling the fresh, clean outdoor air mingled with the musty, repugnant odor of the black dust deep inside the long, wide crack in the door. Sunny, dry days were rare this time of year: Soon the rain would return again, and the tantalizing soft dirt would once again disappear into a mess of gloppy mud.

Gently scolding us, our mother called us away from the door; and not for the first time that day. She enveloped us in a thick, warm quilt; probably one of the many quilts our grandmother Margaret had sewn together.

Associating the blanket with bedtime, we both resisted for a moment, then surrendered to the comforting warmth and softness.

This all happened on a cold, clear day in wintertime, and we both had been afflicted with weak, sickly lungs since early infancy; and had only just finished healing from another bout of pneumonia: Being born female had nothing to do with our having to stay indoors.

But at three years old, I was too young to understand such things. As a three-year-old I hadn't paid much notice when my mother argued with the apathetic slumlord, protesting that the long gap in the back door was unacceptable in wintertime for a family with two sick toddlers. I only learned of this many years later, when my mother told me her side of the story.

This apartment had been the best home she could afford for us, this run-down apartment with a dreary, barren backyard and a badly broken back door that let in the winter wind. But at three years old, I didn't know we lived in poverty, or that life was better for other toddler girls with wealthier parents. I only knew that our big brother Reuben was a little boy having fun in the dirt; and that Drea and I were little girls standing indoors, staring through a crack in the door, watching our brother have all the fun by himself.

Deuteronomy

12:32    All the word that I *am* commanding you, be careful to do it: you shall not add to it, and you shall not take away from it.

Proverbs

30:4    …What *is* His name, and what *is the* name *of* His Son? Because you will know!

5    Every saying from His[46] God *is* pure—He *is a* shield to *those who* trust in Him.

6    Do not add to His words, lest He reprove you, and you be *found* a liar.

Psalm

119:103    How sweet *are* Your sayings to my palate; *sweeter* than honey to my mouth!

104    From Your commandments I have gained understanding: therefore I have hated every false way.

105    Your word *is a* lamp unto my feet, and *a* light unto my path.

—Deuteronomy 12:32[47]; Proverbs 30:4-30:6;
Psalm 119:103-119:105

174

1    …Who, therefore, is greater in the kingdom *of* the heavens?
2    And Yeshua, calling *a* little child forward,
      stood him in their midst,
3    and said: Truly I say *to* you, Except you turn around
      and become like the little children, you will not enter
      into the kingdom *of* the heavens.
4    Therefore, whoever humbles himself like this little child,
      that *person* is the greatest in the kingdom *of* the heavens.
5    And whoever receives in my name *one* such little child,
      receives me.

10   …See that you do not despise one of these little ones;
      because I say unto you, that in *the* heavens their angels
      always see the face of my Father which *is* in *the* heavens.

------Matthew 18:1-18:10

CHAPTER TWENTY-FIVE:
# Miracle Mouse

In the winter of two thousand two we moved to Idaho, so that my cousin could go to the university there. And she found a house for us: And in that time we were three adults; and three children; and seven hamsters: Because Benaiah had saved seven hamsters from the mouth of a snake: Five babies and their two mothers. And one baby hamster was Manasseh's, which he'd named "Cute Mouse": Because these were Siberian Dwarf hamsters, and they looked like chubby cute mice without tails.

But, more than all her siblings, Cute Mouse loved to escape.

And in the morning of September 20, I dreamed that Cute Mouse had died in a mousetrap in our kitchen. But, when I got up to see, she was still in her cage with her mother. But I asked Benaiah to remove the mousetraps, because of the dream that I dreamed.

But he said: "Did you dream once, or three times? It's only a dream…If you dream this dream twice more, then we will remove the mousetraps. Is not this a stress dream, because tonight is the first day of the feast of Tabernacles, and because Manasseh had named her 'Mouse'?" And my heart said, *No, but this is a true dream.* But I waited quietly. The next morning, the first morning of the holiday, I found Cute Mouse in the same mousetrap as in my dream, dead.

And I carefully removed her body from the trap: But her chest was crushed, and she had no life or breath in her. And I put the body in the hands of Manasseh Raphael.

Because of the feast of Tabernacles, for almost a week I had taught my firstborn son, six years old, about the miracles of the Lord, and how important it is to trust in Him. And with the faith of a child, Manasseh began to pray, and Benaiah and I also prayed with him: And I begged, and said, "Lord, Lord, if you don't give her her life back, my little son will never believe in my words of your miracles again: Please, Lord, return her life to her: Because surely this is a very small thing to you, but very, very big and beautiful to my trusting little son."

Then a tear from Manasseh fell upon the tiny body together with a tear from me, and the hamster began to breathe.

And Manasseh changed the name of his hamster from "Cute Mouse" to "Miracle Mouse."

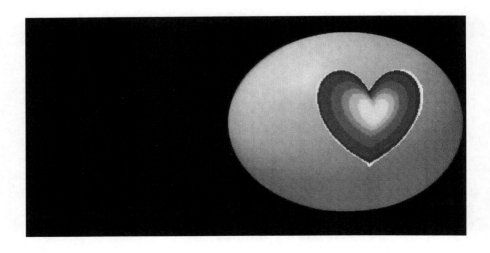

6   Humble yourselves therefore under the mighty hand of God,
    that He may exalt you in due time:

7   Casting all your cares upon Him; because He cares for you.

—First Peter 5:6-5:7

CHAPTER TWENTY-SIX:
# And Yet He Listened

In the book *Heaven is Real*, Pastor Todd Burpo tells the true story of how, while his precious little boy Colton lay deathly ill on a surgeon's table, Todd—a leader of his congregation—was *NOT* reciting some perfect pious prayer—he was throwing furniture and yelling at God, throwing a temper tantrum as if he were no more mature than his three-year old child.

Who would expect God to hear or to answer a prayer like *THAT*? Could it even be called prayer? (Well, yes, prayer is talking to God, but is *YELLING* at God *also* prayer?)

Yes, we should be respectful when we pray. And, yes, we should also be humble, trusting, compassionate, wise, forgiving, and grateful when we pray. But if one of my precious sons were ever trapped in the trunk of a car, and he was running out of air, and another of my sons came to me screaming, throwing things, and blaming me, would you expect me to wait for him to ask *NICELY* before I rescue his little brother? Of course not! And if I, a foolish and sometimes downright mean human woman, would listen and would answer, What would a totally wise and completely loving Father do for His child? Yes, God heard—*and He chose to answer*—this desperate daddy's shouts of rage and fear.

I know a young girl who had seen far more troubles than many others. Tormented by demons; tormented by her family's past; tormented by the same cruel young mob which tries to force conformity on each child in every classroom; this child ran alongside the highway until she came to the quiet little meadow belonging to my church. And she climbed up onto the stage, so she could be that much closer to God. This was a good place to pray. Our brother Pastor Pedro found her perched upon the churchyard's outdoor stage (like a ragged lost bird stripped of its feathers), screaming and cursing at God with all her strength.

I very much doubt that the word "prayer" was mentioned when Pedro described her outlandish behavior to the police.

Even so, God heard. And the healing hand of God began to transform her life.

What a Friend we have in Jesus,
All our griefs and sins to bear!
What a privilege to carry
Everything to God in prayer!

Oh what peace we often forfeit,
Oh what needless pain we bear!
All because we do not carry
Everything to God in prayer.

Are we weak and heavy laden,
Cumbered with a load of care?
Precious Savior, still our refuge,
Take it to the Lord in prayer.

Do your friends despise, forsake you?
Take it to the Lord in prayer!
In His arms He'll take and shield you;
You will find a solace there.

Blessed Savior, You have promised
You will all our burdens bear
May we ever, Lord, be bringing
All to you in earnest prayer.

Soon in glory bright unclouded
There will be no need for prayer
Rapture, praise and endless worship
Will be our sweet portion there.

—Joseph M. Scriven

I've already written about the nightmare that was our life until the day the real God heard my prayer, and Mother took us into our aunt's car and we rode away to safety. We three children felt safe; but for our mother, the nightmare never stopped. She knew all too well that at any moment the man who should have been a father to us might find us and do what he wanted, restraining order or no.

The story did not end there: Dale Stuart Veach would not allow it to end there. Like Pharaoh, his heart was hardened. He followed us; he hunted us, his playthings, from daycare to daycare; he hunted my mother, his toy, from job to job, harassing her at work until her bosses fired our mother just to get rid of her violent alcoholic stalker. Our money dwindled; our time together often came in tiny snatches on the way to new places where we had no friends yet; in truth, my sister Drea and I were often each other's only companion: Reuben was almost always in a different classroom because he was older.

Then, for a short time, we lived with Grandpa Ding-Ding and Grandmother Margaret, and we were happy. I felt safe there— except during the thunderstorm. It was just outside our attic bedroom window, which was an open square hole that stretched from ceiling to floor with no glass and took up most of the wall. The unpredictable crackling lightning flashes and the noisy thunder that followed seemed to be right there just outside the house; perhaps the next one would enter the open window; Drea and I were both terrified; the storm was all made up of violent erratic outbursts; the storm reminded us of *him*, but even bigger.

We hid under the mattress.

Soon afterward, as was true for most of our early childhood, we fell ill, and it was our mother's turn to be afraid because of the big open window with no glass: Summer was ending, and we needed to stay warm at night. Drea and I would gladly have slept anywhere at all, even in a cupboard, just to keep living with our grandparents, but our mother was convinced we needed a proper bedroom.

When we offered to trade bedrooms with Reuben David, she didn't say *anything*—she just *looked* at us like we had asked permission to keep our brother in the kitchen oven, or on top of the roof. Now, Reuben was the sort of little boy who was both constantly adventurous, and too smart for his own good. She never said it out loud—perhaps she didn't want to give our brother any ideas—but our mother *certainly* wasn't about to put our brother Reuben in *there*: There was no telling *what* that mischievous little man-child might think of to do in an attic bedroom with a huge open window. We moved away, back to the life of one home after another, of the sort my mother could afford.

God's holy Law of mercy, justice, and compassion says to put such a man to death, but Dale Stuart Veach wasn't punished with so much as a weekend in jail. He continued to live unmolested and free for more than two decades, with continued access to countless other little girls; and so I continued to live in his shadow. But now I had moved on with what was left of my life; and, twenty-three years later, I was already a mother with three children of my own, one of which was a carefree, trusting little girl. I was a mother now, with a tiny daughter—*his* first granddaughter, already the same age I was when at last this man stopped doing the unspeakable.

There should be no statute of limitations on sexual crimes against toddlers, stalking with intent to kidnap, or attempted kidnapping with intent to rape.

Our laws should not leave it up to sexual offenders to decide for themselves to keep registering: Such men as this man should at the very least have highly visible permanent tracking bracelets on both legs. It is totally unacceptable that this man's victims, having successfully fled to safety, were very nearly kidnapped back from within a daycare which he should never have been able to enter into in the first place.

It is also totally unacceptable that our laws have become so thoroughly corrupt that what he did was not even recognized as a capital crime. And I do agree that, given the alarmingly high rate of false convictions of all manner of crimes, including capital crimes, it is a necessary evil to outlaw the death penalty. Even so, to abolish the death penalty is not the right long-term solution: This is no more than the best temporary solution, while the laws of criminal prosecution are being re-written to conform to the Law of God, which says: "By *the* mouth *of* two witnesses, and *of* three, every utterance shall stand.[48]"

Dale Stuart Veach encountered no such courtroom: He was never even charged with a crime of any kind because of what he did to us: In the family courts of the United States, the cases are heard as if they are neither civil nor criminal. This is done in order to bypass entirely the United States Constitution and, ultimately, give the presiding judges godlike authority over the families they are destroying. They dissolved a marriage, nothing more. He was never a defendant in that courtroom, and never in danger of any further punishment than a totally *UN*-enforced permanent restraining order.

Since Elishevah Yael's fourth birthday on September 7, two thousand two, the nightmares were becoming more and more frequent: I dreamed I was a tiny child again, too young to know the words for his crimes:

In these nightmares, *he* would come to me in a dark dead-end alley, or in an empty house without any lights on, and there was no one to hear my cries. Why was I afraid? How could I so easily forget to pray to the God who had already rescued us so, so many times already?

…What *is* for you here, Elijah?

—First Kings 19:9

What a Friend we have in Jesus,
All our griefs and sins to bear!
What a privilege to carry
Everything to God in prayer!

Oh what peace we often forfeit,
Oh what needless pain we bear!
All because we do not carry
Everything to God in prayer.

Why was Elijah afraid of puny little human Jezebel, when he'd already seen God's fire fall down from heaven[49] and devour his sacrifice, together with the water, the wood, and the very stones and dust of the altar? Why were the Israelites afraid when they found themselves trapped between the Egyptian army and the sea, when they had already watched the ten plagues destroy the splendor of the most prosperous and glorious nation in the world?

But afraid I *was*.

Then, on December 16, two thousand two, after twenty-seven years of living in his fearful shadow, I could bear these nightmares no longer: The knowledge burned in me; it tormented me almost every night that the man who should have been a father to me was still out there in the dark, still free to find other little girls and to do the unspeakable to them. And so, overcome for their sakes, I cried out to my heavenly Father, my only father; overcome not only for these other children's sakes, but also by the gnawing fear that one day this man of darkness would learn that he has a granddaughter. And so I looked down at my sweet sleeping baby girl who had known only safety and love, and I prayed: I do not remember my exact words, but these were the cries of my heart:

*Father, take away, please take away these nightmares; take away this shadow from my daughter's life: Even if I can keep her safe, even if I can keep her safe her whole life, What of his other victims? Please, please: We have revealed his crimes to our nation, and they do nothing to protect the daughters of our nation, your daughters, from what he might do; and from what he has already done.*

*Your Torah commands us to put such a one to death, but this nation did not even send him to jail for one day.*

*I do not want to be unforgiving—If he has truly repented and been saved at his last baptism, please tell me so, so that I can live without this nighttime terror in the dark; without these nightmares. But if in truth he will not change, Is not every life in Your hands? We are powerless to sentence this man to death. These gentiles won't even bother to punish him at all. Please. Save my daughter. Save Your daughters. Save my baby girl.*

Was this prayer pious? Was this prayer wise? Did I humbly trust, when I prayed this prayer, that God was already handling the situation in the very best way possible? Was I being grateful for what God had already done, and had already decided to do? More importantly, was I being compassionate and forgiving toward the man who should have been a father to me? And who (other than another victim of incestuous pedophilia), would not immediately wonder upon reading this, *HOW DARE THIS WOMAN* ask our merciful, compassionate God to *KILL* someone for her?

And I even went on to ask Him for a sign, by which we would know that it was the hand of God: And because my sister and I were born on the Hebrew New Year's Day for trees, I asked that a tree would be involved in his death, as a silent witness that at last my sister and I were avenged.

If Todd Burpo's prayer for his little son Colton was a bad prayer, mine for my daughter was *HORRID*.

But, as bad as this prayer was, I know that God heard me: Because then in that same instant peace came upon me—not slowly, but in a flood: I knew, I *knew*, while I was yet speaking, that I had been heard: I knew that God's judgment would come upon this man before another daughter was harmed. And so I slept in peace that night, never again to face this man in my nightmares.

For me, this was one of the greatest lessons Yeshua has ever taught me in my walk with Him: I can talk to God about *anything*, and I don't have to have the proper words, or thoughts, or to express only the socially acceptable emotions, like when I talk to other human beings. And this is something that I *never* have been good at, and never *will* be good at, because I was born with Autism Spectrum Disorder. With other human beings, I often have to hold back from saying important things because they won't come out right. (It's easier to write books, because the words stay there for me to look at.) But I can talk to God about *ANYTHING*.

What a Friend we have in Jesus,
All our griefs and sins to bear!
What a privilege to carry
Everything to God in prayer!

19:9    …And behold, *the* word of Adonai *came* to him, and *He* said unto him, What *is* for you here, Elijah?

10    And *he* said, I have been jealously jealous for Adonai God *of* armies: because *the* children of Israel *have* forsaken Your covenant, *they have* thrown down Your altars, and *they have* slain Your prophets with *the* sword; and I, *even* I only, I remain; and they seek my life,[50] to take it away.

11    And *He* said, Go forth, and stand on the mountain before the face of Adonai. And, behold, Adonai passed by, and a great and strong wind tearing *into* the mountains and breaking in pieces the rocks before the face of Adonai; *but* Adonai *was* not in the wind: and after the wind an earthquake; *but* Adonai *was* not in the earthquake:

12    And after the earthquake a fire; *but* Adonai was *not* in the fire: and after the fire a still small voice.

13    And it was *so*, when Elijah heard[9] *it*, that *he* covered his face in his mantle, and went out, and stood *in the* opening *of* the cave. And, behold, *there came* a voice unto him, and said, What *is* for you here, Elijah?

14    And *he* said, I have been jealously jealous for Adonai God *of* armies: because *the* children of Israel *have* forsaken Your covenant, *they have* thrown down Your altars, and *they have* slain Your prophets with *the* sword; and I, *even* I only, I remain; and they seek my life,[50] to take it away.

15    And Adonai said unto him, Go, return to your way…

—First Kings 18:21-19:15

CHAPTER TWENTY-SEVEN:

# Weeping (part two)

It was some days after my horrible prayer when I heard the news—it was the date that struck me first, and the word "tree," and the time of day, and then I heard the whole message with amazement. On the night of December 16, two thousand two, on the same night of my desperate prayer, a huge Ponderosa pine tree had fallen in a windstorm, and crushed the man's trailer home as he slept: The entire half of his trailer which had his bedroom was flattened by that enormous pine tree, and the sound of the crash woke up what may well have been his last victim, my youngest stepbrother. The child stumbled out of his bed, saw the crushed remains of the other end of the house, and screamed.

I did not weep that day: Another ten years would come and go before I was able to weep for the man who should have been a father to me.

In reality I didn't have in those years the ability to shed tears: Like a dam, the wall of stone around my heart never allowed the tears to pass. The poetess Alice Walker said, be afraid of those who cannot weep. And she was absolutely right.

There is an ancient Hebrew tradition which teaches us about the Hebrew word for "hand", which is *yad*: Nearly every Hebrew noun has a gender, either male or female, but the word *yad* is neither, because the two hands must be united, like a man and a woman in marriage: The masculine right hand of strength and victory must be married to the feminine left hand of sorrow and compassion. And so, the plural of hands, *yadáyim*, is the dual plural of a matched pair, each incomplete without the other.

Without the right hand of victory, sorrow becomes the weakened hand of those who sink into despair: Lacking courage, they cannot love. When Rachel named her baby "Son of my sorrow", Jacob added the name *Ben-Yamín*, "Son of my right hand", because the right hand turns useless sorrow into healing compassion. Mahatma Gandhi said, "A coward is incapable of exhibiting love: It is the prerogative of the brave."

Likewise, without the left hand of compassion the right hand of strength, without true victory, becomes the distorted right hand of the Crusader, the Nazi, the Islamist *jihadi* who comes only to destroy: Blinded by a lack of compassion, such as these cannot know how to (or even why they should) have compassion on their fellow human beings: Having rejected and suppressed the feminine half of their own people, their cultures become spiritually harsh and indelicate, like a man with no left hand.

There is another ancient Hebrew tradition which teaches us that after the waters of the Red Sea had been parted, when the Israelites rejoiced by the riverbank with singing and with tambourines and dancing, an angel came to them from Adonai and rebuked them, because their joy should have been tinged with sorrow: God's Egyptians, created in His image with His breath of life, were slain, drowned in the river; their wives were widows; their children were fatherless. The angel did not rebuke the Israelites for rejoicing: He rebuked them for not mixing a little sorrow with their joy. And so it is that, when we celebrate the Passover, we spill out ten drops from our cup of wine—our cup of rejoicing—in mourning for our Egyptian brothers who were slain by the hand of God for our sakes: Our cup of joy is also our cup of mourning. We celebrate the saving power of God's right hand, but we must also remember God's left hand of sorrow and compassion.

Yeshua grew up in this tradition, as the son of a Judean father and a Levite mother, with the right hand representing strength and victory, and the left hand representing sorrow and compassion: And it is in this context that our Jewish Messiah Yeshua's words must be understood which he spoke, saying,

31    And when the Son of man shall come in His glory,
and all the holy angels with Him,
then *He* will sit upon *the* throne of His glory,

32    and all the nations will be gathered before Him;
and *He* will separate them one from another,
as a shepherd divides the sheep from the goats;

33    and *He* will set the sheep by His right *hand*,
and the goats by *the* left.

34    Then the King will say to them by His right *hand*,
Come, *you* blessed of my Father...

—Matthew 25:31-25:46

Exodus

15:1    ...I will sing to Adonai, because in victory
            *He* has triumphed: *the* horse and *his* rider
            *He* has thrown into *the* sea.

2      Adonai *is* my strength and *my* song; and *He* is my salvation:
            this *is* my God, and I will rest *in* Him; my father's God,
            and *I* will exalt Him.

3      Adonai *is* a man *of* war; Adonai *is* His name.

4      Pharaoh's chariots and his army He has cast into *the* sea;
            and his chosen *captains* third *in command*
            *are* drowned in *the* Sea *of* Reeds.

5      *The* depths covered them;
            they went down into *the* depths like *a* stone.

6      Your right *hand*, O Adonai, *is* magnificent in power...

11     Who *is* like You, O Adonai, among *the* gods?
            Who is like You—magnificent in holiness,
            fearsome *in* praises, working wonders?

12     You stretched out Your right *hand*,
            *the* earth swallowed them.

13     In Your mercy You led forth
            *the* people You have redeemed...

—Exodus 15:1-15:18

I did not weep that day. My stepbrother was able to weep, because his heart was better than mine.

I praise my God that He has heard my prayer, and has granted us this mercy, even as He held back the waters of the sea for the frightened and cornered sons and daughters of Jacob, and even as He released the waters of the sea upon the soldiers who had so long abused the slaves under their power. And, even as it is the Way of our people to spill out ten drops from our Passover cup of rejoicing, in mourning for our brothers the Egyptians, I have also spilled out my tears, even for this man whose death was Adonai's act of great mercy.

But I did not mourn when I first heard this news: For ten years afterward, because of the pain he inflicted on our souls, I was never able to weep for this man. But on the first morning of March, two thousand thirteen, I awoke to find myself doing something I had

not done in perhaps thirty-three years: I wept for the man who
should have been a father to me.


The tears I cried
You didn't see
Wanting your love
So desperately

Needing you
To want the love you'd made

Not one thing changed
The day you died
Just one more soul
You pushed aside

You just still weren't there
Same as always

Baptized five times
So I've been told
Just five more lies
A conman sold

I wish the last one
Had been true
It wasn't you
It was the wine
What can I answer
This painful line

When I never saw
Just who you were before the wine

I was not planned
You made that plain
One boy, one girl
But still I came

Wanting you

To want the love you'd made

Learned how to love
How to forgive
Learned how to trust
How to open up and give

But I did not learn these things from you
God is my Father

For the first time
In all my life
I want you here
I don't want to say goodbye

No second chances
In the grave

Goodbye forever

You shall not sow your vineyard with mutually imprisoning[51] seeds; lest the fullness *of* the seed which you shall have sown, and *the* increase *of* the vineyard, be defiled.

—Deuteronomy 22:9

CHAPTER TWENTY-EIGHT:

# A Child Unborn

Benaiah had good work in that town, not much money, but enough; and the work was pleasing to him, to clean toilets for the little schoolchildren in the elementary school: A humble job, but Benaiah prefers to be a humble servant for the innocents.

In one moment, in the beginning of springtime, my life changed: I suffered a *Grand Mal* seizure,[41] which broke my neck a little more than before, so that for three months I suffered seizure after seizure after seizure.

Then, what the doctors before had stubbornly called "hypochondria," they now call "epilepsy." And never once in twenty-four years of seizures had any doctor sent me to any neurologist; despite my family history of epilepsy, and despite the fact that my grandfather had the same symptoms for all his ninety years (and nobody was ever so crazy as to deny that he was sick with some kind of seizures: Yet in all his ninety years, no doctor had ever put a name to his epilepsy, nor cured it: But, since before my mother's birth, they said that he had six months to live).

And we began to study medicinal herbs, while I waited to wean Mattithias: Because the time of his weaning was almost at hand; and the artificial antispasmodics could make the milk deadly poisonous, and are also deadly to unborn babies.

Soon afterward, I was found to be with child; but I miscarried the baby in the first trimester.

And the miscarriage was because of unnatural pollution in our corn oil: And the symptoms were the same as with insecticide poisoning. Moreover, years later, I know the truth that corrupt scientists had mixed corn with insecticidal bacteria.

At that time our desire was to buy that house, which we called "The Plum House" because we had five plum trees in the backyard, each of which bore enough fruit to feed us well for more than a year; So much that we canned, in the autumn of two thousand three, enough jars of plums to last until two thousand nine, and another jar in two thousand ten.

Later, while I worked in my garden, I saw a butterfly flutter to the south (and a little to the west); then a little straight north; and then the butterfly flew a great distance, directly south-southeast.

And the Holy Spirit told me that soon I would likewise make three journeys: First I would go south, and there survive a small tribulation, and then travel a little to the north; where the Lord would give me rest, and heal me, and rebuild my soul stronger than before, in preparation for the third journey and the second tribulation; and after my time of rest, I would then travel a great distance south by southeast.

Our neighbors were two friendly elderly Christians, the mayor and his wife; and Benaiah had a good job there. But not everyone of the town liked us: And in the election of two thousand three, a new mayor was elected: Not a kindhearted Christian, but an anti-Semitic neo-Nazi, who was also a wealthy construction contractor.

At the end of the summer, the outer pane of one of our double-paned windows was broken with a big rock: And because we were still only tenants, Benaiah told the owner that the window was broken; and our intention was to repair the window ourselves, and buy the house: But the owner's insurance company required a professional repairman. And the company chose the new mayor to repair the window.

Then with a lot of money and a big pretend smile, the contractor announced that he would wait until the winter, when the construction costs were reduced, and then he would not repair the expensive window, but rather make a big hole in our wall, about eight feet high and eight feet wide, while it's snowing; and that the hole would remain there a week or longer in freezing weather; and finally he would replace our good two thousand dollar window with a single-pane Plexiglas window, designed for a mobile home, not even fit for a stick-built home of the lowest quality: Because the insurance company wanted the work done as cheaply as possible.

And the Plum House was small, and built simply; but very old, and *good*, from the days of the colonists; and our intention was to restore the house for an historic building.

At that time we had two little sons and a little daughter, and our hamsters: And the winters in that town are very, very cold. And I was five months pregnant.

Therefore, we rented a U-Haul truck, to return to Oregon. And in the same hour that the truck was filled, and on the road headed westward, the first snowstorm of the winter came from the east. And all the day that we traveled across Washington, the blizzard cloud seems to me to have been twenty or thirty feet behind (because whenever we were stopped at a red light or a sign, the snow was at first about half a telephone pole length away); but Ben says the cloud was more probably a mile or two behind.

And because of the snow, and the blizzard close behind us, our U-Haul truck stayed at its top speed from Idaho to the Columbia River; then, the surreal cloud turned and left us just before the riverbank. We rested nowhere in any part of Washington, but fled from the snowstorm all the day.

Then at the first gas station across the bridge we slept, and ate, and slept again.

9   *If* I take *the* wings of *the* dawn,
     *if* I dwell in *the* uttermost *parts* of *the* sea,
10  Even there Your hand will lead me,
     and Your right *hand* will catch hold of me.

——Psalm 139:9-139:10

# Section Four:

# *The Storm*

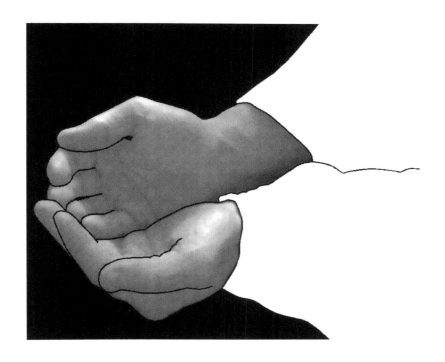

12   What shall I return unto Adonai
     *for* all His benefits toward me?
13   I will lift up *the* cup of salvations,
     and call upon *the* name *of* Adonai.

15   Precious in *the* eyes of Adonai
     *is* the death of His merciful[1] *ones*.

------Psalm 116:12-116:15

CHAPTER TWENTY-NINE:

# A Prophet and a Raven

On the fifth day of January, two thousand four, in my mother Shoshanna's double-wide mobile home, I gave birth to my son Yehudah Isaiah; and a second snowstorm came from the north in that same day. Then in the third day after the birth, the snow in our city was so deep that travel was altogether impossible; that a floating dock and more than a dozen houseboats sunk in the river by reason of the weight of the snow, and that many roofs also collapsed.

Then, in the kitchen with my mother and grandmother, Yehudah Isaiah[2] (three days old) was against my heart in a Snuggli, while my mother made tea.

Suddenly the baby sneezed his first sneeze: And with an expression of utter astonishment, Yehudah Isaiah said, "*Huck-a-POO!*" And he was completely astonished again, because of our sudden laughter. And from that day onward, our family says that, if "Huckapoo" never before meant "I sneezed," his new word surely *ought to* mean "I sneezed" from now on.

In the third night after Yehudah Isaiah's birth, my baby Yehudah Isaiah was asleep in a cradle; the same cradle in which my babies Elishevah, Mattithias, and (later) Abram and Esther also slept. And as we slept I dreamed three dreams:

Here is the first dream: I was in a great cavern, deep, with many caves therein, of the same colors as the Grand Canyon: And there were no openings to the sky; nor any sunlight; yet all the caves were brightly lit. And I saw a child, a seven year old boy, fall into the cavern, and land unharmed, and jump up to run and play. And I knew that the child was my little newborn son Yehudah Isaiah.

194

An elderly Native American man, compassionate and kind, was suddenly together with me: And in a soft voice he said that the child must remain in the great cavern seven years, without any sunlight, but never in the darkness. And, without words, the Holy Spirit then gave me to know that this old Indian man would protect my son all the seven years, in the Spirit.

And suddenly I was under the open sky, and the old Indian man with me, whose hair was long, and very thick, beautiful black hair: And his clothing was not modern (but rather of a tribe which I knew not); it was beautiful, and with lovely embroidery of his people. And we were under the nighttime sky. And the gentle Indian raised his open hand toward the stars, and said the Choctaw name of my baby boy Yehudah Isaiah; and he forbade me to reveal this name during the seven years: But he said that, in the end of the seven years underground, the people shall know his Choctaw name; for this son shall be manifested to all the people, but only at the established time, after the seven years.

I dreamed this first dream in the night of January 9, two thousand four (which date I remember, because my fourth child was four days old).

And the second of these three dreams, I dreamed it for the third time in my life: First in nineteen eighty-seven, and again when Manasseh was still a baby.

My spirit was troubled within me, when I saw a man from this dream, because then I knew his face and his name; I dreamed of two mountains and two men, and this second dream was in two parts:

There were two mountains, whose appearances were the same, and like Mount Gerizim[3] and Mount Ebal, like two great hills, round, and golden in color, and the land was dry and barren. A native tribe, which I knew not, worshipped upon one of the mountains, for they believed that it was a sacred mountain. But they were mistaken: Because the knowledge was given to me that the other mountain was in truth the sacred one: Because foreign conquerors had carried their ancestors away captive, and this generation had returned to the land of their fathers, but they knew not how to distinguish the one from the other. But the other mountain was also accepted in the eyes of the Lord, for their sakes.

And I was old, and my hair was long and white. Two men were also with me there: an old man, the same Native American from my first dream that night: Who was an elderly and honorable man; and his soul was very beautiful, because his heart was pure and full of fire for his Lord Messiah Yeshua. His hair was long, thick and black with streaks of silver. His clothing was not modern, but rather it was as in the first dream that night: Clothing like that of his ancestors, and magnificently hand-embroidered.

This man was the chief of his people, and his soul was beautiful, because his face shone brightly with the Holy Spirit. And to his left hand was a youth named Stone: a man whose face looked so like the face of the elderly Native American that I was sure he must be his son. But the youth was unlike this old Indian chief, because his face was proud, and his heart full of fire to protect his people. And his clothing was unlike the chief's clothing, but rather was modern; the clothing of a modern businessman; and his hair was thick like the older man, but short and black.

And, without his father's consent, the young man was preparing to sell the mountain upon which I stood, for he said in his heart that this was a small matter, so long as the people still had the holy mountain: Because he had authority over the money and the land of his people, and they were very poor, and the need was great.

A crow-sized[4] raven was with us upon the mountain; because although the people (which were beloved of God) knew not that this was the holy mountain, in truth God always knew, and the Lord my God had it in His heart to restore pure worship[5] to it: Therefore God sent the raven; and therefore God also sent me to the people of the two mountains.

Therefore was the raven put on the mountain with me, because the proof of the matter was in the mountain: Because only the sacred mountain concealed the lost graves of their ancestors, which tombs the conquerors had hidden when they destroyed every sign of the people of that native tribe, for hatred. And when the raven landed, behold a pile of stones; and the raven commanded me, "Mark;" and I obeyed. And it landed upon another grave, and again commanded me, "Mark." In this manner we placed a stone upon each grave: Perhaps there were twelve graves in all which we found. And at the last grave, behold a shovel. And the raven commanded

me, "Dig." And I obeyed (digging perhaps one or two feet), until he
commanded me, "Stop!" And, behold, a hand trowel was at the
raven's feet, and he again commanded me, "Dig." And I dug
carefully, and found ancient cloth, a hand-woven shroud, more than
a century old but well preserved in the dry mountain.

Then was the youth quietly angry with me, because of the
poverty and suffering of his people, and also because I had put him
to open shame; in that he had secretly endeavored to sell the
mountain from his people's hands, without the knowledge of his
chief, and I had found out the matter openly (although not I alone,
but also the raven with me discovered the graves, by the hand of the
Lord).

This is the first part of this dream; and the dream is true: And
here is the second of two parts:

Again the two men were with me upon the sacred mountain,
and they were among an uncounted multitude, the whole tribe under
this chief's authority. And I stood upon the top of the mountain, and
under the authority of this chief; because for yet a short time the
chief had put the matter in my hands, to teach them the forgotten
law of the sacred mountain, because it seemed good in the eyes of
this chief to put his people under my hands in this matter.

The raven was also there; a living creature sent by the Lord,
but to be unto the people for an omen, and for a witness; and for
hardship, and trouble; and for fear. Therefore, although the raven
was sent by Adonai, the men did not want it there.

The raven was now upon my left shoulder, and Adonai
commanded me to hold it firmly there (because a leather strap was
upon the raven's foot, as upon a trained falcon). Because the
knowledge was given to me, that if the raven should escape, great
hardship and great oppression shall come upon the people.

All the people surrounded me at my feet upon the mountain,
to listen to me attentively, but some heard me not with love.

The youth named Stone (who was, as before, to the left hand
of the chief) kneeled behind me, to my left: and he took up in his
right hand a smooth round stone with which I had marked one of the
graves; because he feared for the people because of the raven upon
my left shoulder; to kill the raven, in order to protect his beloved
people. With great force he hurled the stone; but as soon as the stone

had departed from his hand, he saw that the stone flew not straight forward: the raven would not be the one to die. The youth was not able to call the stone back into his hand: And so he watched the trajectory of the stone in helpless horror, and his anguish was more painful to me than the pain from the stone in my skull—for the stone struck me just above and to the left of my neck, in my skull: And I fell to the ground as dead.

And the raven, free, ascended to the heavens; and as he rose, he grew bigger and bigger, until his wings overshadowed all the people; and this evil omen was more painful to me than my own destruction; and the raven's shadow covered every face from the light of the sun.

And I dreamed a third dream, of the same kindhearted chief: I was in the doorway of a modern café, and my mother was with me, and my little son Yehudah Isaiah was in her arms, still a newborn babe. And my mother, with the baby, sought out a table in the café to the right: But I walked straight ahead, because I saw the same chief from the first two dreams, with his friends at a table. And in this dream, his hair was short, so short that his hairs stood up like porcupine quills; and his clothing was modern, casual clothing, blue jeans and a polyester fleece jacket. And he was not so old as in the other dreams, neither had he any silver hairs that I saw.

And I asked him what the raven means to his people: And he did not want to say, but I saw fear in his eyes because of the word "raven." And the Native American chief again commanded me, strictly, never to reveal to the world Yehudah Isaiah's Choctaw name during his captivity, until the end of the seven years.

Then all these dreams ended and I awoke, and the entire household with me, because of the sound of a great crash: And we saw that the roof of the carport was on the ground, tilted like a lean-to, because of the weight of the snow in one night.

43     And having said this, He cried *with a* loud voice,
       Lazarus, come out!

                                                    —John 11:43-11:47

Faithful *are the* wounds *from a* loving[6] *friend...*
——Proverbs 27:6

## Always in the Palm of God's Hand

And in those days, soon after Yehudah Isaiah's birth, I began to attend classes at Chemeketa Community College in McMinnville, Oregon: Because at the same time my cousin Rosalinda began to attend classes there; and so I was able for a time to go with her, in her van, and my husband and three children with me—three, not four, because in those days Manasseh lived with his paternal grandmother, to be her helper: Because her left wrist was broken, and she is left-handed. And our hope was for me to become a schoolteacher because my disability excluded me from minimum wage jobs: I still needed constant supervision, and I could not operate machinery nor drive a vehicle.

But we both saw that I was a competent teacher for my children: And if I were to be able to teach in a school, then Benaiah would also be free to work for money: Because we were certainly not so wealthy as to hire a caretaker for me, and a babysitter for our small ones, and to pay tuition for our school-age children—all to free one father to earn minimum wage.

And in those days, I dreamed a dream in which I saw my baby girl as an adopted daughter of strangers, and from such an age that she knew not my face, nor my heart: And for seven or more years her adoptive parents believed that she was the daughter of worthless[7] drug addicts, and that the man who gave her to them was her rescuer and savior:

In this dream I was without feet from the knees downward, and without my right arm from the shoulder, and I was in a wheelchair, with a broken back; and the adoptive parents finally knew that I was an innocent mother, and that the man called her rescuer was a kidnapper, and a murderer; and that, to take her, this man had nearly killed me; and that he broke my back, and destroyed my feet, and tore off my right arm; and after all these cruelties, that he slandered us, and sold our children.

But, by the time everyone knew the truth, our daughter had already been sold at least seven years earlier: Because many had believed that the kidnapper spoke the truth, including the judges and the police.

In this dream, I thought, we already had all[8] the other children, whom we had regained one at a time: But our little daughter was already illegally sold before the judges learned the truth; and nobody would say where.

And after the adoptive parents learned that their little daughter was a black-market baby with innocent and loving biological parents, they were afraid for the child, that we would seek to take her: And with many tears I pleaded, and said that we knew deeply the anguish of parents bereaved of children by the hands of a kidnapper, and that we could never cause this anguish to anyone; and, more than all others, to the beloved parents of our own greatly beloved daughter.

With tears of joy I kneeled before the child, and told her of my love, and the love of her biological father and sister and brothers; and I blessed my loving, and just, and compassionate God; because He had given all that I had asked for my little daughter: Because I saw that she was greatly beloved by her adoptive family, and safe, and that her adoptive parents were loving, and kind, and also that they believed in and loved Adonai the Living God.

In this dream I saw the face of the kidnapper in court, a broken and terrified man, his sins exposed. And his face and his name I now know very well, the same face as in my dream.

That dream was more than I could receive, for anguish: And each time that I dreamed this dream, I could not accept that it was a prophetic dream: And each time I said in my heart that it was only a horrible nightmare: And because I could not call this nightmare a prophetic dream the second time, nor the third, the Lord of my soul gave me the dream a fourth time. And still I said in my heart that it was only a nightmare, because in the fourth time, Elishevah was already old enough to remember my face and my heart; and too mature to sell in illegal adoption without her knowledge.

But, when I saw the face of my stepdaughter Hannah-Joy, I knew that she was not the older sister in my dream: But that

Elishevah had a face like Hannah's, and that her little sister Esther Sarah Hadiyah had a face like the daughter taken and sold.

But I was still unable to believe that the dream was from God, a prophetic dream, because of the horror: But now, these days, I know that the same dream is a gift of great mercy, which gives my heart great peace, and which also gives my heart certainty that my dear little daughter is still before the Lord's face, and that she is always in the palm of His hand.

Psalm

61:1     Hear my cry deeply,[9] *O* God: attend unto my prayer.

2     From *the* uttermost *part of* the earth I will cry unto You,
when my heart faints: lead me to *the* rock
*that is* higher than I,

3     because You have been *a* shelter unto me:
*a* strong tower from *the* face *of one* who hates *me*.

4     I will dwell in Your tent *for* eternities;
I will trust in *the* shelter *of* Your wings.
(Lift this up and weigh it carefully.[10])

57:1     Be merciful unto me, *O* God, be merciful unto me;
because my soul trusts in You, and I will trust
in *the* shadow *of* Your wings until *the* calamities pass by.

—Psalm 61:1-61:4; 57:1

27  What I tell you in the darkness, speak in the light;
    and what you hear in the ear, proclaim upon the housetops.

28  And do not fear those who kill the body,
    but are powerless to kill the soul[11]...

29  Are not two little sparrows sold *for one* assárion?[12]
    And not one of them shall fall upon the earth
    without your Father.

30  And the hairs *of* your head are also all numbered.

31  Therefore, do not fear: you surpass many sparrows
    *in your* value.

32  Everyone therefore who shall proclaim me before men,
    I will also proclaim him before my Father
    who *is* in the heavens...

37  ...Whoever loves father or mother more than me
    is not worthy of me: and whoever loves son or daughter
    more than me is not worthy of me;

38  and whoever does not take up his cross and follow after me
    is not worthy of me.

39  Whoever finds his life[11] will lose it: and whoever loses his
    life for my sake will find it.

————Matthew 10:27-10:39

CHAPTER THIRTY-ONE:

# A Bitter Lesson

At the end of two years at Chemeketa Community college, my cousin Rosalinda was ready to transfer to a Christian University in Ohio, to complete her education as a music therapist: Therefore, we no longer had her for our driver to McMinnville: So then, I also needed to transfer to the university in Newberg, Oregon; which is George Fox University: Because we had no van, nor any driver's license because of our poverty, after we gave all to obtain my teaching degree.

Then my firstborn son Manasseh Raphael returned to us; because his grandmother no longer needed his help, and because I needed a caretaker with me in the university.

Our next door neighbor was a landscaper, a friendly giant and simple and elderly, whose pleasure was in nature, and gardens, and in serving widows in his job.

He had two daughters, grown women, living in other states. And his ex-wife was a Jewess; but he was not a Jew.[14] And this neighbor was our good friend, because he shared our love of nature, and of wild places; and because he had a big heart, and was a friend to all, without prejudice or fear or disrespect. And his custom every day was to cook his meal in his front patio, and to talk with whomever. And, to many, this neighbor was greatly beloved because of his big heart: But others (who saw only his flesh) saw him as ugly, and fat, and dark enough to be of mixed races, and old, and simple, and poor. And when my sister-in-law DeAnn saw our dear friend, she said with disgust, "*WHAT* is *THAT?*"

And in the autumn of two thousand five, in the Day of Atonement, I felt the voice of the Holy Spirit, putting our neighbor in my heart: And I asked of Benaiah, that he would go to our friend, to see why I needed to remember this man in my thoughts and prayers.

But, because evening was nearly come, my husband said to pray and wait; because our friend would soon come outside in the evening, to cook and to talk. And I prayed, and waited: But he never cooked his dinner, neither that night nor afterward. After three more nights without our friend, he was found dead in his travel trailer, with the same symptoms[15] as the sickness which nearly killed my own family almost four years later.

And, while the police worked, I (and my husband with me) lit a candle in our friend's yard, away from the place where the police were working, and read from the Psalms of David, according to the custom of Hebrew funerals. And with a sneer a police lieutenant, the deputy medical examiner, commanded three times that I move the candle: But the officers never went nor came in any of the places where I'd had the candle; and all three times, I had put the candle exactly where the deputy medical examiner had commanded.

Finally, with a sneer, the man commanded us to go into our trailer and shut the door, so that neither we nor our little children would see the corpse of our dear friend, while the police put his body in the hearse.

Then I told the man that the death was possibly a homicide: Because our simple neighbor had freely given out that he nearly had enough money to get his little house with his own garden; and because the last man whom I had seen speaking with him was a predator of simple-minded people, just before the probable time of his death. But the deputy medical examiner secretly commanded to cremate the body, which I believe is against federal law when any person has voiced any suspicion of murder. And, moreover, four year later, I read the police report: And I learned that the deputy medical examiner had misrepresented many things, and omitted all inconvenient details: For example, the report did not say that I or anyone else had said anything about possible murder, nor that I had said that I saw the predator speaking to our neighbor just before his death, nor that I had said that anyone was a predator; and the report did not say that our neighbor had a lot of cash, now missing, nor that the predator almost certainly knew this; and, although the medical examiner correctly stated the symptoms, he falsely called them the symptoms of a heart attack; neither was the risk of an outbreak of this contagious disease reported, as I believe is required by law (unless, of course, he knew—being the murderer—that our neighbor was certainly the only victim): But no heart attack I know of ever caused purple spots upon the extremities; nor a fever; nor a swollen tongue; although the report said that he had purple spots on his extremities, and a swollen tongue, and also indirect evidence of a fever; and vomit. Moreover, the report said that our neighbor was old and fat, in order to insinuate that his heart was probably unhealthy, but the report did not say what just about everyone in Newberg knew, that this man had pedaled his bicycle many miles six days every week to work.

Moreover, the report did not say anything about our candle, nor that the deputy medical examiner had commanded us to leave off our vigil over the body, nor that he saw any funeral, nor that he had commanded that we return into our trailer and shut the door. Nor—and I think this is strange—that another man also spoke, like myself, saying that he also thought the death was a possible murder: But the sudden death[23] of this other witness was added to my file, although our undocumented suspicions of murder were my only connection to this man.

After these things, our friends wanted to gather for the auction of our neighbor's property; so as to give money for his funeral: But, when we gathered to the auction, all his goods were already sold, more than an hour before the set time, in one lot. And, four years later, I found out from the police report that the deputy medical examiner had put our neighbor's tractor in the same storage: So that the tractor was also sold with his goods before the auction.

And I was ashamed after the death of our neighbor and friend, because I had had it in my heart to go to him on the Day of Atonement, but I had waited: Therefore, I have determined from that day onward always to obey the Holy Spirit's guidance within my heart.

...and I will have mercy upon Lo-ruhamá
(that is, she had not obtained mercy);
and I will say to Lo-ammí (that is, not my people),
You *are* my people; and he will say, *You are* my God.

—Hosea 2:23

CHAPTER THIRTY-TWO:
# A Child named 'My People'

From the autumn of two thousand five, until the autumn of two thousand six, I attended classes at George Fox University in Newberg, Oregon; with the intention of being a schoolteacher.

And my aunt Rachel in her youth also attended the same college, when its name was George Fox College, where she met my blind uncle Evan, the physics professor; and my grandfather Nathan had also attended the same college, when its name was Pacific College: For which reason our family was in Newberg, Oregon for four generations. And while I waited to be admitted into the teaching school (because acceptance into George Fox University is no guarantee of acceptance into its teaching school), I studied Teaching English as a Second Language. And my firstborn son Manasseh was with me, as my caretaker; because he was competent to treat my seizures, and to push my wheelchair whenever I could not walk, and to protect my books and my safety while I was unconscious.

And while Benaiah taught Elishevah and Mattithias the way of the Choctaws in the university's arboretum, I taught Manasseh English and Writing with me: And in that year, Manasseh wrote his first[16] book, "Manny and Goliath," a fiction novel about a young man and his elephant. And many complemented us concerning our educated, and happy, and caring, and attractive children; and especially of Manasseh, that he was very respectful and caring, and an excellent leader of his siblings.

And, as at Chemeketa Community College, I breastfed Yehudah Isaiah between my classes, and changed his diapers, and ate lunch with my family in the arboretum.

And some gave them gifts, because all regarded our children as children of the university, and future students there, as the fourth generation where their mother had studied, and their great-aunt Rachel, and their great-grandfather Nathan.

Although we never planned to conceive another child until after my graduation, in May of two thousand six I conceived a son, during the days after the Passover, which the Jewish people call "the Counting of the Omer," which are the seven weeks between the feast of unleavened bread and *Shavuot*, which the Greeks called the day of *Pentecostés*, or "Pentecost".

In those days in one evening at the end of the Sabbath, our house had an open window, which had a broken screen; and I awoke from a *Grand Mal* seizure,[17] unable to speak or to use my hands. And I awoke again from a second seizure, in the dark night; and afterward, when I was able to move and speak, I knew only that, although I had the other symptoms which follow a *Grand Mal* seizure,[17] and my bowels were empty, I was clean, and the bed also; and, also, I felt that an enemy had visited, and that something was stolen. And my first fear, when I was able to think, was that Yehudah Isaiah was stolen: Because the child was very attractive to look upon, and he often slept in my bed under the broken window. But nobody and nothing was missing from the bed.

And months later, when I knew that I was pregnant, the Holy Spirit opened to me the book of Hosea day after day, and commanded me to name the baby according to these scriptures:

1  Say you unto your brothers, Ammí, (that is, My People[18]);
   and to your sisters, Ruhamá (that is, Pitied[19])...

23  ... and I will have mercy upon Lo-ruhamá
    (that is, she had not obtained mercy);
    and I will say to Lo-ammí (that is, not my people),
    You *are* my people; and he will say, *You are* my God.

——Hosea 2:1, 2:23


And because I saw not a fourth son in my vision when I was eleven years old, but sensed a second daughter, I believed that the babe must be a girl: Because the other two boys in my vision were not mine: But, one is my cousin Benjamin, son of my aunt Judith

and uncle Bruce; and the other is my nephew, son of my brother Reuben. Therefore, we planned to name the unborn baby "Ruhamah"; and also our daughter loved the name Sarah, and greatly desired a sister. And this baby was smaller than all the others, and very calm, and greatly loved to kick and twirl every time there was any music with a good drumbeat.

12    And Asa in *the* thirty and ninth year of his reign was
       diseased in his feet, until his disease *was* excessively severe;
       and also in his disease *he* did not ask Adonai,
       because *he asked* among physicians.
13    And Asa slept with his fathers,
       and died in *the* one and fortieth year of his reign.

——Second Chronicles 16:12-16:13

CHAPTER THIRTY-THREE

# A Living Son

In the autumn of two thousand six, in the fifteenth day of October, at the end of the Sunday after the Feast of Tabernacles, when we took down our tabernacle, a spider fell on my face; and it bit my left cheek. And we didn't think much of this bite, because the spider was not a Black Widow, nor a Brown Recluse.

But, the next Tuesday, I was delirious (and Ben says that my face was gross, and grossly swollen.) And for more than a week I was near death: And, soon afterward, I had to drop out of the university; because I was, for more than six months, more sick than in two thousand three, with seizures almost every week, and half blind because of the seizures.

And from this time until the end of my pregnancy, I could eat no meat, nor tolerate the odor. And after the birth, the babe was likewise unable to digest meat,[20] and never wanted to eat meat; nor were we able to tolerate his smell for three days after he had eaten meat.

And the spider, called "the Newberg Mystery Spider", looks exactly like a Hobo Spider; not of North America but from the south of South America,[21] and its venom is also like a Hobo Spider's poison.

With Western Medicine a Hobo Spider bite in the face is sometimes deadly, and bites in other parts of the body are frequently cured by amputation; and, with Western Medicine, a Hobo Spider bite is also fatal for an unborn baby.

But I did not receive this drastic chemotherapy, and so I did not miscarry the baby; but rather I had healed with raw garlic, and so I gave birth to a living son. I think this is sufficient evidence of the superiority of herbal medicine, at least for Hobo Spider bites, for all of us who value the life of an unborn child. And while I was sick, the university counselors all said that I could return to school as soon as I was well: But when I returned, they said that it's only possible for me to return with documents from a Western Medicine doctor: And that the word of a Western physician is documentary evidence of illness (and therefore needed to temporarily drop out of the university), but the word of an herbalist is merely the word of a man: Therefore I was never able to return to the school. (What? What? The word of an herbalist is merely the word of a man, but the word of a Western physician is more?) As if a physician of Western Medicine is like a god!

18    Because *the* needy will not always be forgotten:
      *the* hope of *the* poor will *not* perish for ever.
19    Arise, *O* Adonai! *A* mortal *man* will not strengthen *anyone*:
      *The* nations will be judged in front of Your face.
20    Put, *O* Adonai, instruction[22] in them:
      *The* nations will know *that* they are mortal.
      (Lift this up and weigh it carefully.[10])

—Psalm 9:18-9:20[23]


    From Saint Valentine's Day until the sixteenth of February the pains of childbirth were with me, off and on; but I had no labor pains on the Sabbath. Nevertheless, from the evening at the beginning of the week, I had labor pains again: And in the night of February 18, two thousand seven, I gave birth to Abram Jedidiah Ammi.[24] But as soon as Benaiah saw the baby, while I waited to hear whether the baby was a boy or a girl, Benaiah suddenly fell silent: So that I was afraid that the baby was dying, or horribly deformed, or stillborn. But, after an agonizingly long silence, Ben said quietly with sadness, "It's a boy." Because the child was bald, and looked like a cross between cute salamanders and space aliens; and he also was evidently premature.[25]
    But the day of his birth was the only possible due date for a child conceived by me and Benaiah, on Mother's day in two

thousand six: And I have never committed adultery in all the years of our marriage.

Moreover, unlike many women of the United States of America, I was provably never alone with any other man in more than three years before the conception: And all the family knew that the boy had to be Benaiah's son, because I was constantly chaperoned since my *Grand Mal* seizures[17] in two thousand three.

Nonetheless, Abram Ammi bore no resemblance to my husband in anything, not in appearance, in sound, in mannerisms, in thoughts, in odors, no: Neither bore the child any resemblance to anyone in our family, nor to my husband's race. And Abram Ammi's face was divided with a subtle cleft from the top of his forehead until the bottom of his chin, and under the roof of his mouth: And the tip of his tongue was also split into two tips. And his eyes were usually the color of ice (but red in some light); and his hair, when he finally had hair, was blond, and his eyebrows were transparent; and his head was curiously square.[26]

And if I had given birth to this son in a hospital, I would never have believed that he was mine: But rather I might have thought until my death that one of the nurses had switched the babies in order to steal my beautiful baby to sell him on the black market. But nobody was with me at the birth except my husband, and our children, and my mother (a retired nurse's assistant).

And we had chosen my mother's double-wide mobile home as the birthplace for Yehudah Isaiah, and Abram Jedidiah Ammi (and, afterward, Esther), because her house is very close to the hospital, and because she had a telephone, and because she was an assistant nurse, with some years of training in the nursing profession at Linfield University in McMinnville, Oregon. (But, in undeserved obedience to her husband, she dropped out of the university after she and her husband had eloped.)

And when we saw that Abram Ammi was by all measures healthy, we returned to our smaller mobile home.

Then in the first day of March, which was the Fast of Esther, Manasseh and I went to the bank to get the rent money: Because I was still in no condition to be alone with my newborn baby, because of the risk of a *Grand Mal* seizure;[17] and, although Manasseh was competent to guard me, he was only ten years old: Still too young to babysit a newborn. And when I and Manasseh returned from the bank with the rent money, he guided me away so that police lights would not give me a seizure, because police lights now surrounded my home: And I sent him to see for which trailer the police had come, and whether there were any firemen or EMTs; and my son returned, and said that the police were in our driveway, and that there were no other emergency vehicles.

And I was afraid for my new little son: Because, although he was healthy by every measure, his appearance was strange, almost not human. And I sent Manasseh to ask the police to shut off the lights, so that I could return to my house: And they turned off the lights, and we returned.

In our driveway were two policemen: And the one had a silver rune with his uniform; and the other had the same rune, but inside a circle, also of silver. But I knew not at that time the meaning of this rune: That it is called a "Life Rune," and was worn much among the Nazi SS. And the meaning of the Life Rune[27] is that its wearers believe it is good for Aryan men to violate white women in order to conceive more Aryans, and so increase the "Master Race."

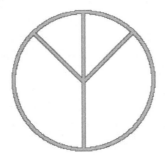

One of them—the same neo-Nazi lieutenant deputy medical examiner who had called purple spots on the extremities a heart attack symptom, and had ordered our friend's body illegally cremated—with the same sneer—"asked" to see my newborn child, and claimed that someone had anonymously called the police and said that the baby looked jaundiced.

But nobody but us had seen Abram Jedidiah Ammi in the last ten days.

And I asked Benaiah, and he said that they'd asked him to see our new little baby; and that he'd said to wait for the mother because Abram was asleep and too easily awakened, because Benaiah had just changed his diaper. And Abram was still sleeping.

And I asked the leering neo-Nazi lieutenant whether he knew what jaundice is, but he could not say.

So I demanded that they send a paramedic, and I would show our little son to a paramedic: Because this leering policeman was clearly unqualified and incompetent to judge my baby's health. Neither did Abram have any jaundice, which is yellowed skin, and quite normal in breastfed newborns, and completely harmless as long as the whites of the eyes are not also yellowed.

Then after the paramedic had come, we showed Abram Jedidiah Ammi to him: And, behold, he wasn't jaundiced. And we put the baby gently into the arms of the ambulance driver, to feel his weight.

The neo-Nazi lieutenant also saw, and with a leer said that my baby looked too small to be Benaiah's son.

Two years later, I read the police report, and I saw that the leering deputy medical examiner had falsely reported that the paramedics were there from the beginning, and that I had put Abram in the paramedic's arms as soon as I came home. And I know not whether the ambulance driver wrote any report of these things, but if so, I believe that this report[28] would show that I came before the ambulance driver: Because the ambulance driver was an honorable man, and no friend of the leering neo-Nazi policeman.

The leering neo-Nazi lieutenant also saw the outside of our trailer, and said with a malicious sneer that our house was very small for two adults and five children, and that he saw ants (who cares about ants living outdoors?), and that the barrier to keep our Elishevah inside our door looked like a fire hazard, and that he knew we Jews light candles every Saturday, and that our candles were dangerous in such a small house. (But he knew not that our family no longer lit candles every Friday night, because Elishevah was inclined to leap about like a little mouse, and she understood no danger.) And I demonstrated that the barrier was very easy to move quickly aside, and said that we mostly only lived in the trailer at night and during storms: Because we love gardens and wild places.

(And I think he already knew this: Because he had watched us very closely since our first day in Newberg.)

After these things, I fled the house with all my little children and walked to my mother's house, and I said that we would never return to our little trailer, because of the leering deputy medical examiner.

And after a month (first in my mother's mobile home, and then in my mother-in-law's apartment), Ben's older sister and her husband bought us a mobile home, the biggest size we could accept, bigger than all the homes of our neighbors, almost too large to move. And we returned to our neighborhood (in haste, because the Passover was near at hand), and we lived next door to our first driveway, so that we had our old western garden for our new eastern garden. And from that day, the leering deputy medical examiner parked his car in front of our driveway nearly every week, to stare, when nobody had called the police to our neighborhood for anything.

Two years later, I read that he had also denounced us to the fire department, because we had no lights on during the eve of the Sabbath, and because we had five children in a mobile home with only three bedrooms and one bathroom. But the firemen had more brains than to respond to such a stupid report, because the danger was obviously imaginary,[29] and because we had broken no laws.

Since that day until the day that my husband and I fled from Newberg and returned, this leering policeman parked his car in front of our driveway for no good reason almost every week, and three times he charged at my husband with his car at night, and three times in one night (at three different street corners) he shined his flashing lights to give me an epileptic seizure, and he invaded both my mother's home and my mother-in-law's apartment without warrants or probable cause in broad daylight, in uniform—and my mother-in-law lives well outside this officer's jurisdiction—all these things being besides the false reports he had filed against us, and finally he testified falsely under oath against us in court.

And his face in the courtroom had the look of mortal terror, and his hands shook: Because he knew that I knew that he is a perjurer, and a neo-Nazi, and an accomplice to murder, if not the murderer himself.

Because I know not whether Dan the predator was the deputy medical examiner's accomplice, or whether the deputy medical examiner was Dan the predator's accomplice, but I know that they both lied together to protect themselves after the murder of our neighbor and friend the pure-hearted and praiseworthy man Barney Edwards.

# SURVIVAL OF THE FITTEST

4    And I say unto you my friends, Do not be afraid of those
     who kill the body, and after that have no more
     that they can do.

6    Are not five sparrows sold for two assárions?[12] And not one
     of them is forgotten before God.

—Luke 12:3-12:7

21　　And you will say in your heart, Who gave birth to these
for me? And I *had been* bereaved of children, and desolate,
*an exile* stripped naked and removed; and these, Who raised
up *these*? Behold, I *was* left *alone*: I *was* alone: these,
where *were* they?

22　　Thus said my Lord Adonai, Behold, I will lift up my hand
to *the* nations, and lift up my banner to *the* peoples: and they
will bring your sons in *their* bosom, and *will* lift up your
daughters upon *their* shoulder.

——Isaiah 49:21-49:22

CHAPTER THIRTY-FOUR::

# Centaurs

During the springtime of two thousand and seven, I dreamed
about my stepdaughter Hannah-Joy, lost to us since the morning of
November 19, nineteen ninety-three: And I saw her face, and the
face of her young husband, and that the young man's name was
Luke. And in this dream they were standing before our door, nude
and unashamed; and she was newly pregnant with a daughter. Three
times I dreamed this dream, and then a stranger began to write to
Benaiah over the internet, saying that she is his daughter Hannah-
Joy. And from the springtime until winter, we learned that my four
stepchildren were alive, but running free like wild pagans.

And for many hours Benaiah wrote to Hannah in emails:
Because he is very dyslexic, and she was very troubled. And, for
two weeks in that summer, I worked as his scribe twenty hours each
day without sleep, except on the Sabbath: And the half of my garden
died of thirst.

And Hannah had a fornicator named Luke: And his face was
the same face in my dream, the face of Hannah's husband, and the
father of her unborn baby, our first granddaughter.

Then, in the Feast of Tabernacles, while we slept, a spider bit
Benaiah in his forehead several times, from the top of his head to his
right eyebrow, and many times under his right eyebrow, and then
down the bridge of his nose, two or three times unto the tip: And we
never saw the spider, but his bites were the same as mine in the
previous year, in the day after the Feast of Tabernacles: The bites of

a Hobo Spider; but we treated his infirmity wisely from the
beginning, with raw garlic and Echinacea purpuera. However, in
addition to blinding him in one eye, the bites made a red formation
upon his face which I had seen in my childhood, in a very symbolic
dream of my future husband and his children.

In this dream, they were centaurs: And Benaiah was alone in
a small empty village of burned huts made of straw: And his face
and his back were both also burnt, until the shoulders of his front
legs, and the burns upon his face were the same as the spider bites
which he now bore in real life: Because they were very like burns,
so that from my memory of the dream I was able to immediately
find the rest of the bites hidden under his hair.

And the centaur Benaiah was alone there in the village,
because of the fire which had caused his herd to flee; until two more
centaurs returned: First his son in his own image, Enoch Micaiah;
and then his daughter Hannah-Joy for but a moment: Then they both
quickly fled. And after a long time, the centaur's firstborn son came,
and left, and returned with his three siblings.

But I had all but forgotten this dream until I saw the spider
bites, because it was so strange and so symbolic that we never
understood it; and because Benaiah was never able to speak much
with me until this day about his firstborn son Elias Luke, for
anguish; nor much about his first daughter Hannah-Joy Elspeth until
the day after she returned to him in two thousand nine: Therefore, to
speak of this dream would have been as if I should thrust a sword
into his heart until the hilt. And so I never spoke of this dream a
second time, nor wrote it down before now.

And I also had another dream in my youth about Benaiah, in
which he was a centaur, and I also, and my mother, and another:
And we four centaurs were running through a forest: And then three
of us, because my mother was no longer with us: And the equine
trail was more and more difficult.

The other centaur was smaller, and African: And his body
was not like a horse, but rather like a strong black pony. And we
were in the midst of a war: And enemies were pursuing behind us:
Therefore we ran galloping; and leaping because of the tree trunks in
our path. And Benaiah was the first, and I second, and the black
centaur farther and farther behind, because his legs were short, and

because of the large tree trunks in the path. Finally, we came to a great log, perhaps six feet in diameter, which Benaiah jumped over easily, and then I with a great flying leap. But the top was nearly up to the black centaur's human chest, so that with all of our strength and with great difficulty we both heaved him over it.

And I know not this African man, but we saw one like him, perhaps the same man, at George Fox University, a Christian refugee whose village had been carried away captive: And his soul was pure and faithful to Messiah Yeshua. But we never spoke with him. Moreover, from the day that we thought to join with this man, something was against us to separate our family from the university.

And Benaiah said not to worry about the African, because if this dream was from Adonai, we shall certainly meet the man at the appointed time.

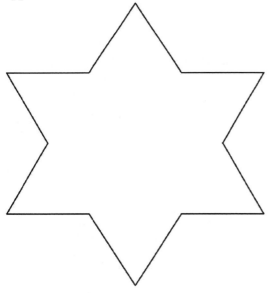

Then, in the summer of two thousand eight, my stepson Enoch Micaiah returned to his father. And his soul and his appearance were the same as Benaiah at his same age: And just as Benaiah was very lost in his youth, a fatherless[30] son, so also was Enoch.

And we all received Enoch with great joy and many gifts; and sent him away again to his brothers and sister, he saying that he would also soon return likewise again, before the Feast of Tabernacles.

But Enoch never returned to us that year; because just before the holiday, Hannah-Joy Elspeth wrote from the hospital that she was very sick with appendicitis; and she also described the symptoms. But the first symptoms which she wrote were like those of the first stages of pregnancy: And the symptoms after she returned from the hospital were very like miscarriage or abortion, including severe depression. Because of this depression, therefore, her faithful brother Enoch Micaiah never returned to us that year, because Enoch stayed with his sister to comfort her.

After this surgery, I never again sensed my unborn grandchild, the daughter of Luke and Hannah.

Exodus

13:1    And Adonai spoke unto Moses, saying,

2    Separate unto me all the firstborn: *the* one who opens any womb among *the* children of Israel, *both* of man and of animal: it *is* mine.

21:22    And if human beings strive, and they strike
a pregnant woman, and her children go out[31] *from her*,
and *yet* there is no mischief, surely *you* shall fine,
according as the woman's patriarchal chief
shall lay upon him; and *they* shall give through judges.

23    And if *any* harm follow, then you shall give life for life,

24    Eye for eye, tooth for tooth, hand for hand, foot for foot,

25    Burning for burning, wound for wound, stripe for stripe.

Matthew

18:10    See that you do not despise one of these little ones;
because I say unto you, that in *the* heavens their angels
always see the face of my Father which *is* in *the* heavens.

—Exodus 13:1-13:2; 21:22-21:25;
Matthew 18:10

In that hour Yeshua rejoiced in the Spirit, and said:
I praise You, Father, Lord of heaven and earth, because
You hid these *things* from *the* wise and understanding,
and revealed them *unto* speechless *babes*. Yes, Father,
because so *it* was well-pleasing in Your presence.

—Luke 10:21

CHAPTER THIRTY-FIVE:

# Birth of a Beautiful Seer
## by Abba

The hardest writing I ever wrote was about Esther. And it
still is...

Her miracle wasn't once in a while; she was all the time in a
miraculous state, day after day... God gave Esther and me a special
bond because He knew—He knew what was going to happen. One
day a princess was born—Esther Sarah Hadiyah[32] was royalty. So
now I can talk about her birth... So, the first time I saw her is when
she was born naked into my arms.

I discovered that royalty was born to me—I had royalty in
front of me. We are all special; our children are all special; but
Esther's specialness was atypical... God gave us a unique bond
which made me realize there was a lot more going on than meets the
eye... it was a big responsibility, just like having a queen being
born, and that's what she is to me, she is like a queen.

They are taking somebody very high and important and deep
and they are messing around and doing whatever they want. Like
Yeshua said,

Matthew
10:24   The student is not above his teacher, nor *is* the servant
        above his lord.

25      ... If they have called the lord of the home *Baál-zevúv*,[33]
        how much more *shall they call* them of His family?

—Matthew 10:24-10:25

220

So we are treated even worse. They did all these horrible things to John the Baptist: Who even knows what they did with his head after they cut it off?… What did they do? All they did is put him somewhere where they can't watch him. There's nothing noteworthy the persecutors can do to us: They can kill her, they can kill us, but all that will happen is we will be connected forever and they won't be able to see *us* anymore.

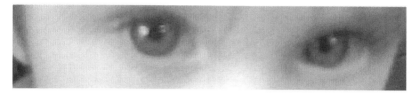

She was… She was more aware; this little baby lived in two worlds. It really opened up my eyes; she was really aware spiritually… A lot of people think their kid is really special. I wondered at first if I was imagining it—I didn't want to be one of those parents who think that their kid is exceptional, just because the kid is theirs. But it was proved to me day after day: I saw many proofs. Esther… has a lot of authority in the spiritual world. And so I know I need to be very humble and submit to her authority… When you meet someone who is clearly higher than yourself and has some great authority, you bow. They tried to get Daniel to bow to the wrong authority. We bow to the real authority; we bow to God: We would be completely idiotic and stupid not to bow. When you meet the King of kings, you won't tell Him a joke (unless He asks you to tell him a joke).

Some of us have experienced lightning and thunder; when I was in the desert I experienced lightning not very far away from me. It feels like it could just blow you to dust. It's scary: Most people run away from it. When you meet true royalty, it's the same way. You bow. You are awestruck.

And now I will end it on a scripture that says the soldiers fell down like dead men when they saw that angel, and it wasn't even Christ—it was only a messenger, and it didn't even say it was an archangel. You don't tell jokes: You tremble: You're scared. Well, this is what Esther is—Regal, Sovereign.

*by Abba*

21   Do not despise, for Your name's sake; do not dishonor
     *the* throne *of* Your glory: remember;
     do not break Your covenant with us.
22   Are there *any* rain-makers among *the* idols of the nations?
     And can the heavens give us rains? Are You not He,
     Adonai our God? And we will hope in You,
     because You do all these *things*.

                                        —Jeremiah 14:21-14:22


CHAPTER THIRTY-SIX:

# The Fire and the Rain

Our people always celebrate *Shavúot*, which is the Festival
of Weeks, fifty days after the Passover, remembering the day that
the Lord spoke to us with His own voice the Ten Commandments
(Three times in the Hebrew part of the Bible, this holiday is called
the Feast of Weeks (*Shavúot*), but three times in the Greek part of
the Bible it is called *Pentecostés*—[that is, Pentecost]).

The Hebrews in the Holy land celebrate the Pentecost one
day of the year, but we celebrate the festival for two days in the
Diaspora: Because in the Diaspora the Jews celebrate every divinely
commanded festival one extra day, to ensure that the correct day is
kept according to Adonai's Law: and in May 30, two thousand nine,
in the second morning of Pentecost, which was also a Sabbath that
year, I looked outside the windows and saw, to the east side of our
trailer, rain (and no rain was expected that week); but, to the western
side, sunlight.

Then, on Sunday morning, I went outside to water the
garden: And, behold, an ugly burn newly marred the little seat of my
little daughter Elishevah's little pink bicycle: And our children's
bicycles were locked against the side of our propane tanks; and the
pink bicycle was right next to one tank, just under it, so that any fire
on the seat would certainly touch the propane tank.

But we never reported this arson to the police: Because we
knew very well that the leering deputy medical examiner had a
fascination with fire, and with Sabbath candles.

In the next Tuesday, which was the second of June, we walked to my Aunt Rachel's house, and told Rachel these things. But she said that this rain was certainly a miracle, and a sign that we had no cause to fear, because the hand of the Lord is our shield. So I could not prevail in my desire to flee with the children, because all the family was with her in these things, and they dismissed my fears and nightmares as paranoia.

But I began to prepare to move away from Newberg. But Benaiah said that we needed more money; and that I still needed a caretaker twenty-four hours a day; and that he was not able, therefore, to work outside the home.

Therefore we continued in our work to publish one of our books, until I should be able to return to the university.

1 Hear deeply,[9] *O* God, my voice in my prayer;
  keep my life from terror of the hater.
2 Hide me from *the* secret council *of the* wicked,
  From *the* rage of *the* workers of iniquity,
3 Who sharpen their tongue like *a* sword.
  *They* guide their arrow, *even a* bitter word,
4 To shoot in secret *at a* complete *one*:
  Suddenly they shoot at him, and they do not fear.
5 They strengthen themselves *in an* evil *matter*:
  they write to hide snares, saying, Who will see them?
6 They search for iniquities;
  they perfect *the* concealing and searching out
  *of a* hidden *snare*:
  And *the* inward *thought* of *every* man and heart *is* deep.
7 Yet God will shoot an arrow at them;
  their wounds will be sudden.
8 And they will fall: their *own* tongue *will be* against them:
  all *who* see them will flee *away*.
9 And every man shall fear,
  and they *will* declare *the* work *of* God;
  And in wisdom they will understand of His doing.
10 *The* righteous will be glad in Adonai, and will trust in Him;
  and all *the* upright in heart will praise.

——Psalm 64

108   Accept *the* freewill *offerings* of my mouth, I beg You please,
      Adonai; and teach me Your judgments.

169   My cry comes before Your face, Adonai:
      according to Your word give me discernment.

                                   —Psalm 119:108; 119:169

CHAPTER THIRTY-SEVEN:
# An Answer to my Prayer

To live within the safety of the holy Law of our God, we
need to be allowed to choose what to teach our children: We need to
be free to give our children a Torah-centered education: No
civilization can even *continue to exist* if it is not also the civilization
being taught to the next generation: If I have a plant in my garden
that is an annual, and I don't plant its seeds, it won't come back the
next year.

To live within the safety of the Torah, we must surrender,
and so we must be free to surrender, every aspect of our children's
lives to the holy Law of our God: It is completely meaningless only
to *learn* what God has commanded us to do; this knowledge *is not
enough*: Nor is it enough only to have the freedom to *teach our
children* what God has commanded us to do—Clearly, beloved
fathers, to live within the safety of the Torah also requires us to
actually *obey* the holy Laws of Adonai our God.

What is my duty as a mother? Indeed, What is the whole
duty of any mother toward her sons and daughters? Is it merely to
quietly know and remember the household rules, while letting the
babysitters do all the decision-making? Or is it my duty only to
know and to teach the household rules, but not to obey them, nor
teach my children to obey?

This, then, is my whole duty as a mother: To raise my
children in accordance with the laws of my family, my tribe, my
nation, and—above all—in accordance with the Laws of my God.
And so, when the Laws of the Torah disagree with other nations'
human laws, then we mothers are forced to choose whether to obey
God or men: Rome did not send Christians and Jews into the jaws of
lions because of which songs they sang or which prayers they

prayed: Rome sentenced these martyrs to death because they disobeyed Roman Law by refusing to teach their children to worship a human emperor.

More recently, the Soviet Union, and other Socialist nations since then—while congratulating themselves on granting full religious freedom in all areas except for teaching and healing—tried to destroy both Judaism and Christianity by forbidding us from teaching our beliefs to our children, and by forbidding us from teaching our children to live as we believe.

There can be no peace in a nation which does not protect the right of its people not only to believe as we do, but to do as we believe: Not only the right to speak what we believe to be the truth, but also the right to live according to what we believe is the truth. As mothers and fathers, we must defend to our last breath the right to choose our children's teaching, and we must defend to our last breath the right to choose our children's healing.

The most important issue which faces mankind today, Beloved, is whether a human government is competent to make such choices for us, or whether we have, and must necessarily continue to have, the right to live as we believe.

Thomas Jefferson said we must. We *must*; we absolutely *must* have both the freedom and the courage to raise our children within the safety of the Law of our God.

Let us therefore return to Adonai our God, our Beloved Father, our *Abba*, and obey His voice according to all that He commanded us that day, and also our children with us, with all our heart, and with all our soul: There is no room for compromise.

Here is the story of the day when I asked to be used of my God as a martyr for this cause; I praise my King and my Redeemer that He has granted me this gift, although it was hard to receive—even so much so that I nearly died from the bitter anguish in my frail, tiny soul: Who am I, that He should use me? What am I, that I should be counted as a worthy sacrifice for anything? And yet, trusting, like a child trusting that Daddy can put anything at all under his Christmas tree, I dared to ask, for the sake of the family of a little girl who, to protect what remains of her family's privacy, I will here call *Havalah*, a Hebrew form of her given name:

On the evening of March 8, two thousand eight, shortly before the tribulation of my own earthly family, a toddler who I will call *Havalah* died suddenly during the night, as a victim of a rapid bacterial infection.

Havalah's parents were not judged as the Torah commands, "By *the* mouth *of* two witnesses, and *of* three, every utterance shall stand.[34]" I very much doubt that the American justice system or the tax-funded history books will ever acknowledge just how thoroughly unjust Havalah's parents' trial was. But I will not be silent.

I have never yet met young Havalah or her family; and yet, her story and mine have become so intertwined that the true story of her life has every right to be written in my own:

In the year two thousand nine, Havalah's father and mother were accused of contributing to their daughter's death by medical neglect: But the entire case was heard and judged, and the father finally sent to prison for sixty days (the maximum penalty for the only, and scarcely related, accusation of which the jury was able to convict this innocent father)—it didn't seem to matter much that he was found innocent of 2nd degree manslaughter: The news reporters seemed only to notice that he was found guilty of *something* (a misdemeanor, and nearly unrelated to the case)—and that he was sent to a county jail.

The final autopsy results confirmed the medical examiner's original diagnosis in March, two thousand eight, of death by sepsis, showing that Havalah's parents could not possibly have predicted nor prevented Havalah's sudden death from a rapid bacterial infection.

The shameful slanders against Havalah's father and mother came from the lips of one Daniel Leonhardt, MD.: Daniel Leonhardt testified under oath that Havalah's death was partly due to her "malnutrition," a claim which he based entirely on the fact that she was far below the national average size for her age on the growth charts. But Daniel Leonhardt conveniently forgot to mention[35] that this was because she was a *slightly obese dwarf*, having inherited her mother's congenital dwarfism.

Rejecting the expert testimony of Dr. Janice Ophoven of Minnesota, a respected scientist with thirty years' specialty experience in autopsies of children, Daniel Leonhardt testified under oath that Havalah's death was partly due to the large, soft cyst on Havalah's neck, which he claimed caused the child to slowly suffocate over a period of months, while her parents looked on and did nothing to have this cyst removed.

But Daniel Leonhardt conveniently forgot to mention[35] that Havalah's mother has an identical cyst on her own neck, caused by the very same congenital dwarfism, and that this cyst had never once impeded the breathing of Havalah's mother. Daniel Leonhardt also conveniently forgot to mention[35] that right up until the last week of Havalah's life, her photographs showed her to be pink and smiling. Suffocating children are not pink, unless they are suffocating because of carbon monoxide poisoning. Suffocating children, in my experience, do not smile either. Havalah was *not* slowly suffocating: Moreover, since the cyst was obviously completely harmless, it would have been reckless and foolish for Havalah's parents to request its surgical removal at so tender an age, before she was even old enough to be embarrassed about looking different from the other girls her age. Moreover, it would have been criminal malpractice for any surgeon to grant such an abusive and outrageous request, to perform a totally elective major surgery on a toddler—and an undersized toddler at that.

Daniel Leonhardt testified under oath that Havalah's mother contributed to Havalah's death by a delay of approximately two minutes—the time this mother spent hysterically screaming in utter anguish before anyone thought to call 9-1-1 after finding her daughter dead in the bed. Daniel Leonhardt conveniently forgot to mention[35] that Havalah wasn't *dying* while her mother was busy screaming hysterically: Havalah was—indisputably and obviously— *already dead*: She had died soon after her parents fell asleep the night before.

Daniel Leonhardt testified under oath that the child's runny nose the night before was a clear sign that Havalah needed to be rushed to the hospital. I speak from experience on this one—any child brought into the emergency care unit with nothing more than symptoms of a common cold will *not* be treated there—at least not while there is a higher priority patient: Which is to say, in most cases and in all large cities, until bulls start wearing bloomers.

The real issue was, and remains, the religious convictions of Havalah's family: Quite simply, Daniel Leonhardt wanted to see Havalah's parents go to jail because they prayed for their daughter's healing instead of going to human doctors. Never mind that it has yet to be established that Havalah's runny nose even had anything to do with the rapid bacterial infection which killed her.

The simple fact of the matter is that, if Havalah's parents had done *nothing at all* about her runny nose, they would *never* have been charged with a crime. They were accused of criminal neglect because they prayed. Daniel Leonhardt wanted to make an example out of them because of his own hatred of families that actively prefer God as their primary physician, and who often only turn to human doctors as a second choice. Daniel Leonhardt hated Havalah's parents because they prayed.

They were accused of criminal medical neglect because they are Christ-obeying Christians.

Daniel Leonhardt wants all prayers for miracle healing of all American children to be outlawed, and branded as medical neglect in the United States: It is an abomination to him that the First Amendment was ever written to protect our God-given rights to raise our children in accordance with our own beliefs.

We Jewish Americans do not have a right to stand in the sidelines and watch this destruction happen: We are commanded to turn back to God, and to seek His direction both for our own lives and for the life of our nation, and to live according to His holy Law. As mothers and fathers, we must defend the right to choose our children's healing.

In the summer of two thousand nine, while two of my older children and I watched this case come to its twisted conclusion, and having seen the sneer of utter hatred on Daniel Leonhardt's face—this video recording should be available as public record in the news archives—I prayed for God to bring down this enemy of the Church, and I offered myself, asking my God to make me a witness to this cause.

When Benaiah heard this prayer, he objected,[36] saying that I, as a mother, owed it to my children not to pray for their mother's martyrdom, who had never asked to be martyrs with me, and at such

228

a time when three of them were still too young to even consider such a choice.

Even so I answered my husband, protesting that with all my heart I would hope for my faithful children to gladly pray the same for themselves; but I also agreed that the three oldest should certainly have a say in the matter (and Yehudah Isaiah also— because I did not agree with Ben that Yehudah was too young to decide). So I asked Manasseh, Elishevah, Mattithias and Yehudah to consider the matter for their own selves, whether they were willing for their mother to be sacrificed to save the Christian families of America; and, moreover, that if they were willing to suffer with me for the sake of the Cross they would pray in agreement with my prayer; and I also prayed that God would honor their choice above my own on this matter.

Yehudah Isaiah, only five years old at the time, and his big sister Elishevah Yael, both immediately looked at me with the same serious, thoughtful, and sad look on both their faces, and they both turned aside to Elishevah's bedroom to pray. I knew not what they prayed; neither did I intrude upon their walk with God by asking. Manasseh Raphael also looked at me with a quite serious and thoughtful gaze, although I did not see him stop to pray.

This was the last news broadcast our family ever watched together.

Soon I would meet Daniel Leonhardt in person, and hear Daniel Leonhardt's slanders[35] against me and against my husband, accusing us likewise of medical neglect, because of my son Abram's own rapid bacterial infection, which—but for the power of answered prayer—would certainly have also claimed Abram's life, and Elishevah's, and Yehudah's.

But Benaiah and Mattithias and Esther were spared the ravages of this rare and brutal disease; and Abram, although marred more than all, was spared the sudden death which Satan had appointed for him that day. Without the hand of God, it is unlikely that any of the eight of us would have survived—and we all lived, even the two babies Esther and Abram, for whom the first symptom of Meningococcus would have been death, had not Abram fallen ill with an even more rare mutation of this rare disease, and so had begun to thrash wildly, suffocating and changing colors, rather than to simply pass quietly away in his sleep like Havalah.

Praises be to our God for His mercy.

And for His justice.

As mothers and fathers, we must defend to our last breath the right to choose our children's teaching, and we must defend to our last breath the right to choose our children's healing.

This is not an issue of whether I raised my children properly, or whether I could have done a better job as a mother. This is not an issue of whether the few minutes we spent praying for Elishevah's fever and ankle rash helped save her life, or merely caused unnecessary delays. This is only the issue of whether a human government is competent to make such choices for me, or whether I have, and must necessarily continue to have, the right to live as I believe.

I praise my God that He has walked with me, and that He has allowed me (a mere stubborn human) not exceptional in any way—at least, not in any *good* way—to also walk with Him. And with Him is where I will walk.

I am a Christian Jew. With or without the Government's permission, I will strive with my whole being to wholeheartedly obey the commandment,

Deuteronomy

6:4  Hear deeply,[9] O Israel: Adonai our God, Adonai *is* one.

5   And you shall love Adonai your God in all your heart,
    and in all your soul, and in all your strength.

6   And these words, which I command you this day,
    shall be on your heart;

7   And you shall sharpen them unto your children,
    and shall talk of them in your sitting in your house,
    and in your walking by *the* way, and in your laying down,
    and in your rising up.

8   And you shall bind them for *a* sign upon your hand,
    and *they* shall be for frontlets between your eyes;

9   and you shall write them upon the doorposts *of* your house,
    and in your gates.

11.1    …And you shall love Adonai your God, and you shall keep
His guard, and His statutes, and His judgments,
and His commandments, all the days.

30:6    And Adonai your God will circumcise your heart, and the
heart of your seed, to love Adonai your God with all your
heart and with all your soul, so that you will live.

8    And you will return and you will hear *the* voice *of* Adonai,
and you will do all His commandments
which I command you today.

11    Because this commandment which I command you this day,
it *is* not hidden from you, and it *is* not far away.

12    It *is* not in *the* heavens, that *you* should say,
Who will go up for us *to* the heavens, and bring it unto us,
and cause us to hear *it*, that we may do it?

13    And it *is* not beyond *the* sea, that *you* should say,
Who shall cross over to beyond the sea for us, and bring it
unto us, and cause us to hear *it*, that we may do it?

14    Because the word *is* very near unto you, in your mouth
and in your heart, that you may do it.

——Deuteronomy 6:4-6:9; 11:1-11:21; 30:1-30.16

Here is my testimony. Let us take up the Law of Love gladly
and with both hands: Let us return unto our God: There is no room
for compromise.

...therefore choose life...
———Deuteronomy 30:19

# CHAPTER THIRTY-EIGHT:

# Fourth of July

1    And Adonai spoke unto Moses, saying,
2    Command *the* children of Israel that they send out of the
     camp every leper,
     and everyone flowing, and everyone *with a* defiled soul:
3    Both male *and* female you shall send out; outside of *the*
     camp you shall send them, and they will not defile their
     camps, in the midst whereof I dwell.
———Numbers 5:1-5:3


On June first, two thousand nine, my five year old nephew
Samuel had the swine flu. And his mother, my twin sister and close
neighbor Drea Michelle, did not believe in quarantining sick people
from others, but rather she believed in vaccinating and then living
free. But there was no vaccine available against the swine flu until
the following autumn.

And my twin sister tried to give us some of Samuel's hand-
me-downs for Abram Ammi, saying that the clothing was clean,
straight from the dryer: But I saw that her snot-nosed five year old
had the laundry basket in his hands; and that his snot still made a
slimy green and yellow waterfall of mucus on his mouth and chin
and shirt. And I commanded my children to go inside the house,
saying, No, Thank you. But when my mother Shoshanna Miriam
came to visit her grandchildren, my sister returned with the same
clothing, to give the clothes to my son Manasseh: But Manasseh
would not accept them from her.

Then my sister turned as if to leave, but instead turned again
and tossed the clothes to our mother, who tossed them into my son
Manasseh's hands. And he did not want to receive them; but he did
not want to dishonor his grandmother either, so in a moment of
confusion he hesitated just long enough to breathe in the disease.

And so, two or three days later, Manasseh was very sick with the swine flu, and he separated himself for six days: But in the seventh day of his sickness, Yehudah Isaiah went to his sick brother of his own self-will. Three days later Yehudah Isaiah had the swine flu, and the next day Elishevah, and Mattithias, and then me, and then baby Esther Sarah Hadiyah. But the fever came suddenly and left quickly, so that we had no need of or much time for any healing herbs to treat the fever, although it caused the heart to race. Then, until a week after the last symptoms, we put ourselves in quarantine: Because the Torah *does not* say to vaccinate and then live free, but rather commands the Hebrews to put in quarantine, and to have all sickness in abomination.

In the sixth day of healing for Mattithias and Esther and Yehudah Isaiah, which was the first day of my healing, and also Elishevah's, then my stepson Enoch returned to us with his sister Hannah. And they gave gifts to our young children their half-brothers and their half-sisters; and walked with their father Benaiah and with Manasseh: But we sick folk remained in quarantine, and only allowed that the children remain in the doorway, with Enoch and Hannah their half-siblings, and open the gifts there. Then they returned to their homes. But I had the swine flu three more days, because I had gone outside too soon in order to talk to my stepdaughter Hannah-Joy Elspeth; and I kept at a distance, and did not touch her.

And neither Abram nor Benaiah ever caught that flu.

And so I was sick again until the second day of July: And in the late morning of July 3, the second day of my healing, I went outside with Manasseh to the yard to water the garden, but not until the leering policeman left: Because his car was in our driveway that morning as it had been almost every other day, about three times a week; and he was also prowling about our yard that morning like a predatory animal on the hunt.

But while I watered the plants, I smelled an odor like a kitten's flea collar: And I thought that the landlord must have contaminated my garden on the east side of the house (again); and accordingly I moved to the west garden to avoid the poison. But the smell followed me. Immediately I turned off the water, and went to return to the house, and so I passed in front of the mouth of the garden hose: And I saw white foam, with the same smell as a kitten's flea collar, thick and white. And I called for my son Manasseh (because he was not right with me, but nearby): But I had no voice.

And I awoke upon the hood of our car, unable to speak, and my first thought was to flee and hide, and to die alone like a cat, so that the enemy policeman would gain no opportunity to frame my severely dyslexic husband as a murderer. And I prayed, but the Lord put strongly upon my heart to stay alive for my children, that they should not become orphans. And I answered that they would not be orphans without their mother, because they would still have their father.

But Yeshua said, "No. Live."

And I signaled to Manasseh, but he wasn't watching.

And I awoke again upon the hood of our car, unable to speak or to raise myself, and made a sign again to Manasseh. And I awoke again in my husband's bed, and three more times I awoke, the third time in the evening, with symptoms[37] of poisoning.

Then I felt severe pain surging through my wrists; and I saw that my right wrist was so broken that the bone pierced the skin. And I showed my broken wrist to Benaiah, but he only looked confused, and returned to our daughter Elishevah: And I looked at my wrist again, and the wound had disappeared.

I awoke again at the beginning of nighttime, and found that Benaiah had not understood that I was hallucinating, because his mind was on Elishevah, who now had a mild fever, with tiny purple spots on one ankle.

And the mild fever left when Benaiah and Manasseh prayed for her, but it returned, and left when they prayed again: And now they were waiting until I woke up, to seek help: Because he had never heard of any sickness like this, which wasn't smallpox, nor chicken pox, nor anthrax. But Benaiah had had no choice but to wait for me to wake up on my own, because waking me up out of dream sleep could easily trigger the first of a series of seizures. So Ben had to wait until I woke up on my own before he could ask me whether this might be cowpox: Because he didn't know what cowpox looked like, but he knew I'd had cowpox in my childhood.

But I said, No, it isn't.

So we began to plan a walk to the hospital, right away or else at dawn: Because she had a fever, and her brothers were still weak from the flu, and we certainly didn't want to be so sloppy in our haste as to expose her brothers to this strange rash which looked like some kind of poisoning, but might also be some contagious sickness we'd never heard of.

And I was no help most of that day; and very little help that night, because of the poisoning from the water hose.

And Ben was weighing the merits and risks of waiting until dawn (with a daughter whose rash was of a sort we'd never even heard of) against the merits and risks of walking in the night (for at least two or three miles alongside a poorly lit highway, and in the cold night air with four healthy children still weak from our recent flu; one of whom would have to be physically restrained from leaping like a little mouse into the road; while leading an epileptic wife who was still fairly useless because of the poisoned water hose).

Meanwhile, I was not thinking clearly enough to recognize that Benaiah had not slept for days, nor eaten anything for quite some time,—even today, I *still* have no idea *how* long—and that his blood sugars had therefore fallen dangerously low, and that we were both in a state of emotional shock because we couldn't imagine how Elishevah had gotten any disease at all, let alone a totally unfamiliar sickness, when we had been in quarantine for more than two weeks.

While we were still weighing the merits and risks of waiting until dawn against the merits and risks of walking in the night, our two-year-old son was dancing with joy in his crib, wearing only his diaper, laughing at our strange behavior: Because only Abram and Benaiah never caught this flu, and baby Abram had never been sick in his whole life, and didn't understand.

Exactly at midnight (because we had an "atomic clock",[38] guaranteed to keep perfectly accurate time, and I looked to see the time), our happy dancing Abram suddenly dropped down limp in the bed, and rested calmly.

So I felt his forehead with my hand, and the other children's foreheads to compare: And because his temperature is normally nearly two degrees cooler than his brothers and sisters, and was now about the same, I said that Abram Jedidiah Ammi had a very mild fever.

So of course Benaiah took his temperature with our thermometer: And Abram did have what was for him a mild fever, which was a little past 97.8 degrees Fahrenheit,[39] and no other symptoms, except possible lethargy. (It was only a borderline fever, however: The same temperature would not have been a fever for his sister Elishevah Yael.) Still, we didn't want to expose his mild fever to the night air. Therefore, two and a half hours later, we were almost in agreement to wait for the morning, and to walk to the hospital at first light. Because I knew that my little boy was healthy by every standard measure: But I also knew he was not healthy.

I did not know that Benaiah was eighteen days and eighteen nights without sleep. And now both of us were in shock, because Elishevah Yael had a new sickness in quarantine, of which neither of us had heard in all our lives; neither gave I any thought to the fact that the leering deputy medical examiner had been in our driveway just before I went out to water the garden.

In my distress I called upon Adonai, and I cried
unto my God: From His temple He heard my voice deeply,[9]
and my cry came before His face, *even* into His ears.

————Psalm 18:6

While we were still speaking (exhausted, confused, amazed, and in shock; and Benaiah sleepless for eighteen days and nights and ready to pass out from dangerously low blood sugars), all this time with my eyes upon Abram Jedidiah Ammi asleep in his bed, suddenly Abram began to thrash wildly. I yelled to Ben. Matt yelled to Ben. Manasseh yelled to Ben. And Ben moved fast.

The child was not breathing, and he was burning hot, and his throat was swollen shut. And after Benaiah sought to cool the baby in water, he yelled to me to go to our neighbor and call 9-1-1. And, because we didn't have a telephone, I ran outside, still in my underwear, to call for an ambulance.

3:4　*With* my voice I called unto Adonai,
and He answered me out of His holy mountain.
(Lift this up and weigh it carefully.[10])

5　I laid me down and I slept; I awaked,
because Adonai sustained me.

6　I will not fear ten thousands *of* people,
that have set *themselves* against me round about.

18:6　In my distress I called upon Adonai, and I cried
unto my God: From his temple He heard my voice deeply,[9]
and my cry came before His face, *even* into His ears.

18:16　He sent from on high, He took me;
He drew me out of many waters.

3:4　*With* my voice I called unto Adonai,
and He answered me out of His holy mountain.
(Lift this up and weigh it carefully.[10])

——Psalms 3:4-3:6; 18:6; 18:16

When the ambulance came, the EMT was very young, and
he looked too young to have a driver's license (much less an
Emergency Medical Technician's certificate). And he began to
argue, saying that the little child was not sick, but had a food
allergy, probably to peanuts: And while the young man argued, with
his back to my dying son, Abram's skin began to change colors, his
veins deep purplish black, and the skin of his face reddish purple:
And he was upon the hood of our car, on his little blanket, for the
convenience of the EMTs.

I yelled—perhaps in my haste more harshly than the
situation warranted—for him to get a tube into my baby son *NOW*,
and then I would explain in the ambulance *why* this sickness was *not*
a peanut allergy.[40] Then the boy turned to look at the baby, and
began to argue all over again, saying that Benaiah shouldn't have
put his fingers down the child's throat. And I yelled again, "***Put a
tube in the baby's throat—NOW!***"

237

And Benaiah had been trained as a paramedic, and lacked only the temperament for the job, and he knew well how to open the throat with his fingers: Without which his beloved son would have died, or suffered brain damage. And I marveled at the ignorance and youth of the young paramedic, and that these last four hours were like a curious nightmare from the depths of hell. I hadn't even given my own health a single thought at this point, nor did it occur to me that Ben might have been looking out for both of us when he sent me in the ambulance with Abram: I thought I'd already recovered from the biocide poisoning. I was just a frantic mother staying with my deathly ill child.

Meanwhile, Benaiah was alone with the children; exhausted, confused, amazed, and in shock; and I knew not that he also hadn't eaten that day, nor slept in eighteen days, and was probably in immediate danger of a diabetic coma, because of the shock of seeing our little son change in seconds from borderline healthy to dying.

In the ambulance, I watched while Abram's skin continued to change: His feet turned purplish black, and his fingers, and a big patch on his right arm, and upon his chest, and his left earlobe. And in the hospital I stood beside the stretcher, upon which lay my beloved baby boy, limp and pale, his feet black and rotting before my eyes; and now he also had purple spots on his black feet. And I almost fell to the floor.

And while a nurse brought a chair to put under me, she said, "Look—she has spots too!"

After three or four hours of x-rays and observation, the doctors in Newberg declared that they didn't have the technology for this disease, which they called "meningococcus." And they sent Abram Jedidiah Ammi in an ambulance to Portland, to Legacy Emanuel Hospital, without his mother: Because the EMTs had only brought one ambulance, and said that because of my sickness they didn't want to endanger the child with my presence: Because if I also suddenly started dying, the EMTS would be distracted from the care of my little son.

And I knew not that the journey to Legacy Emanuel was three hours or more, nor did I think to doubt the wisdom of the doctors: Because I did not know to say to them to send a helicopter[41] for Abram Jedidiah Ammi, and to bring me in the ambulance.

And they sent me with my sister and her husband in their Volkswagen camper; and I asked my brother-in-law to bring his nephews and nieces, and their father, to the hospital. But I later found out that my sister's husband had not even tried to bring any of them anywhere, nor passed on the news of our difficulties to anyone else. I also asked my twin sister to tell Manasseh and Benaiah that Elishevah, and possibly everyone in the house, had been exposed to meningococcus, a horrifyingly fast deadly disease, and to bring everyone to the hospital *NOW*. But I later found out that she had communicated nothing to either of them about haste, or contagion, or about mortal danger, and that Benaiah—already in shock and in immediate danger of a diabetic coma—thought that his batty sister-in-law had said that Elishevah had mononucleosis.

After three hours in the Volkswagen camper, my sister's husband dropped me off in front of the hospital door without a word to the doctors to ask about their dying nephew, neither did either one of them get out of the camper, neither did they watch to see whether I went in or collapsed on the pavement.

And the nightmare continued.

And in the hospital, I asked about Abram Jedidiah Ammi, and I asked to see my little son: And they said that his condition was serious, but stable (it actually wasn't stable at all), and my little son was in an induced coma. And they put me in a room alone. And doctors, with many medical students, came to stare, and to speak in low voices.

I asked repeatedly for someone to call my family and to tell my aunt Rachel to take her nephews and nieces to the hospital: Because my wrists and my hands were completely useless, and swollen to almost double their normal size. And a nurse gave me the telephone, but couldn't be bothered to dial the number; and she explained grumbling that this was a waste of her time, because they had already told my family all these things. But I later found that nobody in my family had heard anything, except what I said to them with my own lips, part of which was gibberish.

And five times I said to the nurses that Benaiah was diabetic, and that he would probably be almost passed out when he came, because of his diabetes: And two of those times the nurses said yes; and in the fifth time, the nurse rebuked me, saying that this was an insult, to tell them how to do their job, when they already knew to test his blood sugar. But nobody ever checked his blood sugar; but rather they appear to have assumed that Benaiah was delirious with Meningococcus, although he had no other symptoms of anything but severe emotional shock and exhaustion, except for the usual early warning signs[42] of a diabetic coma. Hour after hour, I asked whether my family had arrived at the hospital, and asked them again and again to call my aunt Rachel to send my children and my husband to the hospital. And every time the nurses insisted that my family already knew, and would be there soon.

But no: Nobody in Newberg Providence Hospital, nor the ambulance drivers, nor my sister and her husband, nor the hospital in Portland, nobody except myself ever said anything to my family (except that my twin sister did tell Benaiah that our baby son was very sick, which he already knew).

And finally I sensed that my family was there: And also that every demon in the building had immediately swarmed together in the same place where Benaiah was: Eight demons: So that every other part of the hospital was suddenly spiritually clean. And so I asked again about my family: But now there was no reply but frowns. And soon afterward they put me in the intensive care ward, where there were no telephones. And I saw that it was already night. And I asked a nurse to use her cell phone, after I had seen her talking on it to her family: But the nurse said with a frown that it was against regulations[43] for any patient in intensive care to talk on a telephone.

And police officers came, from Portland, and Newberg, and Washington County, and Yamhill County, and from Oregon, and a very stupid social worker, to interrogate me while I was still delirious with hallucinations: And I asked why I could not speak to my aunt Rachel or my husband, but even so they *had* brought in this crazy woman to talk to me. And they said that the law did not allow them to deny her access to anyone.[44]

Then, after almost a day, they put me in the adult ward: And more police officers came, health officers of Washington County, and health officers of Oregon, to ask about our sickness. And they said to me that it's not possible to catch Meningococcus from animals, or from contaminated objects, because the bacteria needed uniquely[45] human proteins—two, to be precise.

Still I asked whether it is possible for mice to be carriers, because we had found a mouse nest just before our flu. But they said no: Only humans are able to be Meningococcus carriers. And I asked what the incubation period is; and they said, less than twenty-four hours before death. And I asked whether this sickness was able to appear like swine flu for three weeks: And they said No: Because the victims die in the first or second day.

Then I asked whether it is possible to get the bacteria from a garden hose (Three times I asked this): And three times they said no: Because the city water travels more than five hours to come to our garden hose, and the bacteria can only live less than five minutes outside of a human being. So I asked, "And what if someone puts the sickness directly into our hose, less than five minutes before I put the water in my garden?" But they began to get angry, and never answered the question, but said rather that I had lied to protect the carrier. This was while I was still in shock day and night because of the death of my beloved son's legs, and still delirious half the time.

Then the crazy social worker came again, and asked more weird questions, many of them about Messianic Judaism.

And I used nearly all my strength to speak and sing to my comatose son, in the pediatric intensive care unit; and to read to him from the Holy Bible.

And a nurse rebuked me, and forbade me to read any scriptural passages which she called "negative:" Because I had read with the Holy Spirit's guidance from the book of Isaiah to Abram Jedidiah Ammi, in a very "negative" passage: And I sensed Abram's spirit while I read, and at first I sensed deep affliction in his soul; but, with the words of the prophet, I sensed peace, and an assurance in his little heart that I knew his affliction, even though he wasn't able to cry out in his coma. I obeyed, even though the nurse was wrong, and also well outside her authority to command me which of the Scriptures I could read to my Jewish son, to comfort him in his isolation and pain.

And I also visited the other children in the pediatric ward: And I saw that Manasseh was healthy, and strong, and an excellent foster father to his little brothers and sisters; and that neither Manasseh nor Esther had ever caught the Meningococcus. But I was more often with Abram Jedidiah Ammi, because the doctors did not allow him to be visited by any of his brothers or sisters.

But the nightmare continued: Because Benaiah was now missing, and nobody said where; but rather, moreover, the nurses asked *me* where—As if *I* could know; when they were the last people to see him alive!

Psalm

142:1    *With* my voice I cried out unto Adonai;
       *with* my voice unto Adonai I did make my supplication.

2    I poured out my prayer before His face;
       I declared before His face my affliction.

3    When my spirit fainted against me, You knew my path.
       In a way wherein I walked, they have hidden a snare for me.

4    Look to *the* right *hand* and see:
       There is none *who* would recognize me:
       Refuge failed me; there is none *who* asks about my soul.

18:3    I will call upon Adonai, who is *worthy* to be praised,
       and I will be saved from my haters.

4    *The* bonds of death compassed me,
       and *the* floods of futile *men* made me afraid.

124:2    If it had not been Adonai who was on our side,
       when men rose up against us:

3    Then they had swallowed us up alive,
       when their wrath was kindled against us:

4    Then the waters would have overwhelmed us,
       the stream would have swept over our soul;

5    Then the proud waters would have gone over our soul.

6    Blessed *be* Adonai,
       who has not given us *for a* prey to their teeth.

7    Our soul *is* escaped like *a* bird out of *the* snare *of the* fowlers: the snare *is* broken, and we *are* escaped.

Psalm

124:8  Our help *is* in *the* name *of* Adonai,
maker *of the* heavens and earth.

37:18  Adonai knows *the* days *of the* complete *ones*:
and their inheritance shall be forever.

19  They *shall* not *be* ashamed in *the* evil time,
and in *the* days of famine they *shall be* satisfied,
20  because *the* wicked will perish; and *the* haters of Adonai
*shall be* like *the* precious lambs: they *will* vanish;
into smoke they *will* vanish *away*.

14  *The* wicked have drawn out *the* sword,
and they have guided their bow, to cast down
*the* poor and needy, to slay *the* upright of conduct.
15  Their sword will enter into their *own* heart,
and their bows shall be broken.
16  Better *is the* little that *a* righteous *man* has,
than *the* riches *of* many wicked:
17  Because *the* arms *of the* wicked shall be broken;
and Adonai upholds *the* righteous.

18:6  In my distress I called upon Adonai, and I cried
unto my God: From His temple He heard my voice deeply,[9]
and my cry came before His face, *even* into His ears.

3:4  *With* my voice I called unto Adonai,
and He answered me out of His holy mountain.
(Lift this up and weigh it carefully.[10])

——Selections from Psalms 3, 18, 37, 124, and 142

Hide me from *the* secret council *of the* wicked,
From *the* rage of *the* workers of iniquity…

—Psalm 64:2

CHAPTER THIRTY-NINE:
# Blind

A hospital is like a small city, in which the physicians are both the kings and the priests, with total authority: And like any other city, a hospital has both generous and greedy people, prudent and foolish people, Christians and pagans, competent and inept people, righteous and wicked: All who choose to put their trust in any hospital are choosing to trust all of these.

On the fourth of July, two thousand nine, we gave my precious little son into the hands of a brave, valiant, just, competent, skillful, and caring surgeon named Nick Eshraghi, a man of God, guided by the Holy Spirit. Great is our gratitude to God for this man, this excellent surgeon. But, in order to give our precious Abram Jedidiah Ammi into Nick Eshraghi's hands, we also had to choose all the other paramedics, and nurses, and doctors, and the entire multitude of Legacy Emanuel Hospital.

Benaiah gave his precious little daughter Esther Sarah Hadiyah, and his dear son Manasseh Raphael, into the hands of our enemies; although these two children were both healthy and strong; neither had they any need of a physician; in order to save our precious little daughter Elishevah Yael and our dear son Mattithias Lazarus from the talons of a horrifying carnivorous disease called Meningococcus, which ate the feet of our precious, loving, and pure hearted Abram Jedidiah Ammi; and also Benaiah chose to send his beloved wife to our enemies, and he also came to them himself.

But the deputy medical examiner, the man of hatred, knew which hospital our family had come into (because only the Oregon Burn Unit at Legacy Emanuel Hospital had the best capacity to treat Abram's wounds, which were like burns): And so this police officer—filled with hatred—already had all his friends in the hospital waiting for our family, to steal and to kill and to destroy.

But the hand of the Lord was with His beloved little children, to save his servants Benaiah, and Manasseh, and myself from death, and also to save our babies Esther Sarah Hadiyah and Abram Jedidiah Ammi, to frustrate the plans of the Enemy, and to turn away backwards and put to shame those who sought our lives.

And I saw another man different from the surgeon Nick Eshraghi: This man Daniel Leonhardt, MD, was not a man of God, but rather full of lust for wealth and power. And I saw his eyes upon our little children, and our faithful son Manasseh Raphael, and I saw and felt the snares[46] which the deputy medical examiner and Leonhardt laid for our family (Although in truth these two were not my enemies: Because in truth they were no more than slaves of the Enemy). But without fear I say to the Lord of my soul, both then and now,

119:109 My soul *is* continually in *the* palm *of* my *hand*;
and I do not forget Your law.

110 *The* wicked laid *a* snare for me,
and I did not distort Your commandments.

111 I have inherited Your testimonies forever:
because they are *the* rejoicing *of* my heart.

——Psalm 119:109-119:111

My brother Reuben and his wife Cindra were the godparents of Abram Jedidiah Ammi since his birth (although they knew not, but only I, and Benaiah, and our son Manasseh); according as I saw in my vision[47] in nineteen eighty-seven of my children, which same vision I had never told to Reuben: Because I saw in nineteen eighty-seven a beloved youth, a son of my brother Reuben; and also at the same time not his son: And I understood this not until I saw our new little son, my beloved Abram Jedidiah Ammi.

(And because I was only eleven years old, in my innocence I asked the adults nearby—pagans all—how this was possible, that the youth should be my brother's son, and at the same time not his son: And they began to speak shamefully against my future sister-in-law Cindra, with disrespectful slanders; and then they began to blaspheme the Holy Spirit. And I was ashamed because my words to those pagans had caused them to slander and to blaspheme.)

Because of this dream, therefore, both I and Benaiah knew that it is God's will that my brother Reuben adopt Abram Ammi for his own son: But this knowledge grieved us greatly: Neither, therefore, said we any word of these things to the Goldensteins, because Benaiah said, "If this is from the Lord, we don't need to tell them, because it is the will of our all-powerful God."

Therefore, in accordance with the vision, in the evening of the fourth of July and the beginning of the fifth of July; my brother Reuben asked to adopt his nephew Abram Jedidiah Ammi, because my sister-in-law Cindra was only able to have one living baby, my nephew Noah Ezra Goldenstein, with much medical help, and she miscarried all the others; and because Abram Jedidiah Ammi is almost the same age as his cousin Noah; and also because Reuben knew that the child would need many surgeries, and that my family was too poor to bear his medical expenses.

Therefore, when Reuben called, I already knew that Benaiah's will and the Lord's will were with me to say "Yes."

But, in the evening of the next day, at four thirty in the evening, a person ran to my bed furtively, and secretly warned me never to say who told me, but that the state of Oregon has seized custody of my children secretly, and (illegally) commanded all the nurses not to tell me until the twenty-four hour hearing, so that I would be unable to obtain an attorney to reveal the truth: And this person said that the twenty-four hour hearing was the next morning: I only had fifteen more hours, and only half an hour before the end of the business day. And the hospital had made the telephone unable to call McMinnville, where the jurisdiction was.

1 Hear deeply,[9] O God, my voice in my prayer;
 keep my life from terror of the hater.[48]

2 Hide me from *the* secret council *of the* wicked,
 From *the* rage of *the* workers of iniquity,

3 Who sharpen their tongue like *a* sword.
 *They* guide their arrow, *even a* bitter word,

4 To shoot in secret *at a* complete *one*:
 Suddenly they shoot at him, and they do not fear.

5  They strengthen themselves *in an* evil *matter*:
   they write to hide snares, saying, Who will see them?
6  They search for iniquities; they perfect *the* concealing
   and searching out *of a* hidden *snare*:
   And *the* inward *thought* of *every* man and heart *is* deep.
7  Yet God will shoot an arrow at them;
   their wounds will be sudden.
8  And they will fall: their *own* tongue *will be* against them:
   all *who* see them will flee *away*.
9  And every man shall fear, and they *will* declare *the* work
   *of* God; And in wisdom they will understand of His doing.
10 *The* righteous will be glad in Adonai, and will trust in Him;
   and all *the* upright in heart will praise.

——Psalm 64

And after the hearing, at the end of the day, while I was returning to my room, I began to suffer an autistic meltdown; and afterward, in my bed, I was hardly able to breathe, and I felt as if there was a great stone upon my chest; and I was dizzy, and very weak: and I began to go blind.

So I asked three different nurses for help, and told them my symptoms: Which they (and not I) knew to be the symptoms of a classic female heart attack. But the nurses asked, "What do you want us to do?" And I said, "I don't know: You are medical workers, not me: If you don't know what's going on, please call for a doctor." But no doctor ever came to help: Neither did anyone in the hospital say that this was a heart attack.

Then, before I saw that nobody would be coming to help, a male nurse came with a document of authorization, and asked me to sign the document quickly, saying that it was very important right away for insurance reasons that the hospital should have this document in their files. And he did not want me to read the papers first (And he made as if this were because he was in a hurry), but I insisted. And at that time I could still read, because my vision was only just beginning to fade away. And I saw that the papers were a permission document, saying that Legacy Emanuel Hospital had authority to kill me, if they should believe that I was like dead, or

that my quality of life is poor: And there was no place at all to sign
"No," but only "Yes;" and so I wrote in my own words on every
margin of the document, saying "No," "Never," and "No Way."

But when the male nurse hastily returned to immediately
take the document to the files, his face fell; and now, the nurse
didn't want to take or even touch these words, but rather he changed
his words completely to command me to keep the document in my
own bag. But I already knew well that no one wanted to touch that
bag, for fear of the carnivorous disease Meningococcus which had
eaten Abram's feet.

So, I called two friends on the telephone, to tell of these
things, and that in no way, no never, would I want this wickedness,
to slay me like Terri Schaivo.[49]

Then night came, and I could not call any more friends
because everyone was in bed. And my custom every night had been
to read the Holy Bible, but now I was blind: And so I called for a
chaplain: And she read to me from the Holy Bible until I was able to
breathe easily, and to read large print. Then she rose up to leave,
saying that others also needed her help: And I saw with surprise that
she had read to me all night, and now the sun was shining in the
window. And she opened up a large print Bible, and told me that I
should read Psalm 121:

1      I will lift up mine eyes unto the hills;
       where does my help come from?
2      My help *comes* from Adonai,
       maker *of the* heavens and earth.
3      He will not give your foot *to* slip:
       He who guards you will not doze off.
4      Behold, He who guards Israel
       will not doze off and will not sleep.

—Psalm 121:1-121:4

But the Lord of my soul covered the pages with shadow, so
that I was still unable to read His words: And again I became more
and more blind, without the chaplain there to read. So I prayed,
asking to live and to see, so that I could read His holy words; and I
was ready to swear an oath to read the Holy Bible every day for all

my life. But the Holy Spirit put it in my heart to remember that many men have sworn many things great and small to the Lord in the day of trouble, and forgotten their vows: And the Spirit said, "Take heed[50] that you swear no false oath to your God."

His warning pierced my soul, so that I opened my mouth and gasped with anguish, because I was not able to cry out: And I begged the Lord not to give me my sight, except only to restore my sight day by day, only when I read His holy words, and to take away my sight day by day, if I forget and begin to depart from my vow. Immediately I was able to see, but the hand of the Lord still covered the page of Psalm 121 with a shadow, so that I couldn't read: But the other page, Psalm 120, was shining brightly:

1    In my distress I cried unto Adonai, and He answered me.
2    *O* Adonai, deliver my soul from lying lips,
     *and* from *a* deceitful tongue.
3    What will *He* give to you, and what will *He* add
     unto you, *o* deceitful tongue?
4    Sharp arrows of *a* mighty *one*, with burning *coals* of juniper.
5    Woe unto me, because I sojourn in Meshekh,
     *and* dwell among *the* tents of Kedar!
6    My soul has long dwelt with *a* hater *of* peace.
7    I *am for* peace: and because I speak, they *are for* war.

—Psalm 120

And until this day, my God has given me sight day by day, every day in which I am faithful to keep my vow. I have no words for the enormous difference between my gratitude toward my God, and the gratitude of which He is truly worthy.

How easily I turn toward the darkness, and see only my own pain, and not the multitude nor the greatness of the endless blessings that my precious Creator and Savior has poured out into my life, and the lives of my children! There is no way to describe the depth of my pain to anyone who has never experienced such a tragedy in their own home, but by the hand of the Almighty God, we all survived.

I could easily have survived this tragedy with no other family than my Father God and my Brother Yeshua, but even this would have been a greater blessing than I could ever in my life deserve. Benaiah could easily have survived this rare and hideous disease alone, utterly bereaved of his wife and children, or our six children could easily have survived this disease as orphans, but instead by Adonai's grace they can hope to get their parents back someday.

Blessed be Adonai the God of Israel, who has given me what I asked of Him: And with His own loving hand He has taken away from me my sight day by day, every day in which I have begun to depart from the Holy Bible, to keep with His handmaiden my vow to my beloved *Abba.*

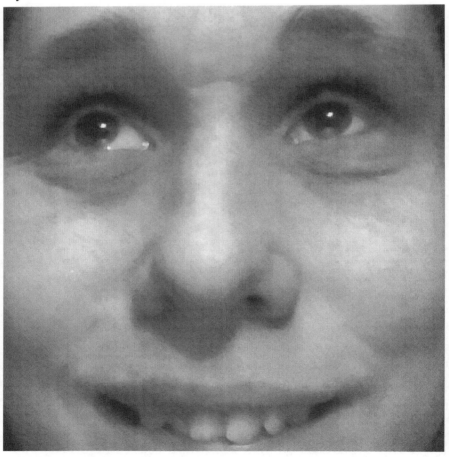

16 Better *is the* little that *a* righteous *man* has,
than *the* riches *of* many wicked:
17 Because *the* arms *of the* wicked shall be broken;
and Adonai upholds *the* righteous.
18  Adonai knows *the* days *of the* complete *ones*:
and their inheritance shall be forever.

—Psalm 37:16-37:18

CHAPTER FORTY:
# The Ivy and the Tree

To kidnap a little child is not only to drive a dagger into the hearts of the child and his parents, but also into the tender hearts of his grandmothers and grandfathers, a terribly cold iron dagger. When I left the hospital, my skin was dark like an Arab because of the toxic antibiotics which blackened my blood (for a full week beyond what was medically indicated, to facilitate with fraud[51] the theft of my small ones); and I kneeled at the feet of a loving grandma, who also had a cold dagger penetrating into her tender soul.

Already there was a wound on this soul, with the sudden death of her dear grandson Abram's feet, and with fear for his life, and the lives of three other precious grandchildren. And now, on top of all this horrible anguish, was the torture and confusion of betrayal: The kidnapper is her beloved America, the United States of America, her beautiful nation; our homeland of freedom of religion and conscience and expression; the homeland of the Constitution of the United States of America: Moreover, one of the reasons why this crime was possible is because this loving grandmother had begged and pleaded with us not to bring her precious grandchildren away from that Homeland of Freedom, away from the safety and security of the Constitution of the United States of America.

With patriotic passion like the passion of a girl in love, this grandmother had taught her grandchildren with me her own love for the nation that stands for liberty; and I also had taught them to understand and to cherish the Bill of Rights; the first ten amendments to the Constitution, the heartbeat of our homeland.

Manasseh, Elishevah, and also Mattithias already knew the First Amendment by heart, which is a sacred law for every faithful American.

## ARTICLE [I]

Congress shall make no law respecting an establishment of religion, or prohibiting the free exercise thereof; or abridging the freedom of speech, or of the press; or the right of the people peaceably to assemble, and to petition the Government for a redress of grievances.

And now, What? Are there any words in any language of the earth, with which I could now persuade Manasseh, or myself, to believe that the First Amendment, the heart of the heartbeat of our nation, is still alive? Because not only my family was destroyed, but many other families also, and no one stirs a wing, nor opens a mouth to peep, while hundreds of our precious little sons and daughters are stolen like eggs from the nests of the poor, the unapproved religions, the disabled, and the political activists; for hatred and for greed our little children are taken like eggs from the nest, And for a bribe![46]

What, then, What to say to my heart, or to the broken heart of this beautiful grandmother, my precious mother of my husband?

She was my friend, and she is my sister in Messiah Yeshua, but now she can't even bear to look at my face, for the horribly painful knowledge that my Messianic Judaism, my faithfulness to the Torah, is the reason for the iron dagger in her caring soul. And now, What? Because I have chosen to love the Torah above all, the Word of God written for us, and also the Word of God made flesh for us, which is Messiah Yeshua my king, to obey Him not only unto death, but also unto the piercing with cold iron of the hearts not only of Manasseh, and Elishevah, and Mattithias, and Yehudah Isaiah, And Abram Jedidiah Ammi, and Esther Sarah Hadiyah, but also the hearts of everyone of us who love them. And now, when I say to my precious mother of my husband, "I love you," she says to me, "I don't think that you *know* what love *is*."

But while this beautiful little grandmother was still able to receive[52] my love, I kneeled at her feet, to serve and to comfort her; although I did not have much strength because of the poisonous antibiotics in my blood.

At that time my blood was black, and I had a fever, and only enough strength to serve her two or three hours in a day, and to have only four hours of Bible study, and to force myself to eat: Because every food tasted like sawdust, and every meat had a metallic flavor, and like a rotting carcass: And I lost more than twenty pounds; and, although Benaiah says I looked like a gorgeous model, I felt that I looked like a walking skeleton. And from the sixth of July onward, I was more and more epileptic.

And one day in July or August, I was working in this grandmother's garden to separate a little tree from an English Ivy plant, a beautiful herbivorous weed: Which in her innocence this grandmother had thought harmless and lovely, a good companion to her tree, but the tree was almost dead of starvation. And she said to me, not to harm her ivy if it was possible to save both plants: But I saw that the English Ivy's roots were surrounding the root of the little tree: Their appearance was like two arms with hands, and one little root for every finger: Ten small roots, fingers and thumbs, unto the root of the tree: And it was impossible to separate them, except I break both arms.

So then I told these things to my husband's mother; and this grandmother said, "Break them, then, so that you don't hurt the tree: But don't break it any more than you have to, to separate them, and then please plant the broken ivy." But after I had shown her all the harm which English Ivy does, eating whole forests, every plant and tree, she said not to save her ivy.

When I went back into the house, both she and Benaiah were studying the Bible; and I washed my hands and joined my husband on the sofa. And I was ready to tell them about the roots like two arms, complete with hands and thumbs and fingers, but this grandmother said, "No: But we need to first read Scripture, and then talk." And the word was the thirty-seventh Psalm:

Psalm

37:1  Do not burn *with rage* because of evildoers;
do not be envious against *the* workers of iniquity.

2  Because like grass they will soon be cut,
and wither like green grass.

3  Trust in Adonai, and do good: dwell *in the* land,
and be fed *the* truth,

4  and delight yourself in Adonai,
and He will give you the requests of your heart.

5  Turn your way unto Adonai,
and trust in Him, and He will do *it*;

6  and He will bring forth your righteousness
like *the* light, and your justice like *the* noonday.

7  Be quiet before Adonai, and suffer for Him.
Do not burn *with rage* at *a* prosperous *one in* his way,
at *a* man who does wickedly.

8  Forsake anger, and forsake fury:
do not also burn *with rage* to *do* evil.

9  Because evildoers shall be cut off:
but those who wait *for* Adonai, they will inherit *the* earth.

10  And for yet a little *while*, and there will be no wicked *one*;
and you will consider his place, and he will not be *there*.

11  And *the* humble will inherit *the* earth,
and will delight themselves in *the* abundance *of* peace.

12  *The* wicked plots against *the* righteous,
and his teeth grind against him.

13  Adonai[53] will laugh at him:
because He sees that His day is coming.

14  *The* wicked have drawn out *the* sword,
and they have guided their bow, to cast down
*the* poor and needy, to slay *the* upright of conduct.

15  Their sword will enter into their *own* heart,
and their bows shall be broken.

16  Better *is the* little that *a* righteous *man* has,
than *the* riches *of* many wicked:

Psalm

| | |
|---|---|
| 37:17 | Because *the* arms *of the* wicked shall be broken; and Adonai upholds *the* righteous. |

37:17  Because *the* arms *of the* wicked shall be broken;
and Adonai upholds *the* righteous.

18  Adonai knows *the* days *of the* complete *ones*:
and their inheritance shall be forever.

19  They *shall* not *be* ashamed in *the* evil time,
and in *the* days of famine they *shall be* satisfied,

20  because *the* wicked will perish;
and *the* haters of Adonai *shall be* like *the* precious lambs:
they *will* vanish; into smoke they *will* vanish *away*.

21  *The* wicked borrows, and does not fulfill;
and *the* Righteous *One is* merciful and generous;

22  because His blessed *ones* will inherit *the* earth;
and His cursed *ones* shall be cut off.

23  *The* steps of a strong *man are* ordered by Adonai:
and He delights in his way.

24  *A strong man* will not be cast down because he falls:
because Adonai upholds his hand.

25  I have been young, moreover I am old;
and I have not seen *a* righteous *one* forsaken
and his descendants begging *for* bread.

26  All the day *long* he *is* merciful, and *he* lends;
and his descendants *are* for *a* blessing.

27  Depart from evil, and do good, and live forever.

28  Because Adonai loves justice, and does not forsake
His merciful *ones*: they are guarded forever.
Yet *the* wicked descendants will be cut off.

29  *The* righteous *ones* will inherit *the* earth,
and live upon it forever.

30  *The* mouth *of the* righteous whispers wisdom,
and his tongue will speak *of* justice.

31  *The* law *of* his God *is* in his heart: his steps will not slip.

32  *The* wicked spies on *a* righteous *one*, and seeks to kill him.

33  Adonai will not leave them in his hand,
and will not condemn them in his judgment.

34  Wait *for* Adonai, and keep His way,
and He will exalt you to inherit *the* earth:
in the cutting off of the wicked, you will see.

35  I have seen *the* wicked terrifying, and making *the land* bare
    like *a* flourishing bay *tree.*
36  And he passed away, and behold, he was not *there:*
    and I sought him, and he was not found.
37  Watch *a* complete *man,* and look at *an* upright *one:*
    because *the* end of *that* man is peace.
38  And *the* rebels will be destroyed together:
    *the* end of *the* wicked is cut off.
39  And *the* salvation of *the* righteous *ones is* from Adonai,
    from their strength in *the* time of distress.
40  And Adonai will help them, and deliver them:
    He will deliver them from *the* wicked, and save them,
    because they trust in Him.

—Psalm 37

*Thelma Elizabeth Cooper*
*daughter of Henry Edward Cooper*
*and future mother of Benaiah*

But the Comforter,[54] *which is* the Holy Spirit,
whom the Father will send in my name,
the same will teach you all *things* …

—John 14:26

# CHAPTER FORTY-ONE:

# Little Samson

Mattithias has always been the sort of child who demands excellence, perfection even, both of himself and of his family, and he was also physically quite strong from the very beginning, holding his head up for several minutes on the same day he was born.

Unfortunately, he had also inherited his paternal grandmother's emotional instability, with very swift mood swings from completely relaxed and happy to utterly miserable, without any apparent cause, as sudden as a lightning bolt from the clear blue sky.

And, just like his paternal grandmother, his sudden moods would sometimes be violent. But both of their moods could be kept in check simply by making sure that they both got plenty of hugs, so I learned real quick to always put Matt in Grandma's lap and try to keep him there as often as we visited her; and several times a day I would also remind Manasseh, Elishevah and Yehudah to hug their brother Matt so he wouldn't get sad or angry or depressed. And this worked quite well—usually. But we all learned never to let him get hold of any pencils, knives, pens, or any other kind of pointed sticks. Most of the time, though, Matt has always been a very passionate, caring, intelligent, creative, and loyal brother and son; and, spiritually speaking, even a spiritual father both to his parents and also to his brothers and sisters.

His childhood nickname was Little Samson, and we also called him Mackerel, because when he was three he couldn't say "Matt" yet, so he kept calling himself "Mack," and so we would joke that Mack was short for Mackerel. (We had such silly nicknames for every child.)

Mattithias has always been a very respectful, polite little guy (except on the rare but very memorable occasions when his sudden anger spells would get the best of him), and he always tried to excel at whatever his hands found to do. And so he was a very good student, quickly showing himself intelligent and talented in just about every subject I taught him. But he never showed any interest in botany. He didn't learn much music, either, because Benaiah couldn't trust such a moody boy to stay calm and gentle while holding the guitar, and we wouldn't have been able to afford a new one if Matt suddenly got mad and smashed it. But Mattithias did advance quickly in the few music lessons he had.

There were only two reasons Mattithias ever lost his temper: He could never accept imperfection in his own artwork, and he could never tolerate anyone disrespecting anyone he loved. So we learned to try every day to be respectful of one another, and we also all got just a little bit nervous whenever he decided to do an art project. But Ben and I certainly didn't want to let anything stifle his creative genius, so we were both always lecturing him at the beginning of every art project to try to be tolerant of imperfection, because no artist can ever create their perfect masterpiece.

Elishevah Yael disagreed with this approach: She never put much faith in her brother's ability to learn self-control: She absolutely never approved of letting Matt start an art project in the first place.

Moreover, whenever she saw Matt start to get excited about any new creation, Elishevah very conspicuously went as far away

258

from her moody little brother as the length of the house would conveniently permit.

But, most of the time, Matt and Elishevah did just about everything together. They were best friends from the very start,

and from the very second Elishevah first met that baby boy, she was as doting a big sister as any child could ask for. And sometimes folks would ask me if they were twins, because—until Elishevah's body began to change—they looked so much alike, and were nearly the same size, despite being about two years apart in age.

Mattithias Lazarus was always obedient, loyal, and brave, an excellent son, really, except that absolutely nothing could persuade him to eat his onions, either raw or cooked. I don't know what Mattithias had against onions, but I do know that he has most certainly been a most stubborn young man from the very day he was born, and so I was rather inclined to spoil the child a little bit, and cater to his food preferences rather than let him get as skinny as a willow.

And there were also some curious problems with having such a strong little boy: For example, Mattithias once decided to rip the bathroom door off its hinges when he was four years old.

Moreover, it took the both of us working together to change his diaper whenever Matt decided he didn't want to wear one—and, being a very clean and proper little fellow who disapproved entirely of having to touch anything sticky or slimy, Mattithias most certainly *never* wanted to wear a diaper. But this proved a very effective motive to cause Matt to potty-train himself at an uncommonly young age. And there were some of my relatives who said I was potty training the boy too young, but in truth I never did potty train Matt at all, because he had already trained himself before I was even done potty training his elder sister.

And I knew from the beginning that Matt would be a bit different from his siblings, because the voice of the Holy Spirit had commanded me, before I even knew I was pregnant with Mattithias, that the child in my womb should be a Nazarite from birth like Samson, as is written in Judges 13:1-13:24; and in Numbers 6:2-6:21. But in our last year together, Mattithias was often wondering why this was so, and why he should be set apart as a Nazarite when his brothers and sisters were not, and I could never give an answer, except that this was the Holy Spirit's command, and that he would have to keep the vow, at least until he became a *Bar Mitzvah*[55] in the summer of two thousand thirteen.

There were also days when Mattithias was glad to be a Nazarite, and said that he would probably keep the vow, but at other times he would say that he intended to end the vow on his thirteenth birthday, and we made plans together to donate his long beautiful hair (which had never been cut) to Locks For Love, which is a charity that makes donated hair into wigs for bald children.

For nearly ten years Mattithias was set apart to God, from his earliest days within my womb, until he fell into the hands of a government that knows no god but Money.

But in the year two thousand ten, a proud judge commanded against these words of the Holy Spirit—because indeed it was the Holy Spirit, and not I, who had commanded that the hair of this young servant of Adonai should grow uncut: But in defiance of the Constitution of the United States of America, a proud judge dared to command against this Law of the King of kings and Lord of lords:

All *the* days of *the* vow *of* his separation no razor shall pass over his head: until the days are fulfilled which he has separated unto Adonai, he shall be holy; *he* shall grow *the* exposed hair *of* his head.

—Numbers 6:5

And the hearing was not for this matter, neither was any warning given. And when my court-appointed attorney asked a second judge to re-establish justice according to the Constitution, the second judge neither restored justice, nor answered a word to the matter. Nor did the judge answer a word when my court-appointed attorney asked that Mattithias sweep up his sacred locks, and take the hair of his sacred locks and offer them for an offering to Adonai; nor when my attorney asked that one of the kidnappers should not throw the sacred locks in the trash, did the judge seem to even care that it is written in God's holy word:

13  And this *is the* law of the Nazarite, in *the* day *when the* days of his separation *are* fulfilled…

18  … And *at the* opening *of the* tent of *the* congregation the Nazarite shall shave *the* head *of* his separation, and shall take *the* hair *of the* head *of* his separation, and give *it* upon the fire which *is* under *the* sacrifices *of* peace offerings.[56]

—Numbers 6:13, 6:18

We had no way to speak to Mattithias about any of this because, after I had secured an order commanding the state of Oregon to allow our Jewish children to keep the Passover as commanded in the Bible, the caseworker had immediately cut off all of our visits with the children: And since that Passover unto this day, my children have not been allowed to even see our faces.

In those sad days our three oldest children were approaching the age of seeking marriages, guided only by strangers not of our faith, and who had shown themselves hostile to our faith: And in our little book *Burning Coals*, we wrote this letter to Mattithias:

# The Book of Mattithias

by Benaiah and Naomi Levell
(An excerpt from *Burning Coals*)

Woe *unto* the legislators *of* idolatrous[57] decrees, and writers *who* prescribe labor;[58] to turn aside *the* poor from judgment, and to rob justice *from the* afflicted *of* my people, so that widows may be their prey; and they plunder orphans!

—Isaiah 10:1-10:2

Mattithias, my beloved son, unrighteous decrees may have robbed you of your earthly father, but not your father's love nor the words of your heavenly father. Here are some of God's words, followed by a ghost story:

> Woe *unto one who* causes[59] his neighbor to drink! *Woe unto you,* who join your wineskin *to them,* and also make *them* drunken, that you may look upon their nakedness!

> —Habakkuk 2:15

Mattithias, my son, many educators make us drunken with their seductive lovely lies about sexuality.... Once there was a teenage boy who felt lonely because his parents were not there for him. An educator told him to get some lovers to ease his loneliness. So he did. Because he was a good-looking vibrant youth it was easy for him to find a couple of teenage girls to be intimate with. He lost himself in their sexy voices, their sensuous eyes, their curvaceous shapes, and their voluptuous movements. He went into their private rooms and closed the doors,[60] thinking no one else could see. But God saw everything. God knew their thoughts, their sensations, and their souls' trepidation.

Later on, this young man's buddy asked him, "How many girls did you 'do it' with?"

The young man replied, "Two." His buddy laughed and said, "I've been with dozens, more like *fifty*-two...You're slow!" he said, wagging his head.

The young man listened to other friends too. They said things like "Love the one you're with." "If you really love her, you'll share her." "Let her have freedom and don't be jealous." The young man took their advice, and soon he discovered that there were many sexy ways to have females. He started calling his females "chicks"[61] and talked with his buddies about all the creative ways to make love to all the willing females. There were blondes, brunettes, and redheads, all gorgeous and young and sexy, and some would even stay for a while. Night after pleasurable night, he kept himself and all his females from being lonely.

This young man was now respected by his buddies because

he had had dozens of sexual encounters like them—he felt smug and content. But soon things would change.

He noticed that after a few years of this "free love" lifestyle many of his romantic memories began to merge together. Then he caught a venereal disease and spread it to some of his "chicks." It was embarrassing to hunt for ladies he had set free to tell them that they were now sharing a venereal disease with their new lovers. These fornicating ladies didn't want to tell all their sex partners about their disease either, so it spread dangerously. Many of these ladies also got abortions and ruined their lives. They couldn't stay married; and many divorces occurred. Confusion and drugs and suicide began to occur among the young man's friends. And soon the young man was confused, drunken, and suicidal too. Maybe getting lovers to ease loneliness was not such a good idea.

He had learned to quickly spot a potential sex partner by sensing her amorous spirit. He would then let his animal instinct take over and let his romantic passion explode like a flood of welcome pleasures all over her spirit. This impassioned embracing of body and spirit seemed to heal both of their lonesome souls—but only for a few moments or only for a night. Like a full moon lights up the darkness for a time, their night was bright. But then the moon set and the stone cold darkness surrounded them once again.

Mattithias, this young man in his despair wanted to die;[62] but instead, he turned to God and became a born-again Christian. He repented of all his sins and, after ten years of growing in the knowledge and wisdom of God, he got married. His new wife was as glowing and lovely as a springtime flower garden. He wanted to make a beautiful family with her—children's innocence and a wonderful family at work and play seemed a future heavenly blessing.

One night, just the two of them, husband and wife, hand in hand, went into their bedroom and closed the door. The closing of the door reminded this now thirty-year-old man of something sinful[63] in his past. But he was a born-again Believer now, so he tried to forget his evil thought. He kissed his lovely Christian bride's virtuous lips. The kiss seemed sinfully familiar—it was just like a remembered one years ago. He tried to forget those years and those fornicating times. He focused now on his bride's lovely shape and her beautiful graceful movement. Her dark eyes were so sensuous. However, her eyes were like those he'd seen before.

He couldn't forget! "Maybe if I turn the light out," he thought. As he switched it out he heard his bride behind him say, "Come." Her voice was too sexy, too much like the ones he had heard before. "She doesn't deserve this inattention from me," he thought. "Because of my extra special deep love for her, and because I am a valiant groom and she is my one and only bride, I will do my best to make love to her like the impassioned animal I know I have in me. I gave this passion to all the other women in my past—This good woman, my wife, deserves even more. I, enthralled by her exquisite beauty; and she, enthralled by my experienced powerful *lovemaking*: we shall be one in sexual ecstasy."

He turned, intending to bestow all his soul's deep passion upon her. He froze in his steps. There, crowding his bride on her bed, were a dozen or more specters—Ghostly voluptuous figures of some of the very women he had been with, all earnestly waiting and yearning for him....

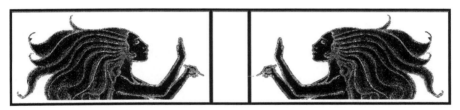

Mattithias, seek marriage soon. This is God's holy way. The world's unholy way is pleasure without purpose, avoiding marriage. Man makes himself sexy and lusts after many things unnatural. Seek a wife—*Seek a home*—Make a family! These are natural, having a good purpose. These are good, and full of many great and wonderful surprises. Remember, Mattithias, those unholy people around you are confused, ignorant, and sometimes desperate. Have compassion on them, pray for them, but don't take part in their foolish sex crimes. These crimes appear innocent to people who never grow up. They never understand that every one of their sexual memories will haunt their future wedding beds, and that each and every one of their love partners (real or imagined) will be an intimate, unwelcome specter chained forever between them and their holy spouse—fools, trapped with no escape!

265

Sexy ladies who shan't have babies
Handsome men who lust within
Fornicators, Educators
Encouraging our kids to sin
While throwing God's miracles out, they say:
"Evolution is here to stay!"
Eating to eat,
Sexy and gay
Shunning truth, they throw marriage away;
Shunning truth, they throw marriage away.

*—By Abba*

Just as food is purposed for health and lovemaking is purposed for making babies, so you and I are purposed for God. Be holy, my good son Mattithias; get married and have delightful fun with your wife and kids. But let the foolish educators and fornicators alone, except to have pity on them to save their trapped and tortured souls.

## The Moth in the Garden
By Imma

Beloved Mattithias, there was a tiny creature I once held in my right hand, which had astonishingly delicate, soft wings on her furry back. Her tissue-thin wings were a lovely design made of hundreds of tan and brown scales smaller than fine dust; and her slender feet tickled as they firmly grasped my skin; and her graceful antennae waved thoughtfully as she gently explored the open palm of my hand. You were still a very small boy on this day, Mattithias, so I do not know if you will remember watching her as she timidly meandered up my index finger to the very tip, spread out her dusty brown wings to gather the warm breeze, and then fluttered helplessly into our garden where we had found her. Once again, I gently scooped her up into my palm, taking care not to touch the scales of her wings. Death would find this creature long before the next morning's pale light, for she had already lived out her whole life, and finally laid one of her jewel-like eggs with great care on each of our newly sprouted apple seedlings.

She trembled in my hands, as if astonished to be conquered by such a mild breeze. Soon her pure, innocent spirit would fly free of its temporary delicate vessel; returning to where it had come from.

Beloved Mattithias, from the moment this innocent creature first mightily struggled free of her papery chrysalis, she never harmed any other living creature: She was never violent, destructive, or abusive in any way to anyone as she mastered the powerful winds in her search for a clean, healthy, tender-leaved garden for her unhatched children.

Son, we taught you to live by the Choctaw Way:[64] invasive of nothing, in harmony with the rest of Adonai's creation, a compassionate little king and not an intrusive tyrant over the earth. "Gently, gently…" Many times I have said the word "gently" as I taught you in the garden. Gently, you helped me nourish the soil with healthy, organic manure that would not harm the earth. Gently, you poked your shiny new apple seeds into the soil. Gently, you poured clean, shimmering water onto each seed. Gently, you welcomed each new apple sprout into this world with a prayer. Gently, you tugged out of the soil several invasive weeds which would have strangled your precious apple seedlings. Gently, we lifted each newborn tree from its seed bed and into a small pot.

And gently we examined one day this fragile, elderly moth, brushing not one scale from her aged wings; and gently we let her die in peace, shaded by the short grass in our little lawn.

Beloved Mattithias, the lovely brown flying creature we examined in our garden is called a Gypsy Moth, and her children are called Tent Caterpillars. She was completely harmless, but her children were very harmful for our tiny apple seedlings. So, even though she herself was completely harmless, this creature would probably have been destroyed if she had been found by *Wasíchu* gardeners.[65] It would have been cruel, though, to harm this dying creature, Mattithias, because she would never harm us. She only had a few minutes to live, and it would not have been kind of us to take those last few minutes away. It is not the Choctaw Way[64] to invade. Likewise, it is not Adonai's way to manipulate, interfere, or bother anyone with bossy rules that protect nobody. Because Fornication is a destructive moth in Adonai's human garden, His seemingly oppressive marriage laws are truly gentle and fair.

Beloved Mattithias, listen closely: Just as we were distracted together by a lovely little moth's delicate beauty, Fornication powerfully sidelines young men like you with fleeting earthly delights. Fornication and her children are intrusive and oppressive. And, like this lovely little moth in our garden, Fornication's delightful distraction is usually long gone when her children (Abortion, Divorce, and Venereal Disease) emerge unseen and begin to devour us, Adonai's human garden. Beloved Mattithias, Adonai intentionally chose to invent sexual pleasure as an important part of His children's holy, pure marriages. A kindhearted and wise Creator gave us many good pleasures, and He put within each of us a natural instinct to seek these good pleasures.

More than a baby's sigh, more than the taste of fresh, hot bread, we turn strongly to seek sexual pleasure. Every creature suddenly ignores every other sweet pleasure when it comes of age to find a mate. Eagle or turtle, squirrel or boy, frog or ladybug, every awkward teenager of every sexual species is suddenly distracted in a startling new way like nothing else has ever distracted anyone before.

God wants us to strongly want the good pleasures of marriage. He made the desire so strong because marriages are so important to Him: Good marriages build up good families, which in turn build up strong, fair and merciful nations pleasing to our Creator and loving lawgiver.

Mistaking the moth of Fornication for a harmless butterfly in their garden, many people ignorantly reject Adonai's marriage laws. These people do not understand that their Creator's loving laws of marriage protect us from Fornication and from her children; such as Abortion, Divorce, and Venereal Disease. Adonai's marriage laws seem oppressive to many people, who do not see any harm in Fornication's sweet pleasures.

Adonai never makes bossy or unfair laws. Our Creator is never oppressive either: His loving commandments are intended to rescue people from oppression.

All of Adonai's laws in the Torah, without exception, are

merciful and fair. Merciful, fair laws are a blessing, protecting the people from harm. Adonai's Torah is always fair; and obeying His Torah brings us pure pleasure without regrets.

# Self-Control
## By Abba

Hanging in space: that's what lack of control feels like. Nothing to hold to; nothing to grasp; no security ropes, wires or platforms connected to your body.

The other morning, I was almost late for an important appointment. All I had to do was brush my teeth, and I would be right on time. Brushing my teeth was quick and easy unless something went wrong. But what could go wrong? I had my red toothbrush in a perfect grasp in my right hand; and the tube of paste securely in my left. I'd done it countless times before. If I was proficient at anything, it was tooth brushing. Then it happened—my pride got the best of me, I was overconfident, and somehow my clean, well-held immaculate toothbrush mysteriously leapt out of my grip and, like a bullet, flew unabashedly down into the toilet. Splash! I watched it quickly sink to the bottom.

I glanced at the clock, hoping it was earlier than I thought. It wasn't. I could feel my anger rising inside. It was getting late, my breath stunk, and I had an open tube of perfectly good toothpaste in my left hand, waiting to squeeze toothpaste onto a brush that was now silently gloating at me like a brat at the bottom of a germ-infested toilet bowl. My temper flared, and in a surprise attack a foul word that I dread came from my lips. Now I had three things against me: I was late, I had stinky breath, and I had foul language. My face was now flushed with rage and embarrassment. My heart was throbbing and my breathing was labored—I was stressed. Four things were against me now: Late, Stinky, Foul, and Impatient. I had missed my appointment and was definitely not happy with myself. Which was worse—my corrupted toothbrush at the bottom of the toilet, or me: stressed, foul-mouthed, and impatient?

Because I love Adonai, I repented of the sins of that morning; and I asked Him in His Son's name to keep me from those kinds of sins. I felt like I was hanging in space and had nothing to hold onto. Then, Adonai showed me my death—the end of my life with no more opportunity to improve on my earthly experience. He showed me some others who were like me, yet who had already died. They were beyond and outside of their earthly existence forever. Even though they could not return here, they wished that they had done better during their earthly lives. In this way, God made me more serious.

I then worked hard and carefully on myself because I wanted to be a tool in Adonai's hand and useful to Him. Soon something else happened to send me out of control, but I seriously stayed calm; and although staying calm felt unnatural and harsh to me, Adonai rewarded me. He immediately gave me relaxation: Beautiful relaxation in the midst of a small disaster. I had the kind of peace and joy that passes all understanding. Later, on a different day, another small disaster occurred and I willed to stay calm again…nothing to hold onto, except love of God and wanting to be used of Him as a tool in His hand. Then Adonai rewarded me again. Time! Adonai gave me the gift of more time: By staying calm, my heart stayed healthier, my breathing stayed healthier, and my mind continued to think more clearly. So Adonai gave me relaxation and a longer life with a clear mind to continue my chosen work for Him and His Son in peace and tranquility.

Mattithias, getting serious about life, about marriage, about self-control, this is more important than it first appears.

Letting our emotions have the liberty to sway loosely will allow the pestilence of sin to swarm into our souls. Tighten your God-given self-control, Mattithias, to keep all those dirty, destructive sin-bugs out.

# The Faithful Mother

There was an Indian mother in a canoe with her child on a river; and the canoe capsized, and they both fell in the river, and were separated and swept downstream. The mother made it to shore, but she could not find her child. And the woman searched and wept and prayed for her child all day. Night came, and she continued to search and weep and pray. She was wet because she kept jumping back into the water to search, and she was getting very cold. But she would not stop searching, even though she was very hungry, tired, and cold, because she was afraid she would not be there to hear when her child cried for help.

A preacher came to the mother as she wandered shivering in the dark and said to her, "Think of what is true. Think of what is noble and right.[66]" And she said, "What is true is that my child fell in a river. What is noble is that God loves my child even more than I do, and that He will search for him. What is right is for me to stay warm and dry, so that I can stay alive to help my child." So the mother came to the campfire and dried herself.

At the campfire, a teacher came to her and said, "Think of what is pure and lovely and admirable.[66]" And the mother said, "What is pure is that I love my child. What is lovely is that God loves my child even more than I do. And what is admirable is that I also love all the other children in my village. So I shall eat, so that I will have strength to help my child, and also protect all the other children from falling into the river." So the mother ate some food, even though she had no appetite, and got some strength. But she still was not ready to return to the river, because she was exhausted; and a little blind for lack of sleep.

Then a prophetess came to the mother, and the prophetess said, "Think of what is virtuous, and excellent, and praiseworthy:[66] What is virtuous is for you to remain faithful to the LORD. What is excellent is for you to help all of the children, so that they may not fall in the river. And what is praiseworthy is that God will unite you and your child. Keep your thoughts on the Lord,[67] and sleep, that you may have the strength and vision to seek your child in the morning. Therefore get rest, so that you will be able to build bridges and watchtowers along the river so that the other children may not fall in as yours did; knowing that God loves all of these children more than you do." So the mother went to her bed and slept, trusting the LORD.

But some of the people said, "This proves that she does not care!"

But every day, throughout all her days, the mother worked to protect all of the children, and she became known throughout the land as a great person of God.

And one day when she was old, a young man walked up to her and gently took her by the hand, and said, "I am that child you lost in the river all those years ago. I am honored to have such a hero for my mother, and we shall never be parted again." And as they went on a long walk together, the son told her that her godly work to save children had inspired him to create a canoe that children couldn't tip over.

Love, *Abba and Imma*

Matthew Lazarus

P.S.    We thank you very, very much, our great artist Mattithias, for all your lovely and inventive treasures you have ever made for us. We would like to take them to heaven with us when we go. Please, with your great creative talent, invent an indestructible vessel for us to carry them in from earth to heaven—or, if you can't do that, just bring them within yourself.

The sky and the earth will pass away,
but my words will never pass away.

———Mark 13:31

# CHAPTER FORTY-TWO:

# Dust

In the first hearing, the date was set for the second hearing, and the judge heard many false, baseless accusations (which she called "facts"), but she did not accept one word from me, nor from our family, nor our friends: And neither I nor Benaiah had any attorney. Moreover, the judge refused to appoint any attorney for Benaiah for the second hearing without him being there: And still none of us knew where my husband was; or whether he had brain damage, or was kidnapped, or hallucinating, or dying.

And the judge thought nothing at all of the fact that all the accusations were against me and Benaiah; even though the godparents already had legal custody, and were therefore the correct defendants.

The judge heard that my brother Reuben and his wife Cindra were already the legal godparents and adoptive parents of Abram Jedidiah Ammi: But she still denied them custody of Abram, saying—falsely— that an oral contract is not legal and binding, and therefore our contract had been signed too late, because we had not signed the contract in writing until after the state had secretly taken custody.

But the truth is that an oral contract is in fact legal and binding in Oregon, and therefore that their custody of their new son was taken from them illegally: Because the state of Oregon had the wrong defendants, and the true defendants were Reuben and Cindra Goldenstein of Virginia. And even if the oral contract had not been legal, Lydia and Scooter Phillips were still the legal godparents of the other five, and would have been to Abram also.

Moreover, under the ICWA treaty (Indian Child Welfare Act) with the Choctaw Nation, because Abram and his brothers and sisters are Choctaws, it is illegal to take custody of them without first making every reasonable effort to avoid the removal:[68]

Therefore, the timing of their secret custody grab is irrelevant, because the state of Oregon had no legal custody when the contract with Reuben and Cindra was signed. (And this same judge had already acknowledged that ICWA law is thus, and that ICWA applied to our six children.) But she denied—falsely—that Abram's custody had been taken illegally without the slightest effort to avoid the removal; moreover, she chose to ignore the fact that the social worker had made flagrant efforts at every opportunity to avoid our every effort to avoid the illegal removal.

Moreover, this same judge herself clearly had an opportunity to avoid her own theft of Abram Jedidiah Ammi Goldenstein's custody from his godparents Reuben and Cindra Goldenstein of Virginia, who are his legal guardians, godparents, and adoptive parents under ICWA law.

And in the second hearing, the third hearing was set to be heard on *Yom Kippur*, the Day of Atonement commanded in Leviticus as a day rest: And this same judge knew and acknowledged these things. Moreover, she also recognized that the caseworker had made accusations against our faith; and against the way of our people; and the judge forbade these accusations, but refused to remove this woman of hatred from our family, saying that she was only to be with us for a short time, until the third hearing. But the third hearing was set for *Yom Kippur*, in October.

And the next months were hellish.

Here, by way of example, are but seven of the many torments which threatened (and were intended) to drive us mad, or into the grave: Our little daughter Elishevah's foster mother had sent her to her first day of school in tears with verbal abuses, dressed like a prostitute so that she tried in vain to cover her lap with her schoolbook, shivering in the foggy morning, on her eleventh birthday; and finally, on another day, this abusive foster mother had forgotten Elishevah altogether, so that the child left the house, trying to go to school by herself, a mentally disabled eleven year old virgin, who still had a stalker in the same town.

Moreover, our little Mattithias Lazarus' Nazarite vow was illegally annulled by a secular judge, and Mattithias and his older siblings were forced with fraud to work and to eat on the Day of Atonement; and, afterward, to break the Feast of Tabernacles; and, afterward, to break the Passover. Moreover, the anti-Semitic social worker, when she was finally replaced, was replaced with another anti-Semite—whom she had chosen and trained. Moreover, our little son Yehudah Isaiah lost his smile, and stuck out his chin in angry silence when I asked him to thank God for his food. Moreover, the appeal judges found many of the slanders against us to be false, but had nonetheless remanded the case back to the same court that had already found against us falsely, with the other member of the same relay team of cruel judges. Moreover, our little son Abram Jedidiah Ammi never again saw nor heard nor touched his parents, and probably thinks that he is an orphan. Moreover, our little daughter Esther almost died a slow death of legume protein in her food,[69] until the day in which Esther did not come to our visit, because she had gone to the hospital, unable to breathe because of the rash which had spread from her inner ears into her sinuses.

And these were only seven of the torments against our children.

I cried out to the living Lord within my soul, praying for Abram Jedidiah Ammi: Because although the judge had twice ordered to send him to his godparents, and to permit him to visit with his parents and brothers and sisters, Abram Jedidiah Ammi was still alone, without any face he knew, from the day in which he awoke from his coma.

Neither, until this day, have I or Benaiah seen his face, nor has Abram seen us, nor heard our voices, nor touched us, nor had any way to know that he is not an orphan. From the depths I cried unto my Savior one night; and in the depth of our tribulation, while we were in a TRI-MET bus in the city of Portland, Oregon, I cried out within my soul to the living Lord, praying on behalf of Abram Jedidiah Ammi, to give this pure heart to his caring godparents.

Immediately, an SUV was outside the bus window in the night, with the initials A.J.A.G. written in the dust upon the rear window: Abram Jedidiah Ammi Goldenstein. And a flood of peace washed over my soul, so that many tears poured down my cheeks: and I had not been able to weep much since my early childhood, for the depth of anguish.

# Section Five:

# *The Daughter*

26    And I will give to you *a* new heart,
    and a new spirit I will give within you;
    and I will take away from your flesh *the* stone heart,
    and I will give to you *a* heart *of* flesh.

27    And my Spirit I will put within you, and my statutes
    I will cause you to walk in, and my judgments you will keep,
    and you will do *them*.

—Ezekiel 36:26-36:27

10 And he carried me in spirit onto *a* great and high mountain, and showed me the great city, the holy Jerusalem, descending out of the sky, from God,

11 having the glory *of* God. And her light *was* like unto a precious stone, which *was* like *a* crystallized jasper stone…

23 And the city has no need *of* the sun, neither of the moon, to shine in her: because the glory *of* God illuminates her, and her light *is* the little Lamb.

24 And the saved nations will walk in His light…

27 And any defiler will certainly not enter into it, and *any* maker *of an* abomination and *a* lie: but only the *ones* written in the Lamb's book *of* life.

—Revelation 21:10-22:5

CHAPTER FORTY-THREE:
# Portland in God's Eyes

And in another night in the city of Portland, Oregon, soon afterward, I cried out to the Lord from this city, this place of asphalt, gangsters, cars, robbers, trucks, pesticides, herbicides, kidnappers, leaf blowers, rapists, lawnmowers, and every kind of pollution of the air, and of the earth, and of the soul.

But the Savior of my soul opened my eyes to see the city as He sees it: Not the ugly temporal things, but as a galaxy of lovely stars: Each soul a star: Some shining brightly with the glory of His love, others dim without their Messiah and Savior: And all the temporal things I saw even as the Lord sees them: As dust and shadows.

And Benaiah and I were in a bus heading southward from Washington; and until this moment I was afraid: But God opened my eyes to all the souls around me: And I saw that those of whom I was afraid, the same were also afraid of me and of one another: And nobody of all of them was an enemy. And I saw a soul in the C-TRAN bus in North Portland that night, a man with tattoos and a fierce countenance, a dimly glowing star, yet struggling to shine: And I had been afraid of this fierce man: And when I saw his poor soul, I asked the Lord for him, that he would come to be our brother in Christ.

And in all my life I had never understood the prophecy, that there is a glorious city in heaven: Because cities were always hellish and ugly in my eyes: But now I understood: The holy city is a glorious galaxy of souls, each one shining like the sun with the glory of the immense love of the Author of Creation.

And I saw all the souls around us all the night, through four buses, and the MAX train, and four bus stops: People of every race, all of them alone, and many in fear one of another. And my desire was to gather them unto myself and to comfort them, but I could not because of the wall of fear and isolation: Even as the desire of our Holy Father is to gather unto Himself all of His children.

But many of us never put our trust in our loving Father: And those who don't trust in Him, these ones lose more and more their shining light; until the fearful soul becomes as pale as a fading ember. But every soul which trusts in its loving Father, the light of this soul grows greater and more beautiful; but the only soul that I saw shining like the sun is Messiah Yeshua, the living Lord.

43 You have heard that *it* has been said,
You shall love your neighbor, and hate your hater[1]
44 But I say unto you, Love your haters,[1] bless the *ones*
cursing you, do good *to* those hating you,
and pray for those slandering you, and persecuting you;
45 So that you may be children *of* your Father in *the* heavens:
because He makes His sun to rise on malicious and good,
and rains *rain* on righteous and unrighteous.

——Matthew 5:43-5:48

CHAPTER FORTY-FOUR:

# Mustard Seed

After we published *Seven Flames*, we continued to learn
more about the Beast which shall have great iron teeth; spoken of by
Adonai's prophet Daniel and then in more detail by Yeshua's
disciple John: For example, we learned that human beings in
Florida, Mexico and Europe have actually embedded microchips in
their right arms, in which their social security numbers are digitally
encoded; and there is a growing movement in the United States
Senate to require all American citizens/subjects to carry a universal
ID card, which would serve as an ID, and a driver's license, and a
Social Security card, and a credit/debit card, as does the today-
optional microchip in the right arm; which would allow the
government to advance its "War on Terror" by phasing out and
eventually outlawing the use of physical money:

Revelation
13:16 And everyone, the small and the great, and the rich and the
poor, and the free and the slaves, made him so that he might
give an engraving on their right hand, or on their foreheads;
17 and that none could buy or sell, except whoever has the
engraving, or the name of the beast, or the number of his
name.
18 Here is wisdom. Whoever has understanding, count the
number of the beast: because it is the number of a man; and
his number *is* six hundred sixty six.[2]

——Revelation 13:16-13:18

But the most important lessons we have learned since then are these: That Adonai deeply loves all His little humans He has created, including our haters the cruel children of the Beast and of the Antichrist; and therefore He wants His servants to learn how to love our haters, as our Lord Yeshua commanded:

Matthew

5:43   You have heard that *it* has been said,
       You shall love your neighbor, and hate your hater.[1]

44     But I say unto you, Love your haters,[1] bless the *ones*
       cursing you, do good *to* those hating you,
       and pray for those slandering you, and persecuting you;

45     So that you may be children *of* your Father in *the* heavens:
       because He makes His sun to rise on malicious and good,
       and rains *rain* on righteous and unrighteous.

——Matthew 5:43-5:45

And again,

Luke

6: 26  Woe *unto* you, when all men speak well of you!
       Because their fathers did likewise *to* the false prophets.

27     But I say *unto* you who hear, Love your haters,[1]
       do good *to* the *ones* hating you,

28     bless the *ones* cursing you,
       and pray for the *ones who* slander you.

29     *Unto* those striking you on the *one* cheek offer also
       the other; and from those taking away your *outer*[4] garment,
       forbid not *to take* the tunic also.

30     And *to* everyone that asks *of* you, give;[5] and from those
       taking away what *is* yours, *do* not ask *them to return it*.

31     And as you desire that men *would* do *to* you,
       do you also *to* them likewise.

——Luke 6:26-6:31

In the early winter of two thousand eleven, we wrote *Mustard Seed* to our daughter Elishevah, and soon afterward we wrote *Burning Coals*. And then, when in two thousand twelve we published the second edition of *Seven Flames*, we replaced *Deir Yassin* with our new chapter, *Mustard Seed*, as follows:

# *Mustard Seed*
## by Benaiah Levell

Elishevah, your little sister was born strong in God's Spirit. She knew more and felt more than that which was expected of a newborn. She was a noble and beautiful child that peered deeply into the souls of those around her. And she was exceptionally sensitive in body and soul. We sometimes called her "*Esh*", which is Hebrew for "fire".[6]

Seven months passed, and your little sister Esther Sarah Hadiyah grew more and more beautiful. During those first seven months of her life, she sensed deeply the soul of Abba. Sometimes, when Abba was rocking Esther Sarah Hadiyah, they would weep deeply together; that is, Abba and Esther would connect in soul and in the Holy Spirit. And then the Holy Spirit would let the two of them weep together for the sad things in the world.

Esther was born November 1, two thousand eight; and was carried into danger on July 4, two thousand nine. On that horrible day, Abba carried his Esh and all his family into a trap. Abba thought he was just having medical experts help him and his family heal the flesh. He would soon be shocked into a frightening spiritual reality.

Modern men call it a "medical facility" or a "hospital building," but from the eyes of a certain little spirit called "Esh," it appeared like this:

> Bright lights everywhere
> Blinding to look at
> Shadows of faces
> Shadows of faces
> Bright lights everywhere
> Blinding to look at
> Shadows of faces
> Blocking Abba's love

Gentle Abba disappears
Pain and blood and piercing poke
Gentle Abba reappears
Tears, blood, fleeting hope
Poke, poke
Shadows and faces
Sharp and blood
And flowing faint
Crying, pain
Searing pain
Gentle Abba
Here and again

Gone, Gone
Surging sadness
Bright lights, shadows
Clamoring madness
Abba, Abba
Sadness, Sadness
Internal pain
Infernal madness
Abba's gone
Forever sadness....


Elishevah, Imma said she has no [human] enemies,[7] Only people who think they are her enemies. Abba had a dream about a strange enemy: He dreamed of a huge black shadowy wall standing before him. Abba could not see the top of it because it was too high and in the dark. He could not see the sides because they were far away and also in the dark. He, in truth, knew that it was evil; that it was an enemy of goodness, purity, and all things holy.

Abba had a large double-edged sword in his hands.

With all his might he lifted the sword by its sturdy handle and thrust it down on the wall again and again, harder and harder, until Abba's arms became exhausted and the large sword began to feel too heavy. Abba didn't want to give up. So, with all his remaining strength, he painfully continued to hit down on the giant dark wall with this sharp double-edged sword. Abba was sweaty and out of breath and just about ready to collapse. His arms were trembling.

Then an angel told him to grasp the sharp blade and thrust upward into the belly of the wall. So Abba grasped the sharp blade with one hand and the handle of the sword with the other hand. He stabbed upward with the heavy sword into the belly of the wall. Again and again, grunting and groaning, Abba forced himself to painfully stab the evil wall. His hand was bleeding and he was very tired. However, because the sword was strong, the wall fell. It was a victory over a big evil in Abba's path.

Later, Abba remembered the dream, and he named the handle of the sword ***Don't hate*** and the blade of the sword he named ***Don't doubt***. A real wall of enemies[1] soon came into Abba's and Imma's life. And to conquer this big wall of enemies,[1] Abba and Imma knew that they needed a sword like the one in Abba's dream. For many months Abba and Imma tried to make their souls have a perfectly strong sword—but the handle always had weak spots of hate, and the blade had holes of doubt. Finally, two things helped: First, the words of Yeshua strengthened the handle by teaching Abba and Imma to not hate their enemies. Secondly, the miraculous little mustard seed completely formed a perfect double-edged blade ready for a glorious victory.

Here is how it happened: Yeshua told Abba and Imma to turn their sword over. It became a cross. The handle called ***Don't hate*** then became ***Love***. (Like Yeshua said: Love your enemies,[1] bless the *ones* cursing you, do good to those hating you, and pray for those persecuting you.[8]) This means, be as God made you: Truthful, noble, pure, and loving. The small-hearted ones are trying to change you into what they are—Hateful. Don't change into what your enemy is. Continue to be like God. Don't hate, no matter what, or you will make God hurt. He is your big-hearted friend. Be big like Him, not small-hearted like your small enemy (who is—*in truth*—small).

Abba likes to say "When you hate those that hurt you, you hurt those that love you."

As the handle ***Don't hate*** became ***Love***, Yeshua said: "Your blade that you named ***Don't doubt*** becomes ***Faith***."

He meant not big faith, or a faith that's difficult to get, but a tiny little seed. Faith as small as a mustard seed is the secret. Believe Yeshua—That's all. Just believe, and the blade of **Don't doubt** will have the tiny edge of faith sharp enough to cut through the belly of any evil beast of any size. Remember the edge: It can barely be seen, yet it is the most deadly part of the whole blade…

Elishevah, here's a hint of advice that might help in the latter days of the Beast. Each moment of each day choose which good to think about and choose which bad to forget. Choose, and don't let anything from the Beast choose for you. Adonai gives us the power to forget any evil. He has given us a forgettery that can block the attacks of an enemy who wants us to tremble and faint. Forget them after their moment of evil—every time. Choose to forget their repeated attacks again and again. Only remember what you choose to. Forget what your enemy is trying to make you hate him for.

Forgetting hate and remembering love: This is one way to deal with an attack from the Beast. But the little mustard seed of faith is still the most powerful weapon of all.

# THE LAST SHALL BE FIRST

Children weeping
In ashes and flame,
The heat is upon you, but God is the same.

Death is no victor,
Though dark is your sky,
How deeply you suffer yet keep sinless eye

Children weeping
In ashes and pain,
No hatred be in you! Be always the same!

Though blasting and blood
And their murderous sin
Surround you, Beloved, stay lovely within

Oh poison! Oh pollution!
Oh bombs from the sky,
My children are eternal and also am I.

Though you bruise them and burn them,
Your hour to destroy
Is but seconds on a clock to our eternal joy.

My children weeping
In ashes and flame,
The heat is upon you, but God is the same.

Death is no victor,
Though dark is your sky,
How deeply you suffer yet keep sinless eye

How deeply you suffer, yet keep sinless eye.

Love, *Abba*

CHAPTER FORTY-FIVE:
## The Book of Sarah
## by **Benaiah Levell**
(An excerpt from *Burning Coals*)

# *THE BOOK OF SARAH*

## *By Abba*

22 He who sits upon *the* circle *of* the earth,
and her inhabitants *are* like grasshoppers;
He who stretches out *the* heavens like *a* curtain,
and spreads them out like *a* tent to dwell *in*;
23 He who gives monarchs to nothingness;
Judges of *the* earth He makes as nothing.

—Isaiah 40:22, 40:23

Hear O mountains of the earth: cometh now the King of planets, the Prince of stars, and the Lord of miracles.

The voice of the LORD thunders. He is arrayed with glory and beauty. He is the Almighty God—Creator of the heavens and the earth.

He breathed on me, and I arose. I came into being by the breath of His mouth. He lifted me into His gentle bosom and embraced me with His everlasting strength. He put me into a mother's care and gave me mothers and fathers without number. My children were many, like the stars of the sky, and my enemies had fallen into pits like beasts without escape. Then I sinned in my anger. I was simple in my thoughts. The world became my dungeon. Breads eaten in secret were pleasant. In the depths of hell, I fell into the whorish woman's lair. I delighted in her enticements. I kissed her deathly lips.

Philosopher, Confusion, Demon Devil;
Sorcerer's delusion, deception and revel.
I could not see God in the midst of my hell;
And in the dark of my dungeon, oh how I fell.
Drunk in despair, down on the floor
A-whoring, abhorring myself—a whore!

Hear O mountains of the earth: cometh now the King of planets, the Prince of stars and the Lord of miracles. The voice of the LORD thunders. He is arrayed with glory and beauty. He is the almighty God—Creator of the heavens and the earth. He breathed on me, and I arose!

When the morning stars sang, I arose. And at the dayspring I became alive; I became earth. I was naught and became a living being, and like the earth I was carefully designed and measured out by the Great I Am. Who are you, O man, who has knowledge but a little? Where were you when God laid my foundations? Where will you be after your death? I will trust in the Lord who is the beginning of me—who takes me where He will. Whether in heaven or hell, being in His hands is better than being a written memory in your dusty museums of your doomed cities.

You were given a pleasant earth; and I a pleasant daughter. From within the earth you came, and my daughter came from within me. You loved your earth and I loved my daughter. O happy birth, breath of life, wonder, beauty, smile of delight. I loved her, so tender, so small and so new; your earth was just as beautiful too.

And the Lord God took the man, and put him into the garden to dress it and to keep it. And the Lord God took the *abba* and gave him the baby child to keep it. And they polluted the earth, its lifeblood, with every kind of pollution known to man. And they took the baby child from the *abba* and caused her pain she had never known, piercing, searching her tiny body for every pollution, spilling her lifeblood unnecessarily. But they found no pollution.

And now the Great I Am will in like manner search and spill the lifeblood of the earth, and *will* find pollution, because man committed sin against his own body, against his own earth, against his own child; and Yahweh, the Great I Am, will find it and will judge: because they put all manner of pollutions into their baby child Earth. They have sinned and are guilty: the prophet's precious tiny daughter was not polluted. But their precious daughter is....

Repent therefore, restore the man his baby daughter; because he is a prophet, and he shall pray for you and you shall live.

Oh, let my streams of tears hide my sins against You, O Lord my God. Let me be a deep dark ocean. Let my hard breathing of remorse deafen for a moment Your lovely ears. Let me be a storm of thunder, and let my bursting repentant heart disperse into a covering cloud of misty blood drops to cover my sinful soul from Your beautiful eyes. Let me turn into red soil hidden beneath Your perfect feet, and cover me with discarded angel feathers, the forgotten tattered robes of saints, and all the broken lashes fallen from the little children's weeping eyes, that Your beautiful feet never feel the moist tear-filled dust of my forgotten sins. And now therefore the LORD God says:

> Sing and rejoice O Israel; because your time has come and your Messiah is near. Though heaven and earth pass away, you will be blessed again. I will raise you up O Jacob, and you will once again take delight in my name; because I will dwell in you like a beating heart, and will stir you up like a thundering, swelling ocean—a holy tempest for the LORD.

—Benaiah 1:1

And now return the man's wife *to him*; because he *is a* prophet, and he will pray for you, and you will live:
And if you do not return *her*, know that dying you will die: you, and all that *are* yours.

—Genesis 20:7

# A Secret Heaven Peek
## for Esther Sarah Hadiyah

Horses with wings,
Unicorns singing,
Little children bringing
Flowers in their hands.

O my Lord,
Lovely are Your presents
Kissing us, giving us
Holy golden things.

Living emeralds
Dropping like raindrops
Poppies popping
Under dancing lambs.

Angels and lions
Peaceful, undying,
Flying and flying,
Shining rainbow land.

No crying, no tears;
No lying, no fear,
Rejoicing in music
And flowers once again.

O loving embrace,
Friendship eternal,
Everlasting waterfalls,
Diamonds in the hand.

Easy walking,
Trusting, talking,
Swimming, warm waters,
Luscious on the sand.

Pools and swirling
Clouds of color,
Never ending wonder,
Creatures so grand.

Vastness everlasting
Forever eyes casting
Deep loving glances
With holy desire.

Turtles and doves
And myrtle and love
And herbs recognized
And earth once again.

Horses with wings,
Unicorns singing,
Little children bringing
Flowers in their hands.

O my Lord,
Lovely are Your presents
Kissing us, giving us
Holy golden things.

—*From Abba*

## *Star Princess*

Though Hannah was first to bring tears to my eyes
Your eyes, blue and blue, outshined heaven's sky.
But for Yael: a friend taught to hate
It's too late for her sorcerer: alas, too late!
Oh Esther Hadiyah, my gift from God's throne
My empty arms ache to feel you are gone.
I came bringing treasure to your new royal bed;
In my arms I held you high and cradled your head.
Then it happened, the libelers and the liars came 'round
Denying Yeshua—His throne and His crown.
I cut out my heart. It's the head of God's shaft;
Speed straight, true arrow, to the sorcerers' craft.
Hadiyah: Star princess; see the arrow strike near,
Strike fear in the enemy—terrifying fear.
Behold, he is dead now, killed by my heart
For God was with you right from your start.

Let fathers and mothers witness this feat:
A libeler lay conquered by an *abba's* heartbeat.


This poem is to my graceful dancing princess who may have
been kept under the feet of arrogance and blind pride: A princess is
not a slave, nor is she to think of herself as less than she really is.
Don't lie down at your enemy's feet, beloved daughter.

Let Yeshua lift you up to your rightful place, and array you
in your royal apparel, O Queen Esther. I am your good father who
knows your high place of honor. And I give homage to you and
bestow upon you all the flowers of God's Kingdom.

Love, *Abba.*

P.S.    Beloved Esther, some of us can see your beauty, while others cannot. I am one who can see in you certain lovely qualities that my grandmother Grace had. You have brought them to life again. She was there with me in my very first years, in my very first memories of God's love. She showed me His love. I was new, small, and just learning like you are now. She tenderly took me with her, while she worshipped God. She sang to Him and raised her hands high to Him. And with those same hands she gently guided me, when I was a very small boy, towards Adonai. I had not seen that exact spirit or those exact hands for many years until you were born into our home, Esther Sarah Hadiyah. Now I see her in you and you in her. I thank your great grandmother Grace for showing me how to strum her guitar to God with my tiny fingers, and I thank you, Hadiyah, for letting me teach your tiny fingers to strum.

I don't know how these family connections work. They are a beautiful mystery. Just know, my sweet daughter, that I long to give you this joy that I have; this deep, deep joy of knowing our ancestors, of knowing a little of who we are and who we came from.

> Sweet fingers of my grandmother's hand
> I see you anew in my new gentle lamb.
> A brutal world breaks in and steals her
> But her Beautiful God steps in and heals her.
> Sweet fingers of my grandmother's hand
> I see you anew in my new gentle lamb.

*The Beginning...*

33 And Adonai spoke unto Moses, saying,

34 Speak unto *the* children of Israel, saying,
In *the* fifteenth day of this seventh month *shall be*
a celebration *of* the booths *for* seven days unto Adonai.

35 In the first day *shall be a* holy gathering:
you shall not do any work of service.

39 …in the first day *shall be a* little sabbath,
and in the eighth day *shall be a* little sabbath.

40 And you shall take to yourselves in the first day the fruit
*of the* citron tree, leaves of date palm trees, and branches
*of* interlaced trees, and willows of *the* brook; and you shall
rejoice before the face of Adonai your God seven days.

41 And you shall celebrate it with dancing
*as a* celebration unto Adonai seven days in *the* year,
*an* eternal statute unto your generations;
in the seventh month you shall celebrate it with dancing.

42 In booths you shall dwell seven days;
every native in Israel shall dwell in booths:

43 that your generations will know that I caused *the* children
of Israel to dwell in booths when I brought them out
from *the* land *of* Egypt. I *am* Adonai your God.

—Leviticus 23:33–23:44

CHAPTER FORTY-SIX:

# Xenophobia

On October 8, two thousand ten, the day before the Festival of Trumpets, Benaiah and I came to the end of our northward journey from Newberg, Oregon to Vancouver, Washington, and from Vancouver to Ridgefield, Washington, and from Ridgefield northward again; and we hastened to close the rental contract at our new trailer court before the holiday, which is a day of holy convocation:

And in the seventh month, in *the* first of *the* month, shall
be to you *a* holy gathering; you shall not do any work of
service: *it* shall be unto you *a* day *of* blowing trumpets.

—Numbers 29:1

And we arrived, and Benaiah blew the shofar, and we rested
in holy convocation: and we had rest from our journey.

And I give thanks to God, for my aunt (and my sister in
Christ) Judith, who changed the day of the third hearing from the
Day of Atonement: But with the new day came a new judge; and he
was a man of hatred, and friends with each of our enemies in his
presence. And in the third hearing, the enemies had improved their
slanders and frauds with each hearing, and the new judge saw only
their final effort, twice improved.

And without recourse the new judge pardoned every
contempt of court of our enemies.

Moreover, this judge heard and recognized that my autism
spectrum disorder was illegally used against us: But he still
convicted me of five counts of what he knew to be symptoms of
autism spectrum disorder.

And because of many abuses, my epilepsy grew worse, until
the judge in his pride denied during the eighth hearing that I had any
medical reason to close my eyes in court, and so forced me with
blackmail to have an epileptic seizure in the courtroom: And even
while I was being taken to the ambulance on a stretcher, we heard
the judge continue the case without the slightest pause, nor any word
of recognition that I was gone.

And in this hearing we were to regain visits with our six
children: Because when I had spoken against the anti-American
cruelty that for hatred the kidnappers had denied to my children their
right to keep and celebrate the Passover according to the word of
God, they had retaliated by canceling all our visits with five of our
beloved children:

And now, since that moment in which I was taken to the
hospital from the courtroom on May of two thousand ten, with an

epileptic seizure which the judge had caused, we have not had any visits with any of our children.

And Benaiah faced all these things with Post-Traumatic Stress Disorder (PTSD); and still without the help of any attorney. But with a strong hand the Lord of Hosts drove us more and more northward, as the Spirit had said to me in two thousand three that He would bring me southward, then a little northward with a small tribulation, and then give me rest; and in the north He would prepare my heart for the third journey (a long journey to the south-southeast with a greater tribulation).

Then, on *Yom Kippur*, October 18, two thousand ten, I saw one of our neighbors cast a very wary glance at me, as if I was an enemy.

And this neighbor was a Mexican, and I recognized his face as a young man of Beaverton, Oregon, who in two thousand three had driven our family from our apartment, so that we were homeless at the birth of Yehudah Isaiah: Because like a wolf with his pack (the Los Lobos gang), the youth had watched us in the kitchen door; which was a large window, without curtains. And while Benaiah was away buying groceries, the young man toyed with the fly of his trousers, then licked the fierce dagger in his hand, a beautiful Spanish dagger, and toyed with his fly again.

I had already been raped twice, as a runaway foster child on the streets; and so I had recognized and felt deeply this young man's lust—the cruel, raging lust of a conquistador.

But at the moment that I saw this young warrior I considered, and said nothing, because I knew well that the frightened mind can see falsely; and that the Enemy's desire is always to rob me of my rest: All the more so because this day was *Yom Kippur*, the Day of Atonement, of which it is written:

Leviticus

23:27    Surely in *the* tenth *day* of this seventh month *there shall be a* day *of* the atonement: it shall be unto you *a* holy gathering; and you will humble[10] your souls, and you will bring near *an* offering of fire unto Adonai.

28    And you shall not do any work in this same day: because it *is a* day *of* atonement, to atone for you before *the* face of Adonai your God...

296

31  You shall not do any work: *it is an* eternal statute unto your
generations in all your dwellings…

—Leviticus 23:27-23:32

Then, as is the way of neighbors in many neighborhoods
these days, I watched, and hid, hoping to see whether the neighbor
was an enemy or not, and whether he was that young man from the
Beaverton Los Lobos gang: But (like a cautious soldier) the man hid
his face from me, according to the custom of many modern
neighbors. Yet I gave him little thought: He was only one of
thousands of strangers in an unfriendly world; and only one of
countless worries with finding our place in the new neighborhood:
Because, in the common garden of our trailer park, the picnic table
had a neo-Nazi sign engraved in the wood. Moreover, two or three
of our new neighbors, young white men, stared at us with narrowed
eyes.

Then, after the Day of Atonement, we had to prepare for
*Sukkot*, the Feast of Tabernacles.

*Sukkot* is a big holiday; a holiday for the children. In this
holiday, every Hebrew family builds a tabernacle—a temporary
dwelling, like a tipi or a yurt without any roof except for some leafy
branches—with rugs or blankets for the walls.

A *sukkah* is a peculiar dwelling, useless against rain or wind:
More like a Christmas tree than a house; and every family decorates
their sukkah with ornaments and fruits, and Christmas lights, and
candies, and every other decoration: And with thousands upon
thousands of illuminated *sukkot*, Jerusalem is never more lovely
than in the nights of the Feast of Tabernacles.

Our family had prepared a fire in our *sukkah* almost every
year, and in the previous year my firstborn son was to have prepared
the fire himself alone, without matches or any lighters, a glory of
manhood for a Choctaw Indian youth. However, instead of this rite
of passage in this happy and glorious holiday, two disconsolate
parents sat in a scarcely decorated booth, without any fire; and we
sat silent upon the floor, like those who mourn the dead. And our
children had no *sukkah*, because of the hatred of the anti-Semitic
social workers.

But this was another year, and a new neighborhood. Here, no policeman of hatred was watching like a hunter; and here, no one knew us as parents without our children.

But this was a holiday for the children, and the only children that I saw were those of the Mexican stranger next door: And I watched them sadly, because I saw that these children kept their distance. And I watched carefully, because a small child cannot practice hypocrisy: Therefore, I could see in their faces what their parents had taught them about us, whether I was an enemy in their eyes or not: And I saw no hatred in their eyes, but they were very careful to keep their distance from me. And my desire[11] was to hide—but the Feast of Tabernacles was almost here: Moreover, we had to build our tabernacle in our garden, in full view of their front yard. And we thought that, when we built our *sukkah*, the curious little children would bring our families together: Never again to be strangers, but either friends or enemies: Because a *sukkah* is impossible for a little child to ignore.

Every *sukkah* is different, unique; and many Hebrew families keep their *Sukkot* ornaments as family heirlooms, and also make and buy new ornaments every year. But many of our ornaments were in storage, in another city, in another state, and we had no money to find and bring them. And because our little children were captives, unable to celebrate the Biblical holidays, for the first time in my life I adorned the *sukkah* alone, and with tears.

Our favorite ornaments are always all that are pleasant and exciting and good for the children: Apples, drums, elegant rattles, tiny pumpkins, brightly colored flags flying in the wind. Some tabernacles of other families have mirrors, and exotic flowers, and laces as delicate as spider webs, and ornaments of expensive crystal, but never in mine: Because for me, the glory of the tabernacle is the children within it; living the stories of the Bible and joyfully learning the way of our fathers, with their own eyes and tongues and ears and hands.

And this year, we bought for the children a windsock, and red feather boas, and sturdy plastic purple snowflakes: And with green blankets we hung not only these, but a small tapestry of horses, and golden Christmas ornaments; and our leafy roof was intertwined with thousands of bright golden leaves: And from the branches I hung the purple plastic snowflakes, and the red feather boas, and the windsock.

And I knelt alone on the floor of dirt, gravel, and pitiable grass which struggled to survive in that poor clay between the gravel; with my face to the east after the Hebrew custom, as is written in Solomon's prayer in the eighth chapter of First Kings, and in chapters five, six, and seven of Second Chronicles; and according to what the living God had responded to His servant Solomon: Thus I knelt on the floor of the *sukkah*: Because my greatest joy in every holiday is always to talk with my beautiful Father and my Savior, the Lord of my soul. But Messiah Yeshua did not talk to me, nor did I hear the sweet voice of the Holy Spirit in my heart. And day after day I searched my heart and my ways for sin,[11] and found no evil work: And I cried out to my God, but He did not answer me one word.

Then in the *sukkah* I felt utterly alone, an unworthy servant, a Hebrew foreigner in a gentile neighborhood, a childless mother, completely alone without my only faithful friend Adonai.

And without the voice of my beloved God, I had no desire for any other: So I cried to my God with all my heart to cleanse my soul of its hidden sin: Then fear came to me, and became my constant companion: I felt all my enemies, and saw every danger, and my nights were filled with sweat and nightmares. I cried out to my Savior, but fear was my companion night and day. And my only consolation, apart from Adonai, was little children: But the tabernacle did not entice them near. And I knew well that in the face of the innocents I could see the heart of their parents: Because hypocrisy is impossible to teach to a small child.

And I thought that I was alone in the *sukkah*, but no.

Then the Enemy put in my mind the memory of the Spanish dagger, and the ancient memory of my people with the Spanish blade in our bellies; the abomination of mixing the holy blood with the unclean bile and feces and urine, so that *kashér*[12] burial was impossible. And I knew well the reputation of the Los Lobos gang, that they also loved this abominable death: The white gang members in the neighborhoods of my youth said that a Lobo would thrust the dagger in his victim's belly, so that the victim usually dies of shock from the tremendous pain; but sometimes not, but rather lives on for one, or two, or three days in torment until the infection in his unclean wound kills him.

And the Enemy put within my heart, that certainly my death would probably be slow, because the first pain would give me an epileptic seizure, and the Lobo would think that I'm dead. And I had purposed, if possible, to throw myself from the bridge, so that Benaiah would not find my defiled corpse, and die with me of a broken heart, or live in anguish all his earthly life. But my great fear was that I would find his defiled body, and live without him all my earthly life. And because I saw that my Lord was silent with me, I prayed silently upon my knees; and I prayed, and prayed, three days; although I knew that His silence was for the sake of mercy.

And the memory of *Kristallnacht*[14] was with me day after day, the ancient memory of the broken windows and of thousands of the homes of our people burned down in one night: The beginning of the Nazi war against the European Hebrews.

And in the last morning of the Feast of Tabernacles, one of our front windows was broken.

And every one denied any knowledge of when or how or why: Neither had we any money for repairing such a broken window: And, now, it was impossible to move the house: Because nobody accepts a trailer with a huge broken window in front.

Then, despairing of my life, I curled up on the bed and wept, and wept, and wept, until I had lost all strength to cry, until the night.

3:1 Upon my marriage bed in *the* nights I searched
for *the one* whom my soul loves: I searched for him,
and I did not find him.

2 I will rise—please—and I will go about in *the* city: in *the*
marketplaces, and in *the* streets, I will seek *the one* whom
my soul loves—I searched for him, and I did not find him.

5:5 I, I arose to open to my beloved; and my hands
dripped *with* myrrh, and my fingers *with* myrrh,
going upon *the* handles *of* the lock.

6 I, I opened to my beloved; and my beloved had turned,
*and* was gone: with his speaking my soul had gone out.
I searched for him, and I did not find him;
I called him, and he did not answer me.

7 The guards found me *that* went about in *the* city;
they struck me, they wounded me; the guards of the walls,
my veil they lifted up from upon me.

8 I charge you, *O* daughters *of* Jerusalem, if you find
my beloved—What will you tell him? That I *am* lovesick.

—Song of Solomon 3:1-3:2; 5:5-5:8

CHAPTER FORTY-SEVEN:
# A Call to Surrender

And although I knew well that the silence of my God was for
mercy, I still arose from my bed, returned to the *sukkah*, and prayed
all the more: I cried out within my heart all the more, saying,
"Punish me, beat me up, torture me, tear my soul to shreds: For
there is no torture that I would not gratefully accept from Your
hands, only to hear Your beautiful voice, only to be with You, only
to feel Your touch, no matter how painful: Touch me, punish me;
chastise me with any other punishment than silence: Give me the
gift of Your wrath, the gift of Your voice, please chastise me, please
punish me; punish me; punish me."

And thus I cried out silently in the night upon my knees in
our little tabernacle: No matter that my knees were pierced with the
sharp gravel, until I heard His beautiful, beautiful voice, His sweet
reproach:

"You have pity on your husband, that he should not find your defiled body, and die of a broken heart or live in sorrow as a widower; and you have pity upon yourself, that you should not find his defiled body, and live without him as a widow: But have you no pity upon your two Latina neighbors, that you can cry out to me, to deliver their husbands, the fathers of their children, into your hands? And should I not rather have pity on them? Why? How can you ask me to choose between your life, and the life of my servant? And why would you think that I should choose your life above the life of my servant, when you are already separated from your children, and you are in a broken body, but my servant is healthy, and strong, and has three little children and their mother who depend on his job to live? Are you not ready to come into my arms?

And what of his soul?—for you, little daughter, are ready to be with me, but if my servant dies in the sin of murder; then, What? Is it not much better that my servant should live, and repent, and return to my will?" I had been sitting there with a sword in my hands, afraid, and I had asked God to protect us, and to deliver my enemy into my hands; but God did not have respect for this prayer: Instead, He had given me over to my own fears, until terror all but consumed me.

Now I understood my Quaker grandfather's teaching that the violent man harms himself, and not the other person.

The words of my Yeshua pierced my soul as with a sword, and I saw well that truly His silence had been in mercy: Because I saw that my words had pierced His soul as with a sword. Yet still I chose to suffer, for love of His voice. And His words were like a hot knife through cold butter: Because my King had not called me His servant as before times, but He called the Latino man, of whom I had been afraid, His servant.

And in the final day of the Feast of Tabernacles, and then in the following night, which was the last holiday of the seventh month, *Simkhat Torah*—that is, *Rejoicing in the Torah*—I was in the *sukkah* alone, unarmed, in a house without locks, and with blankets for walls; deeply aware in the night that I was utterly defenseless, an Hebrew foreigner in a gentile neighborhood; and that thirty feet from the house was the house of a man whom I now knew to be a servant of my Messiah, a brother, beloved of my Lord, who looked upon me as a foreigner and possibly as an enemy; Moreover, I knew well that my Savior had no desire to deliver His Latino servant into my hand. Then I asked my Lord and Savior to tell me what to do: But Messiah Yeshua said, "Surrender."

And I cried out for mercy, but the Lord of my soul said yet again, "Surrender."

Like two lions, my will to survive struggled with my desire to die for my Messiah Yeshua, my Messiah; my reason to live. And their teeth shredded me: But my desire to please my Lord, in life and in death, was the victor: So that I was finally ready to die at the feet of my gentile brother, and neither to protect nor avenge my life, for love of my Messiah Yeshua. And I surrendered in the darkness after the last day of the Feast of Tabernacles, in the *sukkah*, and I didn't care at all when the rain began at the end of the holidays: Still I prayed, kneeling in the mud until the night came, with my knees cut by the gravel; and in the darkness in the rain, my tears mingled with the rain.

Then, in the moment of surrender, in the thirty-fifth year of my life, at last I deeply understood the reason and the meaning of the Feast of Tabernacles. And I saw my sin for which my Friend and my King had been silent with me: Because the way of my people commanded me to invite my neighbors to our *sukkah*, but I in my fear had said nothing to them, but only invited people whom I had met at the churches: And in this I had been outside the will of the Messiah from the day that we came to this town in the beginning of the Feast of Trumpets, because of my fears. From the moment of my surrender I understood that, like my native nation the United States of America, I had allowed myself to be polluted by terror after September 11, two thousand one.

On Christmas Eve of nineteen ninety-five, Benaiah and I came to our first home, a tiny trailer in California: And our new neighbors were Mexican Catholics; and I had knocked on their door, and had given the mother an apple pie, and I said to her two of the few Spanish words I knew: *"Feliz Navidad"*—"Merry Christmas." And for four years, we were friends with her four little children Rocio, Francisco, Olga, and Victor. And her firstborn daughter

Rocio (pronounced as *Rosío*), as pure and lovely as the dew, was our good friend.

And now, here, (more than fourteen years later,) in the night after *Sukkot*, the soft, kind voice of my Lord said, "Was it truly so difficult to knock on your new neighbor's door and to say, 'Feliz *Rosh HaShanáh*',[15] and give her an apple pie? Is her family so very different from your friend Rocio's family—or have *you* changed?"

Then I wept bitterly, because I knew that fear had polluted my heart; and I asked the Lord of my soul why He had not simply told me to do with my new neighbors as I had done with my friend Rocio's family.

I had a dream that night, in which I asked again, "Why did you give me over to my own fears, when I had asked for mercy?"

Then Yeshua whispered to me: "Listen…"

I listened; and He asked me in a whisper,
"I want to give my servant a gift—is that okay?"

And I said, "Yes, *Adón Nafshí*,[16]
You know that all your gifts to all your servants
are sweet to my soul." And again He asked,

"I want to give my Latino servant a gift—is that okay?"

And I said, "Yes, my dear King, give your servant a gift."

And He said to me,

"Look—I want to give this gift to your neighbor
my servant—is that okay?"

And I looked, and behold a silver armband, magnificently engraved. And I said again, "Yes, *Adón Nafshí*,[16] please give your servant this armband."

Then my King Yeshua showed me an ugly rock and said, "Behold: this is good silver mixed with clay and stone: Is it a good gift? What would your neighbor my servant do, if his friend should give him this rock?"

The rock was very ugly: Therefore I said, "I suppose he would probably keep the rock a short while, for his friend's sake, then throw it away."

My Messiah asked, "Then, What? Is it good to purify the silver with fire?"[17]

And I said, "Yes, purify the rock."

Then Yeshua showed me a simple armband, never carved nor polished; and He said to me, "What would my servant likely do, if his friend should give him this armband?"

The armband was good, but plain, not in the Latino fashion: And I said, "I suppose he would probably keep the armband for a while, for his friend's sake, then sell it, perhaps to buy a better car for his family."

So my Lord asked, "Then, What? Is it good to carve the armband with a blade?"

And I said, "Yes my King, please carve the armband deeply with a sharp blade, as you showed me, to make it beautiful in your servant's eyes, then your servant will surely accept his gift with gratitude, and wear it with sincere joy."

My Lord answered, "You are this armband; Do you understand now why I gave your heart over to your own fears?"

And I said, "I don't know, my King: Why?"

He answered in a soft voice: "You were the ugly rock,[18] but now you are purified with fire: And now, What? Do you want me to engrave your heart with a sharp blade?"

And I said again, "Yes, *Adón Nafshí*,[16] engrave deeply: Carve my heart with your blade: You know that all your gifts are sweet to my soul: Give me the gift of your painful wounds."

But He turned His face away and wept quietly: Because His Father had set at our feet the beautiful Spanish dagger.

In the darkness, in a whisper, my Messiah Yeshua said to me, "May I give you a gift? Is it okay?"

I said, "Yes, Beloved."

And He asked me, "Can I be your *Sukkah*?"

And my tears in the rain were tears of joy: because in the thirty-fifth year of my life, at last I understood deeply the reason and the meaning of the Feast of Tabernacles: And I rejoiced in Messiah Jesus, my tabernacle, my only perfect refuge, my *Sukkah*.

Psalm
20:7 These in *the* chariot, and these in horses; but we,
in *the* name *of* Adonai: we will remember our God.

Isaiah
45:18 …thus said Adonai, creator *of* the heavens
(He *is* the God *who* formed and made the earth;
he arranged it; *He* did not create it in vain: *He* formed it
to be inhabited): I *am* Adonai, and there is none other.

19 I did not speak in hiding, in *a* dark place *of* the earth:
I did not say to *the* seed *of* Jacob, seek me in vain:
I Adonai speak righteousness, declaring fairness.

21 …there is no other God except for me:
*the* righteous God and *the* Savior: there is none beside me.

22 Face toward me, and be saved, all *the* ends of *the* earth:
because I *am* God, and there is none other.

—Psalm 20:7;[19] Isaiah 45:16-45:22

CHAPTER FORTY-EIGHT:

# A Bunny Rabbit

In the first night of the winter of two thousand ten, on a cold, rainy, windy, and very dark night under the clouds and the new moon in November, Benaiah was returning alone from the grocery store when a huge black rat, soaked with the rain and fierce with hunger, leaped out onto his feet from underneath the steps of our front door: So Benaiah jumped backward, away from the surprise attack—But no: The ferocious beast was not a big rat at all, ready to tear his boots and ankles—it was only a very small black rabbit, identifiable only by its long ears, well hidden within the filth of its own blood, mingled with the mud and its own excrement; the tips of its ears in bloody shreds well hidden underneath all this filth—a tiny rabbit, shivering in the black night in the rain. Benaiah called to me to come and see; and, behold, the poor creature was one of the most miserable in the world; shivering; its eyes fixed on Benaiah's boots, ready to follow those big black boots anywhere; because they were its best and final hope, the last things in its world with the slightest resemblance to its mother.

315

The rabbit was clearly no wild animal, certainly not one of the cottontails that lived here among the briars.

I gave the creature a pear; and with a moment of pitiful indecision the rabbit looked first at the boots, then at the pear, then again at the boots, and at last crawled like a newborn bunny toward the pear; desperate enough with hunger to leave the comfort of the boots and approach me, a huge predator. The rabbit was nearly blind, and small enough that I could put its whole body in one hand: But first I had to win its trust. And the creature's bunny-crawl was deceptive: Despite its wounds, it could run and leap like any rabbit; and nobody had ever given it any reason to trust in man.

I was asking this animal for an enormous hop of faith: Humans had already betrayed its whole litter to their deaths, abandoned to cars, and hawks, and starvation, and thirst, and to be food for a nest of little owls: And now its sensitive nose could smell that I was a meat eater, and that in the big friendly boots was an even bigger meat eater.

But we had food, and the *boots*, and so—with enormous faith—the bunny allowed me (a carnivore more than twenty-six times its own height) to take its whole trembling body in my hands.

And this night was the sixth of November, the first day of the Hebrew month *Kislev*.

For three days, the little bunny waited to either live or die alone in a metal cage, almost as quiet as the teddy bear I had put under its muddy feet: The rabbit's only sounds were to grind its teeth, and to purr in agony.[20]

Then, in the fourth day and the fifth, Benaiah gave the rabbit its first bath: But it had to be bathed thrice more to be clean: The tip of its left ear was torn off, hanging like a living fishhook stiff and bloody, too dead for surgery, too alive to remove, too painful to touch, so that we had to wash and protect the creature's ear four times every day against infection for three weeks, until the dead tip fell away from the living ear. And the dead tip fell off on the twenty-sixth of November, a Friday; and then Benaiah gave the rabbit its first *full* bath.

Later, when the bunny at last understood that our laughs were a happy sound, it also began to imitate the sound with its own laugh—a rabbit is not mute with its trusted friends, but rather its sounds are all very soft: Trills and chirps, bossy honks, rude grunts, friendly beeps: all in a *very* soft voice.

Then the Holy Spirit said to my soul without words, "How many times have my people put their trust in other things, even as your rabbit trusted in the black boots—But these my people ran away from the only true Savior! And, What was in your heart, when the bunny wanted to choose the boots? How much, How much more is my love for my own little children, than your fondness for a stray animal! And, What was in your heart, when the bunny finally chose your hands?"

Then I felt the sorrow of our faithful Savior every time any soul chooses a useless idol instead of the only Lamb of God: And I felt the joy beyond words of our Savior every time—*every* time— any soul meets its true Savior, the only Lamb of God, who was sacrificed for us, for every soul, from the beginning of the world; and His desire to carry every, every, *every* soul, as a new believer, in His faithful hands.

And we named the shabby bunny Bonito,[21] and the bunny rabbit began to be beautiful.

4:16      ...God is love; and the *one who* stays in love, stays in God, and God in him...

4:18      ...Fear is not in love; but complete love casts out fear: because fear holds *a* punishment; and the fearing *one* has not been perfected in love...

——First John 4:7-5:3

CHAPTER FORTY-NINE:

# Christmas Eve

In one of those days soon after the Feast of Tabernacles, Benaiah had a dream in which were two little goats: And his custom is to tell me his holy dreams, so that I may write them: Because I am his faithful scribe.

But in this morning, when I asked Benaiah to show me his dream, behold, our delightful, godly friend Daisy came to us. And so Benaiah said, "I'll tell you later." Then, while Daisy was visiting with us, our friend saw one of our Latino neighbors—the same man of whom I have already written—and she ran to him and his wife, and led him to us by the hand, and introduced him to us: And his name was Rodrigo. And when Rodrigo heard that we are Messianic Jews, Believers in Messiah Jesus, his face showed surprise, and he said that he had thought that we had some other religion; and Rodrigo invited us to his church. And I remembered well the commandment, "Surrender."

But while he yet spoke, Daisy interrupted him, asking Rodrigo to ask his pastor Pedro to give her the two little goats; saying that the pastor had discussed this with her: Three times Daisy asked Rodrigo to ask the pastor for the two little goats, saying the third time, "I want my two goats!" And I nearly laughed, because Daisy was so like a little goat herself, and because Rodrigo was so unimpressed: Rodrigo obviously knew our friend well enough; and he never blinked an eyelash. And I saw Rodrigo's face for the first time in broad daylight: And the likeness between him and the gang member from Beaverton *was* quite notable, but Rodrigo's skin was a shade darker, and his face a tiny bit wider; and his eyes were the beautiful eyes of a gentle farmer, eyes that never knew the bloodlust

of the conquistador. And while Benaiah walked back to our front
door, I said nothing: Because although in hearing the name 'Pedro
Bernabe'[22] my soul had leaped for joy within my heart, still I had to
wait until the Spirit also called Benaiah to this church: Because I am
a wife, and Benaiah is my head: And so by his word, not mine, we
would go to this church: Neither had I any words to say how I knew
that this was our new church that God had chosen.

Then with a mischievous smile Benaiah said: "Daisy's never
gonna get her two goats—you know why?"[23]

And I said, "I don't know—Why?"

And Benaiah answered, "Because we are the two little goats:
We're Pastor Pedro's goats—and she can't have us!" And we both
laughed with joy (although I knew not his dream).

Later in that same day I asked Benaiah to reveal to me his
dream of the two goats, but he had partly forgotten, and never again
remembered all the details of his dream unto this day. And Yeshua
had bound my soul to the souls of this new congregation; and one
soul, to which my High Priest Yeshua had bound my soul, was in
tears day after day, a broken mother without her three little sons.
Then I asked my God one day, when we were returning to our
house, "Please, Yeshua my Messiah, teach me a better love."

And in the same moment of my prayer, a cold iron dagger
pierced through my heart, and I fell upon my knees: And the dagger
was the anguish of my little sister, whose family is shredded.

And I saw more: I saw that when my little sister had looked
to her brothers in the Lord to comfort her soul, they thrust an iron
dagger into her heart, which was that dark side of the Prosperity
Doctrine: The cold dagger of false judgment: The dagger so, so cold
which was piercing my heart was not from the blind world, but from
the apathy within the church, the spiritual brothers of our broken
sister.

Two nights and two days, from the evening of the fifteenth
of December until the beginning of the Sabbath in the evening of
December seventeenth, the dagger pierced my heart, so painfully
that I could not leave my bed. And all the time in which I wrote
these things, the pain shot through my whole body so that I
struggled to breathe; with tears, and sweat, and my body
outstretched upon the bed—My spine at times arched and drawn

tight like a bow—But in His mercy my kindhearted God gave me rest from the spiritual blade for one day, until Saturday evening.

Then from Saturday evening onward, the dagger pierced through my heart again; so I wrote all these things, but still had no rest from the blade so, so cold: And I wept and I cried out to Yeshua for His mercy, saying, "Why? Why?" The Holy Spirit said quietly, "Your little sister doesn't understand English, nor do her cold brothers: You have to show in Spanish what I have revealed to your heart." Nevertheless I wept, saying, "But I don't know Spanish!" But the Holy Spirit said again, "Write."

And so I began to translate my words into poor and clumsy Spanish: And the pain faded a little, dull and cold: Until I put in the pastor's hands the two letters of these things, one in English and the other in Spanish. This was the first time in which I saw Pastor Pedro's face clearly; then joy and fear came into my soul together: Joy, because I saw clearly that Pedro Bernabé was my beloved gentle Indian chief from the dream of the two mountains, and because I saw his soul filled with beautiful fire for my God; and fear came also, because surely the young man (the one who would take my life) was near to the chief.

And when the pastor put his hands upon the paper, the cold dagger was gone, and the wound was closed up. And I knew that we had found our church, because I was powerless to leave: Like a lost animal my shepherd Yeshua had bound my horns, and my chest, and my legs, utterly defenseless at the feet of this pastor; who had the strong arms of a man, and the pure eyes of a beautiful little child. And then, when I saw the face of this brother, I was troubled: Because I saw the spirit and the face of the Indian chief in the dream of the two mountains: The same is Pastor Pedro Bernabé.

With consternation I watched for the young man named Stone, with the stone in his hand; but the Lord in His mercy had hidden from my memory the young man's name, and hidden also his face from my eyes when I saw him. And my Lord and Savior forbade me at that time to show who is the strong-willed young man, until the stone is in the air, lest I put a stumbling stone before my beloved brother, a faithful servant of my God.

I was afraid because of the dream; but the Lord of my soul said to me: "Don't be afraid." And—because I feared the face of my killer—I wanted to run; but my Lord Yeshua bound my soul to the soul of the beloved Chief, and also to the soul of every lamb of his flock, saying "I will surely hold back your death with my own hand." And behold, He has also caused me to see the end of all these things; so that I have loved not only the people and their chief, but also even the stone in the young man's hand, because truly the end is as beautiful as the beginning is painful, so much so that I have loved even the stone in the young man's hand.

The Lord also commanded me, at that time, to conceal these things from the man until the stone is in the air, lest he should unwittingly fight against God's hand, and thus the Lord's faithful servant would break himself to protect my heart.

And I had another dream, of which I soon afterward told the first part to Pastor Pedro, for concerning this dream the Lord had commanded me to conceal the part which had yet to come to pass: The first part I told to Pedro, saying: I saw two young goats, a male and a female, which a gentle farmer gathered to himself, and bound the horns with two strong cords; and the name of the little he-goat's cord is "Brotherhood," and the name of the little she-goat's cord is "Trust." This farmer then brought them to a beautiful temple, a tabernacle, which was colorful and magnificent. Then, within, the farmer put them both gently into the arms of a faithful Levite, who in turn put them gently in the arms of the Eternal High Priest.

This gentle farmer is Rodrigo, and the he-goat bound with the cord named "Brotherhood" is Benaiah, and I am the she-goat bound with the cord named "Trust," and the faithful Levite is Pedro. This first part I told to Pastor Pedro, but then the Lord, the High Priest Yeshua, put His hand over my mouth, and commanded me to conceal the part which was still in the future. And this is the commandment to me, concerning the congregation Fuente de Vida: That I shall not depart from this people.

Although not of any tribe known to be Hebrew, nor numbered among the sons of Levi the son of Jacob; even so, Pedro Bernabé is called and chosen to be a Levite for His High Priest Yeshua: This holy dream, and the holy dream which I saw three times in my eleventh year, the same bear witness of him, that Pedro

Bernabe is a Levite for Messiah Yeshua. Concerning this Levite, four commandments are given to me: To do all that he asks; to strengthen his heart; and also to lift up his head, and not to bow down his head with grief.

Behold, here is the second part:

In this same dream, I saw Benaiah no more.

And I was in the High Priest's arms, with the cord named "Trust" upon my horns. Then Yeshua bound up my whole body (to bind my soul, so that I may trust in His people); and the two ends behind my neck, then across my chest (to bind my heart to this church, Fuente de Vida); and then the High Priest Yeshua bound up my four legs, with the center of the cord upon my horns (to bind my strength to serve, and that I should not desire my freedom from the faithful Levite's hands).

Then He put me in the Levite's hands, although my desire was to remain with Him; and never in the hands of a mortal man. And I cried out in great fear, for fear that the man's foot should stumble, and I should fall from his hands and break. And, when I cried, then instead of comforting words He gave me a bitter promise, that surely the human Levite's foot *shall* stumble, and the Levite shall certainly break me: And instead of gentle words, the High Priest gave me a bitter choice, to choose how much pain to suffer: Because He gave me to know that the measure of my pain by the Levite's hands is the measure of my love for the Levite and his flock. (Behold, He has caused me to see the end of these things, so that I have loved even the pain, and desire not my own safety, for joy of the consequences, which are in truth beautiful, lovely beyond all words: So much so that my heart longs even to fall and be broken.)

Then I wept for fear of failure, for fear that I should fear to love the people with great love, according to the will of my High Priest, the Lord of my soul. Then the Messiah also said that, if I should love this church enough for the pain to destroy me, "Surely I will hold back your death with my own hand."

Therefore I cried in bitter prayer for a promise, that I should not fail to love this people enough to please the Lord of my soul, even enough to die.

But my words were bitter to Yeshua, and He wept. Then was my heart shredded, that because of my words Yeshua had wept. He did not want to promise this bitter promise, which was very bitter to him, lest I break His heart with great pain, should I change my mind and weep and cry out bitterly for His mercy, because He cannot change His promises.

However, although His tears shredded my heart, I wept bitterly and would not be turned aside, begging and crying for this bitter promise, protesting that I could not bear the burden of this uncertainty. But I also wept afterward, saying that if He asks it of me, then with a broken heart I would willingly bear unto death the pain of uncertainty, because I could not bear to provoke my beloved King to any more tears. Throughout the night He walked with me, His little goat, in His arms, declaring to me many things, to teach me the truth and beauty of the cross, until I understood deeply both the beauty and the necessity in the words:

> No one takes it from me, but I lay it down from myself.
> I have authority to lay it down, and I have authority
> to receive it again. I have received this commandment
> from my Father.
>
> ——John 10:18

And also I understood the beauty and the necessity when our Lord was saying:

> Father, if You are willing, remove this cup from me;
> nevertheless not my will, but Yours, be done.
>
> ——Luke 22:42

And I understood deeply that Yeshua had conquered not only at Golgotha, but also in the garden of Gethsemane; and not only upon the cross, but also upon His knees.

In this way for three nights and three days my Lord walked with me, and at dawn He said that His greatest joy is to bear all the burdens that we cannot; and also that His tears were not only of pain, but also of deep joy. And my Messiah declared to me, also, that for my happiness He wanted to give me this beautiful, beautiful gift of great joy, to suffer for my brothers and sisters. And, as for the promise that I had desired, my Messiah declared to me that He would establish His covenant with me. In the dream, throughout all the night He walked, with His little goat in His arms, until dawn. Then my High Priest Yeshua said: "This is the sign of the covenant which you shall establish between me and you: The young man shall not kneel and take up the stone in his hand; but you, my servant, shall put it in his right hand with your own hands."

I doubled over gasping, even while my heart sang with joy; for in all these things, every joy was with pain, and every pain with joy, to teach me about the cross. Moreover, the Lord of my soul said:

"I will put the stone in your hands to give to the young man; and I will reveal the stone in that time. If you don't want this, put it in the hand of another, to give to him. And this is the sign of the covenant which I shall establish between me and my servant (And I am not able, like a man, to change my promises): My servant shall embrace the stone above his heart."

In this way, for three nights and days, Yeshua gave me many holy dreams, and rest for one day, then three more nights and three more days He gave me holy dreams: To teach me many things concerning the cross, to purify my heart from the fear of man; and then He gave me rest for one day: Therefore, with the twilight, I rested.

Then, at the next sundown, which was Christmas Eve, our congregation celebrated with a *vihilia*.[24] But my gifts were not ready because, for more than a week, I had been outstretched upon my bed in fear before the voice and the face of my Holy Lord. But my husband Benaiah had prepared one gift for one friend our beloved brother, which was our two books that we had written together, to tell our little children of the things of God.

Then in the time of fellowship, Benaiah put in my two hands the two books (which were audio books on five CDs); and Benaiah asked of me that I would give them to our friend: And then came the word of my Lord to me, that the gift in my hands was the stone. And in a whisper He spoke softly to me (and it hurt my heart to hear these words) that I did not need to give the gift to the young man myself, but it was acceptable to put the gift in his daughter's hands; and she would be faithful to give him the gift for me; and so I would remain free. But I was fearless, except for the fear that, when I am tested, I should be found cowardly and weak.

And I sought the man's face. Twice I found his daughter, but I found not the man. A third time, I found him with his daughter, and she saw me, but he did not see me. And I stood before him until they had ended their conversation, and so I gave the stone to the man: But he did not embrace the stone above his heart, but only said, "Thank you," and hurried away with his eyes down. And I waited patiently upon my High Priest's promise, although my heart felt as if in a vise, because I understood that this was only a test of whether I trusted in my king.

And when our brother preached about Yeshua, the first and best Christmas present, he lifted up our gift to himself, and embraced the gift above his heart...

Then I gave thanks to God for the stone, and for all His gifts, and—more than all—I thanked God for Yeshua, the first Christmas present. And when I prayed to our Redeemer thanking Him for His amazing, beautiful, magnificent, precious son Yeshua (whose name is Salvation in Hebrew), tears poured down over my cheeks: And they were tears of joy.

16  *The* right *hand of* Adonai *is* exalted;
    *the* right *hand of* Adonai acts courageously.

17  I will not die, because I will live;
    and I will declare the works of Adonai.[25]

18  *With* punishing Adonai[25] punished me,
    and He did not give me over unto death.

19  Open to me *the* gates of righteousness:
    I will go into them; I will thank Adonai.[25]

20  This *is* the gate to Adonai:
    the righteous will enter into it.

21  I will thank You because You have answered me,
    and You are my salvation.

—Psalm 118:16-118:21

13     *Is* anyone among you afflicted? *Let him* pray. *Is* anyone
cheerful? *Let him* sing, playing a stringed instrument.[26]

14     *Is* anyone frail among you? *Let him* call *for* the elders
*of* the congregation; and *let them* pray over him,
anointing him *with* olive oil in the name *of* the Lord:

15     And the prayer *of* trust will save the fainting *one*;
and the Lord will raise him up; and if he has committed sin,
it will be forgiven him.

16     Confess to one another your fallings, and pray for
one another, that you may be healed: *an* effective prayer
*of a* righteous *one is* greatly capable.

—James 5:13–5:18

# CHAPTER FIFTY:

# Healed through Prayer

In those same days, my brothers and sisters had already
begun to see the mighty works of God, with great miracles of
healing: But sometimes Benaiah and I did not come to church
because of my epilepsy, which threw me down upon my bed, with
my spine drawn backward like a bow: Then when the pastor knew,
he prayed for God to heal my epilepsy—which prayer others had
already prayed many times (myself and Benaiah more than everyone
else), but God had always answered, "Not yet:" And again, after
Pastor Pedro's prayer, my Lord said to me, "Not yet."
But when Pedro asked Yeshua specifically to heal the pain, in the
very same moment all my pain was gone. And I began to pray every
day concerning my epilepsy, "Heal me, Heal me."

And the second time in which the pastor, and two other
brothers, prayed for God to heal my epilepsy and my spine, then I
also silently asked, "Please my Lord, Please don't say again, 'Not
yet.'" So Yeshua answered, "Soon."

But I remembered that He had said, nearly two thousand
years ago, "Behold, I am coming soon."[27]

So I whispered, "When, Lord, When?"

"Why not right now?"

And He said, "I want to show my strong hand to my servant
Pedro." This second time was the twenty-seventh of February, the

326

Sunday after the Sabbath in which I had given my testimony in the ears of the church.

And in the next Thursday night, while I was singing to the Lord with my sisters, the pain shot through my spine: And I sensed that within moments I was likely to be on the floor with a *Grand Mal* seizure;[28] possibly with a broken back:[29] And I remembered that my Yeshua had said, "I want to show my strong hand to my servant Pedro." But I was not able to speak well, because of the pain, and because of the scrambling of my language before every *Grand Mal* seizure;[28] but I could still walk: And I took my husband Benaiah's arm, and he helped me toward the altar: Because I could no longer walk without help. Then I knelt by the altar at Pastor Pedro's feet, so that he knew to pray for me: But my language was already confounded.

Then I felt a hand on my shoulder and spine—which is painful to autistic people; neither was I able to complain—and the pastor began to pray.

Instantly, the pain was gone.

Moreover, the flesh of the broken place at the top of my spine, where my epileptic seizures began, was hot, and it was also tender, like the flesh of new babies.

In those days soon afterward, I found—for the first time in my life—that I had good balance without any walker or wheelchair, and that I had rhythm; and that it doesn't hurt anymore to feel my brothers and sisters patting my back; and that the nerves in my body had changed: Because since my early childhood I had bitten the flesh of my hands and my wrists to control my pain: And the bites had felt good, and had taken away the pain in my spine. But not anymore: I had to learn what things I can do now.

Nine miracles of healing, in my lifetime, I had seen with my own eyes (although the first time I don't remember, but I heard of it from my mother): When my sister and I were only three years old, we were both hospitalized, dying of double pneumonia. And day after day the nurses kept telling our mother that we would certainly heal soon—but no.

Then, after the nurses could no longer look in my mother's eyes and say that we would live to see our fourth birthday, she took us both out of the hospital the next Sunday, and she carried her two twin daughters to her church, and set us before the altar, and prayed: And in the same hour our pneumonia was gone.

And this I remember, which I saw with mine own eyes: Fourteen years later, soon after I was baptized, one of our brothers in the Lord sent me to a Christian camp meeting, where the theme of the sermons was healing through faith. Then at the end of the camp meeting, while we were walking to the vans to return home, my left knee buckled (because I had broken my knee two years earlier, neither had any doctor even tried to repair my broken knee).

And I fell in the dust, and stopped breathing because I had had asthma since the ninth hour of my life. And I had suffered much under many physicians, and was nothing bettered by any: But rather they said that I would outgrow the asthma. Nevertheless the scars in my bronchia and lungs remained. (In my sixteenth year, the doctors stopped saying that I would outgrow my asthma.)

So when I fell in the dust, my bronchia closed and I stopped breathing.

Then, with my last breath, I was only able to pray two words—"Lord! Help!" And I kneeled in the dust, and my knee was restored, and my breathing also, unto this day. The year was nineteen ninety four, and I was eighteen years old.

Nearly ten years later, on the first day of the Feast of Tabernacles, I watched my firstborn son Manasseh take a dead hamster in his hands, and pray; and I saw the hamster, which was dead, begin in the same moment to breathe; and I saw when she awoke in the hands of my faithful little son, even as I have written in the chapter "Miracle Mouse."

Then, in two thousand nine, when I was blind for several hours and ready to die of a broken heart, my God healed my heart; and every day He gives me sight, but only for the word of God, even as I have written in the chapter "Blind."

These seven miracles I had seen with mine own eyes, and in two other times I had heard faithful testimony that my prayers for the healing of others were heard: Because in the same day as the birth of our "Little Samson" Mattithias, twice the Lord had commanded me to pray for the safety of my new cousin; and my new cousin Benjamin Nathaniel was saved, as I have written in the chapter "Twin Cousins."

Moreover, in two thousand nine, by everyone's prayers who prayed for Abram Jedidiah Ammi, his surgeon Nick Eshraghi was called by the Holy Spirit to come to work at night, in order to be ready to save the life of our Ammi, when the little baby's bronchia were closed up by pneumonia and bronchitis.

And now, in the Thursday night of March 3, two thousand eleven, I saw a new healing miracle, which is the healing of my epilepsy: And this night was the twenty-eighth of the Hebrew month *Adar*, the eighteenth anniversary of my baptism; (and, to us Hebrews, eighteen is the number of life[30]).

In some Hebrew fonts, the Khet gets to wear a little crown, because Khet is the Hebrew letter that represents humility.

To *the* Chief *Musician*; with stringed instruments.
A song; *a* hymn sung with a stringed instrument.[31]

1    God be merciful unto us, and bless us (His face shines
upon us: lift this up and weigh it carefully[32]);

2    That Your way may be known in *the* earth,
Your salvation in all nations.

3    *The* peoples thank You, *O* God;
*the* peoples thank You, all of them.

4    *The* communities will be glad and shout,
because You will rightly judge peoples,
and You will give rest[33] to *the* communities in *the* earth.
(Lift this up and weigh it carefully.[32])

5    *The* peoples thank You, *O* God;
*the* peoples thank You, *even* all of them.

6    *The* earth gives her produce;
God will bless us, *even* our God.

7    God will bless us; and all *the* ends *of the* earth
shall fear Him.

—Psalm 67

# CHAPTER FIFTY-ONE:

# Stars

Listen to me, please; pay attention; here is a word which was proclaimed from the beginning, and yet it is hidden from many: Listen carefully; and cherish well this secret which is no secret: When I was young (even though I had a poor sense of balance), my most treasured possession was my skateboard—until I traded my skateboard for a bicycle. And I did not regret that trade, but rather rejoiced to have the bicycle for mine own. Which of the two, then, did I value more? Is not the value of a thing certainly known by the price which men willingly pay to gain it?

There was a wealthy landowner who kept a great flock, with rams and ewes of every breed of sheep: But rustlers came in the night and carried away all his sheep.

In the morning, a ram and a ewe had escaped, and they returned to the fields of their beloved shepherd; and these two he patiently nourished and protected, until he had made a great flock of their descendants; and many said of this wealthy shepherd that surely he loved his second flock more than the first, which was carried away, and that this second flock was surely his favorite breed of sheep. And in time, a young ewe brought forth a perfect lamb: Healthier, stronger, bigger, and much more comely than any other lamb of his great flock: And that lamb followed the shepherd everywhere, and joyfully obeyed his every command; so that many said, "Surely the shepherd loves this flock above every other flock, and of this most precious flock, he loves that one lamb more than all other lambs in the field." But then, this shepherd sold his only perfect lamb to buy back all the sheep which were stolen—and then, soon afterward, he sold the whole flock from which his perfect lamb had been born, to regain the remnant which had not yet been returned.

Now, I speak as a ewe of this flock (because this wealthy shepherd is the Creator of the heavens and the earth): I speak as a ewe lamb sold, whose flock was sold with me, as it is written:

Romans
11:25    Because I am not willing, brothers, that you *should* be
         ignorant *of* this mystery… that, in part, a blindness of the
         eyes and a hardening of the heart has happened *to* Israel,
         until the fullness *of* the nations comes in;
26       and so all Israel shall be saved: as it is written,

         Out of Zion the Liberator will come,
         and will turn away ungodliness from Jacob:[34]
27       And this *is* the covenant from me to them,
         when I will take away their sins.[35]

                              ——Romans 11:25-11:27


This is because neither our Jewish Messiah, nor His Father, was contented that Yeshua should be a shepherd only over His flock Israel; therefore to His Jewish followers Christ said:

16       And I have other sheep, which are not of this fold: I must
         also bring them, and they shall hear my voice, and there shall
         be one flock, one shepherd.

                              ——John 10:14-10:16

And this scripture about the combining of these two flocks was a hard word for His apostles, who *still* struggled to understand when the non-Jewish believers began to join the Church through the words of His holy apostle Paul.

The first time in which Benaiah and I spoke with our brother Pedro Bernabé, Pedro called us the "Chosen People;" and he was visibly excited to have two of the Chosen People[36] in his congregation. But I was not excited. My heart cringed (although Pedro was in the right, and I, I should have *rejoiced*); the hearts of our people *cringe* when we hear the words "Chosen People."

Why?

Wherefore was our nation chosen by God?

Is it not to be sacrificed for every other nation that we are chosen, even as our Lord and King of the Jews was chosen for a sacrifice for every soul? My nation is chosen unto persecutions, tribulations, and sorrows.

Unto what am I chosen?

For persecutions, mourning, poverty, nightmares, and to feel in myself the suffering of my brothers, and of my beloved Lord on His cross—and yet, today, I sing with joy to be chosen.

In the Sunday which was the first of May of two thousand eleven, our brother Tim's parents came, who had been missionaries in Southeast Asia for many years; and  they spoke to our congregation about the ingathering of the nations:  Because already we are in the final age of the human race: Already, the fullness of the nations is coming in, and so the Messianic Jewish Movement has begun in all the earth, as it is written: "…until the fullness *of* the nations comes in; and so all Israel shall be saved…" And also,

Romans

11:1    I say then, Has God rejected His people?
        It will not happen…

11       …Have they stumbled that they should fall? It will not
        happen! But rather through their stumbling salvation is come
        unto the nations, for to provoke them to jealousy.

12       And if their stumbling is the riches of the world,
        and their lack the riches of the nations,
        how much more their fullness?…

15  …Because if the loss of them is the reconciling of the world,
    what shall the receiving of them be,
    but life from among the dead?…

28  …concerning the chosen,
    they are beloved for the fathers' sakes.
29  Because the gifts and calling of God
    are without repentance…

—Romans, chapter eleven

Beloved sisters and brothers, behold therefore the eternal covenant of God with the children of Jacob:

38  And they shall be a people to me, and I will be God to them;
39  And I will give them one heart, and one way:
    that they may fear me all the days, for their good, and *the good* of their children after them:
40  And I will make an eternal covenant unto them, that I will not turn away from doing good to them; and I will put my fear in their heart, that they shall not depart from me.
41  And I will rejoice over them to do them good,
    and I will plant them in this land, in truth,
    with all my heart and with all my soul.

—Jeremiah 32:38-32:41

And, also;

Psalm
2:8  Ask of me, and I will give nations *for* your inheritance…
Zechariah
8:20  Thus has Adonai of armies said: that even more peoples shall come, and the inhabitants of many cities;
21  And inhabitants of one *city* shall walk to another to say, Let us go: we will go to plead before Adonai's face, and to seek Adonai of armies: I will also go.
22  And many people and strong nations shall come to seek Adonai of armies in Jerusalem, and to plead before the face of Adonai.

Zechariah

8:23    Thus has said Adonai *of* armies: that in those days ten men
shall take courage, out of all the languages *of* the nations,
and they shall seize *the* hem *of* a Jewish man, saying,
We will go with you: because we have heard[37]
*that* God is with you.

2:10    Sing and rejoice, daughter of Zion: because here I *am*;
Come; and I will dwell in *the* midst of you, says Adonai.

11    And many nations shall be joined to Adonai in that day,
and shall be to me for a people, and I will dwell
in the midst of you; and you shall know
that Adonai of armies has sent me to you.

12    And Adonai shall inherit Judah his portion on the holy land,
and shall choose Jerusalem again.

13    Be silent, *O* all flesh, before the face of Adonai:
because He is stirred up from His holy habitation.

—Psalm 2:8; Zechariah 8:20-8:23; 2:10-2:13[38]

When our brother Tim's father and mother had nearly
finished speaking, they called all who were willing to give their
lives to Adonai; these ones they called up to the altar to be
missionaries to proclaim the glorious good news of our Salvation
Yeshua. And I kneeled before the altar in total surrender: And I felt
a finger put oil upon my head: And from the moment in which I was
anointed, I fell into a trance: And I saw a vision in which the
physical world became completely invisible: And my soul began to
fly upward into the heavens: And I looked downward while I arose,
and saw at first the souls of everyone in our little church, and then in
our little town, and then in the whole Pacific Northwest; higher and
higher I arose, seeing every soul as a little light; some pale, others
brilliant: A great constellation of thousands of thousands of
thousands of stars, every star a human soul, a constellation in the
shape of a great sphere: And I knew by the shape[39] of this spiritual
constellation that these stars were the souls of every human upon the
earth.

Arise, *O* God, judge the earth:
because You shall inherit all nations.

—Psalm 82:8

334

# This next chapter was written by my beloved friend and spiritual sister Laura:

5 Trust Adonai with all your heart;
  and lean not unto your own understanding.
6 In all your ways know Him,
  and He will make your paths straight.

—Proverbs 3:5-3:6

CHAPTER FIFTY-TWO:

# Saving James
## by Laura Snider-Seal

My son James is five, but he was three back then. He has blue eyes, and straight blond hair. He's kind of got a little round cherub face. He's fearless. And he takes responsibility. He does. If I tell him not to do something, because he's going to get hurt, and he does it anyway, when he gets hurt he doesn't cry; he apologizes to me for not listening.

His feelings get hurt very easily but he's super-quick to forgive. And he loves hugs and kisses. He can be a little bratty to his older brother, Johnny. He gets his brother in trouble sometimes, but that's normal sibling stuff. James is really smart; he understands and he remembers. I told him that I didn't know if he could bring his toys to heaven; but if they weren't there, then there would be something even better. And a week later he told me that if he didn't have his toys in heaven, he would have something better. And it would be lots, lots better. But that was recently.

When my son James was three, we were going through a difficult time. My mother died that year, a couple weeks before my stepfather's birthday in November. Shopping trips with James were usually expensive, time consuming, and stressful. He had not yet learned that he couldn't have everything he wanted.

The closest store was the Dollar Tree across the street, and we needed a couple things. James' Dad was working in the shop. I told my step dad where I was going and that I'd be back soon, and I snuck out when James wasn't looking. As I was walking up and down the aisles, adding things to my basket, a man came up to me. I had seen him walking around town. He was always clean, with a cheerful, Santa-like smile, but he was different from the people I normally hung out with. He had long hair and a long salt-and-pepper beard, and he walked around town, usually with a wheelchair or a shopping cart to carry his things in. When he smiles, his whole face smiles. I like that about him. It lets me know that even though he's different from me, he's not scary. He walked with a younger woman who always wore a long head scarf and seemed very shy. I liked them: they were always polite and friendly, and once they had purchased small toys for my two boys when the three of us were shopping. I didn't know their names.

He asked me if I was James's mother and I said I was. He told me that my son had just tried to follow me to the store, across the fairly busy street in the dark.[40] He said that he and his wife had just come by and seen him there alone. Then they took him to the nearest house to see if that was where we lived,[41] but not to worry, because he was with his grandpa now.

Instant panic froze me for a moment, and a dozen pictures of horrible things that could have happened flashed through my brain. But I took a big breath and forced myself to think. If James was hurt, the man would not be smiling. There would be sirens and all was quiet.

I told him thank you and immediately paid for my items and left the store. If I allowed panic to make me leave without my things, I would just have to come back later, and if I showed up frightened, I might scare James.

I came across my step dad and my son, going for an after-dark walk. Apparently, little James had gotten his own shoes on, gotten Grandpa to help him with his little wind-breaker (Grandpa thought he was playing a game), opened the door all by himself and started off. He was at the corner, waiting for his chance to cross the street when Ben and Naomi found him and brought him home. The next time I saw Ben and Naomi, I had learned their names and they told me that they never, ever went for walks before sunset on the Sabbath day, but that a little voice inside[42] had told them to that night.

I thank God that He sent Ben and Naomi for a walk that night.

They think James is special, and I think so too.

But I'm not sure it was James they were mostly there to save. Losing my mother was extremely difficult for me. Aside from the grief, her death made me the oldest surviving member on my branch of the family tree, and the only girl. Losing my baby could easily have been more than I could bear. It could have been the breaking of me. There is no doubt in my mind that if they had not been there, I would have lost my son. It was dark and rainy: no-one would have seen him. They heard[42] the Voice of God. Any other voice they would have ignored because of their normal Sabbath night routine, and the weather.

Why would God have sent them if my boy was going to be safe without them?

Perhaps they were sent because James is special. Perhaps his destiny is a great one. It could be; I think he's got the brains and the heart for an important future. It is also in my mind, though, that God only gives us what we can handle. I am made stronger by every trial I am sent to bear. I am a stronger person than I was when I was younger. I am also a person who gives up and surrenders fairly quickly when things get hard, and my lessons and trials have been much gentler than lessons I have watched other people bear. In the end, it doesn't matter why they were sent.

Saving James, saving me, some other purpose or blessing related to others, I will not be given an explanation of His motives. I have thought long and hard about that night, and I have what God intends me to have. I explain to my son now why he can't do certain things—why things are dangerous. I trust God to give me the words my son can understand without scaring him. I don't go out of my way to say goodbye when I'm crossing the street for a few minutes, but I don't sneak out, and he knows I'll always be back soon. I have learned my lesson, and I hold it to my heart with gratitude for both the lesson itself and its gentle delivery. I humbly accept that though I am important to God, my lesson was only a part of what happened that night.

James is safe to live out his future; all the drivers on the road that night were protected from a driver's worst nightmare, and any blessings our heroes have taken from their part.

Ben and Naomi saved my son's life that night, and they saved me as well. They are Servants of God, and favored by Him, and I am grateful to be here on this Earth with them. God's will surrounds us. His motives and methods amaze, delight, and terrify. His Hand is everywhere, touching all of us and the complexity and repercussions are mind-boggling. I am just grateful for what is, and the blessings we are given.

*It's a pretty amazing blessing,*
*for me, just to be called Laura's hero...*

*...but I think that our amazing God was the real hero that rainy Sabbath afternoon, when He spoke to Benaiah in the thunder, and also gave him a vision of James' grandfather, and then sent us out just before sunset, leading us both down the dark rainy streets to find a little boy who He had been watching with so much care...*

10  Create for me *a* clean heart, *O* God,
    and renew *a* right spirit within me.
11  Cast me not away from Your face;
    and take not Your Holy Spirit from me.
12  Return unto me *the* joy *of* Your salvation;
    and uphold me *with a* willing spirit.
13  I will teach transgressors Your ways;
    and sinners will return to You.
14  Deliver me from blood, *O* God: God will save me;
    my tongue shall sing *of* Your righteousness.
15  My Lord, You will open my lips,
    and my mouth will declare Your praise.
16  Because You do not desire sacrifice (and I will give):
    You will not desire *an offering* sent up.
17  *The* sacrifices of God are *a* broken spirit,
    *and a* broken and contrite heart…

—Psalm 51:10-51:17[43]

CHAPTER FIFTY-THREE:

# The Shining Armband

From October of two thousand ten until February, the Lord
cut more and more deeply into me: Neither have I ever written the
greater part of the many painful nightmares in these five months:
For that in His great love and mercy my loving Lord had granted me
my request, to deeply engrave my heart.

Then, I never saw the dagger again—that is, after I had
understood that the dagger was my own—because in a dream in
which I had thought that my Savior had shown me the murderous
sin of my new brother, it was not so: The truth is that a knife had
been in my own right hand to slay, and the death which I had
suffered in that nightmare was the same death which I had prepared
in my great wrath for my own father (who, like a wasp upon a
defenseless caterpillar, had enjoyed the helpless silence of his quiet
daughter).

Yet my Savior my Messiah in His mercy had not allowed
me, His new friend, to commit the murder.

But the poison called hatred had still remained hidden within me, poison building a wall of stone around my heart ever since my fifteenth year, until I had a heart of stone: Very slowly my Shepherd of my soul had cut away this stone; slowly, in order to protect His delicate servant from the blade: Because hatred is a very potent poison.

But in the Feast of Tabernacles I had begged, and asked, and begged my King to reveal and to cleanse my hidden sin: Therefore, then, the wall of stone—which I had built for three years before my salvation—the Lord of my soul had cut away in less than five months, according to His beautiful loving word, to deeply engrave my soul in order to give His servant a worthy armband.

Now the time of the dagger was finished, because His silver armband was ready to receive its shine: One thing, therefore, was necessary:

And I will give to you *a* new heart, and a new spirit
I will give within you; and I will take away from your flesh
*the* stone heart, and I will give to you *a* heart *of* flesh.

—Ezekiel 36:2

Then in the night of July twenty-ninth Benaiah and I were in the church, singing to the Living Lord; and, in a worship song, I began to raise up my fingers toward God with all my strength, to touch His great loving heart with my little soul, so that after a while my arms began to tremble with pain.

Then I felt His great holy finger, touching my newly exposed heart: He touched my heart; and like the flesh of my brain which had been renewed, like the tender flesh of a tiny baby, now in the same way my heart was also delicate and warm; so that, struggling to breathe, with amazement, I kneeled on the floor before my brothers and sisters with my right hand over my hot heart.[44] Therefore, then, some of my sisters asked if I was okay: And I—too amazed to find any other words—said [in Spanish], "God touched my heart!"

Then my heart was hot and pounding all that night, and that whole Sabbath day.

19    And I will give to them one heart, and I will give *a* new spirit
      within you; and I will take the stone heart out of their flesh,
      and will give to them *a* heart *of* flesh;
20    So that they will walk in my statutes,
      and keep my judgments, and do them: and they shall be
      to me for *a* people, and I will be to them for God.

——Ezekiel 11:19-11:20

342

He was oppressed, and He was afflicted, and He did not
open His mouth: like *a* lamb He was carried to the slaughter,
and like *a* ewe before her shearers is silenced;
and He did not open His mouth.

—Isaiah 53:7

CHAPTER FIFTY-FOUR:

# And I See the Raven

In the thirteenth of August, two weeks after my Creator had
touched and renewed my heart, our congregation gathered together
to celebrate with three other bands of Christian musicians, Believers
from three other churches, and three different cultures: And all the
day that Sabbath, we worshipped our Living Lord together with
whites, and Latinos, and African-Americans, and people of native
tribes; and Benaiah and I also sang with the congregation in Hebrew
and in Spanish; and we danced to the Lord in the Hebrew way; and I
also danced to God with a Native tribeswoman, in the way of her
people; and all the day both Benaiah and I were serving as Levites in
the Temple.

The native band was of different tribes; and was called the
Black Dog Drummers; they are evangelical ministers who travel to
prisons to bring light to the prisoners, worshipping our God in the
native manner with drums and flutes.

The Black Dog Drummers gave a big drum to our church,
consecrated unto worship, and called forth drummers from our
congregation to beat the drum: And Benaiah was among these. And
because he was the last to come, there was only one place for his
drumstick: And Benaiah saw that the drum was painted with a
raven, whose talons were toward the sun, and whose mouth was
opened to speak: And the only place for Benaiah to beat was the
raven's beak, so that his hand made the raven to speak: And Benaiah
heard his Lord saying that Benaiah is that raven. And while his
band was preparing to leave, one of the native musician ministers
said that Benaiah is now the guardian chosen for this sacred drum.

Two days afterward, in the evening of August fifteenth, two
thousand eleven, while Benaiah and I were singing in the chapel

sanctuary with our pastor, I saw that same drum for the first time up close in good light: And I saw and knew that the raven was the same raven with eyes like an albatross, which I had seen thrice in my lifetime in the dream of the two mountains: And I remembered that Benaiah had told me that he is the raven painted on the drum: And I asked Benaiah again, if by the word of our God he is surely the same raven, and Benaiah said, "Yes, I know that I am that raven."

Then I knew that the time had come for my service at the feet of the people of the two mountains, by the word of the raven sent from my God: I also knew that Benaiah had spoken the truth, because I felt again the same heat in my heart.

20     And I do not pray for these *ones* only, but also
      for those who will trust in me through their word;
21     that they may all be one; as You, Father, *are* in me,
      and I in You, that they also may be one in Us...

—John 17:20-17:23

CHAPTER FIFTY-FIVE:

# Yeshua's Feather

I rejoice, Beloved, when I see the eyes of my little brother Johnny: Because they are full of such light, the light of Adonai's love shining from his reborn soul. No longer does Johnny bear the black, black eyes of a killer's wounded soul, eyes that speak silently of death; of friendship with death. His eyes have God's fire.

This autumn, we were awakened (later in the morning than I care to admit) by a happy, excited voice outside our windows. It was a man's voice, but it had such joy, and such excitement, and such love of life, that it was like the voice of a little boy on Christmas morning. And I knew the voice, and wandered sleepily outside to watch: It was the voice of my brother Johnny, shouting like a rambunctious schoolboy about the wonders of Adonai's love. Sheepishly, he apologized for his loudness, but I grinned. There is no better way to be awakened than by the happy shouts of innocent children expressing their joy (even though Johnny is a full-grown man).

A month or two earlier, I had offered Johnny a part of this book's first draft to read; but he returned it the very next time he saw me. Then, soon afterward, he apologized that he hadn't read it; because he and his wife were too busy reading the Bible.

No apologies needed, my brother. None at all—How could I ever be jealous of *that* Author? May you always be too busy with God's word to read any words of mine.

Beloved Sisters and Brothers in Messiah Jesus, nearly two thousand years ago our Messiah prayed for His twelve apostles, and also for you and for me, saying to our Heavenly Father,

20 And I do not pray for these *ones* only, but also
for those who will trust in me through their word;
21 that they may all be one; as You, Father, *are* in me,
and I in You, that they also may be one in Us;
that the world may trust that You have sent me.
22 And the glory which You gave me I have given them;
that they may be one, *even* as We are one:
23 I in them, and You in me, that they may be completed
in unity; and that the world may know that You sent me,
and have loved them as You have loved me.

——John 17:20-17:23

But, Are we one yet? In this rather small city alone, there are more churches than I have found the time to attend, even after more than a year in this town.

There are not only more Christian denominations on the earth than I can easily number, but each language and each tribe also has its own churches: And here, as small as our city is, the English-speaking Seventh-Day Adventists and their Spanish-speaking counterparts both seem mutually unaffected by the other's existence. And yet none of these churches in our city is of my denomination, or of my tribe, or of the language of my ancestors. And even though the original church in Jerusalem was of Messianic Jews like me, many Christians even wonder whether we Messianic Jews are Christian at all.

Are we one?

How important was this prayer that our Lord Jesus Christ prayed so many centuries ago? Should our doctrines and rituals and traditions divide us? No. We share one Bible. Should our tribes and nations divide us? No. We share one Father, one King, and one Kingdom. Should our languages divide us? No. We share one Bible.

Are we one?

No. But we should be one, and in the future we shall be one.

I do not know the stories of other peoples as well as I know the stories of my own, but I suspect that we are not so different in our hopes, fears, dreams, and needs.

Hatred is something our peoples also share in common; and also Hatred's parents, which are Pride and Fear. Like many Jews, I have known well what it means to be hated, and I also know that Hatred is a very potent poison. I don't think I need to tell you that our people have also been hurt, and given every reason to hate; and fear; and hide our faces from foreigners.

There was a time when my own heart was poisoned with Hatred's father, Fear. Two autumns ago, in two thousand ten, as my husband and I prepared to move to this town where we now live, I was searching for churches we might attend here; and one which I saw, and completely ignored, was nearly next door to our future new home. Why didn't I want to worship at that one? It had a Spanish name, and we didn't speak Spanish at all. We could never fit in, right?

But, even before this little church had begun to exist, God had already made up His mind to bring us to this church.

In the nineteen-eighties, some young Israeli visitors to Guatemala were horrified to find Guatemalan soldiers brutalizing and murdering hundreds of Mayan Indians, intending to genocide their people just as Hitler's army had slaughtered so many thousands of Jews and Gypsies, nearly destroying the Gypsy race from the face of the earth. But what hit these young Hebrews the hardest was that these Nazi-like soldiers were wearing Israeli uniforms, and shooting Israeli bullets out of Israeli guns.

When my husband and I were staying at a small hotel in the Land of Israel, a Jewish woman walked up to me and asked me to ask my husband to remove the feather from his hair, explaining that it was a Palestinian custom to wear Indian feathers, and that some people were offended to see a fellow Jew with an Indian feather in his hair. Now, our ordinary custom is to avoid hurting anyone's feelings unnecessarily, and so I would have said "yes"; but before I could answer, I heard Yeshua's voice saying clearly, "That's *my* feather."

And so I said to the woman, "No. My husband is a Choctaw Indian, and the feather in his hair is a sacred sign…You don't tell an American Indian not to wear his feathers."

I did not know at that time why the people of Palestine were wearing Indian feathers (except for their glaringly obvious shared status as smaller cultures being colonized and threatened with extinction by newcomers to the land with white skin). No one had ever told us of the atrocities done to the Mayan Indians and to other southern tribes with Israel's own bullets and weapons: I knew only that my Lord and Savior had just whispered in my ear, "That's *my* feather."

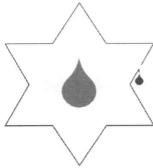

I can't even write this without feeling like I've just been kicked in the stomach.

Today, I have Mayan brothers and sisters in Messiah Yeshua, to whom my heart is bound by an unbreakable cord. I don't deserve the forgiveness of my beloved Latino brothers. Nor will I ever deserve the forgiveness of Messiah Yeshua, whose blood made this kind of love possible, and real, and stronger than my very desire to live. Outside this little church, an awkward little electric sign proclaimed in two languages a laughably improbable message of multicultural brotherhood between foreigners who don't even share a language in common.

In the autumn of two thousand ten, I committed a sin; and for this sin Messiah Yeshua, the Lord of my soul, turned away and was silent when I prayed. This He did for love; this was an act of mercy; this was a fulfillment of His promise to bear within Himself the punishment for all of my sins. But I wept. I cried, and wept, and cried, and begged for mercy: I didn't want His silent forgiveness; I wanted His voice; His face: I wanted His friendship.

Being free from the curse of the Torah, I chose a burden that was no longer mine. It was my Savior's burden, except for the sacred and unchangeable promise in the book of Isaiah:

9 For my name's sake I will defer my anger, and *for* my praise
I will refrain for you, so as not to cut you off.

10 (Behold, I have purified you, and not *as* with silver;
I have chosen you in *the* furnace *of* affliction.)

11 For my sake, *even* for my *own* sake, I will do *it*...

——Isaiah 48:9-48:11

Then I heard Yeshua weep, He showed me His tears; He wanted to turn His face away and continue to bear my sin alone.

But I begged relentlessly.

At the beginning of October, right after the Feast of Tabernacles; and at my own request, the Lord of my soul taught me, He thoroughly chastened me, He painfully cut away from my heart a spiritual tumor I hadn't even known was within me. From October of two thousand ten until February, the Lord cut more and more deeply into me; Neither have I ever written the greater part of the many painful nightmares in these five months: For that in His great love and mercy my loving Lord had granted me my request, to deeply engrave upon my heart.

If you can imagine a heart surgery without any anesthesia, with the surgeon cutting so slowly that his patient would not die of the pain, for five months this was my life. At first, I sometimes begged for mercy. But in time, I came to understand that His mercy was always there with me. For five months the Lord of my soul purified me like silver, cutting away from my heart a sin which looks so small that many people never even take account of it that it is indeed a sin. I didn't beat up or rob anyone. I didn't commit adultery and then mail my husband a photo of the act. I didn't steal an oxygen tank from a gasping grandmother.

What I did—this sin so great that it took my beloved Savior five months to cut it away—was that I hid my face from my brother.[11] But this seemingly tiny sin of omission was not insignificant to God. It was huge: It was a complete betrayal of God's reason for creating me: It was a betrayal of my Savior Yeshua, the Lord of my soul. During these five months, my soul was bound to the souls of the congregation Fuente de Vida (Fountain of Life), and my heart to their hearts, so that when one of my brothers, a butcher, was stabbed at work, I knew before I heard: because I felt the blade in my own flesh; and the memory of the wound filled my dreams.

Soon after the Sabbath, on November nineteenth, two thousand eleven, our brother David found the electric sign in front of our homely little church building had been uprooted like a tree in a hurricane. Somebody, in the dark icy evening, had hitched the signpost to his car and dragged it down with a mighty loud crash, shattering bits of light bulb glass all over the shoulder of the road. Somebody out there doesn't like the light. Was it random vandalism? Or was it the message on the sign—a simple message of multicultural brotherhood, a message of all nations sharing one Messiah?

The next morning, our brother Pastor Pedro led us in prayer, a prayer of forgiveness for the one who uprooted that electric sign. We could have gotten angry. The worldly people might say we have every right to be angry. But instead we saw love, and sadness mingled with joy, on the faces of our brothers as they gathered around the wreckage with shovels and a pickup truck and a tow rope.

Somebody out there doesn't like the light.

But in the diligent hands and determined faces of a beloved Texan scholar, and of Aztecs, and Mayans, and Jews, and Hawaiians, under a cloudy cold November sky, the light shone brightly that Sunday.

46 While He yet talked *to* the crowd, behold, His mother
and His brothers stood outside, seeking *to* speak *with* Him.

47 And one said *to* Him: Behold, Your mother and Your
brothers stand outside, seeking *to* speak *with* You.

48 And answering, He said *to* him *that* told Him,
Who is my mother? And who are my brothers?

49 And stretching out His hand over His disciples, He said:
Behold my mother and my brothers!

50 Because whoever does the will *of* my Father who *is* in
*the* heavens, the same is my brother, and sister, and mother.

——Matthew 12:9-12:50

CHAPTER FIFTY-SIX:

# Abba means Daddy

Dear sisters and brothers, if there is no other Hebrew word
you ever learn, please learn this one Hebrew word: *Abba* means
Daddy. Adonai does not want to be only your Master. Your belief in
Him is *NOT* enough—the demons also believe, and they tremble.
Your devout respect is *NOT* enough. Honor Him, yes. But more than
that, Love Him. Trust Him. Grab his hand tight, friend, as a good
little child holds tight to Daddy's hand when they walk across the
street.

In the book of the prophet Hosea, Adonai showed Israel that
He was *not* happy about being our "*Baal*"—our "Master." He
wanted reverence and obedience, yes; but, much more than that, He
wants our hearts and souls. He wants us to be in love with Him as a
wife loves her husband, and He wants us to cling to Him as a
suckling child clings to his daddy.

When I was very small, there was a man who was called my
father. His name was Dale Stuart Veach. I wanted him to want me,
but he never did. I wanted him to nurture and protect me, but he was
the one from whom I needed protection. But this book is not about
him. This book is about my *Abba*, my Daddy. When Yeshua was
crying out to Adonai from the depths of His anguish in the garden of
Gethsemane, on the eve of the Passover, with such great spiritual
agony that his sweat was as great drops of blood, He prayed,

...Daddy, Father, all *things are* possible *to* You;
take away this cup from me:
nevertheless not what I will, but what You *will*.

—Mark 14:36

He had also told His disciples,

And call no *man* your father upon the earth:
because one is your Father, who *is* in the heavens.

—Matthew 23:9

Yet it has pleased this Father well not only to create us in His image—fragile, foolish, primate shadows of His glory—but even to give to us a very small and temporary shadow of His Fatherhood. This is so, so *amazing* to me. It *ought to* be amazing to *every* earthly father and mother. What am I, this little daughter made of dust and of His breath, that I should ever be a mother, that I should have been blessed with sons and daughters? This I have come to understand, beloved sisters who are called mothers, and dear brothers who are called fathers: The seven children He has blessed me with were never truly my own.

Please know this deeply, dear brothers and sisters who are called fathers and mothers: Your sons and your daughters have only one father, and you and I have been given the truly amazing gift of a vanishing shadow of His Parenthood. These sons and daughters whom He has entrusted to us, we won't get to be their parents forever. These children are in our feeble hands for such a brief moment; and then childhood is but a memory recorded in fading photo albums; but we are *all* of us *always* in the palm of the Almighty's hand. These shadow family relationships of the feeble flesh will vanish like a vapor of smoke in the wind. But, God willing, our sons and our daughters may also be counted among our eternal and true brothers and sisters.

The true Father has chosen and anointed you to be a shadow of Him, and to teach your sons and daughters what it means to have a Father. This is an enormous responsibility, at which I *promise* you that you *will* sometimes fail; and it is also an enormous blessing.

Take this chance; grasp it with all your strength: Take this opportunity to learn more deeply about His real-life Fatherhood, and about His truly amazing love for us.

If you have ever visited the Grand Canyon, or studied astronomy in college, or wrestled a living from the sea, then you have some idea of how very small you are. King David wrote,

3      When I see Your heavens, *the* work *of* Your fingers,
        *the* moon and *the* stars, which You have prepared;
4      What *is a* mortal, that You remember him?
        And *a* son of man, that You visit him?…

9      *O* Adonai our Lord, how glorious *is* Your name
        in all the earth!

——Psalm 8:3-8:9[45]

Yet it has pleased the author of all creation not only to be mindful of tiny little us and to visit us, but even to make us His own sons and His own daughters, even brothers and sisters of our great Redeemer and Brother Yeshua His Messiah, as it is written,

14     Because all who are led *by the* Spirit *of* God,
        these are children *of* God.

15     …you have received *the* spirit *of* adoption,
        whereby we cry, Daddy, Father!
16     The Spirit itself bears witness together *with* our spirit,
        that we are children *of* God:
17     And if children, also heirs: truly heirs *of* God,
        and joint-heirs *with the* Messiah…

—Romans 8:14-8:17

I thank my heavenly father Adonai for every precious moment He gave me with my seven children. I've found nothing on this earth more excellent than these fleeting moments, many of which so easily slip by us foolish human parents, unnoticed in our almost constant struggle to give our children a better future, not heeding the fact that this day may be Mommy's or Daddy's last day, or one of their children's, on this troubled planet. I thank my God for the thirteen years, eight months, and seventeen days which He gave us to cherish and care for our devoted and loyal son Manasseh Raphael. His courage inspires me daily as I remember him in my prayers and as I work: Manasseh Raphael is one of my heroes, and I know that with Messiah Yeshua's help I *can* be the mother this worthy young man deserves.

I am grateful for the enormous gift of Manasseh's life, and I am grateful to God for preserving Manasseh's earthly life on that horrible Fourth of July; and I promise, for the rest of my days, to rely on Adonai, the Holy Spirit, and Messiah Yeshua to become each day the best mother I can be, not merely to my biological sons, but also—and even more importantly—to my spiritual sons in the Lord. I will nurture them, teach them, and I will strive to be the best example I can even in the smallest matters; such as waiting for the light at the crosswalk even when there are no cars coming, just in case a child is watching somewhere.

Manasseh, if you ever get to read this book, I heard all about how diligently you cared for your siblings, and how you were sent away to a "mental health facility" because your captors couldn't convince you to stop teaching Yehudah Isaiah the truth about our amazing God's perfect love. Young man, I'm proud of you; and I can hardly wait for the day you come home, so I can shake your hand. I'm sorry I never bought you that Lego Robotics kit, or sent you to engineering school—and, above all, that I in my anger may have taught you the poison of my own hatred—but you are a man; and with God's help you can make the best of this life anyway.

I thank my God for the twelve years which He gave us to cherish and care for our sensitive and charismatic daughter Elishevah Yael.

I am grateful for the immeasurably priceless gift of Elishevah Yael's life, and I am grateful to God for saving Elishevah's earthly life on that horrible Fourth of July, and I promise, for the rest of my days, to rely on Adonai, the Holy Spirit, and Messiah Yeshua to become each day the best mother I can be;

not merely to my biological daughters, but also—and even more importantly—to my spiritual daughters in the Lord. I will teach them, and I will strive to be the best example I can for them, and I will nurture them in His love and through His holy words of love.

Elishevah, if you ever get to read this book, I'm still waiting for you and loving you, and I always will. I know that you've been taught some very strange slanders against us and against your heavenly Daddy Adonai, but I am confident that your heart will know the truth when you see it. May you return to walk with God when He touches your heart as He touched mine; and may you faithfully hold His hand throughout your remaining days. Amen.

I thank my God for the nine years which He gave us to cherish and care for our courageous and passionate son Mattithias Lazarus. I am grateful for the tremendous gift which is Matt's life, and I am grateful to God for preserving his earthly life on that horrible Fourth of July. I also thank Adonai for sending me one of His holy Nazarites. I'm sorry I couldn't protect his hair or his soul from the cruel ones of this fleeting shadow world below, but I have come to understand that this Mama just can't be the superhero that Matt had ignorantly believed me to be when he was very small. There's only one real-life superhero, and His name sure isn't Naomi Levell. It's been very hard for me to accept, although Adonai had already told me when Matt was still in my womb that Matt is His own child, set apart and sanctified to Him. In truth, from the very beginning, every one of us is in the palm of Adonai's hand; and we all belong to our heavenly Daddy Adonai. Mattithias Lazarus never was my own to begin with. And I promise, for the rest of my days, to trust Adonai that He will be my son's one true Father; and I will trust Messiah Yeshua to be Matt's one true Hero and forever his Friend; and I will trust the Holy Spirit to be Matt's faithful teacher.

Matt-a-tat-tat, if you ever get to read this book, I'm proud of you. I always was. And no matter what your captors have been telling you about favoritism—as if it was God who had sinned against Cain—you are among my six hundred and seven favorite children.[46]

29    And Yeshua answered, saying, Truly I say *to* you,
There is no one who has left home, or brothers,
or sisters, or father, or mother,
or wife, or children, or farmlands,
for my sake, and *for* the gospel's,

30    except he receives *a* hundredfold now in this time
homes, and brothers, and sisters, and mothers,
and children, and farmlands, with persecutions;
and in the age to come eternal life.

———Mark 10:29-10:30

I thank my God for the forty-one days which He gave us to cherish and care for our precious child Yonah[47] whose face we hope to see for the first time in Heaven. Although we hadn't planned on making a fourth child, at least until after I graduated from college, I rejoiced greatly during the two brief days when I knew that little Yonah's new soul was alive and swimming with a tiny new body within my womb. I'm sorry I didn't know that that bottle of corn oil was contaminated. I'm sorry for all the perverse and heartless actions and inactions which have cost the lives of so many immeasurably precious souls like Yonah, who never got to smell this earth's cinnamon, or kitten fur, or the fresh ocean air, and who never got to play with his brothers and sisters.

I know that Adonai loves each child far more than I can, and I know that heaven is an amazingly wondrous place for all the children playing there, but I can't help wishing; and I can't help weeping; and I can't help missing my littlest baby whose tiny toes I never got to wiggle and tickle and kiss. I am grateful for the sweet, sweet gift which was Yonah's life, and I promise this day that I will not be silent concerning the sins of pollution and genetic engineering. While there is still breath within me I will *NOT* be silent; knowing that maybe, just maybe, my words may yet save the life of just one child. And so, when we finally come together again, I may rejoice to find my little Yonah standing among the martyrs. And I will not be silent.

I thank my God for the six years which He gave us in which to cherish and care for our thoughtful and affectionate son Yehudah Isaiah. Yehudah, if you ever get the chance to read this book, please *don't ever* turn your eyes and ears away from the poetry hidden within all languages and throughout Adonai's amazing creation. I'm sorry, Joodlebug,[48] for every moment I ever wasted on preparing for a post-college future which would never even exist, when I should have been dancing with you through the trees and the flowers. Your cute little poems are worth ten thousand times ten thousand more than the best textbooks at the best university, and I hope that every parent who reads this will take notice and take a little piece out of every hour to cherish and fill up each of their children's rapidly vanishing childhoods.

I've made some absolutely rotten mistakes as a human being and as a mother, but in the end my only lasting regret was everything I didn't do because I thought there would be another chance later. And sometimes there isn't. I promise never, ever, to be too busy again for at least a hug, a game of chase, a tickle, a song, a silly face, a smile.

I thank my God for the two years He gave us to cherish and care for our precious, friendly, cheerful son Abram Jedidiah Ammi. Brothers who are fathers, sisters who are mothers, please listen to me and listen well:

In the evening on the third of July, two thousand nine, I put a healthy little bundle of smiles to bed, assuming I would see him there again in the morning, but happy little Abram was too joyful and excited to fall asleep, so he stayed up and danced, shaking and bobbing his funny little square head and flinging his mop of golden hair in rhythm with the drumbeat of our worship music. He danced and he hopped with his big silly grin that was almost too wide to fit on his face. I took the moment for granted, thinking he'd be doing it again in the morning, until suddenly he plopped. Like a kitten plopping down mid-pounce for a catnap, Abram just suddenly, mid-dance step, plopped down in his little bed, limp as a ragdoll.

I checked Abram's temperature with my wrist, and then Benaiah checked Abram's temperature with a thermometer; and it was just a little past 97.8 degrees Fahrenheit,[49] hardly worth calling a fever at all. But somehow it all just felt *eerie*. And then, while we were making plans to carry him to the hospital, in the blink of an eye our little baby boy went from peacefully asleep to violently thrashing with all his strength, unbelievably hot and unable to breathe.

And so to you brothers and sisters who have children, I say, don't ever assume that there will be a tomorrow with your little ones: Despite your prayers, against your will, and despite your very best efforts to protect the ones you love, your child's life can still end without warning, in the blink of an eye.

And I am so, so grateful to my God that Abram's life, as badly as it was marred, didn't end that horrible night. His two little dancing feet died, but he didn't die with them.

There is no way to describe the depth of my pain to anyone who has never experienced such a tragedy in their own home, but by the hand of the Almighty God we all survived. Our six children could easily have survived this plague as orphans, but instead by Adonai's grace they can hope to get their parents back someday. Abe, if you ever get to read this book, you're one of my heroes. I'm proud of you. May your funny faces and giggles brighten up a thousand homes as they once brightened mine.

Your first step was spent dancing in front of your brother Manasseh to the tune of some fiddle music, and the last step your cute little feet ever took was spent joyously dancing in rhythm to glorious worship music. May you never forget, Abram "Jedi",[50] that you *don't* need feet to dance.

I'm sorry I was so careless about our enemy lurking outside our door that summer day, and I'm sorry it was you instead of me who ended up maimed for life by the disease I carried into our house. If I could have taken off my legs and put them on your little knees, I wouldn't even have thought about it twice, but I can't ever go back in time and change places with you.

In these two things I rejoice, my brave little man: First, that I had kissed your little feet and each of your toes when I had the chance; and, second, that you have the kind of heart that is able to overcome the very worst tragedies this world can throw your way.

I thank my God for the one year, seven months, and eleven days which He gave us in which to cherish and care for our deeply sensitive and compassionate baby daughter Esther Sarah Hadiyah. I'm grateful for the eight months I had to hold her in my arms, and for the honor of introducing her to dancing, flowers, music, strawberries, sunshine, and especially to her brother Abram's laughter and baby games. I don't know if she'll even remember me the next time we meet again, but I'll never forget her beautiful summer-sky blue eyes, and her darling brave and regal heart. I am so grateful to Adonai that our delicate little Esther was spared this horrifying sudden plague. Scientists say that at eight months old, Esther Sarah Hadiyah's first symptom would have been death. Indeed, Benaiah could easily have survived this rare and hideous disease alone, utterly bereaved of his wife and children. I hope never to forget Esther Sarah Hadiyah's cute little soft hand that gently slapped me with all her might for wasting some of our precious last hours together by crying.

Beloved *Esh*,[6] if you ever get to read this book, Thank you for that scolding. I'll try never again to waste a perfectly good hug with crying. I will always, always love you, my *Esh*.

And besides these six hearts which the Enemy thinks he took away on the Fourth of July, Yeshua has also promised me sons and daughters a hundredfold, in this lifetime here on earth. And so to my two hundred other daughters[51] in Yeshua I say, don't ever say you haven't got a Mama—I'm right here. And I have learned to love you just like I love my little baby girl Esther. And also to my four hundred other sons[51] in Yeshua I say, I offer this book, and more importantly the Bible, as food to nourish your hungry souls. Don't go away from the table hungry: Let me feed you, because I have learned to love you just like I love my noble-hearted son Manasseh Raphael.

Heavenly Father, I thank You for Manasseh Raphael, Elishevah Yael, Mattithias Lazarus, Yonah, Yehudah Isaiah, Abram Jedidiah Ammi, and Esther Sarah Hadiyah Levell; and I also thank You for my hundreds of spiritual sons and daughters in your eternal family. Thank You for my Grandfather Nathan; and also for Mister Rogers, President Jimmy Carter, Pastor Pedro Bernabe; and especially for my earthly husband Benaiah Zechariah.[52] I never much cared what most other human beings thought of me, but I have desired to make these five brothers proud of me. Thank You, Yeshua my Brother, for all of our brothers and sisters in Your eternal family.

Thank you for Shoshanna Miriam,[53] who is not only my shadow mother of the flesh, but also one of my true mothers in my eternal family, as well as my sister and my daughter. Thank You for all of my mothers, and sisters, and daughters.

*Amen.*

Shoshanna Miriam and her grandbaby Esther

...Woman, Why are you weeping?

———John 20:15

AFTERWORD:
# Jerry's Bright Smile

After a long and sleepless night, lightly tinged with an unexplained spiritual heaviness, I fell asleep on the morning of the Sabbath. Next door to us was the source of the noise which had prevented me from dozing off: A newborn baby boy, astonishingly tiny and oh so precious. Our whole cul-de-sac has been delighted since he came home from the hospital, and even his tiny, feeble nighttime cries are like the sweetest bird song. Still, this song had kept me awake for so long a time that I was glad when he finally rested. The beauty and wonder of a new human life—the anticipation when the due date came and went—I remember the excited little shriek I had made as I ran outside at the news of his arrival.

A son.

Yet there is a greater joy I know of than to gain a son, and that is to watch him grow up into a faithful man of God. How can I think of my son Manasseh Raphael without smiling? I rejoiced greatly at his birth, at his youthful beauty, at the strength in his tiny delicate hands.

But the joy of a faithful son who has joined me on Adonai's path; this joy is deeper; it is both deeper and eternal.

Our sister Mary has also known this kind of joy. I have not spoken to Manasseh or touched his hands in two years, but I know I will. I know that we will be together forever, I and my son. But mingled with this joy are the tears of separation. It's been nearly forty-five months since I stepped into an ambulance and out of Manasseh Raphael's life.

I remember the anguish of that Fourth of July night. My baby boy Abram, my son Abram Jedidiah Ammi, had been happily dancing in his crib, flinging his long golden hair wildly, his lipless goofy grin splitting his face from ear to ear as he twirled his hair and hopped with both feet in time to the worship music. The Fourth of July was about to begin, and Abram knew that he wasn't going to be sent to bed on a holiday. Then, exactly at midnight, as the rest of the Pacific Northwest began a wild celebration, Abram's holiday ended. Mid-dance step, he flopped down limp, and suddenly pale, with the very slightest of fevers. As mild as Abram's symptoms were, their suddenness was eerie and terrifying.

I remember the deep, deep desperation as I sat in the ambulance holding my baby son's hand, trying to comfort him through his very first sickness. In seconds, my Abram had gone from pale pink to dark red, purple, and black. I watched in helpless horror and desperation as his cute little dancing feet turned black before my very eyes. *Don't leave me*, little Abe. *Don't leave me.*

And now, nearly three years later, this desperation was distantly echoed, a dull and distant cloud, and deep. *Don't leave me*, my son. *Don't leave me.* And almost as soon as I fell asleep, the heavy cloud of desperation and heartache pressed upon me, and I began to dream a nightmare.

In this nightmare, I was a man. I was wounded in this nightmare, viciously violently wounded, pierced and cut in my belly and chest as if a machine gun had torn through me, but the physical pain didn't matter. As a good son, I had learned how to keep my eyes fixed on the good things of God. Pedro, my father, leaned over me, his big brown eyes still reflecting the heart of God, but also full of deep desperate fear.

"*Don't leave me*," he said. *Don't leave me.*

My own soul was ready; I wasn't afraid to fly away, and my body was done with me. I wanted to plead with him; I wanted to beg him to understand that I wasn't going anywhere; that I, his son, would never, ever leave his side; that heaven isn't that far away. But Pedro couldn't hear my words: my shredded flesh had nothing to say. So, waiting for my father to be ready, I held onto my failing flesh with all my remaining strength, until the pain had vanished and the darkness had conquered my eyes, and I had no choice but to fly away with the words *Don't leave me* still echoing in the ears that were no longer mine.

Soon afterward, our brother Rodrigo told Benaiah and I that our brother Jerry had passed away.

Mary, my Sister, my friend, I know how it feels to lose a son, and to weep deeply, barely comforted by the distant knowledge that we will only be apart for a very little while. I'm sorry that you had to find out how this pain feels.

Pedro, Mary, there is a saying among the Jewish people that funerals are only for the living. The ones who have already gone to heaven do not mourn, nor do they wish for us to mourn because their time of rest has come. We mourn for ourselves, being left behind, because even though Jerry is okay—he's better than okay, he can even do back flips now—it hurts, it hurts, it hurts to know we won't see him again, perhaps for many years, until we go where he is. Jerry is our brother, our son, and our true friend. He is an inspiration for our dear sister Mary, and for Pedro's favorite miracle sermon. Jerry's bright smile always lifted my heart every time I saw him. Jerry, we love you. We miss you. We're glad you're okay, but still—selfishly, I suppose—we'd rather you were here with us a little while longer.

Heavenly Father, You know the hearts of everyone here on earth, and You know how much death hurts. Throughout the Bible, within the words of the prophets, You have cried out to Your dying children again and again, *Don't leave me. Don't leave me.*

Adonai, Eternal Father, I will never leave You. I'm sorry I made You cry when I was dying in sin. I will never leave You. Thank You for the time we had with Your child Jerry; Thank You for every time You had mercy on us and made Jerry's brief life just a little longer; and thank You for his resurrection and health and joy. I thank You, my Daddy, my *Abba*, that You gave me a vision of Jerry running in a warm, summery field of grass and herbs, and that I saw him turn toward me for just a moment with a big grin, and I saw that his legs were long and strong. I'd never noticed before that Jerry was meant to be a tall man.

After giving me one brief grin, Jerry turned around, did a back flip, and ran away. He didn't even take the time to say goodbye.

Thank You, Eternal Father, for Jerry's bright smile.

…Come out of her, my people,
　　　that you be not partakers *of* her sins…

　　　　　　　　　—Revelation 18:4


And you shall dwell in *the* land that I gave to your fathers;
　　　and you will be to me for *a* people, and I will be to you for God.

　　　　　　　　　—Ezekiel 36:28

# Medical "Care" Limitation Request
## by Benaiah and Naomi Levell:

1.  We, Benaiah Zechariah Levell and Naomi Levell, do not believe that anyone, ever, has a right or a need to be killed for any reason unless they have either done something for which the Bible says to put them to death (and have been convicted of the same in a biblically acceptable manner), or else unless they are a species of animal designated in the Bible as clean for food for the people who intend to eat it. Euthanasia is not medical care.

2.  We, Benaiah and Naomi Levell, do not believe that the hospitals and medical industry in the United States of America can be trusted to honor the sanctity of marriage, or of families, or of human life. We would rather be laid down on the sanctuary floor of a church, or in the garden of a churchyard, than to be taken to any non-Catholic hospital in the United States, all of which dishonor and intentionally destroy families, marriages, or human lives, and all of which have a government-granted "right" and sometimes even an "obligation" to do so with impunity.
    We categorically reject all government-funded ambulances, doctors, and hospitals; we categorically reject all government-sanctioned hospitals; we categorically reject all government-run hospitals; and we categorically reject all hospitals which actively and openly support the Nazi religious doctrine that the murder of individuals for the sake of the community is not only permissible but righteous, and the Darwinist religious doctrine that human beings are apes descended from amoebae.

3.  We do not consent to be organ donors while we are in the United States of America (this is a decision which we greatly regret the necessity of); nor do we consent to be autopsied, or to be embalmed or cremated, or to allow our dead or living bodies to suffer any other shameful abuse contrary to Jewish tradition or Biblical Law.

4.    In the event of our deaths, or the likelihood of imminent death, please call a local Jewish rabbi. We are Christians of Jewish descent, and we have deeply loved the Jewish people and the Torah given by God to the Jewish people, and we humbly request a Jewish burial.

# *Notes*

page 8
1.  πιστευο (Strong's Concordance number *4100*, pronounced *pist-yoo-oh*) is traditionally translated as *to believe*. However, I believe that *to believe* is its secondary meaning, and that its primary meaning is *to trust*: Here, therefore, I have translated *pist-yoo-oh* as *trusts* instead of *believeth* or *believe*. Here are three verses in which the translators of the Authorized King James Version translated *pist-yú-o* thus:

    Luke 16:11—trust
    1st Thessalonians 2:4—trust
    1st Timothy 1:11—trust

page 8
2.  In this verse, I translated απολλυμι (Strong's Concordance number *622*, pronounced *apól-loomee*) as *perish*, as did the Authorized King James Version. The Reina Valera version, which is the Spanish counterpart of the Authorized King James Version, disagrees, saying *se pierda*, which means *be lost*. Here are twelve verses in which the translators of the Reina Valera version of 1960 translated *apól-loomee* with various forms of *perecer*, which means *to perish*:

    Matthew 8:25 and 26:52; Mark 4:38; Luke 8:24, 13:3, 13:5, 15:17, and 21:18; John 10:28 and 11:50, Romans 2:12, Hebrews 1:11, and 2nd Peter 3:9

page 10
3.  *Jesus* is the English form of יֵשׁוּעַ (*yeshúa*), the masculine form of the Hebrew word יְשׁוּעָה (*yeshúah*), which means *salvation* (Strong's Concordance numbers 3442, 2443, and 3444). *Christ* is the English form of the Greek word Χριστος (*Khreestós*), which means *anointed* (Strong's Concordance number *5547*), which is the Greek translation of the Hebrew word מָשִׁיחַ (*Mashee-ah*) (Strong's Concordance numbers 4899 and *3323*)—or, in English, *Messiah*. Thus, *Jesus Christ* means the *Anointed Savior*.

# Section One:
# The Seer

page 13
4.  1st John 4:8; 1st John 4:16

page 18
5.  See note 8 in the notes for *Seven Flames:*
   *Letters to Manasseh.*

pages 18, 29
6.  My mother gave my brother the name Ricky David, but he
   hated the gentile name Ricky so much that he changed it
   almost as soon as he could talk; and when he was eighteen,
   he changed his name legally to Reuben David Goldenstein.

pages 19, 20
7.  *Madhebah* (Strong's Concordance number 4062), translated
   in the King James as "golden", may be the Chaldean name of
   Medeba (Strong's Concordance number 4311), also known
   as Madaba, Jordan. In Arabic, *Madhebah* means *Waters of*
   *Quiet* (the same as its Hebrew name *Mediba*), and Madaba is
   an Arabic city. If the prophet had intended to say that the city
   was golden, Why didn't the prophet Isaiah use the Hebrew
   word for "golden"? And why is there no word for "city"
   here? Certainly, then, *Madhebah* was intended to be read as
   a proper name, not as an adjective.
   I do not believe that the translators' assumption is correct,
   that *Madhebah* is derived from the Chaldean word for
   "gold", but rather that the translators did not take into
   account the possibility that it could be an Arabic word.

page 24
8.  My first memory of Dale Stuart Veach committing incest
   against me happened thus: One night, my twin sister and I
   were very sleepy, but she refused to go to her bed. It had
   never occurred to us that I could go to my bed while she kept
   playing, because we were always together all our life, and
   because it was evident that many, including the man who
   should have been a father to us, clearly thought of us as the
   two halves of a pair of twins. So, I stayed awake with her for
   perhaps fifteen minutes without question, waiting for her to

go to her bed so I could go to mine. But I was very sleepy, and I asked again. But still she refused, asking me to stay awake with her until the morning.

When I asked why, she said to me that she was afraid to return to her bed, saying, "Daddy turns into a monster at night." I didn't understand, but she didn't know how to explain it more than that; and I wasn't afraid of monsters; so I offered to trade beds with her that night to learn in what way the man "turns into a monster at night", and so that she could sleep without fear, because she was even more sleepy than I.

So we traded beds for the night, and the man who should have been a father to us came and sat with me in my sister's bed. (Her bed was beside the door of our bedroom, and mine was on the other side against the far wall.) With his voice, he spoke like a good father, even while with his hands he "turned into a monster".

*page 24*

9.      Exodus 20:12; Deuteronomy 5:16

*page 25*

10.     Actually, I believe that I did have proof (of which, of course, I didn't know at three years of age): I still have physical damage to my secret parts, so that I can scarcely feel it when I need to pee, nor do I have much strength to hold back from wetting my pants, so that I have to change my clothes two or three times almost every day.

I have heard that Medicare would pay to buy diapers for this physical problem, but every time I asked any doctor about this, he/she said that I didn't have any physical damage, but rather that the problem was emotional. (None of them looked at nor tested my secret parts before saying this: They already "knew" because it is said by the "psychologists" to be so.) But I know that this isn't true: Because when a midwife taught me an exercise to strengthen my body for the birth, that is, to pee and then immediately hold back from peeing, I couldn't. So I know that the problem is physical. But I never again want to argue with any doctor who "knows" by the letters after his/her name that I'm a "hypochondriac" without physical problems: I would rather change my pants two or three times a day than bear the pride of men and women with letters after their names.

*page 26*

11.　According to my mother, the two of them were calculating our budget for the month.

*page 27*

12.　This was before the invention of the cell phone, and before the internet: Those of my generation and older had to find other ways to quickly get the attention of the police. For example, we could honk the horn, or drive too fast, or directly over the white line—traffic conditions permitting, of course—then signal "follow me" with the hand. According to my mother, another of her sisters was also in the car with Rachel, but I personally do not remember her being there, nor do I have any other memories of that car ride: One way in which my epilepsy and Autism Spectrum Disorder interacted was that it was next to impossible for me to stay awake during a car ride because of the rhythmic motion of the motor.

*pages 31, 163*

14.　אֶצּוּרְךָ (*etz-tzav-re-khah*); literally, *I moulded you*: from יָצַר (Strong's Concordance number 3335, pronounced *yatzár*).

*page 31*

15.　אֲדֹנָי—In this verse, the Hebrew word *Adonai* is used in conjunction with the Holy Name. (See note 8 in the notes for *Seven Flames: Letters to Manasseh.*)

*page 31*

16.　What is Psalm 22:9-22:10 in the King James Version of the Bible is, in the original Hebrew Bible, Psalm 22:10-22:11

*page 32*

17.　See note 46 in the notes for *The Storm*.

*page 32*

18.　What is Hosea 2:16 in the King James Version of the Bible is Hosea 2:18 in the original Hebrew Bible.

*page 34*

19.　The word κρυπτα (*krooptá*) is a plural form of κρυπτος (Strong's Concordance number *2927*, pronounced as *krooptós*), which is traditionally translated as *hidden, inward,* or *secret* in the Authorized King James Version.

But in Romans 2:16 and in 1ˢᵗ Corinthians 14:25, the King James Bible correctly translates this same plural word *krooptá* as *secrets*.

*page 35*
20.　　What is Psalm 69:7-69:13 in the King James Version is Psalm 69:8-69:14 in the original Hebrew Bible.

*page 40*
21.　　What is Psalm 52:8 in the King James Version is Psalm 52:10 in the original Hebrew Bible.

*page 43*
22.　　I saw with my own eyes a small and delicate little boy who was punished in this manner, when suddenly he stopped screaming and crying, and lost his color so much that he was blue-grey, and his eyes darkened, like death; and when a worker saw that I was watching, she took me by my arm and my head, turning my face to the side with her hand, and took me to the television room, saying, "Quiet now; we don't want to disturb the other children with another child's private business." Soon, I noticed that the little boy and one of the workers were not in the house with us, neither did the boy return home until night.

In the next two days, the workers told us that this little boy had fallen from one of the old apple trees, because the old branches were fragile, and one broke. They also said that the boy's two arms were dislocated from their sockets, and I believe that this part of the story was true.

But I also knew those trees, and none had broken in more than four months; moreover, this child certainly was never a climber of anything, especially those elderly little trees, which all the children knew well never to climb.

For the rest of the month, we were not permitted to enter the apple orchard, allegedly because the trees had been found to be dangerous, but I disobeyed because I was curious to see which of the little old trees had broken—because of this, I can say with certainty that the child had not fallen from any of the apple trees.

Soon (within a month) every apple tree, the entire orchard, was cut, and even the stumps were removed—I suppose that those stumps, being healthy and strong in spite of their age, were likewise dangerous—but dangerous to *what*, exactly?

*page 45*

23.    Her name was actually Aurora Dawn Larsen, but she really hated it, because "Aurora" means "Dawn", so it's as if she has the same given name twice, "Dawn Dawn", which she considered to sound very stupid, although almost everyone else thought that it was a lovely given name. But she did not allow me to say so, nor ever to call her "Aurora Dawn".
(I don't know if the correct spelling of her family name was Larsen or Larson; both family names are very common, and are both pronounced Lárs'n.)

*page 47*

24.    זְרֹעַ (Strong's concordance number 2220, pronounced *ze-ró-ah*) Although I have translated this word literally as *arm*, in Hebrew the arm represents *power*.

*page 47*

25.    מִדְבָּר (Strong's concordance number 4057, pronounced as *midbár*) There are different words in Hebrew frequently translated as *desert*, and *midbár* comes from מִן (Strong's concordance number 4481, pronounced as *min*) (from) and דֹּבֶר (Strong's concordance number 1699, pronounced as *dóver*) (sheepfold).
So, literally, *midbár* means *from the sheepfold*: a *midbár* is not a completely deserted place, but rather wild land commonly used as pasture for goats and sheep.

*page 48*

26.    See note 4 in the notes for *The Daughter*, and also the *letter to Justus* in the book *Seven Flames* by Ben Z. Levell and Naomi Levell.

*page 51*

27.    See note 1 in the notes for *Seven Flames: Letters to Manasseh*.

*page 52*

28.    Daniel 7:5 through 7:23; Revelation 11:7; 13:1 through 13:18; 14:9 through 14:11; 15:2; 16:2 through 16:13; 17:17; 19:19 through 19:20; 20:4; 20:10
"Beast" translates the Chaldean words חֵיוָא (*khey-vá*) and חֵיוָתָא (*kheyva-tá*, Strong's concordance number 2423) and the Greek word *thei-rí-on* (Strong's concordance number

*2342*). A *khey-vá* is a government made by men and submitting, ultimately, to Satan.

See in the book of Daniel, chapter 7, and in the book of Revelation, chapters 11, 13, 14, 15, 16, 17, 19, and 20. The Hebrew word חַיָּה (*khayáh*, Strong's concordance number 2416), and the Greek word ζῷον (*dzó-on*, Strong's concordance number *2226*), are often translated as "beast"; but they have a very different prophetic meaning, and ought to be translated as "living creature"—a *dzó-on*, a living creature, is a government made by God and submitting to Him, like the living creatures in the book of Ezekiel, chapter one, and on the book of Revelation, chapters 4, 5, 6, 7, 14, 15, and 19.

*page 57*

29.　　Philippians 4:8

*page 57*

30.　　Genesis 1:10, 1:12, 1:18, 1:21, 1:25, 1:31—and God saw that *it was* good...and God saw that *it was* good...and God saw that *it was* good...and God saw that *it was* good...and God saw that *it was* good...And God saw everything that he had made, and, behold, *it was* very good.

*pages 58, 68*

31.　　See note 31 in the notes for *Seven Flames: Letters to Manasseh.*

*page 58*

32.　　In saying "the covenant that I made with their fathers in the day *that* I took them by the hand to bring them out of the land of Egypt", God made it clear that this old covenant was not the Torah (the Law given in the Ten Commandments on mount Sinai, which was expounded upon in the other 603 commandments written by the Holy Spirit by means of the hand of Moses because the foolish Hebrews were too afraid of the voice of the Almighty God), because these 613 commandments were given by God the next summer, and not in the day that Adonai took them by the hand to bring them out of the land of Egypt.

On the contrary, the only covenant that God made in the day that He took Israel by the hand to bring them out of the land of Egypt was the symbolic covenant of sacrificing lambs, and marking their doorposts with the blood of these lambs. However, being merely symbolic, this temporary covenant lost all future value since the very moment of the death of the True Lamb, because the blood of those innocent animals never actually had the power to save anyone.

So, because the Old Covenant that these verses promised would be replaced clearly was not the Eternal Torah of our God, clearly the New Covenant did not replace it: On the contrary, Messiah Yeshua added to the Torah a new commandment, saying, "A new commandment I give unto you, That you love one new commandment, saying, "A new commandment I give unto you, That you love another; like I have loved you, that you also love one another." (John 13:34) The Law was never able to offer Salvation to anyone, but only shows us that we are all sinners and that we need the Salvation of God, given through the Blood of the Lamb of God.

Unlike the Torah, the Law which God explicitly called Eternal and unchangeable, the covenant of offering the blood of sheep and goats and birds and bulls was intended to be temporary from the beginning, because it was symbolic of the Sacrifice of the Blood of Messiah Yeshua, so that Adam and all his descendants could symbolically accept the True sacrifice before the time of the crucifixion of the Lamb of God. Just as we, who were born after the day of the crucifixion, have the opportunity to accept this Sacrifice for ourselves now, even so all who died before the day of the crucifixion had the opportunity to accept this future Sacrifice for themselves then.

There is no purgatory, there is no limbo, there is no cosmic waiting room in which the almost-saved might forlornly await the completion of their redemption: The Salvation of God, which was already ordained and which began to be proclaimed since the day Adam breathed his first breath, has always been available to every soul who trusts in Messiah Yeshua, so that even Job, who faced his infamous tribulation before the first words of the first book of the Bible were ever written by human hands, was able through the Holy Spirit to say, "And I know *that* my Redeemer lives, and *that* He will arise at last above *the* dust." (Job 19:25)

*page 58*

33.　פָּרַר (Strong's Concordance number 6565, pronounced *parár*). By translating *parár* as *brake* (an archaic form of *broke*) instead of *annulled*, the translators of the King James Version hid the comparison here with divorce in "my covenant which they annulled, although I was a husband unto them": This verse is the deep heartfelt cry of the faithful husband, divorced by a treacherous wife without cause or reason, when she decided to turn away from His freely given Redemption and rely instead on her own (embarrassingly feeble and futile) attempts to be so righteous that she would not need to be redeemed.

*page 58*

34.　כִּי (Strong's Concordance number 3588, pronounced *kee*), and not אֲבָל (Strong's Concordance number 61, pronounced *avál*).

*page 58*

35.　This Hebrew word for "know" is plural.

*pages 58, 63*

36.　What is Jeremiah 31:31-31:34 in the King James is Jeremiah 31:31-31:34 in the original Hebrew Bible.

*page 59*

37.　What is Joel 2:27 through 2:30 in the King James is Joel 2:27 through 3:3 in the original Hebrew Bible.

*page 59*

38.　This prophetic premonition was only my first, and was like this: One bright morning, my sister Drea and I had been drawing in the kitchen (and our brother was also in the kitchen, playing on the floor behind us), while our mother sat at the table with the sunlight shining in her long hair, which made her hair look as if it were made of gold, transparent like glass. Briefly, Drea and I both stopped, quietly watching the sunlight in her golden hair; then Drea asked me to teach her how to draw that lovely hair.

(I was only four minutes older than her! How could it be possible that I would know how to draw any better than her?)

I said, "I don't know", but she insisted, so I said, "I don't know; I don't believe it's even possible with these crayons." Again, we silently watched our beautiful young mother in the light of the window when—without any visions—the knowledge simply came to me without a word that very soon I would never again see my mother as this fair youth, because when I would return to my family, her golden hair would be cut, and her joyful face would be marked by years of worry and anguish. This painful knowledge made me wish very much that I could be able to teach Drea how to draw the fleeting beauty of our happy mother (but even so I couldn't); so I firmly fixed this beautiful image in my mind, and I asked of God that if I should someday forget everything, I want this image to be the last to remain in my failing mind.

page 62

39.     In those days, the hour was the smallest unit with which time was commonly measured. And in many miracles since the invention of clocks and watches with second hands, it has been observed that God heals in the same moment: So I believe that the demon left this child in the same moment that Yeshua healed her.

page 63

40.     Isaiah 59:20 through 59:21

page 63

41.     Jeremiah 31:33 through 31:34 (See note 36)

page 64

42.     See note 11 in the notes for *The Storm*.

page 65

43.     This phrase "my lord" translates perhaps too literally the Hebrew word אֲדֹנִי (pronounced as *Adon-EE*): *Adon-EE* is a form of "lord" (*ad-OWN*, Strong's Concordance number 113), but it is an intimate form normally reserved for a husband, king, or father: The use of it suggests that this was the same servant whom Abraham had adopted and originally named as his heir: A paraphrase "beloved father", although technically inaccurate, would be more true to the cultural connotations with which a native speaker of ancient Hebrew would have understood this text. If this servant had merely intended to convey the idea of "master", he would probably have said "*Ha-ad-OWN shel-LEE*", or "*ba-al-LEE*".

*page 66*
44.     Leviticus 26:12; Ezekiel 37:27; Revelation 21:3

*page 66*
45.     Isaiah 52:11; Revelation 21:7

*page 66*
46.     Second Samuel 7:14; First Chronicles 17:13

*page 66*
47.     See note 51 in the notes for *The Daughter*.

*page 67*
48.     What is Psalm 68:28 in the King James is Psalm 68:29 in the
        original Hebrew Bible.

*pages 68, 163*
49.     The Hebrew word חֲנֻכָּה (*hanukkah*) means "dedication", and
        the festival of dedication celebrates the dedication of the
        altar after the war against Antiochus, who had invaded Israel,
        outlawed worship of Adonai, erected a golden statue as a
        new god, and corrupted the holy altar by offering upon it a
        pig to this same gold statue. This king also required all the
        Hebrews to sacrifice to the statue, and any who refused were
        to be beheaded immediately. The priest Mattithias refused,
        and he beheaded the Hebrew traitor who tried to save his life
        by sacrificing a pig to the gold statue on his behalf. Then,
        Mattithias and his sons rose up in battle and defeated the
        army of the wicked Antiochus, recaptured the Temple
        Mount, and restored lawful worship of the One True God.
        The Apostles Matthew and Mathias were both named after
        this famous hero: Both of these names are forms of the hero
        priest's Hebrew name מַתִּתְיָהוּ (*Matit-yah-hu*).
        This feast is not to be confused with the "feast of dedication"
        referred to in the added passage headings in some
        translations of 2nd Chronicles 5:2 through 7:10 and in 1st
        Kings, chapter 8, which actually took place during the Feast
        of Tabernacles. I personally would never add my own
        passage headings if I were to write a translation of the Bible,
        because it looks to me like a violation of the commandment
        in the following verses not to add to His holy words:

> Deuteronomy 4:2
> Deuteronomy 12:32
> Proverbs 30:5 through 30:6
> Revelation 22:18 through 22:19

*page 69*

50.     See note 63 in the notes for *Seven Flames: Letters to Manasseh.*

*page 70*

51.     *I* knew that I had a serious medical problem with my nervous system, but I'd grown tired of hearing countless times that my only sickness was hypochondria, because—after the doctors had tested me for heart disease and had tested my sister for epilepsy—everyone "knew" that our bodies were healthy, and that our fainting spells were caused by some kind of mental illness.

*page 72*

52.     חָנֹךְ (Strong's Concordance number 2596, pronounced *khanokh*), means *consecrate*, and also *dedicate*, but only in the sense of *sanctify*. The Authorized King James Version translated it as *Train up*, the which translation is quite accurate insofar as the practical applications of consecrating a life include dedicating the beginning of the child's way to the Lord, but it is not merely the physical act of dedicating the actions, but also of dedicating the child himself as a holy being, made in the image of Adonai.

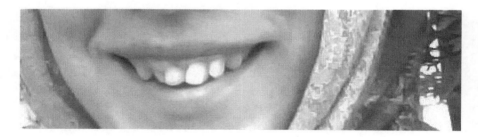

*page 72*

53.     פִּי (Strong's Concordance number 6310, pronounced *pi*), literally means *mouth*.

# Section Two:
# Seven Flames: Letters to Manasseh

*pages 74, 143, 156, 170, 184*

1.  אֶשְׁמַע *I will hear deeply*; a form of שָׁמַע, *hear deeply* (Strong's Concordance number 8085, pronounced *shah-**mah***); as opposed to the milder and unrelated word אָזַן (Strong's Concordance number 238, pronounced *azán*), which corresponds to the English word *hear*, and is closely related to אֹזֶן (Strong's Concordance number 241, pronounced ***oh**-zen*), the Hebrew word for *ear*. See also note 31 in the notes for *Alive and Kickin'*.

*page 76*

2.  Matthew 5:17

*page 76*

3.  Matthew 7:12, Matthew 22:37 through 22:40, Matthew 23:23, and Luke 10:25 through 10:28

*page 76*

4.  Matthew 8:2 through 8:4, Mark 1:40 through 1:45, Luke 5:12 through 5:14, Luke 17:12 through 17:19, Leviticus 13:1 through 13:3, Leviticus 14:2 though 14:32, and Deuteronomy 24:8

*page 76*

5.  Matthew 5:19

*page 76*

6.  Exodus 21:24, and Leviticus 24:19 through 24:20

*page 76*

7.  Matthew 19:17, Leviticus 18:5, Nehemiah 9:29, Ezekiel 18:3 through 18:9, Ezekiel 20:11 and 20:13, Luke 10:25 through 10:28, Romans 10:5, and Galatians 3:12

*pages 18, 77*

8.  *Adonai* (אֲדֹנָי) literally means my LORD. It is the most intimate and personal form of the Hebrew word *adón* (אָדוֹן), which means lord; and this form of *adón* is used only to refer to the LORD God. The name *Adonai* has, for countless centuries, been used by the Hebrews as the proper pronunciation in place of *YHVH*, the holy name of God, which is considered to be so holy that it almost never uttered by the Jewish people. The name *Jehovah* is a hybrid of these two names, which was created when translators of the

Hebrew Bible transliterated the name just as it was written—
the letters *YHVH*, with the vowel points for *Adonai*, which
had been added to remind the reader to say *Adonai* instead of
pronouncing the Holy Name *YHVH*. This pronunciation,
however, is phonetically impossible, since it uses a single
letter *vav* to say two sounds, both "o" and "v".
Interestingly, however, some have noted that *Yehaváh*, with
an "a" instead of an "o" *is* phonetically possible, and also
sounds like *Yé-'hava* (יֶאֱהַב), the word for "he shall love" in
Hebrew. To see that Jesus routinely used the name *Adonai* in
place of *YHVH*, compare the following verses:

1. Matthew 4:7 and Luke 4:12, referencing
   Deuteronomy 6:16
2. Matthew 4:10 and Luke 4:8, referencing
   De. 6:13 and 10:20, and Joshua 24:14
3. Matthew 22:37, referencing Deuteronomy 6:5
4. Matthew 22:44, Mark 12:36, and Luke 20:42,
   referencing Psalm 110:1
5. Matthew 23:39 and Luke 13:35, referencing
   Psalm 118:26
6. Mark 12:29 through 12:30, referencing
   Deuteronomy 6:4 and 6:5
7. Luke 4:18 through 4:19, referencing
   Isaiah 61:1 through 61:2

*page 78*

9. Our children called us אַבָּא (*Abba*) and אִמָּא (*Imma*), the
   Hebrew words for Daddy and Mommy.

*pages 79, 207, 211, 212*

10. At the time we wrote *Seven Flames*, I had not had a single
    epileptic seizure, that I recall, since the day I escaped from
    foster "care". A doctor had said that my "fainting spells"
    were a symptom of extreme emotional stress, and—until I
    was 23 years old—it appeared that this doctor was correct.
    So when Benaiah wrote these words, he thought that my
    "fainting spells" were gone for good, and that I was perfectly
    healthy. (See note 52 in the notes for *Section One: The Seer*.)
    Despite my many visits to the emergency room as a child,
    and despite about twenty-two routine medical examinations

in eleven years, no doctor had ever successfully referred me to a neurologist, and my epilepsy had never been diagnosed, until about a year after Benaiah and I finished writing *Seven Flames*.

Epileptic seizures vary. In all types, the brain activity is entirely disrupted by an electrical surge. After each seizure, I would remember the moments leading up to the seizure, but not the seizure itself. Sometimes, however, I would have a vague impression of having been in the midst of a large crowd of loving people gathered around me talking or singing, but I would not remember who they were or what they said. I had no detectable pulse during my seizures, and I did not breathe, except to sometimes make inhuman sounds by exhaling slowly during a *Grand Mal* or *Petit Mal* seizure. Also, my bowels and bladder would empty themselves as soon as they stopped receiving information from my brain. When I awoke, I would have no sense of balance, and no control over my fingers and toes. How long this problem lasted varied according to the severity of the seizure: Sometimes, after a Grand Mal seizure, I would need a wheelchair for more than half an hour. Also, after each seizure, I would feel fine, very comfortable, peaceful, and even energetic (until I tried to move).

The most infamous type of seizure is the *Grand Mal* seizure, which literally means, in Latin, the "Big Bad."

The "Big Bad" seizure is marked by random, extreme, repetitive, and uncontrolled body movements, which can severely injure or even kill an unsupervised epileptic, by breaking the back or neck, or by suffocation. As far as I know, I only had two *Grand Mal* seizures while in foster "care", but that should have been enough to prompt them to test me for epilepsy. In fact, at least three of my doctors referred me to a neurologist, but these referrals were never followed up on, because the caseworkers were routinely seizing my medical records (and probably destroying them), to prevent my mother's attorney from using them as evidence in court of her innocence.

Following each *Grand Mal* seizure, I had memory loss and scattered memories. For example, I studied an entire course in Level One American Sign Language, earned an "A", then promptly had a *Grand Mal* seizure and forgot all of it (except for the few Sign Language words I had managed to teach to my son Yehudah Isaiah, which he in turn was also able to teach to me).

The second most severe type of epileptic seizure is the *Petit Mal*, which means the "Little Bad". The "Little Bad" is very similar to the "Big Bad", except that the body becomes rigid or has very minor random movements, rather than dangerously thrashing around.

I do not know how many *Petit Mal* seizures I had in foster "care", but I did have many of them between my twenty-third birthday and the day I was finally healed from my epilepsy. Usually, when I had a *Petit Mal* seizure, my spine would stiffen, and slowly bend backward like a bow, so that Benaiah would fear the very real possibility that I might wake up permanently injured, unless he gently and carefully protected me like he'd protected his epileptic grandmother. The mildest type of epileptic seizure (which can also be both the hardest to diagnose and the most frightening) is an absence seizure.

Without modern medical equipment monitoring the victim during a seizure, an absence seizure is indistinguishable from a TIA heart attack (that is, a transient ischemic attack). This type of seizure can be the most frightening, because the victim has no breathing, no pulse, and appears to have suddenly died. (These scared Benaiah the most, before I was correctly diagnosed, making him weep to experience what seemed to be my death and resurrection.)

My grandfather Nathan Mills Whittlesey, Jr. had absence seizures for most of his earthly life, every Monday, because of sensory overload on Sunday at his job as a preacher. And several of his doctors insisted they were transient ischemic heart attacks.

My aunts, uncles and mother were told that it was impossible to diagnose which of the two he was experiencing unless he had an attack or seizure while being monitored at the hospital, which sent his daughters on wild goose chases to try to get him to the hospital fast enough for diagnosis, which of course they never could. But I am convinced that it was absence seizures he was having, because he did have epilepsy, and his symptoms were identical to mine, and because epilepsy runs in his family, and because he showed no other evidence of heart disease.

I had a great many absence seizures during my time in foster "care", and my identical twin had similar fainting spells, which motivated the doctors to order that we be tested both for epilepsy and heart disease.

So, assuming that since we were identical twins, and we had similar symptoms, that of course we must be suffering the same infirmity, they tested my heart, which was healthy, but they didn't test me for epilepsy. They did test my sister for epilepsy, which she didn't have, but unfortunately they did not test her heart: Drea's "fainting spells" were transient ischemic attcks. Her heart disease, like my epilepsy, was not diagnosed until after she was married, and she now sports a pacemaker.

Drea Michelle also differs from me physically in that she was born without an atlas bone in her neck, giving her the ability throughout her childhood to lay on her back on the bed and let her head dangle down over the edge, hanging directly down, which we girls all thought was a really cool trick. The doctors did not agree, when they learned about it, and they put a metal rod in her neck as an attempted repair. The way the doctors found this out was that she fell from a hay wagon while loading hay, and was sprawled out on the ground unconcious with her head tilted at a weird angle from her body like her neck was completely broken, but when she woke up she was fine. So her deformity probably saved her life that day. It was while she was in the hospital to get the metal rod in her neck that her heart disease was diagnosed, because she finally had a transient ischemic attack (TIA) while being monitored by the appropriate medical equipment for diagnosing it.

11.    The verses mentioned in the footnote are as follows:

John 17:20-17:23—

20    And I do not pray for these *ones* only, but also for
those who will trust in me through their word;

21    that they may all be one; as You, Father, *are* in me,
and I in You, that they also may be one in Us;
that the world may trust that You have sent me.

22    And the glory which You gave me I have given them;
that they may be one, *even* as We are one:

23    I in them, and You in me, that they may be completed
in unity; and that the world may know that You sent
me, and have loved them as You have loved me.

1st Corinthians 15:28—

And when all *things* shall be made obedient *to* Him,
then the Son Himself will also obey the One
who caused all *things* to be obedient *to* Him,
that God may be all in all.

Ephesians 1:19-1:23—

19    And what *is* the exceeding greatness *of* His power
toward us who believe, according to the working
*of* the power *of* His strength,

20    which He did in the Messiah, waking* Him
from *the* dead, and He set *Him* at His *own*
right *hand* in the heavenly *places*,

21    far above all principality, and authority, and power,
and lordship, and every name that is named,
not only in this age, but also in the *one* coming;

22    and subordinated all *things* under His feet, and
gave Him *to be the* head over all *things to* the church,

23    which is His body, the fullness *of* that *One*
filling all in all.

* εγειρασ, from εγειρο (Strong's Concordance number
1453, pronounced *eg-**ee**-ro*); literally, *awakening*; but also,
by extension, *raising*.

Ephesians 4:4-4:6—

4      one body, and one Spirit, *even* as you are also called
in one expectation *of* your calling;

5      one Lord, one faith, one baptism,

6      one God and Father *of* all: the *One who is* above all,
and through all, and in you all.

Colossians 3:9-3:11—

9      Do not lie to one another, having taken off
the former man with his actions;

10      and having put on the new *one*,
who is being renewed into full knowledge,
in accordance with *the* image *of* his Creator,

11      where there is neither Greek nor Judean,
*nor* circumcised nor uncircumcised foreigner,\*
*nor* Iranian nomad, *nor* freed slave:
but the Messiah *is* all, and in all.

\* βαρβαρος (Strong's Concordance number 915,
pronounced *bárbaros*): a *babbler*: that is, someone who
speaks unintelligibly; and, therefore, a speaker of a foreign
language. *Bárbaros* is commonly believed to be, like the
English word *babble*, related to the Hebrew word *bavél*
(Strong's Concordance number 894), which in turn is
commonly translated as either *Babel* or *Babylon*, depending
on the context.

John 15:4—

Stay in me, and I in you. As the branch cannot bear
fruit from itself, unless it stays in the vine,
so neither *can* you, unless you stay in me.

John 16:7—

But I tell you the truth: *It is* expedient for you
that I go away, because if I do not go away,
the Comforter\* would not come to you;
but if I go, I will send Him to you.

\*See note 54 in the notes for *The Storm*.

Romans 8:9—

But you are not in *the* flesh, but in *the* Spirit, if *the* Spirit *of* God dwells in you. And if anyone does not have *the* Spirit *of the* Messiah, he is not His.

Genesis 3:9—
...Where *are* you?...

Genesis 1:3—
...*Let there* be light...

John 14:6—
Yeshua said unto him, I am the way, the truth, and the life: no one comes unto the Father, but by me.

For more information, please read *Deceived on Purpose* and *A Wonderful Deception* by Warren Smith, or his online book *Reinventing Jesus Christ: The New Gospel*, and his blog article, *God IN Everyone?*

*page 79*

12.    These two "in" statements are unequal: God in His mercy does *not* dwell in unwilling hearts, but every human being *is* in Him (John 17:20 through 17:23 and 1ˢᵗ Corinthians 8:6): And in Acts 17:16 through 17:32 Paul said to some polytheists that God "is not far from every one of us: Because in him we live, and move, and have our being..." (Acts 17:27-17:28)

*page 79*

14.    He does not have a beginning... Isaiah 41:4, 48:12, and Revelation 1:8, 1:17, and 22:13 teach that God *is* the beginning: It therefore naturally follows that He Himself predated the invention of time.

*page 82*

15.    Earlier editions said "He, in His infinite wisdom, took six days to make all things in the human sphere of knowlege", because Benaiah did not know whether or not God had made other things in other times in other universes.
Which is not that Benaiah meant to say either that there are or that there are not creations unknown to humanity in some other separately created universe somewhere, but rather that we humans don't know of any other creation.
However, it seemes clear to me, from my understanding of

Genesis 1:3 and 2:3, that absolutely *all* physical matter can be traced back to these six days of creation.

*page 82*

16.    Adonai is, of course, God of *all* the nations.

*page 83*

17.    Acts 5:29

*page 83*

18.    Romans 13:1, the most infamous and most abused victim of such pro-totalitarian mistranslations, is discussed in more detail in *Authority* in the chapter *Revelation Revealed*. For a deeper study of both sides of the controversy, I recommend googling the question, "Is it a sin to break the law?"

*page 83*

19.    One could think that it was a mistake to say here "Israel" instead of "Samaria"; but, although 2nd Kings 1:3 says that Ahaziah was the king of Samaria, 1st Kings 22:51 says that Ahaziah reigned over Israel in Samaria.

*page 84*

20.    In the first edition, the order of these two sentences was: "But only Adonai is to be worshipped. To worship means to give great love, devotion, and allegiance to something or someone."

*page 84*

21.    In the first edition, Benaiah had written "their kingdom" instead of "this republic".

*page 85*

22.    There is what appears to be a curious anachronism here: Benaiah killed the monster in this nightmare when he was a little boy, and was a grown man when he was reborn and was baptized. This is because when he was a little boy, trusting in the wisdom and faith of his Christian grandparents, Ben was baptized at eight years of age. Then (when he grew to distrust the limited wisdom of all adults, and to distrust the God who had allowed Ben's parents to divorce) Benaiah lost the true path and turned from the care of his loving Messiah. But Yeshua never turned from Benaiah, but rather God touched him in his hour of greatest need.

*page 86*

23.    2nd Chronicles 7:14, Job 22:29, Psalm 9:12 and 10:17, Proverbs 22:4, Isaiah 57:15, Matthew 18:4, James 4:10, and 1st Peter 5:5

*page 87*

24.     Matthew 6:9 through 6:13, and Luke 11:2 through 11.4
        This prayer is intended to be used as an example, not merely
        as a memorized series of sounds. One lesson that may be
        learned from studying this example is that every petition
        therein is something God is already going to do for us,
        whether we ask or not: For example, we pray, "Lead us not
        into temptation...", but James 1:13 and 1:14 say,

> 13     No one who is tempted *should* say,
>        I am tempted by God: because God is not tempted
>        *with* evil, and He tempts no one;
> 14     But everyone is tempted, *when he* is drawn away
>        and seduced by his own lusts.
>
> ——James 1:13 and 1:14

From this example we can learn that we should not try to
change God's will, which indeed is already perfect, but
rather we should strive to change our will to conform to the
perfect will of our Heavenly Father.

*page 88*

25.     James 5:16—Here, paraphrased the King James Version,
        saying, "The fervent prayer of a righteous soul avails much",
        but my translation says, "*an* effective prayer *of a* righteous
        *one is* greatly capable."

*page 89*

26.     In nineteen ninety-six, when we began to write *Seven
        Flames*, recycling service was nearly nonexistent, smog
        draped some of the large cities in darkness, many of the
        automobiles were huge, unwieldy, and tank-like, and almost
        no one had even seen so much as a prototype of an electric or
        hybrid car. Rachel Carson had tried in her book *Silent Spring*
        to warn everyone that the earth was being destroyed, but she
        was, by many, regarded in her day as a fanatic: Only a small
        minority of uncommonly well-educated citizens (despite the
        warning in Revelation 11:18) was trying to discourage the
        destruction of the earth.

*page 93*

27.     רוּחַ הַקֹּדֶשׁ (Strong's Concordance numbers 7307,
        pronounced **roo**-*akh*, and 6944, pronounced **koe**-*desh*).

page 94
28.    Matthew 7:24 through 7:27; Luke 6:46 through 6:49

page 95
29.    Matthew 10:34

page 96
30.    Absurd, yes, impossible, yes; but this was Benaiah's unreachable goal he set for himself, knowing full well he could never succeed: In order that he might always strive to be better as a father, Benaiah intentionally set the mark impossibly high.

Mahatma Gandhi taught that Adonai likewise set an impossible moral standard for us in the Torah for this very reason. I think there may be truth in Gandhi's theory.

pages 58, 68, 98
31.    מְנַשֶּׁה רְפָאֵל לֵב-אֵל בֶּן-בְּנָיָה לֵב-אֵל In Hebrew, Manasseh Raphael Levell ben-Benaiah is pronounced *Menashéh Refaél Lev-el ben-Benayáh Lev-el. Menashéh* (Manasseh) means Making to Forget, and *Refaél* (Raphael) means *God Heals.*

page 102
32.    The mosque known as the Dome on the Rock is built directly above the place of the altar of Adonai, upon the same stone where Abraham offered Isaac (Genesis 22:1-22:18). It is also the same stone where God stopped a plague from destroying Israel (2 Samuel 24, and 1st Chronicles 21:1 through 21:28) when David sacrificed an ox in repentance of his sin. This rock is the place of the altar.

Compare to Daniel 11:31, Daniel 12:11, Matthew 24:15, and Mark 13:14

An ancient Hebrew tradition also teaches that this rock was also the place where Abraham showed his perfect trust in God by offering up his beloved faithful son.

An ancient Muslim tradition also teaches that this same rock is where Mohammed was taken up into heaven (either in a vision or in the flesh), and that the handprint in the holy rock may have been where Mohammed touched the earth as he was carried skyward.

No doubt this passage will offend at least one Muslim reader, but this is what Benaiah saw: Muslim brothers, we love you. I love you. But you are making me weep.

Don't you know, beloved reader, that the Dome on the Rock is breaking the hearts of your Jewish brothers whom Mohammed commanded you not to oppress, your spiritual brothers who love and worship the same God you worship? Why are you breaking our hearts?

Nor are the Muslims the only guilty ones:

There is a widespread myth in the English-speaking world that Allah and Yahweh are not the same person, and that "Allah" is a masculinization of the Arabic moon-goddess Ella, transformed into a male god to suit the convenience of a profoundly anti-woman society.

No Arabic speaker, however, would make this mistake. *Allah* is the Arabic counterpart of the English word *God*, and if you want to say *"a god"* in Arabic it's *allah*, and every Christian, Jewish, Jehovah's witness, Zoroastrian, Mormon, Catholic, and Unitarian whose mother tongue is Arabic calls God *Allah*.

Moreover (and this is self-evident to all Arabic speakers), the origin of this word is not the name of Ellah the false godess of the moon: The word *allah* comes from the word *il'ah*, which means to *truly exist*: Therefore, although it is the Arabic counterpart closest to the English word *God*, it would be equally accurate to translate *Allah* as *I Am*, or *Yahweh*.

Moreover, the Quran is not a series of clever poems written by Mohammad, as some have said: Mohammad spoke the truth when he said that a spirit who called himself *Jibril* [the Arabic name for the archangel Gabriel] gave him the Quran, just as the Holy Spirit gave Moses the Torah word for word. This angel "Jibril" came from God, and it is the real God he wrote the Quran about, but unless the original Quran has been replaced by a clever counterfeit, this "Jibril" did not tell the truth about his Creator God, because this "Jibril" is a fallen angel, fallen from heaven and fallen away from the truth.

The Quran is an ingenious counterfeit Bible, which has fulfilled amazingly well the prophecy [Matthew 24:24; Mark 13:22] that it would deceive, if possible, the very chosen ones of God.

However, this ingenious counterfeit Bible is utterly lacking the very core message which is the Bible's very reason for existing: The deep love, amazingly deeper and wider and higher than we humans are even able to imagine, it's that big, love in God's heart toward each and every one of us tiny little stubborn humans He has created and then redeemed at such an unimaginable price to His own astonishingly compassionate heart.

Consider this: In the Torah, we find that God is unchanging, faithful, and true, and that He gave us a way to test every prophet, to know whether to accept or reject his teachings: No true prophecy will ever contradict or try to abrogate any other true Scripture from God. Yet the Quran contradicts and tries to abrogate not only the Torah and the Gospel, but even also itself, time and time again: Therefore the Torah, the same Torah which the Quran commands Muslims to read, which was canonized in its current form before Mohammad was born, this same Torah commands us to disbelieve the Quran.

In many "Muslim" nations (quotation marks intentional) it is illegal for Christian missionaries to tell others about this Good News (—even the very same Gospel that the Quran itself commands every Muslim to diligently study)!

Yet, time and time again, missionaries of many different denominations (including Catholics, Protestants, and Seventh-Day Adventists) have told so many variations of the same story—obeying these hate-filled laws doesn't even *slow down* the overwhelming *flood* of Muslims joyously converting to Christianity—sometimes, even, before they have even understood the taboo Gospel message—because they saw something so amazingly beautiful written in the life stories of these censored Christians: God gives individual attention to each one of us personally; God answers our individual prayers: We don't worship a far-off, unknowable Creator, unable to even know which ones of us He will choose to let into His heaven: We worship a God who is *here with* us, *Imanu-El*, who has called *each and every one of us* by *our own names* to have a *personal relationship* with

Him—(This is just so, so beautiful that my throat tightens up at the thought)!—If I can have God, the Creator of the Universe, Yahweh, Allah the Merciful and Compassionate, as my friend (my *friend*!) then, Who even *cares* about any of the blasphemies and the theological heresies the Christians are so often accused of—*I want THAT friendship!*
(Ironically, the Quran forbids the Muslims from passing or enforcing laws which punish Christian missionaries for telling others about the Gospel, inasmuch as the Quran commands the Muslims not to oppress the "People of the Book" lest they cry out to God and He answer.)

*page 102*

33.     The Hebrew name גַּעַל (*Gaál*) means "he has cast out"

*page 103*

34.     Psalm 119:64

*page 103*

35.     Psalm 119:72

*page 104*

36.     All glory and thanks be only to the immeasurably beautiful gift of the cross!—because truly the best of the saints could *never* deserve the amazing mercy of our *Abba* God.
We could *never* obey God's Law completely, and of course *partial* obedience is total *disobedience.*
Nobody except Jesus Christ—whose Hebrew name means *Salvation*—is able to obey the Holy Law of Love that our loving heavenly Father has given us, but—contrary to all human understanding—our Salvation Yeshua has given us *His own perfect righteousness*, and we don't have to do *anything* more than just *trust* in this immeasurably beautiful love: I don't *have* to seek the face of Yeshua my Beloved, I don't *have* to rest in His Sabbath, I don't *have* to worship Him with any church on Sunday or the seventh day (or ever), I don't *have* to read my Bible, I don't *have* to pray—all these things are things that I *get* to do, not things I h*ave* to do.
Such glorious freedom—it sometimes takes my breath away while I'm trying to sing to Him about this freedom—such *amazing, glorious, precious, precious* freedom to have the Holy Spirit ever near me, drawing me ever closer to the Redeemer my Beloved!

*page 107*

37.　διανοια, *understanding* (Strong's concordance number *1271*, pronounced as *dee-áhn-oy-ah*), which comes from *di-á* and *nús* (δια, Strong's concordance number *1223*, which is "*by means of*", and νους, Strong's concordance number *3563*, which is "*mind*").

*page 110*

38.　The title *This is my God* is from Exodus 15:2, which says,

> Adonai *is* my strength and *my* song;
> and *He* is my salvation:
> this *is* my God, and I will rest *in* Him;
> my father's God, and *I* will exalt Him.

*page 111*

39.　His legal name was Mohandas Karamchand Gandhi. The name *Mahatma* means *Great Soul*; it is a nickname given to him by the multitudes who love him. The Hindus also call him a word which means *Daddy*.

*page 113*

40.　When our good friend (a loving Christian nurse) read these words we had written, "This is an evil way to study," she was saddened, and asked us, "What do you want us to do? We need to use animals for research, and these animals often have to suffer in the process, so we can help people who are also suffering. Aren't people more important than animals? Didn't God tell us to eat them? How is this any worse than killing animals for meat, which God told Noah that we can eat meat? The Bible doesn't say anything bad about sacrificing animals for worship or for food; and how is this different? We sacrifice animals to save human lives, and to ease human suffering. What do you want us to do?" Well, that was a lot of questions, and they were good ones, and she was right. But she was also off the point: Yes, it is often necessary to take an animal's life in self-defense, or for food, or for its warm fur, in order to save human lives, and it is said that it is also often necessary to take an animal's life in order to study our own bodies to save human lives. But to do so callously and lightly is wrong. To disregard the animal's pain, and do nothing at all to ease its mortal suffering, is wrong. To curse God and sneer while killing a creature formed with His life—instead of thanking God for the immense gift of the animal's precious life—is evil and selfish and hardhearted and ungrateful.

If a big vicious bear starts ripping through my tent wall in order to eat my baby daughter, and I'm sitting there holding a shotgun in my hand, I probably would not stop to pray for God's guidance before shooting that vicious bear. But there is a time when we should pray for guidance before we act. I must search the Torah written in my own heart, and prayerfully search my own understanding of God's holy Law of Love, and judge honestly whether killing an animal is truly needed in order to save a human life (or to save the lives of other animals).

5      Trust Adonai with all your heart;
      and lean not unto your *own* understanding.
6      In all your ways know Him,
      and He will make your paths straight.

                      ——Proverbs 3:5–3:6

There is a right way to kill, a kosher way to take a life. We Hebrews do not lightly take the life of the animals we sacrifice for food:

We strive to kill as painlessly as possible, and we pray. Kill we must, but we must also be reluctant to kill. And we must thank God for the animal's life. This matters to God.

It is important to Him. And it is important to the animal (yes, I did just say that it is important to the animal): Animals can sense our spirits, and it is not as traumatic for them to die if we apologize to them for what they must lose for our sakes, and if we thank God for the precious, precious gift of their lives.

This is the Hebrew way, and this is also the Choctaw way, and the Way of many other native American tribes; and this is also the way God taught us to live, in His holy Law of love, which we Hebrews call the Torah. Consider, please, the following verses about how to treat the animals over which our God has given us authority:

Genesis 1:26-1:29; 3:21; 9:2-9:3; 9:7-9:17; 24:19-24:25; 24:32; and 42:27;

Exodus 20:10; 21:28; 23:4-23:5; and 23:11-23:13;

Leviticus 22:27-22:28; and 25:7;

Deuteronomy 22:1; 22:4; 22:6-22:7; 22:10; and 25:4;

1st Samuel 17:34-17:37;

Job 12:7-12:10; and 38:39-38:41;

Psalms 8:4-8:9; 24; 36:6; 145:9-145:11; and 147:9-147:11;

Proverbs 12:10; and 27:23;

Isaiah 11:6-11:9; and 66:2-66:4;

Ezekiel 4:2-4:4;

Hosea 2:18;

Jonah 4:10-4:11;

Matthew 6:25-6:34; 10:29-10:31; and 18:12;

Luke 12:6; 14:5; and 15:4-15:7; and

1st Peter 4:10

*pages 114, 115*

41.     Hatred is a very powerful poison. Jews and Christians, especially in the land of Israel, have done many unspeakable things to one another. It is very sad that our Baptist brother, when we came expecting his love and his help, did not see us as brothers in Christ, nor as children of his Messiah's earthly people, nor even as human beings, but only as Jews—that is to say, enemies.

Even as Benaiah wondered whether this Baptist man was really a Christian, saying, 'How could a believer saved by the compassion of God have so little compassion himself?', likewise I do believe that this Baptist man likewise wondered in his heart, 'How could a Jew also be a Christian believer, when the Jews and Christians are enemies?' (But, beloved reader, the Jews and Christians are not by right or nature enemies, but rather only temporarily at enmity, through the very skillful deception of the devil.)

And this man is still our beloved brother, whether he understands this truth or not.

*page 117*

42.     Although none of the popular English translations say any such thing, the original Hebrew Masoretic Text of the Bible states clearly, in a number of verses, that animals have souls

(plural of נֶפֶשׁ, Strong's Concordance number 5315, pronounced *néfesh*).

*page 119*
44.    Benaiah's father and mother both objected when they read this story, saying that his father loved more the beauty of the wild forest, and his mother loved more to fish and to hunt. But what he wrote is what his parents taught him with their actions when he was a boy: It was his father who actively shared his love of hunting and fishing, and it was his mother who actively shared her love of the beauty of the wild forest.

*page 124*
46.    John 2:13 through 2:17

*page 124*
47.    Luke 22:35 through 22:38

*page 124*
48.    John 18:36

*page 124*
49.    Matthew 10:16 through 10:39

*page 124*
50.    In the process of translating *Seven Flames* into Spanish, I was *utterly stymied* when I came to the sentence "We need to follow David's example, and when Adonai or Yeshua commands us not to have pity, we must obey."
Perhaps the problem was merely that the thought being communicated was so foreign to the Christian gals who were teaching me—or at least trying to teach me—because I have never in my life heard a non-Jewish preacher discuss the Biblical teaching that pity is not always an appropriate response.
Nevertheless, it is commanded to us five times in the book of Deuteronomy, "your eye shall not pity": Deuteronomy 7:16; 13:8, 19:13; 19:21; and 25:12—Compassion is good, but if an animal-loving mother can't save her little child quickly enough because she stops to have pity on the rattlesnake coiled under her baby's cradle, that's definitely *not* good. (See also the chapter *The Everyday Miracle of Parenthood*.)

*page 124*
51.    Genesis 9:6

*page 124*
52.    Given the alarmingly high rate of false convictions of all manner of crimes, including capitol crimes, it is a necessary

evil to outlaw the death penalty. Even so, to abolish the death penalty is not the right long-term solution: This is no more than the best temporary solution, while the laws of criminal prosecution are being re-written to conform to the Law of God, which says: "By *the* mouth *of* two witnesses, and *of* three, every utterance shall stand." [2nd Corinthians 13:1— Compare also to Numbers 35:30, Deuteronomy 17:6 and 19:15, Matthew 18:16, 1st Timothy 5:19, and Hebrews 10:28]

*page 125*
53.  Matthew 7:13 through 7:14

*page 127*
54.  Isaiah 55:9

*page 127*
55.  
1.  Exodus 20:13 and Deuteronomy 5:17
2.  Genesis 9:6
3.  Exodus 20:14
4.  Leviticus 20:10
5.  Exodus 20:15
6.  Exodus 20:16
7.  Deuteronomy 16:18

*pages 127, 128, 130*
56.  The word translated "kill" in the King James Version of Exodus 20:13, Numbers 35:27, and Deuteronomy 5:17 is *ratzákh* (Strong's concordance number 7523).
Elsewhere in the Bible, the King James Version consistently translates רָצַח (*ratzákh*) as "murder":

1.  Num. 35:16 (x2) *harotzé-akh, rotzé-akh* רֹצֵחַ, הָרֹצֵחַ
2.  Num. 35:17 (x2) *harotzé-akh, rotzé-akh* רֹצֵחַ, הָרֹצֵחַ
3.  Num. 35:18 (x2) *harotzé-akh, rotzé-akh* רֹצֵחַ, הָרֹצֵחַ
4.  Numbers 35:19 *harotzé-akh* הָרֹצֵחַ
5.  Num. 35:21 (x2) *harotzé-akh, rotzé-akh* רֹצֵחַ, הָרֹצֵחַ
6.  Numbers 35:30 *harotzé-akh* הָרֹצֵחַ
7.  Numbers 35:31 *rotzé-akh* רֹצֵחַ
8.  2nd Kings 6:32 *há-meratzé-akh* הַמְרַצֵּחַ-
9.  Isaiah 1:21 *meratzkhím* מְרַצְּחִים

page 127
57.　מוֹת־יוּמַת　The phrase paraphrased here as *shall surely die* literally means *dying they shall die* (Strong's concordance number 4191).

page 127
58.　The prefix בְ (b'), translated here as *against*, also means *in, with,* and *about*: Remember this when you are tempted to tell a "white lie" in, with, or about your neighbor.

pages 129, 131
59.　"Wonderful", not "deviseth wonders":
The Hebrew word פֶּלֶא (*péle*) is consistently used as a noun or adjective, (Strong's Concordance number 6382), never as a verb. פָּלָא (*palá*) is the verb form (Strong's Concordance number 6381).

marvelous thing
> Psalm 78:12 *péle* פֶּלֶא

thy wonders
> Psalm 77:11 *pilékha* פִּלְאֶךָ
> Psalm 88:12 *pilékha* פִּלְאֶךָ
> Psalm 89:5 *pilakhá* פִּלְאֶךָ

wonderful
> Psalm 119:129 *pela-ót* פְּלָאוֹת

wonderful things
> Isaiah 25:1 *péle* פֶּלֶא

wonders
> Exodus 15:11 *féle* פֶלֶא־
> Psalm 77:14 *péle* פֶלֶא
> Psalm 88:10 *péle* פֶלֶא
> Daniel 12:6 *hapela-ót* הַפְּלָאוֹת

pages 129, 130, 132
60.　תְּנוּאָה (*tenoo-ah*) is the word translated as "breach of promise" in the King James Version of Numbers 14:34 (identified by the Strong's concordance number 8569), which I translated as "alienation". This word is used only one other time in the Hebrew Bible, in Job 33:10, where in the King James Version it is translated as "occasions": "Behold, he findeth occasions against me, he counteth me for

his enemy". The Hebrew word *tenoo-ah* comes from the root word נוא (*noo*), which is variously translated as "break", "disallow", "discourage", or "make of none effect" (Strong's concordance number 5106).

*page 131*

61.     What is Isaiah 9:6 in the King James Version is Isaiah 9:5 in the Hebrew Bible. In the first editions, I wrote the traditional paraphrase "father" instead of "my father", but in *Open Soul Surgery*, I have preferred literal translations.

*page 133*

62.     Matthew 5:39, Luke 6:29, and Proverbs 20:22

*pages 69, 133, 134, 279, 280, 283*

63.     Matthew 5:43 through 5:48, and Luke 6:20 through 6:38 εχθρους, translated here as *enemies* (Strong's concordance number *2190*, pronounced as *ekhthroús*), means *haters*, and comes from εχθω (*ékhtho*), which means *to hate*. (See also note 39 in the notes for *Alive and Kickin'*, and note 7 in the notes for *The Daughter*.)

*page 133*

64.     John 18:22 through 18:23, and Acts 23:2 through 23:5

*page 135*

65.     John 13:34 and 15:12 through 15:13

*page 136*

66.     Romans 12:19; from Deuteronomy 32:35 and Psalm 94:1

*Levell Family Emblem*

# Section Three
# Alive and Kickin'

page 138

1.      נָזִיר (*naz-eer*), which is transliterated in English as *Nazarite* (Strong's concordance number 5139), means *separated*, or *consecrated*.

page 138

2.      חֹמֶץ (Strong's Concordance number 2558, pronounced *khamétz*), here translated as *vinegar* also means *yeast*, *leavening*, and *fermentation*.

page 138

3.      גֶּפֶן הַיַּיִן Literally, *vine of the wine* (Strong's Concordance number 1612 and 3196, pronounced *géfen ha-yáyin*).

page 139, 140

4.      בָּעַר (Strong's Concordance number 1197), traditionally translated here as *kindle*, also means *burn*: Thus, "You shall not burn" would also be a correct translation.

page 140

5.      εθνη (Strong's Concordance number *1484*, pronounced *éthneh*). Here, *nations* is not used to mean *countries*, but rather *non-Hebrew individuals*, *éthneh* being used as a stand-in for the Hebrew word גּוֹיִם (Strong's Concordance number 1471, pronounced *goyim*), commonly translated into English as *heathen* or *Gentiles*; but *goyim* means *nations*.

página 141

6.      עוֹלֹתֵיהֶם, pronounced *owe-lote-ey-hém*, from עוֹלָה (Strong's Concordance number 5930, pronounced *oláh*), is translated here as "their *offerings* sent up". But *oláh* is mistranslated as "burnt offering" throughout the Authorized King James Version, and likewise is translated as "holocausto" ("burnt offering") throughout the Reina Valera version, making blasphemous and slanderous nonsense of Judges 11:29 through 11:31, by falsely accusing Adonai's servant Yiftakh (Jephthah) of vowing, **while the Holy Spirit was upon him**, to sacrifice as a burnt offering to Adonai whatever came out of the doors of his house to meet him after Adonai gave him the victory.

What kosher species of animal could righteous Yiftakh possibly expect would come out of the doors of his house to meet him? Did he have a pet **cow** that slept at the foot of his bed? Who, then, was he expecting to sacrifice to Adonai, if not a slave, or perhaps one of his dogs, neither of which was kosher to burn on Adonai's altar? But donkeys and dogs and slaves were, on the other hand, customarily donated to serve the priests of Adonai's temple as *temple slaves*, which were also called *owe-lote*.

Moreover, continuing the story in Judges 11:32 through 11:38, when his beloved daughter surprised him by running out to meet him at the doors ahead of the dogs and slaves, she says nothing to indicate that his vow sounded in any way bizarre, evil, or expressly forbidden in the Torah, and in Judges 11:37 and 11:38 she does not ask permission to bewail her untimely death, but rather her virginity only, as if she fully expected to stay alive, but never be allowed to marry a man.

Moreover, continuing the story in Judges 11:39 through 11:40, it was a custom afterward for the daughters of Israel to bring gifts to Yiftakh's daughter four days in a year—which word לְתַנּוֹת (*l'tanót*) the King James translators knew full well to be the feminine plural of "to give", from נָתַן (Strong's Concordance number 5414, pronounced *natán*), which is translated *everywhere else* in the Bible with various synonyms of *give*, and yet they intentionally chose to mistranslate it as "to lament" (just as the translators for the Reina Valera version translated it as "endechar"), because they were unable to reconcile the fact of her receiving gifts with the idea that she had allegedly been burned up as a perverse Druid-style burnt offering to Adonai. The Hebrews never had any tradition of giving gifts to the dead. Moreover, adding fraud upon fraud, James Strong created a separate number "8567" in his concordance (deviating in this from his standard format, apparently solely to conceal this mistranslation), to deceive the occasional reader of Strong's Exhaustive Concordance of the Bible, who would not know that the words are numbered according to their primary forms and that *l'tanót* is a form of *natán*.

Moreover, the story ends in verse 11:40 with the statement that this "lamenting" occurred four days in a year, rather than the customary annual mourning which would have followed such a tragedy: Nor would such a tradition have ended, but rather the Jews would still mourn her once a year unto this day, even as we still mourn the tragic murder of Adonai's servant Gedaliah, every year on the third day of the seventh month (See Jeremiah 39:9 through 41:18).

page 141

7.  Here, the Authorized King James Version says, "it shall come, that I will gather", although there are no words here for "that I will", while the Reina Valera says here "tiempo vendrá para juntar" ("time will come to gather"), although there is no word for "time": In the Hebrew Bible, this phrase begins simply with "coming", without saying who or what is coming, leaving the translators to decide for themselves. But the absent noun was declared in verse 66:14, saying "the hand of Adonai", and so I have repeated this phrase in italics.

page 142

8.  (מ, with דַי, Strong's Concordance number 1767, pronounced [*m'*]*die*) "*more* than enough", or "too much", not "from", which would be simply מ.

page 143, 156, 170, 184

9.  See note 1 in the notes for *Seven Flames: Letters to Manasseh*.

page 143

10. גִּדַּלְתִּי (*giddáltee*): literally, *I enlarged* (Strong's Concordance number 1430).

page 143

11. הִתְבּוֹנָן, pronounced *hitbonán*, diminutive of *hitbón*, which means *understands* (from בִּין, Strong's Concordance number 995, pronounced *bean*).

page 144

12. חַיִּין, pronounced *khai-yón*, diminutive of חַי (Strong's Concordance number 2417, pronounced *khai*): The use of the diminutive form indicates and emphasizes that the other beasts' lives, although lengthened, are inherently incomplete and temporary.

*page 146*
14.     Revelation 18:4; see also Isaiah 48:20; Jeremiah 50:8; and 2nd Corinthians 6:14 through 6:17

*pages 146, 147, 148, 150*
15.     αγγελον, "angel" (like its Hebrew counterpart *malakh*) means *messenger* or *ambassador* (Strong's Concordance number *32*, pronounced *áng-e-los*). The Greek word *án-ge-los* and its Hebrew and Chaldean counterparts מַלְאָךְ and מַלְאַךְ (Strong's Concordance numbers 4397 and 4398, pronounced *malakh*), although commonly translated as *angel*, are also used in the Bible to describe human ambassadors of God, as well as Yeshua Himself, the Prince of all of Adonai's ambassadors (Genesis 18:2 and 18:22-18:23 and 19:1; Numbers 22:5, and 22:77; Joshua 6:17, and 2:1-2:5, 2:9, 2:14, 2:17, and 2:23; 1st Samuel 25:5, 25:10, 25:14, and 25:42; and 2nd Chronicles 35:20 and 35:21). And the 7th-Day Adventists believe that Michael, Israel's guardian angel (Daniel 12:1), is Yeshua Himself. (See also *Israel's Angel Extraordinary*, by Robert Leo Odom.)

*page 147*
16.     See the book of Daniel, chapter seven.

*page 148*
17.     Literally, *which has kingdom.*

*page 150*
18.     φαρμακεια (Strong's Concordance number *5331*, pronounced *far-ma-kee-ah*). Literally, *drugging*, or *medicating*, and therefore (by extension) *shamanism*, as involving the prescribing and administration of mind-altering drugs in order to alter the perceptions, behavior, and spiritual state of their patients. See also note 21.

*page 150*
19.     δουλος (Strong's Concordance number *1401*, pronounced *doo-los*); from δεω (Strong's Concordance number *1210*, pronounced *day-oh*). Literally, *slaves*, but not in the sense that the modern non-Jewish reader would understand: The slaves of God have freely chosen that we want to serve Him forever, but the word *slaves* insinuates an involuntary servitude by means of violence: be it physical violence, or emotional violence, like the slavery with which we served the Enemy before our salvation: It must be understood in the

context of the commandments about Hebrew slaves, because all the Christians have been adopted into the family of Abraham and Yeshua (Hebrews both), so all the non-Jewish Christians are also Hebrews, and so this law is also the law for all the Christian slaves, that the Hebrew slave shall be a slave against his will no more than seven years, and at the end of the seven years can only remain in slavery if he refuses to be set free:

16      And *it* will be, if he says to you,
I will not go away from you;
because he loves you and your household,
because to him *it is* good *to be* with you;

17      then you shall take the awl, and give it
through his ear and through *the* door,
and he will be to you *a* servant forever;
and you shall do likewise to your female servant.

——Deuteronomy 15:16 through 15:17

*page 151*

20.     Ιωαννης (pronounced *Yohannes*) from the Hebrew יוֹחָנָן (pronounced *Yokhanán*), which means *Adonai is Merciful*, or *Adonai is Graceful* (Strong's Concordance numbers *2491* and *3110*), from חֵן (Strong's Concordance number 2580, pronounced *kheyn*), which means *grace.*

*page 151*

21.     φαρμακευσι, pronounced *far-mak-**yoo**-see* (plural of φαρμακευς, Strong's Concordance number *5332*, pronounced *far-mak-**yoos***). Literally, *druggers*, or *pharmacists*, or *psychiatrists*, and therefore (by extension) *shamans*, as being those whose profession and authority it was in the Roman Empire to prescribe and administer mind-altering drugs. See also note 18.

*page 152*

22.     μακαριος (Strong's Concordance number *3107*, pronounced *mak-**ar**-ee-os*) also means *happy*, or *fortunate.*

*page 152*

23.     אֱלִישֶׁבַע יָעֵל לֶב-אֵל בַּת-בְּנָיָה לֶב-אֵל In Hebrew, Elishevah Yael Levell daughter of Benaiah is pronounced *Elishéva Yael Lev-el bat-Benayáh Lev-el.* In English, *Elishéva* is Elizabeth,

the middle name of her grandma Thelma Elizabeth (Cooper) LaVelle, Benaiah's mom, and we often called her Elizabeth when speaking in English, because she was named for her grandma Thelma Elizabeth. But when the kidnappers decided to change her name to an English name, they called her *Ella*, the name of the false goddess of the Arabs. It is a very grave insult to change the name of a Jewish child to the name of a false goddess or of a false god. Her *real* name in English is Elizabeth, like that of her beautiful grandmother. The name *Elishéva* (Elizabeth) means *Oath of my God*, or *Promise of my God*; but, like many Hebrew words, the word *shéva* has two meanings; thus, *Elishéva* also means *Seven of my God*, referring to seven aspects of God's character (which are also promises, because God will never change):

1. Almighty
2. Wise
3. Loving
4. Righteous
5. Merciful
6. Holy
7. Truthful

The name *Yael* (Jael) means *Mountain Goat*, but if it were spelled differently, *Yael* would mean *Yahweh is God*. Elizabeth Yael truly had the courage of the heroine Jael in the Bible, and the strength and joy of a mountain goat upon the mountains.

*page 154*

24.    The infamous Dredd Scott case was a very sad matter for the people of the United States, and greatly changed the history of our nation for the worse, and cost many, many lives and much, much pain. It was the first time that the Supreme Court of the United States in its arrogance thought to forbid its Christian people from obeying the Holy Law of God, because the Supreme Court commanded to restore to their owners the escaped slaves, whether or not they were in a state that still permitted slavery, without recourse.

With this new shameful human law, the Supreme Court exalted its own laws over the eternal Law of the great Wise

Judge Adonai, and cast into the dust the very heart of the very liberty that they had sworn to protect, saying that Dredd Scott's master had the right to "his" property, "his" escaped slave Dredd Scott (never mind that everyone knew the slave was a son of people kidnapped from Africa, if not kidnapped from Africa himself, and was in truth *stolen property*, illegal for anyone including his master to possess), even so they said that Dredd Scott's master had the constitutional right to "his property", when in truth the Constitution of the United States only said that his master—*if* he were the *legal* owner of the man—had the constitutional right to be paid his current price in money by the state whose righteous law had freed his slave.

*page 155*

25.      Isaiah 64:4

*page 156*

26.      צְדָקָה (Strong's Concordance number 6666, pronounced *tzed-ah-kah*), means *justice* and *righteousness*, but it is also used the way non-Jewish English speakers use the word *charity*, in the sense of giving to those who have need: There is no exact Hebrew counterpart to the English word *charity*, because giving to the those who have need is social *justice*: Adonai commands us to give to and to protect the widows, the fatherless orphans, and the poor.

*page 159*

28.      אֵלִיָּה In Hebrew, *Elijah* is pronounced *Eliyáh*, and it means *My God is Adonai*.

*page 159*

29.      There are two different Hebrew words translated here as *curse*: In Malachi 4:6 we see the word חֵרֶם (*khéyrem*) translated as *curse*, although its primary meanings are *destruction*, and *thing doomed to destruction* (Strong's Concordance number 2764); and in Deuteronomy 11:26 and 11:28 we see the word קְלָלָה (*kelalá*) translated as *curse*, which is its only meaning (Strong's Concordance number 7045).

*page 159*

30.      What is Malachi 4:5 through 4:6 is Malachi 3:24 through 3:25 in the original Hebrew Bible.

*pages 159, 170*

31.    תִּשְׁמְעוּ *you shall hear deeply*; a form of שָׁמַע, *hear deeply* (Strong's Concordance number 8085, pronounced *shah-mah*); and not the unrelated word יְקָהָה (Strong's Concordance number 3349, pronounced *yik-kah-hah*), which means *obey*. The Reina Valera translates this word as *oyereis* (*you will hear*) in Deuteronomy 11:28, but the King James Authorized Version mistranslates it as *ye obey*. This is a very bad mistranslation, because it changes the meaning of the entire idea to "See, I set before your faces today *a* blessing and *a* curse: the blessing, which you cannot have at all, and the curse, which you cannot escape at all." But I tell you, my brothers and my sisters, that these verses are about a blessing easily obtainable, and a curse just as easily avoidable! See also note 1 in the notes for *Seven Flames: Letters to Manasseh.*

*page 162*

32.    The following Scriptures tell the story of how, at God's command, Mount Ebal became associated with the curses of a sinful life, and Mount Gerizim became associated with the blessings of a God-led life:
Deuteronomy 11:26 through 11:31, Deuteronomy 27:2 through 28:68, and Joshua 8:30 through 8:35

*pages 31, 163*

33.    אֶצּוֹרְךָ (*etz-tzav-re-khah*); literally, *I moulded you*: from יָצַר (Strong's Concordance number 3335, pronounced *yatzár*).

*page 163*

34.    See note 49 in the notes for *The Seer.*

*page 164*

35.    מַתִּתְיָהוּ אֶלְעָזָר לֶב־אֵל בֶּן-בְּנָיָה לֶב־אֵל Mattithias is an English form of his Hebrew name מַתִּתְיָהוּ (*Matityáhu*). Matthew is another English form of the Hebrew name *Matityáhu*, and when we say his name while speaking English we tend to use the names Mattithias, Matthew, Matt, and *Matityáhu* interchangeably, and he answered to all of them. His full Hebrew name is *Matityáhu El-azár Lev-el ben-Benayáh Lev-el*. In English, his full Jewish name is Mattithias Eleazar ben-Benaiah Levell, and his full civil name is Matthew Lazarus Levell. *Matityáhu* means *He is a gift from Yahweh*, and

*El-azár* (in Hebrew ☺) means *God Has Helped*. (But it means something else entirely in Spanish… Oh, well…) (Jews in the Diaspora frequently have two different names: A civil name used when filing government paperwork or speaking to non-Jews, and a Jewish name used when speaking to other Jews.)

*page 165*

36.　רַבּוֹת (*rab-boat*) from רַב (Strong's Concordance number 7227, pronounced *rav*) means both *Many*, and *Great*.

*page 165*

37.　עָצְמוּ (*atz-moo*) means both *more*, and *more powerful*, and comes from עֶצֶם (Strong's Concordance number 6106, pronounced *étzem*), which literally means *bone*.

*page 165*

38.　What is Psalm 40:5 in the King James Version is Psalm 40:6 in the original Hebrew Bible.

*pages 168, 246*

39.　אֹיֵב (Strong's Concordance number 341, pronounced *oh-yave*), from אָיַב (*to hate*, Strong's Concordance number 340, pronounced *ah-yav*); and not related to שָׂטָן, which means *enemy* (Strong's Concordance number 7854, pronounced *sah-tahn*). (See also note 62 in the notes for *Seven Flames: Letters to Manasseh*, and note 7 in the notes for *The Daughter*.)

*page 168*

40.　בַּעֲדִי, (*ba-a-dee*,) from בְּעַד (Strong's Concordance number 1157, pronounced *buh-odd*) means *through me*, and also *for me*, and also *in me*.

*pages 168, 190*

41.　See note number 10 in the notes for *Seven Flames: Letters to Manasseh*.

*page 169*

42.　The dream prophesying the September 11, two thousand one attacks is written in the chapter *Come Out of Her, My People*.

*pages 169, 194*

43.　The King James Version says *saints* instead of *merciful*. But, although the word חָסִיד (*kha-seed*) is translated as *saint* nineteen times in the King James, *kha-seed* (Strong's Concordance number 2623) primarily means *merciful*, and is not related to קָדוֹשׁ (*kadósh*), nor to קַדִּישׁ (*kad-deesh*), nor to קֹדֶשׁ (*kódesh*), the primary hebrew words for *saint*, or *holy* (Strong's Concordance numbers 6918, 6922, and 6944). See also the following verses:

Jeremiah 3:12
2ⁿᵈ Samuel 22:26
Psalm 18:25

חָסִיד (*kha-seed*) is also translated in the King James as *godly*, *good*, and *holy*.

*page 172*
44.     γραμματεις (*gram-mut-ay-yis*) means *writers*, and by extension *scribes* and *secretaries*: plural of γραμματευς (*gram-mut-use*, Strong's Concordance number *1122*); from γραμμα (that is, *writing*).

*page 172*
45.     φαρισαιοι (*faris-ah-yoy*), plural of φαρισαιος (*faris-ah-yose*, Strong's Concordance number *5330*); from the Hebrew *P'rushim*, which means *Separatists*, from *to separate*, which is פָּרָשׁ (Strong's Concordance number 6567, pronounced *par-ash*). The Pharisees, which included several denominations, were the majority, and included almost all of the poor people in Israel. The Pharisees believed in separating themselves from the Greeks and Romans; but the Sadducees (who were few, and wealthy, and held the political power) believed in joining with the peoples around them.

*page 174*
46.     אֱלוֹהַ *His God* (Strong's Concordance number 433, from the Chaldean dialect of Hebrew, pronounced *elóhah*), and not אֵל or אֱלֹהִים (Strong's Concordance numbers 410 and 430).

*page 174*
47.     What is Deuteronomy 12:32 in the King James Version is
        Deuteronomy 13:1 in the original Hebrew Bible.

*page 180*
48.     2nd Corinthians 13:1—Compare also to Numbers 35:30,
        Deuteronomy 17:6 and 19:15, Matthew 18:16, 1st Timothy
        5:19, and Hebrews 10:28.

*page 181*
49.     1st Kings 18:21 through 18:39

*page 184*
50.     The word here translated as *"my life"* is *nafshee* (literally, *my
        soul*). See note 39 in the notes for *Seven Flames: Letters to
        Manasseh.*

*page 190*
51.     Deuteronomy 22:9—You shall not sow your vineyard with
        mutually imprisoning seeds…

| 3610 | 3754 | 2232 | 3808 |
|------|------|------|------|
| כִּלְאָיִם | כַּרְמְךָ | לֹא-תִזְרַע | |
| with mutually imprisoning seeds | your vineyard | you shall sow | Not |

| 2233 | 4395 | 6942 | |
|------|------|------|--|
| הַזֶּרַע | הַמְלֵאָה | פֶּן-תִּקְדַּשׁ | |
| the seed | the fullness [of] | be defiled | lest |

| 3754 | 8393 | 2232 | 834 |
|------|------|------|-----|
| הַכָּרֶם | וּתְבוּאַת | תִזְרָע | אֲשֶׁר |
| the vineyard | and [the] increase [of] | you shall have sown | which |

# Section Four:
# The Storm

*page 194*
1.    See note 43 in the notes for *Alive and Kickin'*.

*page 194*
2.    יְהוּדָה יְשַׁעְיָה לֶב-אֶל בֶּן-בְּנָיָה לֶב-אֶל In Hebrew, Yehudah Isaiah Levell son of Benaiah Levell is pronounced *Yehúda Yeshayá Lev-el ben-Benayáh Lev-el*. The English form of *Yehudah* is Judah. The name *Yehudah* means *Celebration*, and the name *Yeshayáh* (Isaiah) means *Salvation is of Yahweh*.

*page 195*
3.    See note 32 in the notes for *Alive and Kickin'*.

*page 196*
4.    Mexico has a species of raven the size of the crows in the nothern United States. It was a bird of this Mexican species which I saw in my vision. But its eyes were different—very intense and intelligent—and they resembled the eyes of an albatross.

*page 196*
5.    Behold, these are the names of the twin mountains of the Living God: The mountain which is beloved of the Almighty for the sake of His people has four names: The Sanctuary, and Mercy, and Sunday, and Adoption; and the sacred mountain, upon which the God of love put my feet, also has four names: The Church, and Righteousness, and Surrender, and the Sabbath.

All who keep every Sunday as the Sabbath, with innocent sincerity, do well (and Sunday is as the mountain in my dream, which God has also sanctified for the sake of His children); but the knowledgeable Believers who keep the seventh day for the Sabbath, these do better.

The four Gospels bear witness that Yeshua rose from the grave on the first day of the week—the first Easter Sunday—on the morning after the Sabbath:

Matthew 28:1; Mark 16:1 through 16:2; Luke 23:54 through 24:1; and John 20:1

Saturday is *indisputably* the seventh day of the week: Saturday, not Sunday, is the day of rest appointed by God in the Ten Commandments—which are the only words *any* multitude *ever* in the *history of the world* heard spoken *by the mouth of God Himself.*

Furthermore, in the entire Bible, no prophet or Apostle *ever* mentioned *anyone*—except for the Beast of the Apocalypse in the book of Daniel—ever even *trying* to change the times appointed by God.

*page 199*

6.    Although אוֹהֵב (Strong's Concordance number 157, pronounced *ohév*), is translated as "friend" in the King James Version, *ohév* literally means "lover", often in the sexual sense, but also, in certain contexts such as here, simply meaning "one who loves".

*page 199*

7.    Drug addicts are not worthless: No human being made in the image of God is worthless. I used this word only to say that this false belief was passed on to the adoptive parents by the mouth of a liar.

*page 200*

8.    Actually, in this dream we didn't have *all* the other children—Abram Jedidiah Ammi was *not* among the children returned to me in this dream, but since I didn't expect to give birth to my nephew, his absence from the dream went unnoticed at the time: As I have written in the chapter *Visions of a Joy yet to Come*, I was thinking that Abram Jedidiah Ammi would be my nephew, a son of my brother Reuben David Goldenstein.

*page 201*

9.    See note 1 in the notes for *Seven Flames: Letters to Manasseh.*

*pages 201, 210, 237, 243, 330*

10.    The word traditionally transliterated as *Selah* is סֶלָה (Strong's Concordance number 5542, pronounced *sélah*), which is the imperative form of סָלָה (Strong's Concordance number 5541, pronounced *saláh*).

*pages 64, 202*

11.    The word here translated first as "soul"and then as "*life*" is ψυχή (*psookhéy*), which is often transliterated into English as *psyche*, because it has no exact English counterpart: English words beginning with "*psych-*", such as *psychic*, and

412

*psychology*, came from the word *psookhéy*.

The Greek word for "*life*", as English speakers generally understand the idea, is ζωή (*dzo-éy*) (Strong's Concordance number *2222*), from which come the English words beginning with "*zoo-*", such as *zoology*.

*pages 202, 215*

12.  The word ασσαριου (*assárion*) literally means *quarter*, but I don't know how much money the Roman coin *assárion* was the fourth part of.

Perhaps, if one of my readers happens to know the actual price of sparrows, they can write to me and tell me, in which case I'd be able to calculate how much an *assárion* was equal to in comparison with today's market.

*page 203*

14.  Jewish tradition forbids marriages between Jews and non-Jews, because the divorce rate for such mixed marriages is unacceptably high.

Benaiah Zechariah Levell

*page 203*

15.  The death report for our friend and neighbor Barney Edwards is filed under the following: City of Newberg, Number 6544, Newberg Police Department, 401 East Third Street, Newberg, Oregon, 97132 Case Number: 06009321

*page 206*

16.      Manasseh has already written his second book, when he was sixteen years old: *The House of Moses: The Silver Stones*, which has been published online by Amazon Books.

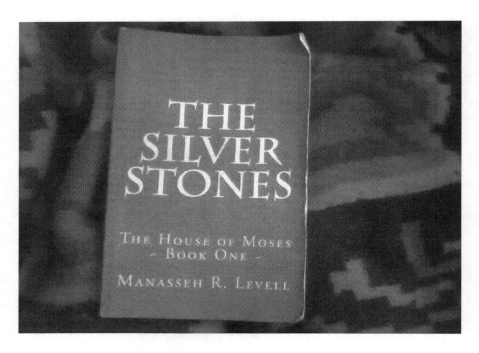

*pages 207, 211, 212*

17.      See note 10 in the notes for *Seven Flames of Fire: Letters to Manasseh*.

*page 207*

18.      עַמִּי (*Ammí*) means *My People* (Strong's Concordance number 5972). *Ammí* is also found within other names, including these: *Ben-Ammí*—[Son of My People], *Ammi-Húd*—[My People of Glory], *Ammi-Zabád*—[My People are a Gift], and *Ammi-Nadív*—[My People are Generous] (Strong's Concordance numbers 1151, 5989, 5990, and 5993).

*page 207*

19.      רֻחָמָה (*Ruhámah*) means *Pitied* (Strong's Concordance number 7355).

*page 209*

20.      We had never heard of the genetic disease PKU, nor do I

believe that it runs in our family, but Abram's inability to digest meat and cheese (and, apparently, the very milk of his own mother), and his strange odors both since his birth and after eating meat or cheese, mimic the symptoms of PKU…

*page 209*

21.     The "Newberg Mystery Spider" is much darker than the typical Hobo Spider. Otherwise, it looks a lot like this…

*Eratigena agrestis*
(Walckenaer, 1802), female - The Hobo Spider
Eugene, Lane Co., OR, September 25, 2014
© Donald H. Gudehus

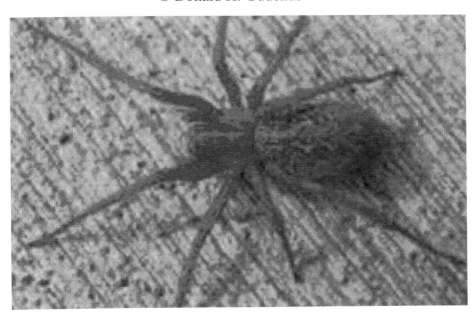

**Donald Gudehus**
April 22, 2015

to me

Dear Mrs. Naomi Levell,

I'm sorry that you had a very bad bite from a Hobo Spider. You may use my spider picture in your autobiography.

Sincerely,
Donald Gudehus

*page 210*

22.    מוֹרָה (*moráh*) was incorrectly identified with מוֹרָא (*morá*) by the translators of the Authorized King James Version. But these two words are not related.

The word *morá* (Strong's Concordance number 4172) comes from the root יָרֵא (*yaré*, Strong's Concordance number 3372), which means *to fear*. So, the translators of the Authorized King James Version incorrectly wrote *fear* in place of *instruction*, the correct translation of *moráh*, which comes from the root יָרָה (*yaráh*), (Strong's Concordance number 3384), which means *to teach*.

*page 210*

23.    What is Psalm 9:18-9:20 in the Authorized King James Version is Psalm 9:19-9:21 in the original Hebrew text.

*page 210*

24.    אַבְרָם יְדִידְיָה עַמִּי לֵב-אֵל בֶּן-בְּנָיָה לֵב-אֵל In Hebrew, Abram Jedidiah Ammi Levell ben-Benaiah is pronounced *Avrám Yedeed'yáh Ammí Lev-el ben-Benayáh Lev-el*.

*Avrám* means *Exalted Father*; *Yedid'yáh* means *Friend of Adonai*; and *Ammí* means *My People*.

*page 210*

25.    His metabolic disorder appears to have caused developmental delay in the womb.

*page 211*

26.    These were symptoms of a metabolic disorder such as PKU, and directly related to the fact that he could not digest animal proteins. This disorder may also be what saved his life, because both *Neisseria meningitidis* and its closest relative have a unique dependence on specific human proteins, and Abram had an infirmity which changed his relationship with proteins, which I think could possibly have made him allergic to *Neisseria meningitidis*. But it's only my own theory, and I am no doctor of diseases of proteins.

*page 212*

27.    Volksfront Life Rune

*page 213*
28.  I do not know whether the ambulance driver wrote any report of these things, but if so, I believe that this report would show that I came before the ambulance driver: Because the ambulance driver was an honorable man, and no friend of the leering neo-Nazi policeman.

*page 214*
29.  It is unfortunate that it did not also occur to them to refer this odd call to the FBI.

*page 218*
30.  Enoch Micaiah was eight years old when he and his siblings and mother all vanished without warning one morning from his father's home. Enoch's father was alive, but the painful loss Enoch suffered from that tragic day and onward was very similar to what a son endures when his healthy father unexpectedly dies.

It is unfortunate that it did not also occur to them to refer this

Benaiah knows this suffering well, because Benaiah was nine years old when his beloved father, who had been a very important part of his life, punched a hole in the wall one night while his parents yelled at each other. The next morning, his father drove away in the car and was gone. His father asked Benaiah to come and live with him and his lovely new wife Dell, and he had wanted very much to say yes, but at that time Benaiah felt obligated to stay with his mother, so he said no.

When a young man's father dies, he mourns, and his loss is seen and understood by all who know the family. The Bible also commands every God-fearing man to care for the fatherless children as if they were his own, and God Himself also promises to be a father to the fatherless children.

But when a young man's father suffers a divorce and quietly vanishes from the home, and the young man thenceforth has no more fathering than an orphan, his loss is seldom seen, his pain and confusion are scarcely understood, and even the slenderest sliver of hope that God may one day heal his parent's shattered marriage, this is torment: As long as both of his parents are still alive, this tiny sliver of hope forbids his wounded heart to mourn the death of their marriage.

31.  As I have said in *Silent No More*, my introduction to *Seven Flames* I have never found an English translation of the Bible more meticulously accurate than the King James Version, although it also has a few serious flaws: It is partly because of its superior accuracy that I choose the King James Version as a reference point for comparison.

Following, read from right to left, is the original Holy Scripture of this translation.

The numbers above each Hebrew word are the Strong's Concordance numbers, which can be used by readers who have a Strong's Exhaustive Concordance to verify or clarify the meaning of these words. (Hebrew Scripture is read in the opposite direction of English, and it was also written without vowel points and without modern punctuation.)

Below each Hebrew word I have placed the English definition of that word:

| 2550 | 802 | 5061 | 582 | 5327 |
|---|---|---|---|---|
| הָרָה | אִשָּׁה | וְנָגְפוּ | אֲנָשִׁים | וְכִי־יִנָּצ |
| pregnant | woman | and they strike | mortals | strive and if |

| 611 | 1961 | 3808 | 3206 | 3318 |
|---|---|---|---|---|
| אָסוֹן | יִהְיֶה | וְלֹא | יְלָדֶיהָ | וְיָצְאוּ |
| mischief | there is | and not | her children | and they go out |

| 7896 | 834 | 6064 | 6064 |
|---|---|---|---|
| יָשִׁית | כַּאֲשֶׁר | יֵעָנֵשׁ | עָנוֹשׁ |
| shall lay | according as | you shall fine | fining |

| 6414 | 5414 | 802 | 1167 | 5921 |
|---|---|---|---|---|
| בִּפְלִלִים | וְנָתַן | הָאִשָּׁה | בַּעַל | עָלָיו |
| through judges | and shall give | the woman | patriarchal chief [of] | upon him |

> And if mortals strive, and they strike *a* pregnant
> woman, and her children go out *from her*,
> and *yet* there is no mischief, fining *you* shall fine,
> according as the woman's patriarchal chief shall lay
> upon him; and *they* shall give through judges.

> ——Exodus 21:22

There is no Hebrew word for *men*: The Hebrew word for
*man* does not have a plural form. In its place, we Hebrews
use the word *anashím*, which is actually the plural of
*enósh*—that is, *mortal*—to mean *men* or *human beings*.
Simple reasoning will show that this verse has indeed
suffered an outrageous mistranslation in the King James
Version:

> If men strive, and hurt a woman with child,
> so that her fruit depart *from her*, and yet no mischief
> follow: he shall be surely punished, according as
> the woman's husband will lay upon him;
> and he shall pay as the judges *determine*.

Problem #1:
If this is referring to fatal premature labor or to miscarriage,
then—even from a strictly economic viewpoint—the
woman's chief has lost whatever financial and physical
security he would have gained by the birth of the child. This
is mischief.
Furthermore, even from a strictly scientific and medical
point of view, the woman will almost certainly suffer far
more severe postpartum depression than if the child had
survived; therefore it is impossible for *no* mischief to follow
an accidental miscarriage. Furthermore, the physical trauma
necessary to cause the child's miscarriage, rather than mere
premature labor, would certainly also fit *any* reasonable
definition of "mischief".

Problem #2:
If whoever hurt the woman is to be punished according as
the woman's <u>husband</u> will lay upon him, then it is the

husband, and not the judges, who gets to decide how much money the horrible lout owes this wife for her emotional suffering and for this wife's and her child's added medical expenses: Exactly *what* determination, then, is referred to in the phrase "he shall pay as the judges *determine*"?

Problem #3:

Verses 21:23 through 21:25 follow, saying,

23   And if *any* mischief follow,
       then thou shalt give life for life,

24   Eye for eye, tooth for tooth,
       hand for hand, foot for foot,

25   Burning for burning, wound for wound,
       stripe for stripe.

*page 220*

32.   אֶסְתֵּר שָׂרָה הוֹדִיָּה לֵב-אֶל בַּת-בְּנָיָה לֵב-אֶל In Hebrew, Esther Sarah Hadiyah Levell is pronounced as *Estér Saráh Hodiyyáh Lev-el bat-Benayáh Lev-el*. אֶסְתֵּר (*Estér*) is a Persian name which means *Star*; שָׂרָה (*Saráh*) is the Hebrew word for *Princess*; and הוֹדִיָּה (*Hodiyyáh*) means *Adonai is my Glory*. But in Arabic, *Hodiyyáh* means *Gift from Adonai*.

*page 220*

33.   Βεελζεβουβ, (from the Hebrew בַּעַל זְבוּב, Strong's Concordance numbers 1176, *954*): *Baál-zevúv*, in Hebrew, literally means "Lord *of a* Fly". It is a name given to Satan by the Canaanites who worshipped him as their god.

*page 226*

34.   2nd Corinthians 13:1—Compare also to Numbers 35:30, Deuteronomy 17:6 and 19:15, Matthew 18:16, 1st Timothy 5:19, and Hebrews 10:28.

*page 226, 227, 229*

35.   He also lied about C. Hamilton: http://www.state.il.us/court /opinions/appellatecourt/2005/1stdistrict/october/html/104 1179.htm

*page 228*

36.   This may seem strange—perhaps even chauvinistic—to many modern Western readers, but in chapter 30 of Numbers the Torah does give a husband the religious authority to

disallow his wife's vow in the day that he first hears of it. This makes sense (from my own patriarchal viewpoint), because if the husband has a duty to protect his wife, then it's only fair that the husband should also have sufficient freedom and authority to actually be *able* to protect his wife.

*page 234*

37.    Meningococcus was mistaken for poisoning at the outset of its first documented outbreak, among the Black soldiers fighting for the North during the American Civil War: The soldiers had been harvesting and eating wild blackberries, and when this strange new plague swept rapidly through the entire group, it looked exactly as though someone had poisoned the wild blackberries before the soldiers picked and ate them. The symptoms tend to vary a great deal, both in order of appearance and severity, and so it looked to us at first as though Elishevah, Abram and I had three unrelated problems. Elishevah was the only one in our house, at first, who bore the telltale purple spots on her ankles. These spots looked like healed-up burns from cigarettes. These spots do not have a darker or lighter center, they do not appear like open wounds, and they are not swollen: They look exactly

like cigarette scars on the ankles and/or the wrists.

Eishevah's only other clear symptom was a mild recurring fever. She was also delirious, but her normal way of thinking was such that this delirium was not immediately obvious until, when Ben tried to get her into my cousin's van to go to the hospital, she decided to sit down on her little brother and pee on him as if he were a toilet.

My only visible (but not obvious) symptom was slipping in and out of consciousness for several hours. I don't think I had purple spots, and I had no strange colors and no obvious fever: I just kept annoying Ben by going back to sleep when he needed my help. I was also delirious, but I guess Ben was a little too busy with the horrifying reality to attempt *mind reading*, so he did not notice my delirium. Neither did I, until I hallucinated seeing a broken bone jutting out of my wrist. This hallucination had been triggered by the severe pain in both my wrists, which I think actually hurt *worse* than broken bones.

Manasseh's only symptom was reported by a perjurer who said under oath that it had been there since birth, but then admitted when cross-examined that it might be new.

Abram's only clear symptom, until his sudden dogfight with death, was sudden lethargy. His temperature was at the high end of a child's normal temperature range: I wouldn't even call it a *mild* fever, except for the fact that Abram was usually at the cool end of the normal temperature range. Abram's purple spots appeared *after* he entered the ambulance; my purple spots appeared at Newberg Providence Hospital; Yehudah Isaiah's one and only purple spot appeared at Legacy Emanuel Hospital. His only other symptom was dangerously low blood pressure.

Esther's only "symptom"—metabolic acidosis—was a symptom of almost dying of thirst after more than thirty hours without liquid while the medical personnel actively refused to give her water. Ben's only "symptom"— incoherent speech—was a symptom of severe emotional shock combined with severe exhaustion and severe dyslexia, together with the normal diabetic reaction to at least thirty or forty hours without food.

Matt's only "symptom"—persistent pain in his joints after he was taken away from the hospital—was a known side effect of the Cipro we were given.

Matt, Ben, and Esther never got the disease at all.

As far as I know, none of us had the commonly reported Meningococcus symptom of neck pain—my neck *was* in pain, as usual, but not more than the normal amount of neck pain I had experienced and learned to ignore since early childhood. None of us were vomiting, belligerently irrational, or otherwise behaving noticeably different than the day before, except for the odd suddenness of Abram's lethargy. Until Abram began turning red and thrashing violently, hotter than any fever I'd ever seen, then turning red with purple marbling while laying limp again, then purple with black marbling and black legs—all within about four minutes of his sudden wild thrashing, which was his first sign of distress—the only unmistakable sign of illness in our house was Elishevah's ankle spots, which we initially thought had been caused by her walking through some kind of poison or allergen.

*page 235*

38.    Actually, of course, the clock was not atomic: Rather, it was controlled by radio waves from an atomic clock elsewhere.

*page 236*

39.    97.8 degrees Fahrenheit is equal to 36.555556 degrees Celsius.

*page 237*

40.    As far as I can recall, I did *not* explain in the ambulance why it wasn't a peanut allergy. I didn't even have the presence of mind to put on the dress Ben had shoved into my hands on my way into the ambulance: I just sat there and stared at Abram all the way to Newberg Providence hospital, in my underwear, because I was in shock. It was all I could do to pray two words: *"Lord. Help."* As for the peanut allergy—which was exactly what Abram's symptoms looked like, from the descriptions I've heard—Abram *lived* on Adam's Natural peanut butter, because he could not digest cheese or meat protein.

*page 239*

41.     One of the primary accusations against us in court was that we didn't respond fast enough to the emergency. But the delays were not our own. Newberg Providence Hospital never called an ambulance for me, nor sent me in an ambulance; and sending me in my sister's Volkswagen instead was *criminal*: They should be charged with the *attempted negligent homicide* of my nephews for doing this. As for Abram Jedidiah Ammi, he did not even *need* the ambulance that should have been for me: Sending Abram in the ambulance, instead of calling for a life flight helicopter, was also criminal negligence, for which they should also be charged with attempted negligent homicide of Abram as well: My brother-in-law never stopped the car until we got there, and yet we were still on the road, on the same route that Abram's ambulance took, for nearly *four hours*. Beloved reader, please learn a lesson from my mistake: Do *NOT* assume that the medical "experts" have *ANY IDEA* what they are doing: If something they are doing does not make sense to you, *HAVE THEM EXPLAIN*. If they can't convince you they know what they are doing, *MAYBE IT'S BECAUSE THEY DON'T.*

*page 240*

42.     Ben was slow moving, and he thought he was speaking clearly, but Rachel could understand almost nothing he said. She has stated repeatedly that Benaiah was babbling gibberish at her.

This *might* partly explain why some of the nurses were not responding correctly when Ben kept insisting that Esther desperately needed a bottle of water. One nurse clearly did see the need, however, and she did try to provide water. But she was prevented by an ominous threat from a frowning doctor, who then isolated Ben in what appeared to be a death chamber as described in Benaiah's poem "Back Room at Legacy" in *Seven Flames and Burning Coals.*

*page 240*

43.     Apparently, it has become a very common problem for hospital personnel to act on the apparent assumption that patients are their temporary property, rather than customers

voluntarily contracting with medical professionals for consultation and services. As a matter of fact, medical personnel frequently have been observed acting insulted and bewildered when their customers treat them like professional scientists instead of voodoo priests. It never once occurred to any of the nurses, for example, that it might possibly be an illegal violation of my constitutional rights to deny me such basic liberties as access to one of the several readily available telephones, while actively imprisoning me with straps in a hospital bed, as if I were a mental patient or something, when I had shown no sign of being a danger to myself or to anyone else.

*page 240*

44.  Actually, the law says just the opposite: It was illegal for them to allow her to interrogate me against my will without a lawyer present to represent me, and all the more so in my obviously altered mental state, when I had not only expressed a clear reluctance, but was arguably incapable of informed consent.

*pge 241*

45.  http://www.ncbi.nlm.nih.gov/pubmed/22509901 "The closely related pathogenic Neisseria species N. meningitidis and N. gonorrhoeae are…"

http://www.ncbi.nlm.nih.gov/pubmed/23699256 "Neisseria meningitidis…exists exclusively in humans…"

https://microbewiki.kenyon.edu/index.php/Neisseria_meningitidis_causing_meningococcal_meningitis

*pages 32, 245, 252*

46.  Courtesy of former president William Clinton, federal taxpayers now provide a bribe of twenty thousand dollars for removing a child from his or her family and placing them with strangers—unless the placement with strangers is permanent, in which case the bribe is twenty-five thousand dollars. For more information, please read this article "The Corrupt Business of Child Protective Services" by Nancy Schaefer:

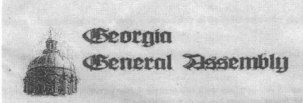

# Georgia
# General Assembly

*From the legislative desk of Senator Nancy Schaefer 50th District of Georgia*

November 16, 2007

## THE CORRUPT BUSINESS OF CHILD PROTECTIVE SERVICES

BY: Nancy Schaefer
    Senator, 50th District

My introduction into child protective service cases was due to a grandmother in an adjoining state who called me with her tragic story. Her two granddaughters had been taken from her daughter who lived in my district. Her daughter was told wrongly that if she wanted to see her children again she should sign a paper and give up her children. Frightened and young, the daughter did. I have since discovered that parents are often threatened into cooperation of permanent separation of their children.

The children were taken to another county and placed in foster care. The foster parents were told wrongly that they could adopt the children. The grandmother then jumped through every hoop known to man in order to get her granddaughters. When the case finally came to court it was made evident by one of the foster parent's children that the foster parents had, at any given time, 18 foster children and that the foster mother had an inappropriate relationship with the caseworker.

In the courtroom, the juvenile judge, acted as though she was shocked and said the two girls would be removed quickly. They were not removed. Finally, after much pressure being applied to the Department of Family and Children Services of Georgia (DFCS), the children were driven to South Georgia to meet their grandmother who gladly drove to meet them.

After being with their grandmother two or three days, the judge, quite out of the blue, wrote up a new order to send the girls to their father, who previously had no interest in the case and who lived on the West Coast. The father was in "adult entertainment". His girlfriend worked

- 1 -

*"Speak up for those who cannot speak for themselves, for the rights of all who are destitute.
Speak up and judge fairly; defend the rights of the poor and the needy" Proverbs 31:8-9*

# Speak up and judge fairly;

as an "escort" and his brother, who also worked in the business, had a sexual charge brought against him.

Within a couple of days the father was knocking on the grandmother's door and took the girls kicking and screaming to California.

The father developed an unusual relationship with the former foster parents and soon moved back to the southeast, and the foster parents began driving to the father's residence and picking up the little girls for visits. The oldest child had told her mother and grandmother on two different occasions that the foster father molested her.

To this day after five years, this loving, caring blood relative grandmother does not even have visitation privileges with the children. The little girls are in my opinion permanently traumatized and the young mother of the girls was so traumatized with shock when the girls were first removed from her that she has not recovered.

Throughout this case and through the process of dealing with multiple other mismanaged cases of the Department of Family and Children Services (DFCS), I have worked with other desperate parents and children across the state because they have no rights and no one with whom to turn. I have witnessed ruthless behavior from many caseworkers, social workers, investigators, lawyers, judges, therapists, and others such as those who "pick up" the children. I have been stunned by what I have seen and heard from victims all over the state of Georgia.

In this report, I am focusing on the Georgia Department of Family and Children Services (DFCS). However, I believe Child Protective Services nationwide has become corrupt and that the entire system is broken almost beyond repair. I am convinced parents and families should be warned of the dangers.

The Department of Child Protective Services, known as the Department of Family and Children Service (DFCS) in Georgia and other titles in other states, has become a "protected empire" built on taking children and separating families. This is not to say that there are not those children who do need to be removed from wretched situations and need protection. This report is concerned with the children and parents caught up in "legal kidnapping," ineffective policies, and DFCS who do does not remove a child or children when a child is enduring torment and abuse. (See Exhibit A and Exhibit B)

In one county in my District, I arranged a meeting for thirty-seven families to speak freely and without fear. These poor parents and grandparents spoke of their painful, heart wrenching encounters with DFCS. Their suffering was overwhelming. They wept and cried. Some did not know where their children were and had not seen them in years. I had witnessed the "Gestapo" at work and I witnessed the deceitful conditions under which children were taken in the middle of the night, out of hospitals, off of school buses, and out

-2-

of homes. In one county a private drug testing business was operating within the DFCS department that required many, many drug tests from parents and individuals for profit. In another county children were not removed when they were enduring the worst possible abuse.

Due to being exposed, several employees in a particular DFCS office were fired. However, they have now been rehired either in neighboring counties or in the same county again. According to the calls I am now receiving, the conditions in that county are returning to the same practices that they had before the light was shown on their deeds.

Having worked with probably 300 cases statewide, I am convinced there is no responsibility and no accountability in the system.

I have come to the conclusion:

- that poor parents often times are targeted to lose their children because they do not have the where-with-all to hire lawyers and fight the system. Being poor does not mean you are not a good parent or that you do not love your child, or that your child should be removed and placed with strangers;

- that all parents are capable of making mistakes and that making a mistake does not mean your children are always to be removed from the home. Even if the home is not perfect, it is home; and that's where a child is the safest and where he or she wants to be, with family;

- that parenting classes, anger management classes, counseling referrals, therapy classes and on and on are demanded of parents with no compassion by the system even while they are at work and while their children are separated from them. This can take months or even years and it emotionally devastates both children and parents. Parents are victimized by "the system" that makes a profit for holding children longer and "bonuses" for not returning children;

- that caseworkers and social workers are oftentimes guilty of fraud. They withhold evidence. They fabricate evidence and they seek to terminate parental rights. However, when charges are made against them, the charges are ignored;

- that the separation of families is growing as a business because local governments have grown accustomed to having taxpayer dollars to balance their ever-expanding budgets;

- that Child Protective Service and Juvenile Court can always hide behind a confidentiality clause in order to protect their decisions and keep the funds flowing. There should be open records and "court watches"! Look who is being paid!

*"Speak up for those who cannot speak for themselves, for the rights of all who are destitute. Speak up and judge fairly; defend the rights of the poor and the needy" Proverbs 31:8-9*

# Speak up and judge fairly;

There are state employees, lawyers, court investigators, court personnel, and judges. There are psychologists, and psychiatrists, counselors, caseworkers, therapists, foster parents, adoptive parents, and on and on. All are looking to the children in state custody to provide job security. Parents do not realize that social workers are the glue that holds "the system" together that funds the court, the child's attorney, and the multiple other jobs including DFCS's attorney.

- that The Adoption and the Safe Families Act, set in motion by President Bill Clinton, offered cash "bonuses" to the states for every child they adopted out of foster care. In order to receive the "adoption incentive bonuses" local child protective services need more children. They must have merchandise (children) that sell and you must have plenty of them so the buyer can choose. Some counties are known to give a $4,000 bonus for each child adopted and an additional $2,000 for a "special needs" child. Employees work to keep the federal dollars flowing;

- that there is double dipping. The funding continues as long as the child is out of the home. When a child in foster care is placed with a new family then "adoption bonus funds" are available. When a child is placed in a mental health facility and is on 16 drugs per day, like two children of a constituent of mine, more funds are involved;

- that there are no financial resources and no real drive to unite a family and help keep them together;

- that the incentive for social workers to return children to their parents quickly after taking them has disappeared and who in protective services will step up to the plate and say, "This must end! No one, because they are all in the system together and a system with no leader and no clear policies will always fail the children. Look at the waste in government that is forced upon the tax payer;

- that the "Policy Manuel" is considered "the last word" for DFCS. However, it is too long, too confusing, poorly written and does not take the law into consideration;

- that if the lives of children were improved by removing them from their homes, there might be a greater need for protective services, but today all children are not always safer. Children, of whom I am aware, have been raped and impregnated in foster care and the head of a Foster Parents Association in my District was recently arrested because of child molestation;

- that some parents are even told if they want to see their children or grandchildren, they must divorce their spouse. Many, who are under privileged, feeling they have no option, will divorce and

- 4 -

then just continue to live together. This is an anti-family policy, but parents will do anything to get their children home with them.

- fathers, (non-custodial parents) I must add, are oftentimes treated as criminals without access to their own children and have child support payments strangling the very life out of them;

- that the Foster Parents Bill of Rights does not bring out that a foster parent is there only to care for a child until the child can be returned home. Many Foster Parents today use the Foster Parent Bill of Rights to hire a lawyer and seek to adopt the child from the real parents, who are desperately trying to get their child home and out of the system;

- that tax dollars are being used to keep this gigantic system afloat, yet the victims, parents, grandparents, guardians and especially the children, are charged for the system's services.

- that grandparents have called from all over the State of Georgia trying to get custody of their grandchildren. DFCS claims relatives are contacted, but there are cases that prove differently. Grandparents who lose their grandchildren to strangers have lost their own flesh and blood. The children lose their family heritage and grandparents, and parents too, lose all connections to their heirs.

- that The National Center on Child Abuse and Neglect in 1998 reported that six times as many children died in foster care than in the general public and that once removed to official "safety", these children are far more likely to suffer abuse, including sexual molestation than in the general population.

- That according to the California Little Hoover Commission Report in 2003, 30% to 70% of the children in California group homes do not belong there and should not have been removed from their homes.

Please continue:

(See Final Remarks next page)

Note added by Naomi: All the "child support" paid to the children's "protective services", and also all Social Security disability and SSI paid to them for the childen, is added to the "general fund", which one of my social workers has freely admitted that this "General Fund" does not pay the children, nor the foster parents, nor the birth parents, for the needs of the children. She actually seemed proud to announce that although, by law, *MY* 400 dollars/month SSI check could *ONLY* be spent on *MY* needs, *NONE* of my many guardians received one penny more for my "care" than for the non-disabled children.

## FINAL REMARKS

On my desk are scores of cases of exhausted families and troubled children. It has been beyond me to turn my back on these suffering, crying, and sometimes beaten down individuals. We are mistreating the most innocent. Child Protective Services have become adult centered to the detriment of children. No longer is judgment based on what the child needs or who the child wants to be with or what is really best for the whole family; it is some adult or bureaucrat who makes the decisions, based often on just hearsay, without ever consulting a family member, or just what is convenient, profitable, or less troublesome for a director of DFCS.

I have witnessed such injustice and harm brought to these families that I am not sure if I even believe reform of the system is possible! The system cannot be trusted. It does not serve the people. It obliterates families and children simply because it has the power to do so.

Children deserve better. Families deserve better. It's time to pull back the curtain and set our children and families free.

*"Speak up for those who cannot speak for themselves, for the rights of all who are destitute. Speak up and judge fairly; defend the rights of the poor and the needy" Proverbs 31:8-9*

Please continue to read:
    Recommendations
    Exhibit A
    Exhibit B

After writing this report, Senator Nancy Schaefer of Georgia continued to carefully study the matter, and to struggle to reform the system. She discovered that the problem is not only within Georgia's government, but also in all the states: Senator Schaefer discovered that the "incentives" granted by President William Clinton, from the taxes of the people, are functioning uniformly in every state of the United States as a very effective bribe. Senator Schaefer also discovered that the infamous Patriot Act was uniting the governments like never before, and is therefore now forming from all the Children's "Protective Services" one single united Mafia. Seeing no effective way to fight against this new Children's "Protective" Mafia within the United States government, Senator Schaefer began preparations to speak to an international council about this grave matter.

Days before the assembly of the council, Senator Nancy Schaefer and her husband were found assassinated in their own home.

The government tried to persuade the public that her husband Mr. Schaefer had murdered his own wife and then committed suicide, but there are too many witnesses to the contrary.

*page 245*
47.     See also chapter seven, *Visions of a Joy yet to Come*

*page 246*
48.     See note 39 in the notes for *Alive and Kickin'*, (and note 63 in the notes for *Seven Flames: Letters to Manasseh*, and note 7 in the notes for *The Daughter*.)

*page 248*
49.     The true story of Terri Schindler Schaivo's legalized murder is briefly recounted in my preface to this book, entitled *God is Love*.

*page 249*
50.     Exodus 20:7; Leviticus 19:12; Numbers 30:2 through 30:16; Deuteronomy 5:11; Deuteronomy 23:21 through 23:23; Matthew 5:33 through 5:37; James 5:12
The Quakers' interpretation of Deuteronomy 23:22, Matthew 5:34 through 5:37, and James 5:12 is that it would be a sin to swear in any circumstances: For this reason the public oaths in the United States say "I swear or affirm" because to force the Quakers to swear would be a violation of the First Amendment, but it would not be a sin if they simply affirm instead of swearing. Other types of Christians believe that these verses simply mean that oaths should be avoided because the commandment never to lie means that every word of a Christian is already equal to an oath, but if I swear an oath, this would insinuate that all my other words are not equal to vows.
I'm not sure which of these doctrines is right, but because everyone agrees that if you should forbear to swear, it will not be a sin in you, I believe that it would be better to live like the Quakers in this most of the time, although I believe that it's better to vow to the non-Christian courts, so that they might understand that our words are equal to vows.

*page 251*
51.     I have a document, a written confession by hospital personnel in their own words, stating explicitly and in plain, clear language that they deliberately kept administering Cipro to me a full week past what was medically indicated,

and also stating explicitly and in plain, clear language that their reason for doing this illegal and harmful activity was to prevent me from doing anything to prevent the legalized kidnapping of my children. They know full well that they lied to me when I asked when I could be safely released, and that they lied to me when I asked how many more toxic Cipro injections were required, and I have a confession in their own words to prove both the crime and the motive.

I was violently ill for about a week after I was released from the hospital: My blood was so black I looked like an Arab, I had a high recurring fever, and I lost more than twenty pounds, because all food tasted like sawdust—except for meat, with tasted like roadkill rolled in sawdust.

This was not because of the Meningococcus, this was because of the intentional and fraudulent overdose of a week's injections of Cipro that my body did not need, and they have confessed in writing to deliberately lying about whether I needed it.

page 253

52.     Yeshua has been healing this beautiful heart, and she remembers again that I do love her.

page 254

53.     אֲדֹנָי—In this verse, the Hebrew word actually is *Adonai*. (See note 7 in the notes for *Seven Flames: Letters to Manasseh*.)

page 257

54.     Παρακλητος (Strong's Concordance number *3875*, pronounced as *par-ák-ley-tos*), comes from the word παρακλησις (pronounced *par-ák-ley-sis*), which means *comfort, consolation,* and *exhortation*: So, it is the Greek counterpart for the Hebrew word נְבוּאָה (Strong's Concordance numbers 5016 and 5017, pronounced as *nevuá*). (See note 7 in the notes for *The Daughter*.) So, *par-ák-ley-tos* is a Greek counterpart for the Hebrew word נָבִיא (Strong's Concordance number 5030, pronounced as *nav-ee*), and so it could also be translated as "*prophet*".

page 260

55.     בַּר-מִצְוָה (*Bar Mitzvah*) literally means "*Son of a Commandment*" or "*Son of a Righteous Action*". Before a

433

young Jew's *Bar Mitzvah* ritual, which consists of his first public reading from one of the five books of Moses, his parents are morally responsible for his actions. After this ceremony, he is no longer considered an innocent child: Henceforth, he is responsible for his own decisions.

page 261

56.    שֶׁלֶם (Strong's Concordance number 8002, pronounced as *shélem*) Although *shélem* is related to the well-known word *shalóm* (שָׁלוֹם, Strong's Concordance number 7965), the primary meaning of which is *peace*, *shélem* and *shalóm* both come from the same root שָׁלַם (Strong's Concordance number 7999, pronounced as *shalám*). This word *shalám* means *to complete* and *fulfil*, and although the Hebrew concept of *peace* is related to and inseparable from the concepts of *completeness* and *wholeness* the primary meaning of *shélem* is *offering of completeness and wholeness*.

(*Shalóm* does not mean the "peace" of the world; an ephemeral and earthly "peace" which is merely the absence of strife, but rather the authentic internal peace which Christ gives us, including in the midst of uncountable wars and struggles, which comes from being complete of soul.)

page 262

57.    אָוֶן (Strong's Concordance number 205, pronounced as *áven*) means *idolatrous*, *wicked*, *evil*, *empty*, *vain*, *futile*, and *worthless*.

page 262

58.    Isaiah 10:1-10:2—

The word כָּתַב (Strong's Concordance number 3789, pronounced as *katáv*) primarily means "write", but it also means, in a legal context such as this, "prescribe".

The word עָמָל (Strong's Concordance number 5999, pronounced as *amál*) means "labour", and is used primarily for hard or troublesome labour. In the King James, *amál* was translated 24 times as "labour", while the only time it was translated as "grievousness" was here (Isaiah 10:1); also, *amál* is translated with various other words in the King James, including once as "miserable", "toil", and "wearisome"; and three times as "travail".

Although it was translated various times in the King James Version as "turn aside", which is also accurate, the first meaning of the word נָטָה (Strong's Concordance number 5186, pronounced as *natáh*) is "turn", and the second meaning is "wrest", as in Exodus 23:2 and 23:6 and Deuteronomy 16:19 of the King James Version.

*page 263*
59.    The word שָׁקָה (pronounced as *shakáh*, Strong's Concordance number 8248) was translated in the King James as "him who gives...drink", but the Hebrew word *shakáh* clearly speaks of an active and causative action of causing to drink, while the translation "him who gives...drink", contrariwise, indicates that the neighbor doing the drinking is making a free and active choice. In the following scriptures, *shakáh* was translated in the King James Version with words clearly indicating that no free choice was given to the ones doing the drinking:

> Genesis 19:32; 19:33; 19:34; and 19:35
> Exodus 32:20
> Numbers 5:24; 5:26; and 5:27
> Psalm 60:3
> Jeremiah 23:15
> Jeremiah 25:15 and 25:17

And in Amos 2:12, although the translators of the King James Version chose the phrase "gave...to drink", it is clear to any Believer who knows and understands most of the rest of the Bible that God would not bring such a harsh accusation against someone who had given His Nazarites an opportunity to freely choose whether or not to break their vows, without any bullying, deceit, or other forms of coercion: It is not the rest of humanity's responsibility to keep other adults' vows for them against their will. And in Amos 8:8 and 9:5, *shakáh* is even translated (twice) as "be drowned".

*page 263*
60.    Because he ignored his God-given instinct to publicly proclaim that he had mated for life, this young man treated these relationships as a temporary game.

*page 263*

61.　　We shouldn't use such disrespectful nicknames for other people. The word "chicks" sounds like (and probably comes from) the more respectful Spanish word "chicas," which literally means "petite," and is used to mean "young women".

*page 264*

62.　　These young people were trying to find family in a worldly way that made no sense, because they were missing—with a pain of deadly loneliness—the family unity their hearts so desperately needed.

*page 264*

63.　　Before he became a Christian, he didn't recognize any sin in his fornication, because he neither understood nor knew Adonai's holy Torah of love. But after he was saved, the young man saw that God's marriage laws are a loving, wise gift to help us live healthy, joyful lives together.

*page 267*

64.　　Earlier editions said "It is not the Indian Way to invade", using the colloquial term "the Indian Way", which actually refers to the Way of a confederation of five particular tribes, including the Choctaws, and of another confederation of five Algonquin tribes. Some other tribes, such as the Apaches and the Aztecs, had no qualms about raiding, invading, stealing, or kidnapping peaceable neighbors for slaves.

*page 267*

65.　　*Wasíchu* is a word used by all the native tribes of the United States which means, approximately, a *White person*, but it does not refer to the color of the skin, but rather to the imperialistic cultures of the Europeans and the Americans. *Wasíchu* is a word of the Lakota ("Sioux") language which means, literally, *"He who takes the fat"*. It is generally not used as contemptuous or insulting, and it is not a cuss word. Historically, it refers to the practice of the conquering white raiders who deliberately killed almost the whole species of the American bisons to extinction, knowing that Lakotas perceived the American bison as sacred gifts from God, in order to debilitate the Lakotas so that they would become easy to conquer.

These *Wasíchus* weren't in it for the money, but they did also wish to get rich, so the *Wasíchus* would wander among the thousands of the slaughtered bison corpses, taking only the tongues, the skin, and the fat, which were the most expensive items to sell, and they would leave the rest of carcasses to rot. This is an abomination to Lakotas, who always had taken great care never to waste so much as a hair or an eyeball of these creatures, these sacred gifts from God.

*page 271*
66.   Philippians 4:8—the word here traditionally translated as *lovely*, which is προσφιλη (Strong's Concordance number *4375*, pronounced as *pros-fee-lay*), literally means *toward-friendly*. In the Spanish Reina Valera, *pros-fee-lay* is rightly translated as *amable*, which means *friendly*. The original meaning of *lovely* was a more accurate translation than its modern meaning.

*page 271*
67.   Benaiah wrote this parable to save my life, and then put it in our letter to Mattithias for all the other fathers and mothers who, like I was, are and will be in danger of dying from PTSD because of their love for their children in danger. Unlike the mother in this parable, I scarcely listened to the three messengers from God until my beloved Benaiah spent an entire day writing and talking with me about the importance of Philippians 4:8 for mothers and fathers in our situation. The Enemy knows this very well, and so his rebellious angels work very hard to deceive the "psychologists" who don't have the continual protection of the Holy Spirit, so that these "psychologists" will teach their clients to do exactly the opposite of what Paul commanded us by the Holy Spirit in his letter to the Philippians. I was deceived for years in this way by some of these "psychologists" who were appointed to manipulate me once a week while I lived in foster "care".

*page 273*
68.   Moreover, because constitutional law forbids discrimination because of race or nationality, federal law requires that all ICWA protections be applied to every family in the United

States. But, as far as I know, this fact has never yet been acknowledged by the United States Supreme Court.

*page 275*

69.    This medical disorder is rare, and little understood, and most likely hereditary: The first documented case of this medical disorder was the legume protein intolerance of the seven children of my aunt Grace (Whittlesey) Hill and Jerry Hill, which seven also nearly died of their disorder in foster "care" due to more or less intentional medical neglect, in their caseworker in California also failing to teach their foster parents about their dietary needs.

Not all of the social workers were so evil: Theresa Lovejoy helped save Esther from dying, by bearing witness on Esther's behalf that Esther was in fact still being fed legumes and at the command of the same hate-filled caseworker who claimed that she had told the foster parents about Esther's legume protein intolerance, and to have explained to them that although it was not an allergy and could not be detected with allergy tests, legume protein intolerance can still be fatal to a very small child.

*Levell Family Emblem*

# Section Five:
# The Daughter

*pages 279, 280, 283*

1. See note 63 in the notes for *Seven Flames: Letters to Manasseh*. (See also note 7 below, and note 39 in the notes for *Alive and Kickin'*.)

*page 279*

2. χξς: khee (600), ksee (60), stigma (6). Take note that the Greek text uses the ancient Hebrew alphanumeric system to build the number 666, rather than spell it out in Greek words, thereby indicating that it is in the ancient Hebrew alphanumeric system that the man's name will equal 666, or else that the number was never 666 in the first place. There have been apocalyptic fiction authors who substituted other alphanumeric systems, often of their own invention, wherewith to count the number of the beast's name, but it is illogical and absurd to do so without also translating this verse according to the same system:

For example, an apocalyptic fiction author who chooses to count the number of a man's name based on the unfounded assumption that a=1, b=2, c=3, and so on up through z=26, he should also translate χξς likewise as χ=22, ξ=14, and ς=18, therefore giving his fictional beast's name the number 54, instead of 666.

*pages 48, 280*

4. For the original readers, who were Hebrews, I believe that the word *outer* is implied by the fact that *garment* is ιματιον (Strong's concordance number *2440*, pronounced *himáti-on*), which is the Greek counterpart of בֶּגֶד (Strong's concordance number 899, pronounced as *béged*), which is the same word in Numbers 15:37 through 15:41, the commandment about wearing *tztziyót*, the "fringes" in their garments.

*page 280*

5. He said, "give", and He did not say that you should give them the same thing they want from you. So, if a beggar asks you for money for food, it is permitted to give him food instead of money.

*page 281, 359*
6.　　אֵשׁ (*esh*) is the Hebrew word for *fire*. The initials of her name being E.S.H., one of her nicknames was *Esh*.

*page 282*
7.　　The well-known Hebrew word *satán* means *enemy*, and Satan, our Enemy, has planted many, many false doctrines and false translations to deceive us into thinking of other human beings, especially those who hate us, as our enemies. Mahatma Gandhi (Mohandas Karamchand Gandhi) and Henry David Thoreau were my principal teachers on this subject, and I highly recommend their writings to my beloved readers, and also the writings of my teachers Oscar Wilde, Ellen G. White, Thomas Jefferson, Hillel, Abraham Lincoln, Pope John Paul II, Saint Francis of Assisi, Cicero, and Jimmy Carter.

My husband Benaiah was also greatly influenced by the writings of J. Vernon McGee, Washington Irving, Plato, J.R.R. Tolkien (*The Hobbit*), George Orwell, John Locke, Rousseau, Jonathan Swift, Dante, Charles Stanley, Doctor Seuss, and William Shakespeare.

*page 283*
8.　　Matthew 5:44 and Luke 6:27 through 6:28. See also Luke 23:34, Acts 7:60, and Romans 12:14.

*page 296*
10.　　I suspect that this nearly consistent substitution of "afflict" in place of "humble" is possibly among the devil's favorite mistranslations. Furthermore, except where *anáh* is used to substitute "humiliate" as a euphemism for "rape", the Hebrew word עָנָה (Strong's Concordance number 6031, pronounced as *anáh*,) never indicates nor insinuates any sort of pain, damage, or abuse. Understand this deeply, my brothers and my sisters: God is love (1st John 4:8), and He would never, no absolutely *NEVER*, oppress or abuse anyone, nor would He *EVER* command us to oppress or abuse anyone, or any creature, including our own souls.

In the following verses, various forms of the word "afflict" have been substituted for "humble", the true meaning of the Hebrew word *anáh*:

440

Genesis 15:13 & 31:50; Exodus 1:11; 1:12; 22:22; & 22:23; Leviticus 16:29; 16:31; & 23:29; Numbers 24:24 (x2); 29:7; & 30:13; Deut. 26:6; Judges 16:5; 16:6; & 16:19; Second Samuel 7:10; 1ˢᵗ Kings 2:26 (x2); 8:35; & 11:39; Second Kings 17:20; Second Chronicles 6:26; Ezra 8:21; Job 30:11 and 37:23; Psalms 55:19; 88:7; 89:22; 90:15; 94:5; 107:17; 116:10; 119:67; 119:71; 119:75; 119:107; and 132:1; Isaiah 53:4; 53:7; 58:3; 58:5; 58:10; 60:14; & 64:12; Lamentations 3:33; Nahum 1:12 (x2); and Zephaniah 3:19

I won't even *TRY* to guess where the translators of the King James Version got their ideas for these oddities of error: I can only say, *HUH?*

| | |
|---|---|
| exercised | Ecclesiastes 1:13 and 3:10 |
| gentleness | 2ⁿᵈ Samuel 22:36 |

But these next ones were invented by substituting English euphemisms for the word *anáh* ("humble"), a Hebrew euphemism for "rape":

| | |
|---|---|
| defiled | Genesis 34:2 |
| force | 2ⁿᵈ Samuel 13:12 |
| forced | J'g 20:5; 2 Sa. 13:14; 13:22; & 13:32 |
| ravished | Lamentations 5:11 |

It may seem harmless to translate *anáh* ("humble"), the traditional Hebrew euphemism for "rape", with other euphemisms such as "defile", "force", and "ravish"; but in reality these following mistranslations serve the Devil's purposes well by reinforcing the misplaced insinuations of violence in this Hebrew word's other mistranslations:

| | |
|---|---|
| dealt hardly with | Genesis 16:6 |
| hurt | Psalm 105:18 |
| weakened | Psalm 102:23 |

And consider also the utter inequality of Sarah "dealing hardly" with Hagar (Genesis 16:6), and then Hagar being commanded by the angel of the LORD "submit thyself" to her abusive mistress (Genesis 16:9); whereas the actual Hebrew word is the same word for both verbs: Sarah *humbled* Hagar, and Hagar ran away, and then the angel of the LORD commanded her, saying *"humble yourself"*.

Other scriptures about humbling our souls which have been likewise distorted by this same mistranslation include: Leviticus 16:29 & 16:31; Numbers 29:7 & 30:13; Ezra 8:21; Psalm 35:13; and Isaiah 58:3; 58:5; & 58:10. In contrast, *anáh* was translated more reasonably in these verses:

| | |
|---|---|
| abase himself | Isaiah 31:4 |
| chasten thyself | Daniel 10:12 |
| humble | Ex. 10:3; De. 8:2 & 8:16; & Judges 19:24 |
| humbled | De. 8:3; 21:14; 22:24; & 22:29; & Ps. 35:13 |
| submit thyself | Genesis 16:9 |

*pages 298, 299, 350*

11.      Isaiah 58:7

*page 299*

12.      While the word "kosher" is usually understood to mean "conforming to the dietary laws in the book of Leviticus", the Hebrew word it came from, *kashér*, literally means *fit*, or *proper*, and is generally used to mean "conforming to God's Holy Law, the Torah". The verb form of *kashér* is *kásher*, which is generally used to mean "to cause to conform to the dietary laws in the book of Leviticus".

*page 300*

14.      *Kristallnacht* was the night that marked the beginning of the *Shóa*, the massacre of fifteen million civilians known as the Holocaust. Literally, *Kristallnacht* means *Night of Glass*— The Nazis broke the windows of German Jews' houses and businesses, and set fire to their houses and businesses as well, both of which were very effective strategies to mislead the Jews into believing that there were many more anti-Semites in Germany than were actually there: The noise and the sight of the broken glass almost everywhere created a panic, isolating the Jews from the other honorable Germans who could have helped otherwise, and the sight of the houses completely burning to the ground while the firefighters used all the water and all their time to save the other buildngs nearby served very effectively to mislead the Jews into believing that the firefighters were also among the enemies

of the Jewish people, although the truth is that none of the firefighters in the whole world could have saved these houses destroyed by arson; and if the firefighters *had* tried to help the Jews, the other houses around them would have been destroyed as well.

In reality many of these firefighters willingly would have given their lives for their Jewish neighbors without a second thought, and this is why the Nazis had to make the Jews mistrust all the firefighters in Germany.

*page 304*

15. רֹאשׁ הַשָּׁנָה (*Rosh HaShanáh*) literally means "Head *of* the Year", because it marks the beginning of the Biblical fiscal year. But its Biblical name is יוֹם תְּרוּעָה (*Yom Teruáh*)—*Day of Blowing the Trumpets* (Strong's Concordance numbers 3117 and 2689), and the actual New Year is in the springtime: Because concerning the month *Avív* (the same month in which we celebrate Passover, and usually Easter as well), it is recorded in Exodus 12:1 through 12:2 that Adonai said to Moses,

> This month *shall be* to you *a* beginning* *of* months; it *shall be* first among *the* months of the year to you.

Thus, all the months in the Bible were counted from the month *Avív*, so that the Feast of Trumpets, although it is often called *Rosh HaShanáh* ["Beginning* *of* the Year"], it was called in the Bible the first day of the seventh month. Moreover, the Hebrew word *avív*, from which this month gets its name, means "springtime."

* רֹאשׁ (Strong's Concordance number 7218, pronounced *rosh*). Literally, *head.*

*pages 306, 309, 312*

16. אֲדוֹן נַפְשִׁי (*Adón Nafshí*) means "*Lord of my Soul.*"

*page 310*

17. Psalm 66:8 through 66:16, Proverbs 17:3, Proverbs 25:4 through 25:5, Isaiah 48:9 through 48:11, Jeremiah 6:29 through 6:30, Ezekiel 22:17 through 22:22, Zechariah 13:9, and Malachi 3:1 through 3:3

page 312
18.     Proverbs 26:23

page 315
19.     What is Psalm 20:7 in the King James is Psalm 20:8 in the Hebrew Bible.

page 316
20.     When rabbits grind their teeth or purr, this means they are in mortal pain. Cats are well known for purring with pleasure, but—like rabbits—cats will also purr when they are dying.

page 317
21.     As I said on the dedication pages, owing to the discovery of a significant error, we rather belatedly changed the rabbit's name to *Bonita*.
        Bonito and Bonita, respectively, are the masculine and feminine forms of a Spanish word meaning "beautiful". The words "bonito" and "bonita" are commonly used for anyone or anything that is both beautiful and cute. (But watch your tongue—"*niño bonito*" is not used to mean "beautiful little boy", but rather it is used to mean "spoiled little rich boy"! If what you want to say is "beautiful little boy", then say, "*niño precioso*", which is pronounced as *NEEN-yo pre-see-OH-so*.) Other Spanish words for "handsome" or "beautiful" are lindo/linda, hermoso/hermosa, guapo/guapa (which also means "sexy"), and bello/bella (pronounced as *béy-oh* and *béy-ah*, because two letter "L"s together in Spanish take on a sound similar to "y").

page 319
22.     Πετρος [Κηφας] Βαρναβας *Pedro* is the Spanish form of *Peter*. In the Greek, *Peter* is pronounced as *Petros*; and it comes from the Hebrew name כֵּף *Kefá*, which is pronounced in English as *Cefas*. As it says in John 1:42, *Kefá* and *Petros* both mean *A Stone*. *Bernabé* is the Spanish form of *Barnabas*. In the Greek, *Barnabas* is pronounced as *Barnabás*; and it comes from the Hebrew name בַּר-נָבָא (*Bar-Navá*), which is traditionally translated as *Son of Consolation*. But this is actually the second meaning: The first meaning of נָבָא (*Navá*) is to *Prophesy*.

page 319
23.     Daisy continued trying to persuade us, until the day she moved to another town, to abandon Pedro Bernabé's

congregation and join the Seventh Day Adventist church she attended. She objected to the Foursquare tradition of "speaking in tongues" in church without an interpreter. Her objection to speaking in tongues without an interpreter is valid (1ˢᵗ Corinthians 12:7-14:40); nevertheless, heresy should not be fled from, but rather should be uprooted by shining light on the truth, and this was the congregation to which God had sent us.

*page 324*

24.     Although the Spanish word *vigilia* (pronounced as *vee-**hee**-lee-uh*) is the exact translation of the English word *vigil*, a *vigilia* does not resemble any vigil I've ever seen in English-speaking churches: *vigilias* are gatherings at which worship songs are sung, and feasts and testimonies are shared.
I don't know whether it's a difference between the Latinos and the whites, or if it's a difference between the "Holy Rollers" and the more sedate denominations like the Quakers and the Presbyterians.

*page 325*

25.     The word translated as *Adonai* in verses 17, 18, and 19 is not the Holy Name *YHVH*, but rather יָהּ (*Yah*), an affectionate short form of *YHVH* much-used in the Psalms of David the king.

*page 326*

26.     ψαλλω (Strong's concordance number *5567*, pronounced *psál-lo*) and *psalm* (a hymn sung with a stringed instrument), both come from ψαω (psao), which is to *strum* or *twang* or *play* the strings of a stringed instrument.

445

*page 326*

27.    Revelation 3:11, 22:7, and 22:12—Note, also, that triple
       repetition in Hebrew raises a statement to its highest
       emphasis, and that although here Yeshua was speaking in
       Greek, Hebrew was nonetheless Yeshua's native language in
       which He thought.
       The King James Version says "quickly" rather than "soon",
       and this translation is also accurate. But I have preferred the
       translation "soon" for this book, because it matches the
       equally accurate "pronto" used in the Spanish Reina Valera.

*page 327*

28.    See note 10 in the notes for *Seven Flames:*
       *Letters to Manasseh.*

*page 327*

29.    A *Grand Mal* seizure is marked by random and extreme
       repetitive body movements, which can hurl a person against
       the furniture and break the spine, causing paralysis or death.

*page 329*

30.    Since before written history, each Hebrew letter has a
       number associated therewith, and therefore every name and
       every word also has a number, which is the sum of the
       numbers of its letters. Eighteen is the number of life because
       it is spelled *Khet Yood* (חי): *Khet* (ח) equals eight, and *Yood*
       (י) equals ten:

| | | | | |
|---|---|---|---|---|
| א | *Alef* = 1 | | ס | *Samekh* = 60 |
| ב | *Beit/Veit* = 2 | | ע | *Ayin* = 70 |
| ג | *Gimel* = 3 | | פ | *Peh/Feh* = 80 |
| ד | *Dalet* = 4 | | צ | *Tzaddee* = 90 |
| ה | *Heh* = 5 | | ק | *Qoof* = 100 |
| ו | *Vav* = 6 | | ר | *Resh* = 200 |
| ז | *Zayin* = 7 | | ש | *Sheen/Seen* = 300 |
| ח | *Khet* = 8 | | ת | *Tav* = 400 |
| ט | *Tet* = 9 | | ך | *Khaf Sofeet* = 500 |
| י | *Yood* = 10 | | ם | *Mem Sofeet* = 600 |
| כ | *Kaf/Khaf* = 20 | | ן | *Noon Sofeet* = 70 |
| ל | *Lamed* = 30 | | ף | *Feh Sofeet* = 800 |
| מ | *Mem* = 40 | | ף | *Feh Sofeet* = 800 |
| נ | *Noon* = 50 | | ץ | *Tzaddi Sofeet* = 900 |

My name Naomi (*Nah-ah-**mee***) is spelled *Noon Ayin Mem Yood*, and my last name Levell (*Lev-el*) is spelled *Lamed Vet Alef Lamed*; and therefore the number of my name is 233, as follows: נָעֳמִי לְב-אֶל

| | | |
|---|---|---|
| נ | *Noon*— | 50 |
| ע | *Ayin*— | 70 |
| מ | *Mem*— | 40 |
| י | *Yood*— | 10 |
| ל | *Lamed*— | 30 |
| ב | *Vet*— | 2 |
| א | *Alef*— | 1 |
| ל | *Lamed*— | + 30 |
| | | 233 |

For the sake of curious Republicans, sorry if this isn't what you want to hear, but the number of the name Barak Hussein Obama is equal to 1,366 as follows: בָּרָק הוּא-שֵׁן אוֹב-אָמָה (*Barák* is not, contrary to popular misinformation, related to the Hebrew word *barúkh*, which means "blessed".)
*Barák* is a Hebrew name meaning "a bolt of lightning", *hoo shein* means "he is a sharp tooth", *ob ámah* means "spirit of a handmaiden"—I am only offering information about his name: God has given me no interpretation thereof: I can say no more than that there are trustworthy prophets and prophetesses who have revealed to me that Barak Obama was placed in his position of power by God, and will not leave office until he has accomplished his appointed purpose for the hastening of the last days.

| | | |
|---|---|---|
| ב | *Beit*— | 2 |
| ר | *Resh*— | 200 |
| ק | *Qoof*— | 100 |
| ה | *Heh*— | 5 |
| ו | *Vav*— | 6 |
| א | *Alef*— | 1 |
| ש | *Sheen*— | 300 |
| ן | *Noon Sofeet*— | 700 |
| א | *Alef*— | 1 |
| ו | *Vav*— | 6 |
| ב | *Beit*— | 2 |
| א | *Alef*— | 1 |
| מ | *Mem*— | 40 |
| ה | *Heh*— | + 5 |
| | | 1,366 |

*page 330*

31.   The word here traditionally translated as *psalm*, I have translated as "*hymn sung with a stringed instrument.*" This word is מִזְמוֹר (Strong's concordance number 4210, pronounced *mizmór*) which comes from זָמַר (Strong's concordance number 2167, pronounced *zamár*), which, like the Greek word *psao*, means to *strum* or *twang* or *play* the strings of a stringed instrument. (See also note 26.)

32.    See note 10 in the notes for *The Storm*.

33.    Here, I break with my usual custom of translating each
       Hebrew word according to its most common and plain usage
       in the King James Version: Although the King James
       Version's translators consistently used variations on the
       theme of "to guide" to translate the word *nakháh*, and never
       rendered it as "give rest", my basic understanding of Hebrew
       grammar makes it self-evident to me that נָחָה (Strong's
       Concordance number 5148, pronounced as *nakháh*) is one of
       three verb counterparts to *yanó-akh, manó-akh, menoo-kháh,
       nó-akh*, and *nokháh* (Strong's Concordance numbers 3239,
       4494, 4495, 4496, 5118, 5119, and 5146, respectively), all of
       which are recognized in the King James Version as
       variations on the theme of "rest". The other two verb forms
       in this word family are *yanákh* ("cause to rest") and *NOO-
       akh* ("to rest"), (numbers 3240 and 5117, respectively).

34.    Isaiah 59:20 through 59:21

35.    Jeremiah 31:33 through 31:34
       The words translated here as "them" and their" (Strong's
       Concordance numbers *846* and *848*) are ambiguous in both
       the original Hebrew text and in the Greek text: These same
       words (in the Greek, αυτος and αυτου, prououced *ow-tóhs*
       and *how-TOO*; and in the original Hebrew, the suffix *–em*)
       also mean "you" and "your" so that it would be equally
       accurate if I wrote "And this *is* the covenant from me to you,
       when I shall take away your sins." But, although "you" and
       "your" would be the more reasonable rendering of the
       original Hebrew in its context, "them" and "their" is a more
       reasonable rendering in of its translation in Paul's letter to
       the Romans, because he was explaining to an audience of
       non-Jewish Believers how to properly understand God's
       ongoing and future relationship with the Hebrews who had
       yet to recognize Yeshua as their promised Redeemer.
       Although the word διαθηκη (Strong's Concordance

number *1242*, pronounced *dee-a-THAY-kay*) is translated both as "covenant" and as "testament", *dee-a-THAY-kay* refers specifically to an inherently unequal covenant, as is reflected in its numerous translations as "testament" (meaning, in modern English, "a will"), including in the phrases "Old Testament" and "New Testament": A *dee-a-THAY-kay* is a will, made by a testator or a testatrix to his or her heirs, of which the only role of the heirs is solely to receive the free gift of their inheritance.

*page 332*

36.     Deuteronomy 7:6; 10:15; and 14:2; 1ˢᵗ Chronicles 16:13; Psalms 33:12; 105:6; 105:43; and 106:5; Psalms 135:4; Isaiah 41:8; 41:9; 43:10; 43:20; 44:1; 44:2; and 48:10; Jeremiah 33:24 through 33:26; and Ezekiel 20:5

*page 334*

37.     See note 1 in the notes for *Seven Flames: Letters to Manasseh.*

*page 334*

38.     What is Zechariah 2:10 though 2:13 in the English translations is verses 2:14 through 2:17 in the original Hebrew Bible (the Masoretic Text).

*page 334*

39.     The roughly spherical constellation looked somewhat similar to the land masses on a globe (except that there were almost no stars in the polar regions), with generally greater density of light around the edges of the continents where the coastal regions would be, and with a few individual stars which seemed to be alone in the sea, and with paths of stars across the seas, which I suppose had to have been the routes generally traveled by ships and airplanes. (See also Daniel 12:3)

*page 337*

40.     Rain had also just begun pouring down, hard and fast, and the sun had just set, and not all of the drivers had yet reacted by turning their headlights and windshield wipers on. In addition, the dark, busy street was where the highway met our small town, and there were many drivers at all hours of the day who were well inclined to drive as if they were still on a highway, rather than in the middle of a residential neighborhood not far from an elementary school.

41.      Benaiah and I knew that it was the right place because he had seen James' grandpa in his vision. When the sun was still up, and the rain was still falling lightly, we were waiting for the sun to set so we could go grocery shopping. Then there was a sudden and brief thunderstorm, in which the voice of God told Benaiah that we were going to break the Sabbath by leaving early, before the sun had reached the horizon. When Benaiah protested, the voice said, "*Yes you will. Go!*"

While we walked, the Holy Spirit guided both of us together in the same direction, until we saw in the distance a very small boy alone in the dark, rainy night at the curb, intending to cross the busy street. Benaiah was older and slower than me, so I ran ahead toward the little boy. He smiled shyly, and took a step backward.

I had seen him once before that I recall, shopping with his mother and brother, but we'd only met briefly and I didn't know their names.

Hoping to buy a little time to give his parent or babysitter time to find us, I asked the child his name, and he mumbled a cheerful little answer—while slowly turning around full circle, facing me again just as he finished speaking. I asked him his name a second time, and again he mumbled his answer while spinning, and came to stop facing me—(which was extremely cute, but not terribly informative: I still didn't know his name yet).

But the delay worked: Ben had now caught up with us, and he bent down to talk to the smiling child. Just then, I heard an old man's voice calling, "James! James!"

Ben had already told me that we were looking for an old man with a white beard, even before we'd left our front yard: He'd been given a vision of an old man with a beard, who was James' grandfather, so that we would know to seek him out and to trust him when we saw him. So when I heard the old man's voice, I ran to meet him; and when I saw that he had a white beard (which is a bit uncommon in this town), I asked the little old man, "Is James a little boy?"—whereupon the grandfather anxiously ran past me in the direction I'd

451

come from, until he reached little James. Then we waited until James was safely in the house again, and—now that the sun was quite set—continued in the way we'd been coming, to go shopping at the Dollar Tree. Benaiah ran ahead of me through the traffic to go find the child's mama, because the little grandfather had told us that that was where James' mom was, who the child had been trying to get to…all by himself, without a care in the world except how much he missed ☹ his mommy ☺…

page 337, 338

42.     Ben heard the big, distant, imperative voice of God. I only heard thunder. (Compare to John 12:29.)

page 340

43.     Psalm 51:10 through 51:17 in the King James Version (and in all the English translations based on the King James Version) corresponds with Psalm 51:12 through 51:19 in the original Hebrew Bible.

page 342

44.     Some of my friends have asked me whether, as I have said described in the chapter "*Blind*", I would still start to lose my eyesight if I skipped reading the Bible for a day. I suppose not, now that my heart has been healed by the touch of God's fingertip, but I have absolutely no intention of testing that theory, at the expense of breaking my vow to Adonai my Beloved One.

Besides, these days, I hunger for His words: My soul pants for hunger and thirst before a full day without Scripture has even come to an end, so that I long for His words as a youth longs for food and water at the end of a day of fasting.

page 353

45.     What is Psalm 8:3 through 8:9 in the King James Version is Psalm 8:4-8:10 in the original Hebrew Bible.

page 355

46.     Matthew 19:29, Mark 10:30. See also Luke 18:29.
My math isn't bad: I had seven babies: Yonah was also mine for a little while, until the miscarriage.

page 356

47.     יוֹנָה The Hebrew name *Yónah*, in English, is *Jonah*.
The Hebrew word *yónah* means *a dove*.

page 357

48.     *Joodlebug* was our nickname for Yehudah Isaiah.

*page 357*
49.　97.8 degrees Fahrenheit is equal to 36.555556 degrees Celsius.

*page 358*
50.　The "Jedis" were the heroes and miracle-workers in the *Star Wars* trilogy of movies.

*page 359*
51.　I mean it! This is *NOT* idle chatter!

*page 360*
52.　בְּנָיָה זְכַרְיָהוּ לֵב-אֶל הָצְשֶׁכְטַהִי In Hebrew, Benaiah Zechariah Levell the Choctaw is pronounced *Benayáh Zekharya-hoo Lev-el ha-Tzshákhtahi*. In Hebrew, Benaiah is pronounced as *Benayáh* (or, to Spanish-speaking ears, "come to way over there" [*Ven-allá*] ☺) and means *Yahweh is Building him*, or *Building of Adonai*. *Zekharya-hoo* means *Remembrance of Adonai*; and *Lev-el* means *Heart of God*.

Our brother Pedro Bernabe calls him the nickname *Béni* instead of "come to way over there". (In the Hebrew, *Beni* means *My Son*.)

לֵב-אֶל (Lev-el), In Hebrew, means *Heart of God*.

זְכַרְיָהוּ In Hebrew, Zechariah is pronounced as *Zekharyáh*. The name *Zekharyáh* means *Remembrance of Yahweh*, or *Yahweh Remembers*.

After Benaiah realized that he would never meet his beautiful baby Justus Zechariah again until Justus became an adult, Benaiah legally changed his own second name to Zechariah, so that his beloved little son would have something of his father's that nobody could take away.

*page 360*
53.　שׁוֹשַׁנָּה [Σουσαννα] מִרְיָם בַּת-נָתָן מְלֹז בֶּן-נָתָן מְלֹז הוּאִתְּלְסִי *Shoshanna Miriam*, in English, is *Susanna Mary*. *Shoshanna Miriam* is pronounced as *Shoshánna Miryám*. *Shoshánna* means *Water Lily*; and *Miryám* means *Bitterness*, or *Rebellion*. Her full name in Hebrew is *Shoshánna Miryám bat-Natán Mills ben-Natán Mills Whittlesey*. Her full name in English is *Susanna Miriam (Whittlesey) Veach*.

# Appendix

*page 455*

54.  Κυριο (Strong's Concordance number *2962*, pronounced *Koo-ree-owe*). Although *Koo-ree-owe* is traditionally translated here as *the Lord*, there is no word here for "the", and its absence means that here (in verse 4:4), *Koo-ree-owe* is a substitute for the Hebrew word *Adonai*.

*page 455*

55.  See note 63 in the notes for *The Storm*.

*page 461*

56.  אֶת (Strong's Concordance numbers 853 and 854, pronounced "et") is not expressed in English translations when it serves only as a prefix to connect a verb with the direct object of the verb, but standing alone it always means "with".

I thank my God upon every remembrance *of* you, …

…being persuaded *of* this, that He who has begun *a* good work in you will complete *it* until *the* day *of* Messiah Yeshua. …

…Rejoice in Adonai[54] always. Again I say, Rejoice!

…*As for* the *things that* remain, brothers, whatever *things* are true, whatever *things are* noble, whatever *things are* right, whatever *things are* pure, whatever *things are* friendly[55], whatever *things are worthy of* good report; if *there is* any excellent virtue, and if *there is* anything *worthy of* praise, think *about* these *things*.

—selections of
Philippians 1:3-4:8

# *Shalom*

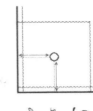

The hole for the fringe is traditionally round, and must be neatly hemmed with stitches after the manner of a button-hole. These button-holes should be placed about five centimeters or about two inches away from the side and bottom edges.

Four strings threaded through the hole become eight. The Shammash String, or Servant String, is a good deal longer than the others because it is used for wrapping around the other 7 strings.

Tie two granny knots before beginning to wind the threads. The loop at the top must be loose enough that the cloth does not bunch up, and tight enough to allow the fringe to hang down from the side of the corner, rather than dangling straight down from the button-hole.

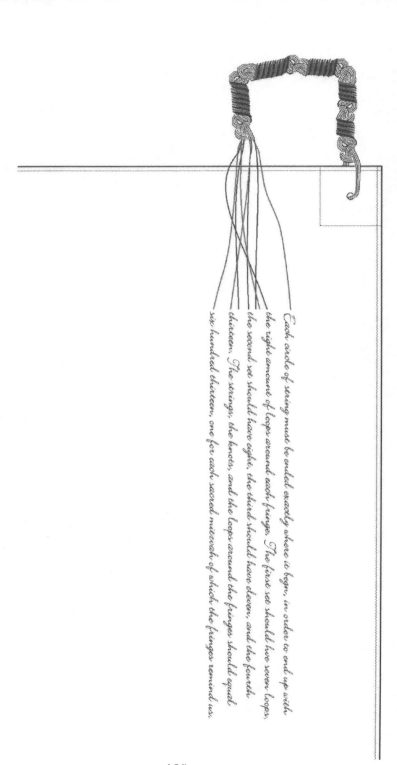

Each circle of string must be ended exactly where it began, in order to end up with the right amount of loops around each fringe. The first set should have seven loops, the second set should have eight, the third should have eleven, and the fourth thirteen. The strings, the knots, and the loops around the fringes should equal six hundred thirteen, one for each sacred mitzvah of which the fringes remind us.

Almighty
Shaddai

Guardian
of the gates
of
Israel

Copy these last nine pages, and then use the copied Bible verses to make a *mezuzah* scroll. Paste the pattern to thin cardboard, let it dry, then cut it out and fold it at the lines, then paste the tabs to make a cardboard *mezuzah* box. Roll up the scroll, place it in the *mezuzah*, and affix it to the doorpost of the main door of your home at about eye level, to remind all those who enter and depart to always keep God's Holy Law of Love on their lips and in their hearts.

Hear deeply, *O* Israel:
Adonai our God, Adonai *is* one.
And you shall love Adonai your God
in all your heart,
and in all your soul,
and in all your strength.
And these words,
which I command you this day,
shall be on your heart;
And you shall sharpen them
unto your children,
and shall talk of them
in your sitting in your house,
and in your walking by *the* way,
and in your laying down,
and in your rising up.
And you shall bind them for *a* sign
upon your hand,
and *they* shall be for frontlets
between your eyes;
and you shall write them
upon the posts *of* your house,
and in your gates.

And *it* shall be,
if hearing deeply
you shall deeply hear my commands
which I command you today,
to love Adonai your God,
and to serve Him in all your heart,
and in all your soul,
I will also give *the* rain *of* your land
in its time,
*rain* of planting and *rain* of gathering;
and you will gather your grain,
and your sweet wine, and your oil.
And I will give grass in your field
to your beasts;

and you will eat, and be satisfied.
Guard yourselves,
lest your heart be seduced,
and you turn aside and serve other gods,
and bow down to them;
and *then* Adonai's wrath be kindled
against you,
and He shut up the skies,
and there be no rain,
and the soil not give its increase;
and you perish quickly from
the good land
that Adonai is giving to you.
And you shall lay these words
upon your heart
and upon your soul,
and bind them
for *a* sign upon your hand,
and *they* shall be for frontlets
between your eyes.
And *you shall* teach them
with[56] your children,
speaking in them
in your sitting in your house,
and in your walking in *the* way,
and in your laying down,
and in your rising up.
And *you shall* write them
upon *the* doorposts *of* your house,
and in your gates;
so that may be multiplied your days,
and *the* days of your children,
upon the soil
which Adonai promised to your fathers
to give to them,
like *the* days of the skies
above the earth.

—Deuteronomy 6:4, 6:5-6:9,
and 11:13-11:21

שְׁמַע יִשְׂרָאֵל

*Shemá, Yisraél:*

יהוה אֱלֹהֵינוּ יהוה אֶחָד:

*Adonai Elohéynoo, Adonai ekhad:*

וְאָהַבְתָּ אֵת יהוה אֱלֹהֶיךָ

*V'ahavtá et Adonai Elohéykha*

בְּכָל-לְבָבְךָ,

*b'khal-levávkha,*

וּבְכָל-נַפְשְׁךָ,

*oov'khál-nafshékha,*

וּבְכָל-מְאֹדֶךָ:

*oov'khál-meodékha.*

וְהָיוּ הַדְּבָרִים הָאֵלֶּה

*V'hay-oo hadevaríym ha-eléh*

אֲשֶׁר אָנֹכִי מְצַוְּךָ הַיּוֹם

*ashér anokhíy metzavekhá ha-yóm*

עַל-לְבָבֶךָ;

*al-levávkha;*

וְשִׁנַּנְתָּם

*v'shinántam*

לְבָנֶיךָ,

*l'vanéikha,*

וְדִבַּרְתָּ בָּם

*v'dibartá bam*

בְּשִׁבְתְּךָ בְּבֵיתֶךָ,

*b'shivteikhá beveytéikha,*

וּבְלֶכְתְּךָ בַדֶּרֶךְ

*oov'lekhteikhá vadérekh,*

וּבְשָׁכְבְּךָ

*oov'shakhaivvkhá,*

וּבְקוּמֶךָ ׃

*oov'kooméikha.*

וּקְשַׁרְתָּם לְאוֹת

*Ookeshartám l'ót*

עַל־יָדֶךָ

*al-yadéikka,*

וְהָיוּ לְטֹטָפֹת

*v'hay-oo l'tetafót*

בֵּין עֵינֶיךָ ׃

*beyn eynéykha;*

וּכְתַבְתָּם

*ookhetavtám*

עַל־מְזֻזוֹת בֵּיתֶךָ

*al-mezoozót beytéikha,*

וּבִשְׁעָרֶיךָ ׃

*oovishe-aréikha.*

וְהָיָה

*V'hayáh,*

אִם־שָׁמֹעַ תִּשְׁמְעוּ

*im- shamó-a tishma'oo*

אֶל־מִצְוֹתַי

*el-mitzvotai*

אֲשֶׁר אָנֹכִי מְצַוֶּה אֶתְכֶם

*ashér anokhíy metzavvéi etkhéim*

הַיּוֹם

*ha-yóm*

לְאַהֲבָה אֶת-יהוה אֱלֹהֵיכֶם
*l'ahavá et-Adonai Eloheykhéim,*

וּלְעָבְדוֹ בְּכָל-לְבַבְכֶם
*ool'avdó b'khal-levavkhéim,*

וּבְכָל-נַפְשְׁכֶם:
*oov'khál-nafsheikhéim,*

וְנָתַתִּי מְטַר-אַרְצְכֶם
*v'natatíy metár-artzekhéim*

בְּעִתּוֹ
*b'itó,*

יוֹרֶה וּמַלְקוֹשׁ
*yoréh umalkósh;*

וְאָסַפְתָּ דְגָנֶךָ
*v'asfetá deganéikha*

וְתִירֹשְׁךָ וְיִצְהָרֶךָ:
*v'tiyrósheikhá, v'yitzharéikha.*

וְנָתַתִּי עֵשֶׂב בְּשָׂדְךָ
*Venatatíy éisev b'sadeikhá*

לִבְהֶמְתֶּךָ
*liveheimtéikha;*

וְאָכַלְתָּ וְשָׂבָעְתָּ:
*v'akhaltá v'savá-ei-ta.*

הִשָּׁמְרוּ לָכֶם
*Hisham-**roo** lakhéim,*

פֶּן-יִפְתֶּה לְבַבְכֶם
*pein-yif'téh levaveikhéim,*

וְסַרְתֶּם וַעֲבַדְתֶּם
*v'saretéim va-avadetéim*

אֱלֹהִים אֲחֵרִים
*elohíym akheríym,*

וְהִשְׁתַּחֲוִיתֶם לָהֶם:
*v'hishtakhaviytéim lahéim;*

וְחָרָה אַף-יהוה
*v'kharáh af-Adonai*

בָּכֶם
*bakhéim,*

וְעָצַר אֶת-הַשָּׁמַיִם
*v'atzár et- hashamáyim*

וְלֹא-יִהְיֶה מָטָר
*v'ló-yeheyéh matár,*

וְהָאֲדָמָה לֹא תִתֵּן
*v'ha-adamáh lo titéin*

אֶת-יְבוּלָהּ
*et-yevooláh;*

וַאֲבַדְתֶּם מְהֵרָה
*va-avadetéim meheráh*

מֵעַל הָאָרֶץ הַטֹּבָה
*mei-ál ha-áretz hatováh*

אֲשֶׁר יהוה נֹתֵן לָכֶם:
*ashér Adonai notéin lakhéim.*

וְשַׂמְתֶּם אֶת-דְּבָרַי אֵלֶּה
*V'sametéim et-devaráy eléh*

עַל-לְבַבְכֶם
*al-levavekhéim*

וְעַל-נַפְשְׁכֶם
*v'al-nafshekhéim,*

וּקְשַׁרְתֶּם אֹתָם

*oo'k'shartéim otám*

לְאוֹת עַל־יֶדְכֶם

*l'ót al-yed'khéim*

וְהָיוּ לְטוֹטָפֹת

*v'hay-**oo** l'totafot*

בֵּין עֵינֵיכֶם :

*beyn eyneykhéim.*

וְלִמַּדְתֶּם אֹתָם

*V'limadetéim otám*

אֶת־בְּנֵיכֶם

*et-beneykhéim,*

לְדַבֵּר בָּם

*l'dabér bam*

בְּשִׁבְתְּךָ בְּבֵיתֶךָ

*b'shevtekhá b'veitéikhá,*

וּבְלֶכְתְּךָ בַדֶּרֶךְ

*oo'v'leikhtekhá vadérekh,*

וּבְשָׁכְבְּךָ

*oo'v'shakh'bekhá*

וּבְקוּמֶךָ :

*oo'v'kooméikha.*

וּכְתַבְתָּם

*u'kh'tavtám*

עַל־מְזוּזוֹת בֵּיתֶךָ

*al-mezoozót beytéikha,*

וּבִשְׁעָרֶיךָ :

*u'vishe-aréykha;*

לְמַ֫עַן יִרְבּ֣וּ
*l'má-an yire-**boo***

יְמֵיכֶם֩
*yemeykhéim,*

וִימֵ֣י בְנֵיכֶ֗ם
*viyeméy veneykhéim,*

עַל הָאֲדָמָ֔ה
*al ha-adamáh*

אֲשֶׁ֨ר נִשְׁבַּ֧ע יְהוָ֛ה לַאֲבֹתֵיכֶ֖ם
*ashér nishbá Adonai la-avoteykhéim*

לָתֵ֣ת לָהֶ֑ם
*latét lahéim,*

כִּימֵ֥י הַשָּׁמַ֖יִם
*kiyméy hashamáyim*

עַל־הָאָֽרֶץ׃
*al-ha-áretz.*

Proof

Made in the USA
Columbia, SC
14 June 2017